For four decades, a brand and a directory you can count on...

Select Registry, Distinguished Inns c⋯⋯⋯⋯uide to exceptional travel and lodging for 40⋯⋯⋯⋯cial place that will make your next trip unforgettable.

Whether you're traveling for business or pleasure, by yourself or with your family, this guidebook will help you to locate extraordinary places to stay throughout the U.S. and Canada. And, no matter what the season or the type of property that you find most appealing, Select Registry likely has something for you.

Most importantly, you can rest assured that our member properties have been selected as among the most comfortable and welcoming—unique and quality assured lodging alternatives in an increasingly cluttered and impersonal travel marketplace.

In years past, the registry book in the lobby of hotels and inns welcomed guests and provided a connection between innkeepers and travelers. The historical registry "quill"—the original instrument of guest registration—has been incorporated into our Association's graphic identity, and the predicates of hospitality, comfort, and authenticity establish our members as "the best of the best"—select properties that will exceed your highest expectations when it comes to lodging.

Look for the plaque with the quill on it when you visit our members' inns, and you'll know that you are "traveling the Select Registry way..."

SELECT REGISTRY
DISTINGUISHED INNS OF NORTH AMERICA

se·lect (sĭ-lĕkt') v. -lect·ed, -lecting, -lects. —tr. To choose from among several; pick out, —intr. To make a choice or selection. —adj. Also se·lect·ed (-lĕk'tĭd). 1. Singled out in preference; chosen. 2. Of special value or quality; preferred. —n. One that is select. [Lat. seligere, select-: se-, apart+legere, to choose.] —se·lect'ness n.

Canyon Villa Bed & Breakfast Inn

www.canyonvilla.com
40 Canyon Circle Drive, Sedona, AZ 86351
800-453-1166 • 928-284-1226 • Fax 928-284-2114
canvilla@sedona.net

continuing
Member Since 1995

Innkeepers/OwnersLes & Peg Belch ❶

Canyon Villa Inn is uniquely located and designed to capture a visual experience of Sedona's world famous Bell Rock & Courthouse Butte. Large common areas and themed intimate guestrooms open from arched French doors onto private balconies or lush garden patios.Guestrooms include cable TV, free Wi-Fi, phone, I-Pod clock radios, irons, hair dryers, and 4 with gas-log fireplaces.Private ceramic bathrooms include jetted tubs, personal amenities, irons, hair dryers, makeup mirrors, and bath & pool robes.Three course breakfast, appetizer hour, and fresh cookies & tea each evening. 1000 volume library with over 100 DVDs, guest computer, and printer. Guests relax daily under the warm Arizona sun by a glass tiled swimming pool, hike desert trails from the premises, & stargaze cool evenings outdoors by fireside. Ranked #1 in the TripAdvisor 2009 Award for "Best U.S. Inns and B&Bs." Past recipient of "Best U.S. Bed and Breakfast" award from Harper's "Hideaway Report". Recommended by Frommers and admitted to Diamond Collection with BedandBreakfast.com. AAA 4 Diamond Award (2011)

❷ **Rates:** 10 Red Rock View Rooms $199-349. 1 Limited View Room $159-199. Discounts for AAA, AARP, Military. Number of Rooms: 11

❸ **Cuisine:** Three course served breakfast includes our award winning Cinnamon Rolls. Afternoon refreshments and appetizers. Guests welcome to bring their own spirits. Harney & Son teas served with original light deserts throughout the entire evening.

❹ **Nearest Airport:** Phoenix Sky Harbor (PHX)

Casa Sedona Inn

www.casasedona.com
55 Hozoni Drive, Sedona, AZ 86336
800-525-3756 • 928-282-2938 • Fax 928-282-2259
casa@sedona.net

Member Since 2004

Innkeepers/Owners Paul & Connie Schwartz

Featured on The Travel Channel "Best of the Best" series and listed in the 2007 addition of "1000 Places to See Before You Die", Casa Sedona is a world-renowned 16-room bed & breakfast inn. Located 6 minutes away from the bustling "uptown" in a quiet area just off the Highway 89A. Relax in our serene landscaped gardens, or on your private patio or balcony, and enjoy inspiring red rock views of Thunder Mountain, Chimney Rock, and "Baby Bell" Rock. Breakfast is served outside - with red rock views – and features mild Southwest Favorites and award-winning French Toast bakes.Afternoon appetizers in the Juniper Garden offer an opportunity for guests to relax, refuel, and share the day's experiences. Guest rooms are up-to-date and well-appointed with AAA ◆◆◆◆ amenties.

Rates: Low Season: $159 – $229 High Season: $179 – $329 Number of Rooms: 16

Cuisine: Two course breakfast. Late afternoon appetizers, beverages, and homemade Coyote cookies. Guests are welcome to bring their own spirits.

Nearest Airport: Phoenix Sky Harbor

10   *SelectRegistry.com*

The guidebook is organized in alphabetical order, by state and province (our Canadian members have a separate section, which begins on page 218). A map of the state or province at the beginning of each section shows the location of each property, relative to major cities and highways. For larger map images, go to the SELECT REGISTRY web site, www. SelectRegistry.com.

Generally speaking, properties are grouped within each state or province by travel area, north to south, east to west. All Camden, Maine properties, for example, are listed together.

For the convenience of our guests, an index of the properties by state and province is provided at the front of the book. At the back of the book, you'll find an alpha-listing of all member properties.

Each SELECT REGISTRY member property is represented with its own page of information in this guidebook. The page includes two pictures, a brief description of the experience a guest can expect at that property, and contact information. The owners/innkeepers are listed so you know who your hosts will be.❶

The Rooms/Rates section gives the number of rooms and pricing structure for the property. ❷ Cuisine describes the food and beverage specialties for which our members are famous, including whether the property serves only breakfast or is full service.❸ The nearest Airport(s) tells you where you might fly in.❹

Because food and wine are important complements to many of our properties, some members are proud to have received the prestigious *Wine Spectator* Awards.

These awards are noted on participating Inns' guidebook page(s), as is any AAA Award the inn has received (confirmed by Official Appointment by AAA). ❺

Each of our inns has a slightly different mix of food and beverage services. Although these are often described in more detail in the Cuisine section for each inn, we want to give our guests a quick snapshot of what each inn offers in-house. The icons near the top of each page tell you whether the inn serves breakfast, lunch, and/or dinner, and whether or not wine or cocktails are available. ❻

Breakfast Lunch Dinner Wine/Cocktails

We hope these instructions help you utilize our guidebook as you plan your travels. For many additional pages of information on each member property, visit us online at:

www. selectregistry. com

Gift Certificates

The gift of an overnight stay or a weekend at an exceptional inn or B&B can be one of the most thoughtful and appreciated gifts you can give your parents, children, or dear friends. Employers are discovering that a gift certificate for a "getaway" is an excellent way of rewarding their employees, while at the same time giving them some much needed rest. A few ideas:

- **Weddings** • **Anniversaries** • **Holiday & Birthday gifts** •
- **Employee rewards/incentives** • **Retirement**

Our gift certificates are valid at any of our more than 400 member properties. We process orders daily, packaging certificates with our complimentary Association guidebook and your personal message. Certificates may be ordered online or by phone, and expedited shipping is available at an additional cost. The next time you think about gift-giving, think about our Gift Certificate Program—the perfect gift for that special person, 1-800-344-5244 or online at www.selectregistry.com/giftcertificates.

The Golden Quill Club: SELECT REGISTRY's guest loyalty program

Coming in 2011 – The New Golden Quill Loyalty Travel Program!

Please go to www.selectregistry.com/goldenquill for complete details on the new program and to learn how to register

Perhaps the most important distinction that sets a SELECT REGISTRY member apart from other inns or B&Bs is our Quality Assurance Program.

SELECT REGISTRY carries out a quality assurance inspection for each of its nearly 400 member properties. This program involves independent inspectors—Quality Consultants, L.L.C.—who are not employees of SELECT REGISTRY and who have handled our inspections for close to 20 years. The inspectors arrive unidentified, spend the night, and evaluate the inn on a detailed point system, which translates into a pass/fail grade for the inn. Hospitality, the physical plant, and cuisine of the property are all evaluated. Inns applying for membership are inspected, as are existing members on a periodic schedule. Not all properties have what it takes to pass the inspections, and this process provides an assurance to the traveling public that a SELECT REGISTRY inn is in a class of its own.

No other online directory or organization of innkeepers has a comparable inspection program.

Guest comments also inform us as we continue to help our member properties meet evolving guest expectations. To add your comments and feedback on a property, go to **www.selectregistry.com/ comments.**

If you see something you like in the SELECT REGISTRY guidebook, and also look for travel information on the Internet, we encourage you to visit our central Association web site or the home web sites of our individual members. On the SELECT REGISTRY site, you'll find thousands of pages of information all in one place, including recipes, descriptions and photos of individual rooms, area attractions and other details that complement the information contained in this book.

The SELECT REGISTRY website includes: user-friendly "Find an Inn" search functions, trip planner itineraries, and innovations such as:

- Recipes
- Calendar of Events
- Packages
- Specials
- Google mapping
- Facebook

In most cases, you'll also be able to check availability and request a reservation online from our members. And, of course, if you want even more in-depth information on a particular member property, there is a hot-link to the home web page for the inn or B&B of interest to you.

On our central web site, you'll also find a place to register for our regular guest e-newsletters, which include featured inns, recipes, stories, and specials. Sign up today, and keep in touch with SELECT REGISTRY on a regular basis!

"Grand Canyon State"

Famous for: Grand Canyon, Painted Desert, Petrified Forest, Copper Mines, Gila Monster, Lake Mead (largest man-made lake in the world), Tombstone (Wyatt Earp's fight at the OK Corral), Cliff Dwellings.

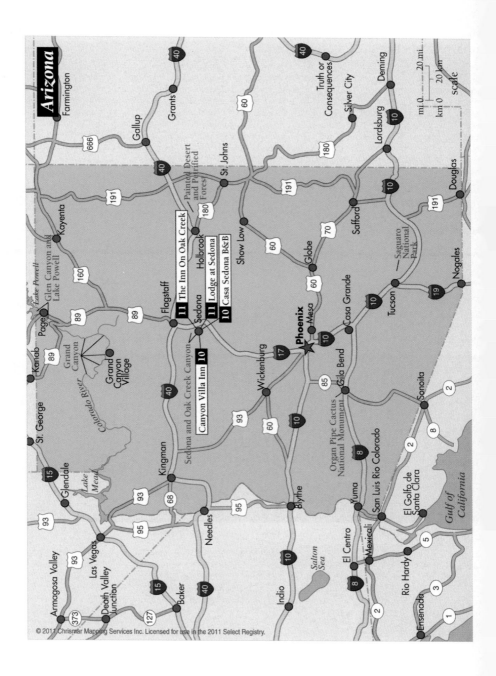

Canyon Villa Bed & Breakfast Inn

www.canyonvilla.com
40 Canyon Circle Drive, Sedona, AZ 86351
800-453-1166 • 928-284-1226 • Fax 928-284-2114
canvilla@sedona.net

Member Since 1995

Innkeepers/OwnersLes & Peg Belch

Canyon Villa Inn is uniquely located and designed to capture a visual experience of Sedona's world famous Bell Rock & Courthouse Butte. Large common areas and themed intimate guestrooms open from arched French doors onto private balconies or lush garden patios.Guestrooms include cable TV, free Wi-Fi, phone, I-Pod clock radios, irons, hair dryers, and 4 with gas-log fireplaces.Private ceramic bathrooms include jetted tubs, personal amenities, irons, hair dryers, makeup mirrors, and bath & pool robes.Three course breakfast, appetizer hour, and fresh cookies & tea each evening. 1000 volume library with over 100 DVDs, guest computer, and printer. Guests relax daily under the warm Arizona sun by a glass tiled swimming pool, hike desert trails from the premises, & stargaze cool evenings outdoors by fireside. Ranked #1 in the TripAdvisor 2009 Award for "Best U.S. Inns and B&Bs." Past recipient of "Best U.S. Bed and Breakfast" award from Harper's "Hideaway Report". Recommended by Frommers and admitted to Diamond Collection with BedandBreakfast.com. AAA 4 Diamond Award (2011)

Rates: 10 Red Rock View Rooms $199-349. 1 Limited View Room $159-199. Discounts for AAA, AARP, Military. Number of Rooms: 11

Cuisine: Three course served breakfast includes our award winning Cinnamon Rolls. Afternoon refreshments and appetizers. Guests welcome to bring their own spirits. Harney & Son teas served with original light deserts throughout the entire evening.

Nearest Airport: Phoenix Sky Harbor (PHX)

Casa Sedona Inn

www.casasedona.com
55 Hozoni Drive, Sedona, AZ 86336
800-525-3756 • 928-282-2938 • Fax 928-282-2259
casa@sedona.net

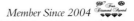

Member Since 2004

Innkeepers/Owners Paul & Connie Schwartz

Featured on The Travel Channel "Best of the Best" series and listed in the 2007 addition of "1000 Places to See Before You Die", Casa Sedona is a world-renowned 16-room bed & breakfast inn. Located 6 minutes away from the bustling "uptown" in a quiet area just off the Highway 89A. Relax in our serene landscaped gardens, or on your private patio or balcony, and enjoy inspiring red rock views of Thunder Mountain, Chimney Rock, and "Baby Bell" Rock. Breakfast is served outside - with red rock views — and features mild Southwest Favorites and award-winning French Toast bakes.Afternoon appetizers in the Juniper Garden offer an opportunity for guests to relax, refuel, and share the day's experiences. Guest rooms are up-to-date and well-appointed with AAA ◆◆◆◆ amenties.

Rates: Low Season: $159 — $229 High Season: $179 — $329 Number of Rooms: 16

Cuisine: Two course breakfast. Late afternoon appetizers, beverages, and homemade Coyote cookies. Guests are welcome to bring their own spirits.

Nearest Airport: Phoenix Sky Harbor

The Inn on Oak Creek

www.innonoakcreek.com
556 State Route 179, Sedona, AZ 86336
800-499-7896 • 928-282-7896 • Fax 928-282-0696
theinn@sedona.net

Member Since 2001

Owner/Manager James Matykiewicz

Initially built in 1972 as an art gallery, then totally refurbished and transformed in 1995, the Inn perches on a bluff overlooking Oak Creek, Arizona's premier year-round spring-fed stream. Within easy walking distance are Sedona's best art galleries, boutique shops, several fine restaurants, and Tlaquepaque shopping village. Almost as close are National Forest trails that will take you to the heart of red rock country. So, while guests are constantly surprised that an Inn so centrally located in Sedona can offer such privacy and relaxation, the luxurious AAA Four Diamond accommodations, professional staff, and culinary delights (Five Star Food!) are what really please them. Additionally, located in the Inn's private owner's quarters is The Art Of Cooking, where professional chefs conduct cooking cooking classes several nights a week. The classes are based on a four course dinner menu, are hands on, and participating guests then partake of their handiwork. Contact the innkeeper for dates, time and price.

Rates: 11 Rooms, $200/$295 DBL; 1 Suite, $350. Creekside rooms have decks w/dramatic views. All rooms include gas fireplaces and private baths with whirlpool tubs. Number of Rooms: 11

Cuisine: Full four-course gourmet breakfast, afternoon beverages, cookies & hors d'oeuvres included. Guests are welcome to bring their own adult beverages. Cooking classes are conducted on Tuesday and Thursday evenings in the owner's quarters.

Nearest Airport: Flagstaff (40 minutes), Phoenix (2 hours)

The Lodge at Sedona

www.LODGEatSEDONA.com
125 Kallof Place, Sedona, AZ 86336
800-619-4467 • 928-204-1942 • Fax 928-204-2128
Info@LODGEatSEDONA.com

Member Since 2003

Innkeepers/Owners Ron & Shelly Wachal

Romance and Intrigue, Comfort & Luxury, Escape and Adventure - the Lodge at Sedona has it all. -AZ News. Elegant & Secluded Mission/Arts & Craft estate set on two acres of grand seclusion in the very Heart of Sedona, Arizona.Awarded Top 10 Inns in US by Forbes.com, Best B&Bs by Phoenix Magazine.Recommended by Small Elegant Hotels, Historic Lodging Directory, Bon Appetit, Mobil Three Star, Fodors.com, and Frommer's. Close to hiking trails,biking, golf, tennis, art galleries and shopping. Spectacular Red Rock views, sculpture gardens, fitness center priviledges and pools adjacent, fountains and a magical labyrinth. King suites with fireplaces, jet tubs, spa robes, large decks, stereo TV. Massage Services, complete concierge service and full gourmet breakfast and snacks included daily. Check our Seasonal Specials and Hot Deals. "The Lodge at Sedona is one of the most romantic Inns in Arizona."- AZ Foothills Magazine.

Rates: 14 Rooms & King Suites: $189/$349 B&B; Kings w/ fireplaces, jet tubs, view decks, stereo TV. Number of Rooms: 14

Cuisine: Professionally prepared and served gourmet breakfast including Sedona Gold coffee, Lodge Granola and yogurt. Sunset appetizers, Spring water & Snacks included daily. Guest beverages welcome!

Nearest Airport: Phoenix (PHX), Flagstaff (FLG), Sedona (KSEZ)

"The Natural State"

Famous for: Natural Hot Springs, The Ozarks, Waterfalls, Diamonds, Oil, Aluminum.

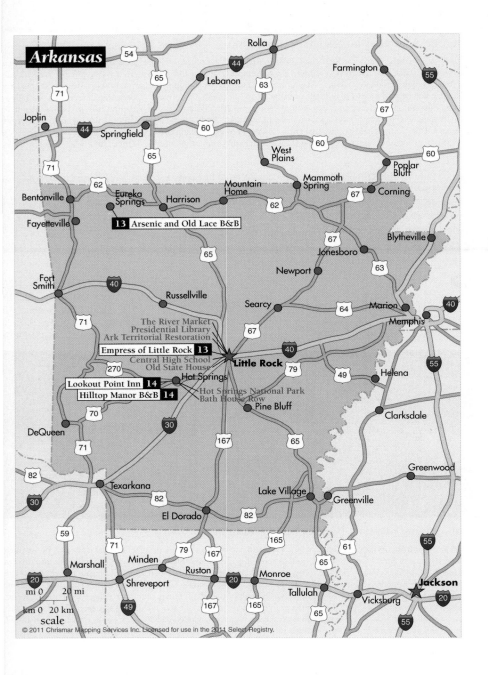

Arsenic and Old Lace B&B

www.eurekaspringsromancebb.com
60 Hillside Avenue, Eureka Springs, AR 72632
866-350-5454 • 479-253-5454 • Fax 479-253-2246
info@eurekaspringsromancebb.com

Member Since 2006

Innkeepers/Owners Beverly and Doug Breitling

Arsenic and Old Lace is located on a heavily wooded hillside in the Historic District of Eureka Springs. The beautiful Ozark Mountains surround the Inn that is a step back to a quieter, more relaxed time. From our Morning Room, or the Chantilly Rose room balcony, guests enjoy the mixed white squirrels, birds, chipmunks and sometimes even deer. A short walk through a wooded area will bring guests to the shops, historic homes and buildings of the Historic Loop. The mood of the Inn is relaxed luxury, as your hosts strive to make each guest feel as if they are at home. The relaxed feel continues into your room, where you will find comfortable furnishings, jetted tubs, Comphy micro-fiber sheets, luxury showers, televisions, VCR/DVD players, CD players and Wireless Internet access. Enjoy the video library to watch a movie, curl-up with a good book or your loved one. Rest, Relax and Recreate. You've stepped back in time without leaving modern necessities. Excite all of your senses with an unforgettable experience!

Rates: $115/$299. Rates vary seasonally and midweek. Number of Rooms: 5

Cuisine: Enjoy custom blended coffee, tea or hot chocolate; our full gourmet breakfast starts with a delicious fruit course, breakfast breads or scones, and a unique main course. Enjoy homemade snacks all day and a well stocked refrigerator.

Nearest Airport: NW Arkansas Regional (XNA)

The Empress of Little Rock

www.theempress.com
2120 Louisiana Street, Little Rock, AR 72206
877-374-7966 • 501-374-7966 • Fax 501-375-4537
Email: hostess@theempress.com

Member Since 2001

Innkeepers/Owners Robert Blair and Sharon Welch–Blair

Stay a century away in the award winning small luxury hotel, THE EMPRESS OF LITTLE ROCK. The historic boutique hotel, ranked as a top ten in the US, was built in 1888 as the largest most opulent mansion in Arkansas. Let your senses be lavished with the most modern spa amenities: hydro–massage therapy, steam, aromatherapy, antique Jacuzzi soaking tubs. Work a 1000 piece puzzle by the warmth of firelight in the parlor. Enjoy an elegant two course gourmet breakfast by candlelight in a dinning room fit for Her Majesty, the Queen. Ascend a magnificent double stairwell as Scarlett to the Chatelaine Suite where a night in a canopied featherbed will have you begging for more. If something slightly more daring piques your interest, retire to the Hemingway Spa Suite with a 1940's "Mogambo" touch, a romantic escape to contemplate the next chapter in your life. Stroll through the Secret Garden where the fountain drums and a romantic hammock beckons. Ah!!! The Empress, where unrushed conversation abounds, along with true Southern Hospitality.

Rates: 9 Rooms, 5 Spa Suites, 3 Mini-Suites, $139/$329 Featherbeds/Cable/DSL/Jacuzzi/Fireplaces. Number of Rooms: 9

Cuisine: Elegant two-course gourmet breakfast by candlelight served 'Before the Queen' w/Victorian pomp and circumstance and a "bow-tied butler." Gourmet coffee, snacks and mineral water available 24/7. Wine social hour and in room complimentary liqueur.

Nearest Airport: Little Rock

Lookout Point Lakeside Inn

www.LookoutPointInn.com
104 Lookout Circle, Hot Springs, AR 71913
866-525-6155 • 501-525-6155 • Fax 501-525-5850
info@LookoutPointInn.com

Member Since 2005

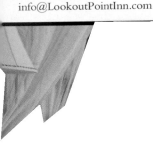

Innkeepers/Owners Ray & Kristie Rosset, Tricia Bradley

Enjoy peace and tranquility, comprehensive pampering and luxury. Savor the views of Lake Hamilton and the low-lying Ouachita Mountains. Experience an exceptional inn, with a fine attention to detail as its hallmark. Delicious breakfasts from one of the Eight Broads in the Kitchen, www.bedandbreakfastfoodie.com, starts your day splendidly. The gardens with waterfalls and meditation labyrinth provide a perfect backdrop for small, intimate weddings. Canoe the bay, watch the birds, nap in the hammock, or soak in the nearby historic Hot Springs bathhouses. A barefoot walk in the gardens or a challenging board game enhances the experience of simplifying life. A one or two bedroom lakeside condominium, called Lakeview Terrace, invites guests to enjoy the 36 ft. deck right at water's edge. Great for a family to enjoy all of Hot Springs fun. Named Best of the Best, Southern Living, Jan. 2010

Rates: $147/$369 for rooms and suites. $297–499 for 1 or 2 bedroom condo. Rates based upon type of room and season. Corporate weekday rates available. Wedding, romance and family fun packages available. Number of Rooms: 13

Cuisine: Fresh and hearty breakfast plus innkeeper's reception features dessert, appetizers, wine and tea. Complimentary snack bar. Soups, salads and hot/cold sandwiches available. Gourmet dinner for two by private chef, with dining by the waterfalls.

Nearest Airport: Little Rock, 60 miles. Air service to Hot Springs airport available from Memphis.

Hilltop Manor Bed & Breakfast

www.hilltopmanorhotsprings.com
2009 Park Avenue, Hot Springs, AR 71901
(501) 625-7829
info@hilltopmanorhotsprings.com

Member Since 2010

Innkeepers/Owners Bob & Faith Kraemer

Legends such as Jessie James and Al Capone have spent time on the Hilltop Manor estate. Is it your turn now? Come visit this award winning 1890 craftsman manor which has been restored to classic elegance. Take refuge from life's stress on this five acre estate which borders the National Park forest and was awarded a "Beauty Spot". Gaze at the waterfall from the expansive front porch. Wander the grounds and explore rock walls and buildings from the past. Meander through the grove of Magnolia trees and stop to smell a rosebud. Whatever you choose to do, we are here so that you can relax. We offer five unique, well-appointed suites most with king-sized bed, whirlpool tub, fireplace, refrigerator and microwave. All with decadent linens, robes and a fully plated breakfast each morning. Relish the morning meal which is served in your private suite, the front porch or the dining room with antique lighting overhead. We also serve an afternoon snack each day with beverages in the common area. Named "Best in the Midwest" by BedandBreakfast.com. Located 5 min. from Historic Downtown.

Rates: Standard Suites $170-$275 — Perfect for an anytime escape!Deluxe Suites $250-$400 (2 Person Jacuzzi Tub, Historic Fireplace, King Bed, 40" Flat Screen TV, Spa Therapy Sound Machine and More) Perfect for a Special Romantic Escape! Number of Rooms: 5

Cuisine: Hilltop Manor is known for its delicious breakfast that is unique each day. There is always a bread item, fruit dish, egg dish and sweet. We promise you won't go away hungry. Happy to accommodate dietary needs; let us know when making your reservation.

Nearest Airport: Hot Springs Memorial Field Airport — 6 Miles and Little Rock Adams Field Intl Airport — 55 Miles

"The Golden State"

Famous for: Spanish Missions, Gold Rush, Golden Gate Bridge, Wine Country, Citrus, Sequoia Redwoods, Hollywood, Disneyland, Lake Tahoe, Sierra Nevada, Yosemite National Park, Big Sur, Earthquakes and Death Valley.

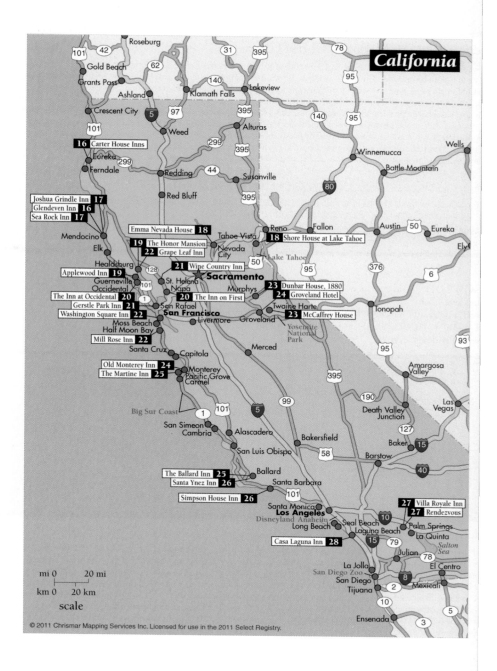

Carter House Inns

www.carterhouse.com
301 L Street, Eureka, CA 95501
800-404-1390 • 707-444-8062 • Fax 707-444-8067
reserve@carterhouse.com

Member Since 2003

Innkeepers/Owners Mark and Christi Carter

Northern California's premier inn is an enclave of 3 magnificent Victorians perched alongside Humboldt Bay in Old Town Eureka. The luxurious accommodations at Carter House Inns and the sumptuous dining at its Restaurant 301 (considered among Northern California's best restaurants) set an indulgent tone for a marvelous visit to the giant redwood forests, rugged Pacific beaches and the other wonders of Northern California's Redwood Coast. Our accommodations and service are unparalleled; our award-winning cuisine is prepared w/local organic products and fresh herbs, greens, and vegetables harvested daily from the inn's extensive gardens. The inn also produces its own wine under the label Carter Cellars (WS 96 pts.)and Envy Wines, specializing in limited production of cabs & merlots from some of the finest vineyards in Napa. Check out our incredible food and wine lovers' packages, featuring romantic dining and accommodations in the heart of the Redwood Empire! We offer Humboldt County's finest accommodations, an outstanding full-service restaurant, full bar, and an e-wine shop.

Rates: 9 Rooms, $197/$380 B&B, 2 Suites, $304/$612 B&B. Open year-round. Number of Rooms: 11

Cuisine: Full service award-winning restaurant open nightly, full breakfast, full bar, Wine Shop with 3,880 wine selections. With a recent 96-point rating from James Laube, Carter Cellars wine is quickly becoming a cult classic.

Nearest Airport: Eureka-Arcata Airport is 16 miles north of Eureka.

Glendeven Inn

www.glendeven.com
8205 North Highway One, P.O. Box 914, Mendocino, CA 95460
800-822-4536 • 707-937-0083 • Fax 707-937-6108
innkeeper@glendeven.com

Member Since 2002

Proprietor John Dixon

As seen in Vogue, Travel+Liesure, Sunset, and New York Magazine, this well appointed 8-acre, ocean-view farmstead B&B offers wood-burning fireplaces, full in-room gourmet breakfasts using farm-fresh eggs, secluded patios and decks, featherbeds, outstanding gardens, 45+ local wines by the glass in its Wine Bar[n] and a complimentary wine and hors d'oeuvres hour.Glendeven is a multi-building 1867 country farmstead situated on a headland meadow with grazing llamas, roaming chickens, manicured gardens, & an organic edible garden.Located 2 minutes south of the historic Mendocino village, Glendeven offers trails to the Pacific headland cliffs, to the beach at its surrounding state park & to its own Forest Trail connecting to Fern Canyon trail along Little River. Its Wine Bar[n] features flight tastings of local Mendocino county varietals in its garden and watertower-view lounge. There is a 2,000 sq ft vacation rental onsite, perfect for couples traveling together.A four-course wine pairing ocean-view dinner is available twice a week at Glendevenâ s farmhouse "host table."

Rates: 10 rooms & suites, $145 to $380. King & Queen beds. 2-3 people per room. Open year-round. Number of Rooms: 10

Cuisine: A 3-course, hot, in-room breakfast begins the day. 4-course wine pairing dinners available twice weekly. Complimentary wine & hors d'oeuvres in the inn's Wine Bar[n] nightly. Coffee, teas & goods always available in the farmhouse lounge.

Nearest Airport: San Francisco, Oakland, and Sacramento

Joshua Grindle Inn

www.joshgrin.com
P.O. Box 647, 44800 Little Lake Road, Mendocino, CA 95460
800-474-6353 • 707-937-4143
stay@joshgrin.com

Member Since 1996

Innkeepers/Owners Charles & Cindy Reinhart

Experience Mendocino at its best.Our Inn sits atop a two-acre knoll overlooking the village and ocean. Park and forget about your car as galleries, shops, restaurants and hiking trails are just a short stroll away. Tastefully decorated, comfortable, and exceptionally clean rooms await you. Charles and Cindy and the friendly staff will attend to your every need, and serve a full gourmet breakfast. Enjoy chatting with fellow guests over evening refreshments in our parlor, or escape to a private, quiet nook in the gardens.Relax on the front veranda and watch the whales spout in the distance. AAA Four Diamond and Mobil Three Star rated.

Rates: 10 Rooms Main House, Cottage, Water Tower, $150-$279 B&B. 2 Ocean View, 2 bdrm, Guest Houses $400/+ Number of Rooms: 10

Cuisine: Full gourmet breakfast served to guests using fresh local ingredients. The highly regarded Cafe Beaujolais is a two-block stroll. Wineshop on premises with selection of premium Mendocino wines. Complimentary wine in room & Cream Sherry in Parlor.

Nearest Airport: Little River Airport, Oakland International, San Francisco International, Sonoma

Sea Rock Inn

www.searock.com
11101 Lansing Street, P.O. Box 906, Mendocino, CA 95460
800-906-0926 • 707-937-0926 • Fax 707-676-9008
innkeeper@searock.com

Member Since 2005

Innkeepers/Owners Andy & Susie Plocher

One of the few inns in Mendocino with ocean views from every hillside accommodation, The Sea Rock Inn beckons with crashing surf and inviting firelight rooms. From your suite or cottage you will experience the true beauty of the Mendocino Coast with spectacular panoramic views of the ocean and dramatic rocky cliffs of the Mendocino Headlands State Park. The setting is perfect for a memorable getaway. Hand-hewn wood treatments accent luxuriously comfortable coastal contemporary design and appointments of virtually every amenity imaginable. Stroll through colorful gardens, curl up by the fire or relax on your deck and watch the sunset from your private ocean view cottage or suite. Hiking trails abound nearby, as does ocean and river kayaking, canoeing and many other outdoor activities. Gourmet dining is a short walk or minute's drive away, and the charming village of Mendocino is a National Historic Register community laden with special shops and attractions. Great rooms, stunning views and nice people. . .The Sea Rock Inn.

Rates: 6 Cottages, 4 Jr.Suites, 4 Suites. $179/$395. Number of Rooms: 14

Cuisine: Guests enjoy an attractive breakfast buffet with daily changing quiche, hard boiled eggs, yogurt, fresh pastries, juices, fruit and more. Upon check in to the room, guests may relax with a complimentary split of fine local wine.

Nearest Airport: SFO or Oakland, 3 1/2 hrs

Emma Nevada House

www.emmanevadahouse.com
528 East Broad Street, Nevada City, CA 95959
800-916-3662 • 530-265-4415 • Fax none
mail@emmanevadahouse.com

Member Since 2006

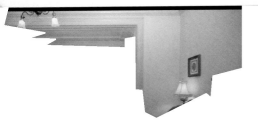

Innkeepers/Owners Andrew & Susan Howard

Enjoy Nevada City's four seasons of food, wine and art in California's best-preserved gold country town. Our welcoming home sits in a quiet enclave of unique and elegant Victorians, just on the edge of the most beautiful town in the Sierra Foothills. Park and forget your car, as the historic allure of Nevada City is just a short stroll away. Beyond the fascinating shops, galleries and history, there are also trails alongside boiling river rapids, and seventeen unique and interesting wineries to visit. All this is capped by a proliferation of exceptional restaurants that will delight even the most cosmopolitan of travelers. It is not uncommon to hear favorable comparisons to the most notable restaurants of San Francisco and the Napa Valley. At the Emma Nevada House, you will find large and comfortable rooms characterized by their fine linens, exceptional cleanliness and thoughtful touches. Wrap around porches, beautiful gardens, and a babbling brook invite guests to linger and unwind in this graceful retreat.

Rates: $179/$249. Number of Rooms: 6
Cuisine: Guests enjoy a sit down three course breakfast that many guests say is worth the trip by itself. Menus are seasonal, with variations on fluffy souffles and fruit or berry stuffed French toast as frequent choices.
Nearest Airport: Sacramento, Reno, San Francisco & Oakland

Shore House at Lake Tahoe

www.shorehouselaketahoe.com
7170 North Lake Blvd., P.O. Box 499, Tahoe Vista, CA 96148
800-207-5160 • 530-546-7270 • Fax 530-546-7130
innkeeper@shorehouselaketahoe.com

Member Since 2000

Innkeepers/Owners Marty & Barb Cohen

The Shore House is the ultimate romantic getaway at the water's edge of spectacular Lake Tahoe. Balconies in front of each room offer fabulous views of the pristine lake and mountains. Relax in the large outdoor lakefront hot tub. Enjoy fine lakefront restaurants, art galleries, and casinos close by. This winter wonderland offers world class downhill and x-c skiing at 29 resorts, ice skating, snowmobiling, and sleigh rides. Summer activities include spectacular hiking, biking, golf, tennis, rafting, para-sailing, and lunch cruises on the Shore House 36' yacht, Lady of the Lake. Kayak right from the Shore House. Enjoy a romantic couples' massage in the on site massage studio overlooking the Lake and Mountains. The Shore House specializes in intimate lakefront weddings with marriage license and Minister on site. Wedding, Honeymoon, Anniversary and Birthday Packages are also offered.

Rates: All King or Queen Rooms, $190-$325. Each room has a gas log fireplace, custom-built log furnishings, TV, Coffee Maker, Hair Dryer, Robes, Beach Towels and Refrigerator. Number of Rooms: 9
Cuisine: Award-winning gourmet breakfasts, wine and appetizers served daily in lakefront dining room or in lakeside gardens. Fresh Baked Treats in room each day. Walk to extraordinary lakefront restaurants.
Nearest Airport: Reno Tahoe International

The Honor Mansion

www.honormansion.com
14891 Grove Street, Healdsburg, CA 95448
800-554-4667 • 707-433-4277 • Fax 707-431-7173
innkeeper@honormansion.com

Member Since 1998

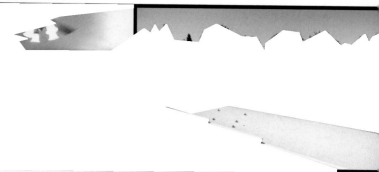

Owners Steve & Cathi Fowler

A Wine Country Resort. Come. . .let us pamper you! The only AAA 4 Diamond property in Healdsburg for 13 years, this luxuriously comfortable resort awaits your arrival. Imagine "world-class" amenities and service with hometown hospitality. Spa services, pool, tennis, PGA putting green, bocce, competition croquet lawn, decks, fountains and walking gardens, all situated on more than 3 acres of landscaped grounds. A pleasant walk to the downtown square which is replete with terrific shops, bakeries and restaurants. The perfect "special" occasion get-away. Romantic and private. Located in Healdsburg at the confluence of the world-renowned wine growing appellations of Dry Creek, Alexander and Russian River Valleys, with over 150 wineries. Come enjoy our passion for this incredible area and discover some of our boutique wineries, as well as those that have been here for over 100 years. Our fully trained concierge staff is at your service. Plan day trips, picnics, get that special wine tour in some of the world's best wineries right in our back yard. You will never want to leave!

Rates: 13 Rooms, $230/$600, 2 guests per room. K & Q beds, fireplaces, soaking tubs, private decks, wifi and more. Number of Rooms: 13

Cuisine: Full gourmet breakfast buffet, as well as room service menu, complimentary evening wine and appetizers, sherry, cappuccino machine, and bottomless cookie jar.

Nearest Airport: Oakland and San Francisco

Applewood Inn

www.applewoodinn.com
13555 Hwy 116, Guerneville, CA 95446
800-555-8509 • 707-869-9093 • Fax 707-869-9170
relax@applewoodinn.com

Member Since 2004

Owners Carlos Pippa and Sylvia Ranyak

A lovely and verdant meadow guarded by towering Redwoods in the heart of Sonoma's Russian River Valley (one of the world's premier growing regions for Pinot Noir & Chardonnay grapes) is home to Applewood Inn and its acclaimed restaurant which is recommended by Zagat and has earned a Michelin star for 2011. Splashing fountains and whimsical statues add texture and interest to the terraced courtyard and gardens that separate the tile roofed and stuccoed villas of this gracious Mediterranean complex. The old-world atmosphere of a "Gentleman's Farm" is evoked in lovingly maintained orchards and kitchen gardens that supply the restaurant through the Summer and early Fall. Gourmet picnic baskets provided by Applewood's kitchen help make a day of exploring the wine country and dramatic Sonoma Coast all the more enjoyable while Day Spa services add a touch of indulgent pampering. Located within a short drive of wineries in both the Napa and Sonoma Valleys, the Sonoma coast and Armstrong State Redwood Reserve.

Rates: $165/$375. Number of Rooms: 19

Cuisine: The Michelin stared restaurant at Applewood offers Mediterranean inspired wine country fare paired with a Sonoma wine list. The inn's romantic dining room features lovely views over a garden courtyard & towering redwoods. Adv reservations suggested.

Nearest Airport: San Francisco/Oakland/Sonoma County

Inn at Occidental

www.innatoccidental.com
3657 Church Street, P.O. Box 857, Occidental, CA 95465-0857
800-522-6324 • 707-874-1047 • Fax 707-874-1078
innkeeper@innatoccidental.com

Member Since 1995

Innkeepers/Owners Jerry & Tina Wolsborn

Inn at Occidental of Sonoma Wine Country–according to The Wine Spectator, "One of the Top Five Wine Country Destinations." The antiques, original art and decor provide charm, warmth and elegance exceeded only by the hospitality you experience. "Tops our List as the Most Romantic Place to Stay" is what Bride and Groom said of the featherbeds, down comforters, spa tubs for two, fireplaces and private decks. The gourmet breakfast and evening wine and cheese reception add to a memorable experience. Excellent boutique wineries, Armstrong Redwoods State Reserve, Russian River, the dramatic coast and scenic drives along country backroads make for a great destination and the perfect hub for exploring the pristine area. Hiking, biking, horseback riding and golfing nearby. Concierge service. All reasons why AAA VIA says of The Inn "The Best Bed and Breakfast in the West. "An Andrew Harper Recommendation. AAA ◆◆◆◆

Rates: 3 Suites, 13 Rooms: Fireplaces, Spa Tubs, Decks $199/$379, 2 BR Vacation House $689. Number of Rooms: 18
Cuisine: Full gourmet breakfast. Local wines and cheeses and freshly-baked cookies provided nightly. Wonderful dining nearby. Special Functions: Wedding, Corporate Retreat, Celebrations.
Nearest Airport: San Francisco (SFO), Oakland (OAK), Santa Rosa (limited service)

The Inn on First

www.theinnonfirst.com
1938 1st Street, Napa, CA 94559
866-253-1331 • 707-253-1331
innkeeper@theinnonfirst.com

Member Since 2008

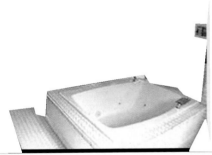

Innkeepers/Owners Jim Gunther and Jamie Cherry

Welcome to The Inn on First. This historic Inn is located in Downtown Napa, just minutes from boutiques, vineyards and fantastic restaurants. The Inn itself boasts 10 luxury rooms, lovely gardens and hand-crafted breakfasts, all of which contribute to the experience that have encouraged our guests to continue visiting. The rooms at the inn are each uniquely appointed and offer a long list of amenities, including internet access. Fireplaces, jacuzzi tubs and private baths in every room accompanied by complimentary sparkling wine, specialty refreshments, house-made confections and snacks. Breakfast is a centerpiece at the inn, with a unique and creative approach, offering whimsical dishes such as breakfast lasagna, omelet corn dogs, and handcrafted noodles with poached eggs in savory broth with prosciutto and onion steamed buns. No matter how often you visit, your breakfast experience will not be repeated. Currently there are over 100 breakfast recipes for the chef to choose from, and more yet to be created! This is definitely an inn for foodies.

Rates: 10 rooms, 5 Mansion and 5 Garden Suites. Rates vary by season. $205- $385. Number of Rooms: 10
Cuisine: Exciting, California Contemporary Comfort food. Guests are served in two courses. The first consists of house-made granola and baked goods, organic fruits, berries and yogurt. The second is a unique and whimsical creation that keeps guests returning.
Nearest Airport: 1-Sacramento. 2-Oakland. 3-San Francisco. Although SFO and OAK are closer than SAC, there is less traffic to SAC.

The Wine Country Inn

www.winecountryinn.com
1152 Lodi Lane, St. Helena, CA 94574
888-465-4608 • 707-963-7077 • Fax 707-963-9018
romance@winecountryinn.com

Member Since 1978

Innkeeper Jim Smith

For over 30 years, 3 generations of the Smith's family have been welcoming guests to this slice of Heaven. The stone and wood Wine Country Inn is a tranquil and hidden oasis in the heart of the Napa, America's center for fine wine and eclectic dining. The tree-lined drive, welcoming common room and friendly greeting set the mood for a memorable experience. Smells of freshly baked granola or evening cookies raise expectations of meals to come. Then with the antique-filled guest rooms, panoramic vineyard views, lush gardens, sun-drenched pool with warming hot tub and massage tent almost in the vineyards, guests find it hard to leave the property. But for those who do, the staff are eager to help map out truly memorable days of sampling the finest the area has to offer. At the end of the day guests gather with the innkeepers to compare experiences over more great wine and tables laden with homemade appetizers. To increase enjoyment the inn offers a free evening restaurant shuttle servicing 12 of the finest area restaurants as well as guided day-tours they call Inn-Cursions.

Rates: 20 Rooms 4 Suites 5 luxury cottages. Rates are $220/$610 Off-season and $285/$680 Harvest Season. All rates include a full buffet breakfast, wine social in the afternoon and evening restaurant shuttle. Call for seasonal special packages. Number of Rooms: 29

Cuisine: Innovative egg dishes, fresh fruit, juices, home-made granola and nut-breads as well as a fun bagel/waffle bar. Family-recipe appetizers with great local wines in afternoon.

Nearest Airport: Sacramento or San Fran

Gerstle Park Inn

www.gerstleparkinn.com
34 Grove St., San Rafael, CA 94901
800-726-7611 • 415-721-7611 • Fax 415-721-7600
innkeeper@gerstleparkinn.com

Member Since 1998

Owners Jim & Judy Dowling

Located 15 minutes from the Golden Gate Bridge and 30 minutes from the wine country, the Inn is in the heart of beautiful Marin County. It is the perfect location from which to explore all of the points of interest in the San Francisco Bay area. The Inn has a country setting on several acres with an orchard, Redwood trees, giant Valley Oaks, Cedar trees and green lawns. Being located at the end of a quiet residential street and backing up to the county's open spaces, it creates a secluded, restful environment as if being in the wine country. The historic estate offers a breathtaking example of comfortable elegance and refinement. In the evening, relax on the veranda during wine hour, play croquet, hike in the woods that border the estate, or pick fruit from the orchard. In the morning, enjoy a full hot breakfast to order at your leisure on the veranda or in the breakfast room. Spacious guest rooms are plush in comfort and color, with fine fabrics, antiques, parlor areas and private decks or patios with beautiful views. There is nothing like this in Marin County!

Rates: 12 Rooms, 4 with Jacuzzi tubs; Cottages and Carriage House Suites with kitchens $189/$275. Number of Rooms: 12

Cuisine: Accommodations include & extensive breakfast menu offering a full hot breakfast cooked to your order during a two hour period. Self service wine hours in the evening & 24 hour kitchen privileges which include a variety of beverages & snacks.

Nearest Airport: SFO-San Francisco and OAK-Oakland A.P., 45 min.

Washington Square Inn

www.wsisf.com
1660 Stockton Street, San Francisco, CA 94133
800-388-0220 • 415-981-4220 • Fax 415-397-7242
info@wsisf.com

Member Since 2006

Proprietors Daniel & Maria Levin

Situated in the very heart of San Francisco's legendary North Beach, the Washington Square Inn welcomes guests with the charm and comfort of a small European hotel. Whether traveling for business or recreation, some of the amenities offered include free wireless Internet access, complimentary breakfast, afternoon tea, evening wine and hors d'oeuvres, and full office services. Rooms feature European antiques, cable TV, soft robes and private baths. Some rooms have sitting areas in bay windows; others offer a cozy atmosphere with fireplaces. Located in the vibrant neighborhood of North Beach-just voted one of the top ten neighborhoods in the US, our historic hotel boasts beautiful views of Coit Tower, Russian Hill, Washington Square Park and the Cathedral of Saint Peter & Paul. The Inn is one of the best San Francisco hotel deals, offering exemplary lodging and service. You'll have a great location from which to explore this beautiful and exciting city! It's just a short cable car ride or comfortable walk to some of the most famous San Francisco landmarks.

Rates: There are 15 guest accommodations (15 with private baths). Double occupancy rate is between $179 and $329. Number of Rooms: 15

Cuisine: Breakfast served in your room or our lobby, includes fresh juices, tea assortment, muffins, croissants, pasteries, fresh fruit, yogurt or toast. Bagels and smoked salmon on the weekends. Fresh coffee every morning and afternoon wine and hors d'oeuvres.

Nearest Airport: San Francisco, Oakland, and San Jose

Mill Rose Inn

www.millroseinn.com
615 Mill Street, Half Moon Bay, CA 94019
800-900-7673 • 650-726-8750 • Fax 650-726-3031
info@millroseinn.com

Member Since 2008

Innkeepers/Owners Terry & Eve Baldwin

For guests who expect extraordinary personal service, warm hospitality and meticulous attention to detail, the Mill Rose Inn of Half Moon Bay is a destination not to be missed. This award-winning boutique Inn is renowned for an exuberant garden of year round color, sinfully comfortable rooms and suites, decadent culinary treats and an easy five-minute walk to beaches, numerous shops, galleries and restaurants of vibrant Half Moon Bay. The Mill Rose Inn invites you to relax and be pampered in the comfortable luxury of an English country garden by the sea. The innkeepers and their staff welcome you into a world of tranquility and romance. Ideally located 30 minutes south of San Francisco and 45 minutes north of the heart of Silicon Valley on the breathtakingly beautiful California coast, the Inn is the perfect venue for a special celebration, a reunion, or a business meeting, as well as an elegant garden wedding and reception. A Mill Rose Inn massage treatment coupled with our spa enhances your total escape.Owned and operated since 1982. Four-diamond AAA rating since 1992.

Rates: Baroque Rose Room $175 – $230, Burgundy and Briar Rose Rooms $235 – $280, Botticelli Rose Room $265 – $310, Renaissance and Bordeaux Rose Suites $295 – $360 Number of Rooms: 6

Cuisine: Our Lavish gourmet champagne or breakfast with vegan options served to you in your room or dining room gets rave reviews from all our guests. Fresh and homemade emphasized!

Nearest Airport: We are 30 mins. from San Francisco Intl. & 45 mins. from Oakland Intl. & San Jose Intl.

Dunbar House, 1880

www.dunbarhouse.com
271 Jones Street, Murphys, CA 95247
209-728-2897 • Fax 209-728-1451
innkeep@dunbarhouse.com

Member Since 2001

Innkeepers/Owners Richard & Arline Taborek

Step into Dunbar House, 1880 and step back into a piece of history, where homes were beautifully decorated with a casual elegance. This AAA ◆◆◆◆ Italianate home is filled with Old World Charm, and offers guests a private haven of relaxation, comfort and ease. Located two hours east of San Francisco, nestled between Lake Tahoe and Yosemite in the Sierra foothills, Murphys has not changed much since the Great Gold Rush. Just steps across the bridge over Murphys Creek, are restaurants, galleries, wineries, seasonal events, and live theatre. Our lovingly tended historic rose garden and surrounding floral gardens are the jewels of our property. Water fountains and lush greenery abound, surrounded by a white picket fence with many private sitting areas. Get a good book, or take a long nap in our hammock for that ultimate, lazy afternoon. An appetizer plate and local bottle of wine await guests in their rooms each day. Grab a fresh baked cookie, a cup of hot chocolate, or a glass of Rosemary Lemonade or Iced Tea, and just sit on our veranda and watch the world go by.

Rates: $210-$290 TV/DVD, wifi, refrigerator, fireplace & AC. Private porches & 2 person Jacuzzi available. Number of Rooms: 5

Cuisine: Enjoy your gourmet breakfast, and our own special roasted coffee blend, served in our cozy dining room by the fire, or in our beautiful century-old garden. Our specialty is our own homemade Mustard Sage Country Sausage, and daily fresh baked goods.

Nearest Airport: SFO-San Francisco, SAC-Sacramento, SJC-San Jose

---

McCaffrey House

www.mccaffreyhouse.com
23251 Highway 108, P.O. Box 67, Twain Harte, CA 95383
888-586-0757 • 209-586-0757
innkeeper@mccaffreyhouse.com

Member Since 2004

Innkeepers/Owners Michael & Stephanie McCaffrey

Pure elegance...in a wilderness setting. This AAA Four Diamond Inn is a delightfully warm and enchanting mountain lodge nestled in the quiet forest hollow of the High Sierras — near Yosemite National Park. Guestrooms are artfully decorated and feature handmade Amish quilts, fire stoves, private bath, TV/VCR, CD players, free wifi, and parking, plus exquisite views of the forest that envelops the Inn. McCaffrey House was designed and built by your hosts, Michael and Stephanie. They had one essential theme in mind: refined luxury blended with comfort and modern convenience. General gathering areas are spacious and beautifully decorated, with a fascinating collection of furniture and art which they acquired during their extensive travels. All appointments have such a welcoming touch that they extend an invitation to come often and stay awhile. In summer, breakfast is served on the decks which surround the inn. Enjoy the romance of this mountain lodge, the pleasure of a family vacation, take over the inn for a reunion or business meeting, or schedule a small wedding.

Rates: $145/$200. Number of Rooms: 8

Cuisine: Awaken to the aroma of fresh coffee. Relax in the dining room for a full country breakfast, prepared by Stephanie McCaffrey. Enjoy fresh fruits & juices, hot entrees, potatoes, muffins, scones, Decadent French Toast, delicious egg casseroles & quiches.

Nearest Airport: Approximately 2.5 hours from SAC, SFO, SJC, OAK Check website under location for directions to the inn.

Groveland Hotel

www.groveland.com
18767 Main Street, P.O. Box 289, Groveland, CA 95321
800-273-3314 • 209-962-4000 • Fax 209-962-6674
guestservices@groveland.com

Member Since 2005

Innkeepers/Owners Grover & Peggy Mosley

Drive to Yosemite 24/7 with a picnic and bottle of wine from Cellar Door Restaurant/Saloon. Tuolumne Rafting, US #1 whitewater river, 100+ species of wildflowers, hiking, golf, tennis, stables, swim at Rainbow Pool or discover God's Bath on the Clavey River. Four seasons — Spring, with songbirds, wildflowers and N. America's tallest waterfall. Summer's roses, hydrangeas, lavender and balmy evenings to herald Fall's brilliant color and crispness in the air. Winter temps suggest hot cider, cozy fireplaces, toboggans, snowshoes and skis. Lots of wildlife — deer, squirrel, bear, etc. Feathered species are varied, including an occasional eagle. Country Inns Magazine named it one of the US Top 10 Inns, and Sunset Magazine called it "A West's Best Inn.' Romantic parlour dining with fireplace, music, fresh flowers and candlelight. Upscale linens surround your warm, snuggly bed. We provide the ambiance — you create the memories! Weddings, receptions, family reunions, company parties, etc. Our Conference Room seats 15 people. Full service business center and FREE Wi-Fi.◆◆◆

Rates: Suites: $235. Decadent Suites: $275/$285. Rooms: $145. Nice Rooms: $155/$165. Luxury Rooms: $175/$185. Rates are for 2 guests. Add'l guests: $25. Pets Welcome — $15/pet /night includes treats and use of bowls. $4.50 Energy Surcharge Number of Rooms: 17

Cuisine: Gourmet Breakfast, Lunch for Groups and Full Service Dining, open to the public. Full Service Saloon and Wine Spectator Award of Excellence Wine List.

Nearest Airport: Approximately 2.5 hours from Sacramento (SAC), Oakland (OAK), or San Francisco (SFO).

Old Monterey Inn

www.oldmontereyinn.com
500 Martin Street, Monterey, CA 93940
800-350-2344 • 831-375-8284 • Fax 831-375-6730
omi@oldmontereyinn.com

Member Since 1993

Innkeepers/Owners Patricia Valletta & Ted Lindsay

'The level of service and accommodations here would rival most any inn or hotel we've visited,' says The San Francisco Chronicle. Set amidst an acre of spectacular gardens on a quiet, oak-studded Monterey hillside, the Old Monterey Inn exudes romance and warmth. The 1929 half-timbered English Tudor Inn's rooms all overlook the uniquely beautiful gardens. Inside, guests find the attention to detail, which is the hallmark of the Inn—memorably fluffy featherbeds and 24-hour access to mineral waters, juices, tea and coffee. A full gourmet breakfast is served bedside or in our Heritage dining room, or, weather permitting, in our gardens. The owner imbues every element with the extra touches that help the Inn achieve near perfection. Recommended by prestigious Harper's Hideaway Report, Conde Nast Gold List, and Travel & Leisure (as seen on a recent Today Show Dream Getaway Segment).

Rates: Cottage, 3 Suites & 6 Rooms w/sitting areas — fireplaces, spa tubs, private baths, air conditioning $269-$449. Number of Rooms: 10

Cuisine: Evening wine and hors d'oeuvres. Extaordinary restaurants nearby. Port and fresh fruit.

Nearest Airport: Monterey Airport — 10 min. San Jose Airport — 1 hr. 15 mins. SFO — 2 hrs. 30 mins.

Martine Inn
www.martineinn.com
255 Oceanview Boulevard, POBox 330, Pacific Grove, CA 93950
800-852-5588 • 831-373-3388 • Fax 831-373-3896
don@martineinn.com

 Member Since 1992

Innkeeper/Owner Don Martine

Just blocks from Monterey's bustling Cannery Row lies a 25-room Victorian villa that Bon Appetit considers "one of the 8 best B&Bs in historic homes" & Conde Nast Traveler calls a "spectacular place for a romantic getaway." Welcome to the Martine Inn, built in the 1890s as a lavish private residence just 90 minutes south of San Francisco. Today it's a meticulously renovated resort, where every fixture and furnishing is an authentic Victorian-era antique, & every room, many with fireplaces, claw foot tubs/or ocean views, has its own name & unique decor. Two sitting rooms afford priceless views of the bay, & other inn extras include a library, piano, game room replete with a 1917 nickelodeon, an 1890's billiard table & Don Martine's collection of vintage MG autos. Miles of coastal hiking/biking are literally at the inn's front door. All the attractions of California's magnificent Monterey Peninsula are nearby, only 3 blocks to Monterey Bay Aquarium & Cannery Row, 1 mi to Monarch butterflies, on 17 Mile Drive, 5 mi to Carmel, 30 mi to Big Sur, and 2 mi to Fishermans Wharf.

Rates: Intimate Room $189, Fireside Room $219, Romance Room $259, Ocean View $339, Family Suite $359 Number of Rooms: 25

Cuisine: Morning brings a full breakfast of a hot entree/fresh baked pastry/fruit/fresh juices, tea & coffee, on silver, crystal and lace. Evening presents wine & hot hors d'oeuvres. Group lunches & dinners prearranged from 20 — 50 up to 12 courses.

Nearest Airport: Monterey — 5 miles, San Jose — 70 miles, San Francisco — 90 miles

The Ballard Inn
www.ballardinn.com
2436 Baseline Ave., Ballard, CA 93463
800-638-2466 • 805-688-7770 • Fax 805-688-9560
innkeeper@ballardinn.com

Member Since 1993

General Manager Christine Forsyth

Voted one of America's Top Ten Most Romantic Inns, our comfortably elegant 4 diamond Country Inn is nestled among vineyards and orchards in the charming, historic township of Ballard. Each of the fifteen rooms possesses its own special charm and character reflecting local history. Many of our rooms have fireplaces, creating an especially romantic retreat. Borrow a bicycle and take a picnic lunch for an adventurous tour of the Santa Barbara wine country. A tasting of local wine & hors d'oeuvres, bed turn down service with home-made cookies, and a full breakfast are included in your stay. The acclaimed Ballard Inn Restaurant features French-Asian cuisine in an intimate 12 table dining room complete with a magnificent marble fireplace. Our Restaurant is open to the public Wednesday-Sunday. AAA ◆◆◆◆.

Rates: $245-$315 not including tax or service charge. Closed Christmas Eve & Christmas Day. Number of Rooms: 15

Cuisine: Breakfast:A delicious full breakfast, included with your stay, is served in our dining room each morning. The Restaurant:The Chef's award winning French Asian fare melds the flavors of eastern & western cuisines to create mouthwatering dishes.

Nearest Airport: Santa Barbara

Santa Ynez Inn

www.santaynezinn.com
3627 Sagunto St., Santa Ynez, CA 93460
800-643-5774 • 805-688-5588 • Fax 805-686-4294
info@santaynezinn.com

Member Since 2004

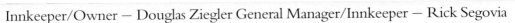

Innkeeper/Owner — Douglas Ziegler General Manager/Innkeeper — Rick Segovia

Our Wine Country Getaway awaits in 14 individually decorated rooms and junior suites. Accommodations feature unique antiques, queen or king-sized beds with Frette linens, remote-controlled gas fireplaces and whirlpool tubs in deluxe marble baths. Most rooms offer a private balcony or patio to savor the beauty and serenity of the Santa Ynez Valley. Take advantage of all that Santa Barbara County has to offer, from wine tasting and antique shopping, to Glider rides and Jeep tours. There's something for everyone in Santa Ynez. After a day of Southern California sightseeing adventures, you may wish to unwind in the heated outdoor whirlpool, lounge on the sundeck, or take a leisurely stroll through the gardens of the Inn. Whatever your needs–whether you wish to arrange for wine tasting tours, shopping, dining, glider rides, bicycle rentals or transportation–our concierge service is eager to assist you.

Rates: $285/$475 Number of Rooms: 14

Cuisine: Full Gourmet breakfast, Evening Wine & Hors d'oeuvres and Evening Desserts.

Nearest Airport: Santa Barbara Airport

Simpson House Inn

www.simpsonhouseinn.com
121 East Arrellaga Street, Santa Barbara, CA 93101
800-676-1280 • 805-963-7067 • Fax 805-564-4811
reservations@simpsonhouseinn.com

Member Since 1993

Owners Glyn & Linda Davies

...the whole effect is like walking into another time, another place of great elegance and wonderful service... This elegantly restored 1874 Historic Landmark Victorian Estate is the only Five Diamond Bed & Breakfast Inn in North America. It's comprised of six tastefully appointed rooms in the original Victorian estate home, four private cottages and four spacious rooms in our historic carriage house. The Inn is secluded within an acre of beautifully landscaped English gardens, yet just a five-minute walk from the historic Santa Barbara downtown area, restaurants, shopping, theater and easy access to the beach. All rooms feature antiques and Oriental rugs. Fireplaces and whirlpool tubs are available in rooms. We serve a delicious full gourmet breakfast, to your room, in the gardens, or our dining room. Afternoon refreshments and lavish evening Mediterranean hors d'oeuvres and wine tasting are not to be missed. Additional complimentary amenities include bicycles and evening dessert. Our concierge can arrange spa treatments, wine country tours, & dining reservations.

Rates: 6 Main House & 1 Garden Room $255-$475. Carriage House Rooms $595/$610. Garden Cottages $595/$610. Sun-Thurs and seasonal rates available. Number of Rooms: 15

Cuisine: Complimentary full vegetarian breakfast, afternoon refreshments & Mediterranean hors d'oeuvres buffet with local wine tasting each evening.

Nearest Airport: Santa Barbara

www.palmspringsrendezvous.com
1420 North Indian Canyon Drive, Palm Springs, CA 92262
800-485-2808 • 760-320-1178 • Fax 760-320-5308
info@palmspringsrendezvous.com

Member Since 2009

Innkeepers/Owners Marty, Barb, & Jake Cohen

Awarded TripAdvisor Travellers' Choice Award for Top 10 Romance & Bargain Hotel in the US by TripAdvisor Users! Your Rendezvous experience starts as you walk through our frosted glass doors and hear our nostalgic 50's music wafting through the air. You then pass into our gorgeous courtyard with pristine pool, hot tub, and blue AstroTurf sun deck. You will want to settle yourself in a lounge chair and wrap yourself in a plush towel and bake in the beautiful desert sun. Our rooms are individually decorated each with great 1950's style. All rooms have California King Beds, 32" Flat Panel TVs, DVD & MP3 Players, a sitting area, refrigerator, microwave, coffee maker, plush robes, and organic bathroom amenities. Most rooms have 2 person whirlpool tubs for added romance. Make sure to schedule a couples massage in our Massage Studio! While this property has all the amenities you could want, the real value comes from the amazing staff. They will make you feel at home, take care of reservations at local restaurants, and pamper you from the moment you step through the door!

Rates: $139-$249 depending on room and season. Number of Rooms: 10

Cuisine: Rendezvous' full gourmet breakfast starts with gourmet coffees and fruit smoothies followed by a fruit dish and fantastic main course. In the evening enjoy our RendezBlue martinis and appetizers. We are happy to cater to individual dietary needs.

Nearest Airport: Palm Springs International airport is 5 miles away. Ontario, Los Angeles & San Diego airports 50-110 miles away.

 *Member Since 2006*

Villa Royale Inn
www.villaroyale.com
1620 S. Indian Trail, Palm Springs, CA 92264
800-245-2314 • 760-327-2314 • Fax 760-322-3794
info@villaroyale.com

Innkeepers/Owners David & Bambi Arnold

Framed by breathtaking mountain views, the Villa Royale's intimate three acres echo an ancient Tuscan estate. Wander through tranquil courtyards overflowing with fragrant citrus, jasmine and lavender, gently cascading fountains, two heated pools and a large jacuzzi. AAA's Westways magazine calls the Villa Royale's AAA Four Diamond Europa Restaurant "a charming hideaway where you'll feel as if you have been transported to an intimate castle in Europe." Europa's bar, with its pool and mountain views, prides itself on its extensive offerings awarded by Wine Spectator Magazine. Luxurious full-service amenities, including full complimentary breakfast and fine dining, a daily newspaper, in-room spa services, and an attentive and caring staff make the Villa Royale Inn your ultimate Palm Springs romantic getaway.

Rates: Four room styles from $99 to $450(Seasonal). Pool Side, Private Patios, & Fire Places are available. Number of Rooms: 30

Cuisine: Cook to Order Complimentary Breakfast.Dinner with Four Diamond cuisine served fireside or by trickling fountains. Small private dinning room for up to 12 ideal for a special occasion or intimate wedding celebration.

Nearest Airport: Five minutes from downtown Palm Springs and the Palm Springs International Airport.

Casa Laguna Inn & Spa

www.casalaguna.com
2510 South Coast Highway , Laguna Beach, CA 92651
800-233-0449 • 949-494-2996 • Fax FAX 949-494-5009
innkeeper@casalaguna.com

Member Since 2004

Proprietor: Francois Leclair /General Manager: Kathryn Mace

Casa Laguna's 1920s mission-style architecture & terraced gardens exemplify a time when Laguna Beach was known as both an artist colony & a hideaway for famous film stars. Expansive views of the blue Pacific are framed by red tile roofs & towering palms. Relax on a secluded patio, or lounge on our sunny pool deck. Take a dip in our heated pool, or picnic at nearby Victoria Beach. Schedule a massage, or toast the sunset with champagne in our by-reservation-only, gazebo soak tub. Dream of our acclaimed gourmet breakfast as you slumber in an antique bed with a cloudlike pillow-top cover & luxurious eco-friendly linens. Our inn is just 1.5 miles from downtown Laguna Beach, with its many shops, art galleries, & summer festivals. We are within walking distance of beautiful beaches & tidal pools. We work hard to maintain a relaxing, romantic ambiance. Room occupancy is limited to one or two guests only, & our inn is not considered appropriate for children or groups. No smoking is allowed anywhere on the property. Well behaved, clean & healthy dogs, are welcome with restrictions.

Rates: Rooms, suites & a cottage: $149 to $649 subject to weekend/seasonal adjustments. All rooms have luxurious bedding, AC, flat-panel HDTV, DVD player, & WiFi/Internet. Some rooms have jetted tubs. Most have ambiance or gas fireplaces. Number of Rooms: 22

Cuisine: Our chefs have won both Silver & Gold Medals at Select Registry's Inn-Credible Breakfast Cook-off, & our inn has become a "foodie" destination. Choose from more than a half-dozen breakfast entrees, plus gourmet wine & cheese reception each evening.

Nearest Airport: Orange County,John Wayne — SNA Los Angeles — LAX San Diego — SAN Ontario — ONT

"The Centennial State"

Famous for: Gold Rush, Mile-High City, Mesa Verde, Cliff Dwellings, Rocky Mountains, Skiing, and Hiking.

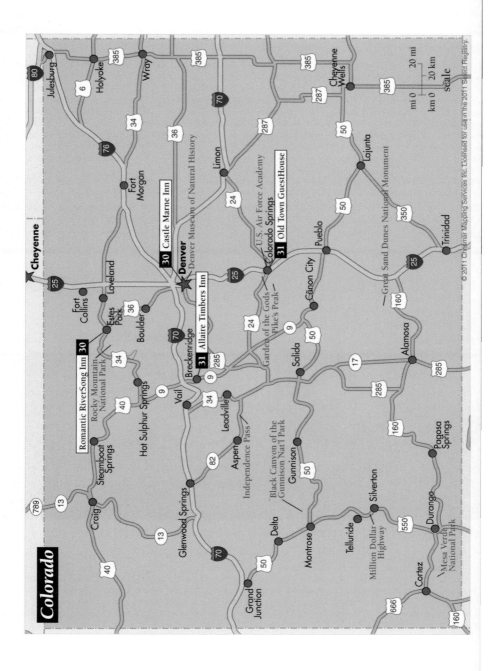

Romantic RiverSong Inn

www.romanticriversong.com
P.O. Box 1910, 1766 Lower Broadview Road, Estes Park, CO 80517-1910
970-586-4666 • 970-586-3223 • Fax 970-577-1336
info@romanticriversong.com

Member Since 1987

Innkeepers/Owners Sue & Gary Mansfield

Romantic RiverSong represents the classic country inn rarely found in Colorado. Located on a quiet backroad, we were was personally chosen by Select Registry's founder Norman Simpson. . . his choice for a unique place that offered "exceptional hospitality" and "good honest lodging." Secluded on 27 wooded acres with towering Blue Spruce and Ponderosa Pines, the inn offers quiet ponds, hiking trails and tree swings. Romantic RiverSong is a refuge for guests, as well as for wildlife. With only ten guest rooms, the inn has achieved a marvelous balance with its luxurious rooms (radiant-heated floors, jetted tubs for two, crackling fireplaces) and surrounding nature with the melodies of songbirds and a rushing stream. After exploring nearby Rocky Mountain National Park and the variety of quaint shops in town, come home to a relaxing "streamside massage." Then, later that evening enjoy our own chef-prepared candlelight gourmet dinner. Our warm hospitality will make your memories of Romantic RiverSong linger long after you've gone from this little bit of heaven in the Colorado.

Rates: 5 Rooms from $165-$195 junior suites ; 5 Suites, $225-$350 with Jetted tubs for 2; real wood burning fireplaces, private decks or flowered patios. Free Wifi on property.Hiking sticks and packs available without charge. Guided hikes Number of Rooms: 10

Cuisine: Mountain morning chill is lifted by a crackling fire and fresh brewed coffee followed by John Wayne Casserole and Happy Trail muffins. Dinner is served on fine china enhanced by soft jazz a glass of wine ..the perfect end to a day of adventure and fun.

Nearest Airport: Denver International (DIA) only 1 hour 45 minutes away , no mtn passes to cross !! Open year round to Estes Park.

The Historic Castle Marne Inn

www.castlemarne.com
1572 Race Street, Denver, CO 80206
800-92-MARNE • 303-331-0621 • Fax 303-331-0623
info@castlemarne.com

Member Since 1991

Innkeepers/Owners The Peiker Family: Diane, Jim, Melissa, and Louie, Louie J, Charlie & Liz

Denver's grandest historic mansion, listed on both National & Local Historic Registers. Built in 1889, features hand-hewn lavastone exterior, hand-rubbed woods, balconies, four-story tower and original stained glass Peacock Window. Beautifully blending antiques and heirlooms to create a charming Victorian atmosphere. Featuring Denver's finest examples of Victorian ceiling art, hand painted from original photos. Relax beside the bubbling fountain. Full gourmet breakfast served in the original Dining Room. Afternoon Tea served in the Parlour. Whirlpool spas and private outdoor hot tubs. Lunch & Private candlelight dinners by reservation. Wedding and Honeymoon packages available. Small weddings and elopements a specialty. The AIA says, "Castle Marne is one of Denver's great architectural legacies."

Rates: 9 Rooms, $115/$270. 2 Suites with Jacuzzi tubs. 3 Rooms with private out door hot tubs. Number of Rooms: 9

Cuisine: Full gourmet breakfast featuring home made muffins and breads. Artistically presented fresh fruit, Elegant Private 6 course Dinners served in the original formal dining room. Afternoon Tea and Luncheons. Evening Sleepy Time Tea and fresh baked cookies

Nearest Airport: Denver International

Allaire Timbers Inn

www.allairetimbers.com
9511 Hwy. 9, South Main Street, P.O. Box 4653, Breckenridge, CO
80424
800-624-4904 Outside CO • 970-453-7530 • Fax 970-453-8699
info@allairetimbers.com

 Member Since 1995

Innkeepers Sue Carlson and Kendra Hall

This contemporary log B&B is the perfect Rocky Mountain getaway. Wonderfully located at the south end of historic Main Street and nestled in the trees. Allaire Timbers offers 10 guest rooms, each with private bath and deck. Two suites offer a special touch of romance with private hot tub and fireplace. Relax by the fire in the Great Room or enjoy the serenity of the sunroom. Retreat to the reading loft, or unwind in the outdoor hot tub with spectacular mountain views. Just steps from downtown Victorian Breckenridge with its many and varied restaurants and shops. Access to the ski area and Breckenridge Riverwalk arts/music amphitheatre via the Free Ride town bus system. Featured in Arrington's Inn Traveler and CNN's Travel Guide.

Rates: 8 Lodge Rooms, 2 Suites $129/$400. Number of Rooms: 10

Cuisine: Full breakfast including homemade breads and sweets, fresh juices and fruits, the Inn's special recipe granola and changing menu of hot entrees. Evenings enjoy fresh baked cookies.

Nearest Airport: Denver International

Old Town GuestHouse

www.oldtown-guesthouse.com
115 South 26th Street, Colorado Springs, CO 80904
888-375-4210 • 719-632-9194 • Fax 719-632-9026
Luxury@OldTown-GuestHouse.com

Member Since 2001

Innkeepers/Owners Don & Shirley Wick

The three-story brick guesthouse is in perfect harmony with the 1859 period of the surrounding historic Old Colorado City. The contemporary Inn offers upscale amenities for discerning adult leisure and business travelers. Our elevator allows the entire inn to be accessible and the African Orchid room exceeds ADA specifications. The soundproof, uniquely decorated guestrooms have private baths and 7 rooms have fireplaces and/or porches overlooking Pikes Peak. Relax in the library or out on the umbrella-covered patio for afternoon wine, beer and snacks, then walk to some of Old Town's many fine restaurants, boutiques and galleries. End your evening with a soak in your own private two-person Hot Tub or your relaxing ensuite Steam Shower. Your morning starts with a gourmet 3 course breakfast served in our dining area. And then it's off to one of the many attractions and activities that the area has to offer (Pikes Peak, Garden of the Gods, Cave of the Winds). Member Pikes Peak Lodging Association, Bed & Breakfast Innkeepers of Colorado and other local community organizations.

Rates: $99/$235 Corporate and military rates available, Private baths, hot tubs, steam showers, fireplaces. Even lower Winter rates November and April with few seasonal blackout dates. Check our website for periodic discounts and packages. Number of Rooms: 8

Cuisine: Full 3 course sit-down breakfast. Hot entree, fruit in season, muffin or sweet bread and a cereal buffet. Evening with wine, beer and light snacks. Dine on our veranda (weather permitting) or in front of the fireplace with semi-private seating.

Nearest Airport: Colorado Springs Airport (~20 min. away)Denver International Airport (~1hr 30 min.)Call for directions.

"The Constitution State"

Famous for: Inventors (Charles Goodyear, Elias Howe, Eli Whitney, Eli Terry), Inventions, Watchmaking, Typewriters, Insurance, Submarines.

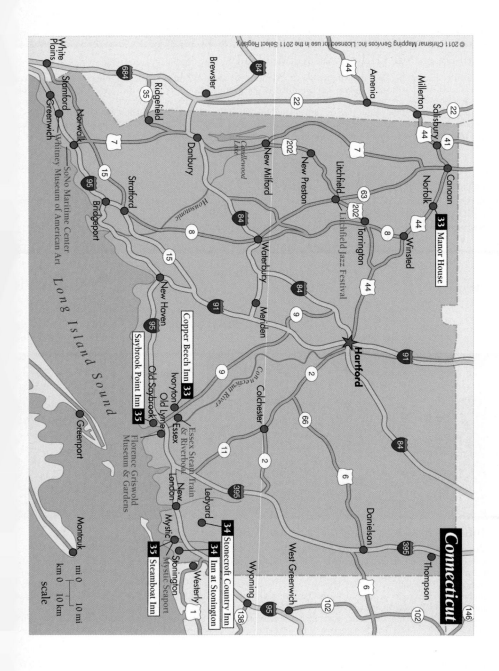

Manor House

www.manorhouse-norfolk.com
69 Maple Avenue, Norfolk, CT 06058
860-542-5690
innkeeper@manorhouse-norfolk.com

Member Since 2000

Innkeeper/Owner Karl Vess & L. Keith Mullins

Surround yourself with Victorian Elegance in this 1898 Tudor Estate described by Gourmet Magazine as "Quite Grand," and designated "Connecticut's Most Romantic Hideaway" by the Discerning Traveler. Featured in National Geographic Traveler, Good Housekeeping's "Best Weekend Getaways," and listed as one of the top 25 Inns by American Historic Inns. All rooms offer views of the spacious grounds and perennial gardens, are furnished with period antiques, and luxurious comforters. Savor a full breakfast made with local ingredients in the elegant dining room, relax by the baronial fireplace in the living room, or read a book in the library, all adorned with Tiffany windows and architectural detail. The Manor House is located at the foot of the Berkshires, and travelers can enjoy an array of outdoor activities, shopping, summer theater, and music festivals. A short walk to Infinity Music Hall and Yale School of Music Summer Chamber Festival. Rejuvenate with a treatment in the Spa Room, massage, facials, body wraps, reflexology or hot stones.

Rates: 7 Rooms, 1 Suite, $180–$255. Four rooms offer wood or gas fireplaces, 3 with whirlpools, and two with private balconies offering sweeping views of our grounds. All rooms air conditioned. Number of Rooms: 8

Cuisine: Two course country breakfast. All baked goods made in-house. Afternoon tea and cookies. Complimentary snacks, boscotti, coffee, tea, hot chocolate and spring water available all day in our bar area, which has a refrigerator, ice and all stemware.

Nearest Airport: Bradley International

The Copper Beech Inn

www.CopperBeechInn.com
Ivoryton, 46 Main Street, Essex, CT 06442
888-809-2056 • 860-767-0330 • Fax 860-767-7840
info@CopperBeechInn.com

Member Since 2003

Innkeepers/Owners Ian S. Phillips & Barbara C. Phillips

Named 2010's "Best Country Inn" by the readers of Connecticut Magazine, and one of "America's Top 100 Hotel Restaurants" by the ZAGAT Survey and USA Today, The Copper Beech Inn in Essex, is minutes from the Connecticut River and Long Island Sound. Just a 2-hour drive from either New York or Boston, the elegant guest rooms and suites with oversize beds feature Italian marble bathrooms and air-jet tubs. The Inn's award-winning AAA Four-Diamond restaurant features extraordinary food and a Wine Spectator award-winning wine list. The menu, created by Executive Chef Tyler Anderson, features sustainable seafood and high quality, locally-raised ingredients from local farms and artisan producers. Andrew Harper's Hideaway Report named the inn as one of the "The Ten Best in New England" and, The New York Times said "The Copper Beech Inn is a lovely example of what Americans look for in a four-star country inn ... the dining experience always marvelous."

Rates: $219-$399. Rates vary seasonally and on weekdays and weekends. Open Year-Round. All rooms with Private Bath, some with Mini-Bars. Number of Rooms: 22

Cuisine: Four-Star French and Modern American featuring an extraordinary menu and 300 plus selection award-winning wine list. "Crystal sparkles, silver shines, ... masses of fresh flowers set the scence for the flawlessly elegant dining" Connecticut Magazine.

Nearest Airport: Hartford 45 mins., Boston 2 hours, New York 2 hours

Stonecroft Country Inn

www.stonecroft.com
515 Pumpkin Hill Road , Ledyard, CT 06339
800-772-0774 • 860-572-0771
stonecroftinn@comcast.net

Member Since 2002

Innkeeper/Owner Jason Crandall

Relax in quiet country elegance on an 1807 sea captain's six-acre estate, only ten minutes from Mystic Seaport, Foxwoods and Mohegan Sun casinos. Ancient stone walls and lush green lawns surround the Inn, consisting of The 1807 House, a sunny Georgian colonial, and The Grange, our recently converted 19th century barn. Romantic guestrooms feature French, English and American country decor, with fireplaces, whirlpools and heated towel bars, wide-screen TV/DVDs and free Internet access. Savor an exquisite country breakfast, fireside dinner in our elegant granite-walled restaurant or the outside garden terrace. One Inn . . Two Styles . . Endless Charm.

Rates: Please check our website for current rates and specials (including our popular Hide n'Sleep Package) at www.stonecroft.com. ($99 — $289) Number of Rooms: 10

Cuisine: Full country breakfast in Grange Dining Room or on the stone terrace. Fine Dining in the Stonecroft Dining Room or enjoy our Garden Menu out in the Summer Gardens. Share after dinner drinks & dessert out around our fire pits on warm summer nights.

Nearest Airport: TF Green (Providence) — 45 minutes Bradley (Hartford) — 60 minutes

Inn at Stonington

www.innatstonington.com
60 Water Street, Stonington, CT 06378
860-535-2000 • Fax 860-535-8193
innkeeper@innatstonington.com

Member Since 2005

Innkeeper/Owner William Griffin

Named by Travel + Leisure as Inn of the Month, this 18 room waterfront inn is located in the heart of Stonington Borough, one of the last untouched and 'historic' villages in New England. The inn offers individually decorated guest rooms with gas fireplaces, baths with oversized soaking Jacuzzi tubs and separate walk in showers. Seaside rooms have private balconies with views of Stonington Harbor and beyond. Common areas include a top floor sitting room with breathtaking views, an intimate bar with adjoining breakfast room, the cozy living room, and a well equipped gym. During your stay, stop by one of the local wineries, visit downtown Mystic or simply take a stroll down Water Street and enjoy the specialty shops and some of the finest antique shops in the area. Enjoy our complimentary wine and cheese before walking to dinner at one of five fabulous restaurants in the village. Area attractions: small beach within walking distance, Stonington area vineyards, Mystic Seaport, Mystic Aquarium, Mohegan Sun and Foxwood Casinos, Watch Hill beaches.

Rates: 18 Guest rooms. Seasonal rates $150/$445. Open Year Round. Number of Rooms: 18

Cuisine: Continental breakfast of fresh baked treats and fresh fruit. Complimentary wine and cheese hour nightly.

Nearest Airport: T.F. Green- Providence, RI or Bradley Internation Airport- Windsor Locks, CT

Steamboat Inn

www.steamboatinnmystic.com
73 Steamboat Wharf, Mystic, CT 06355
(860) 536-8300 • Fax (860) 536-9528
info@steamboatinnmystic.com

Member Since 2009

Owners — John McGee & Paul Connor / Innkeeper — Kate Abel

The Steamboat Inn, offers eleven elegant rooms overlooking the beautiful Mystic River. Located in the heart of Historic Downtown Mystic, Steamboat Inn is just steps from fabulous shopping and fine dining; and just minutes away are The Mystic Seaport, Mystic Aquarium, Foxwoods Resort, Mohegan Sun plus four wineries within 15 minutes of the Inn. Each of our rooms are uniquely decorated with antiques and individually climate controlled. The rooms have private baths with single or double whirlpool tubs. Six of our rooms have wood burning fireplaces. Enjoy breathtaking river views from ten of our rooms. Complimentary wireless internet is offered throughout the Inn. Enjoy a full breakfast each morning in our common room or stop by in the evening for our delicious cookies and sherry! Awarded "most unique setting" two years in a row by Llannier Bed and Breakfast — chosen by the guests of over 8,500 B&B's worldwide. Be among the guests who visit Steamboat year after year, what are you waiting for come explore Steamboat Inn today!

Rates: 11 Guest Rooms. Seasonal Rates $150 — $300. Open Year Round Number of Rooms: 11

Cuisine: Buffet Breakfast includes scrambled eggs, bacon, turkey sausage, fresh fruit, yogurt, cereal, granola, cheeses, fresh bagels, oatmeal, homemade muffins, coffee, tea, and juices. Complimentary sherry and fresh baked cookies nightly.

Nearest Airport: T.F. Green Airport, Providence, RI Bradley Int. Airport, Windsor Locks, CT

 Member Since 2010

Saybrook Point Inn

www.saybrook.com
2 Bridge Street, Old Saybrook, CT 06475
(800) 243-0212 • (860) 395-2000 • Fax (860) 388-1504
info@saybrook.com

Innkeeper/Owner Stephen Tagliatela

Beautiful waterfront AAA Four Diamond Inn on Long Island Sound and The Connecticut River. Spacious and elegant guest rooms with delightful amenities. Full Service European Spa featuring organic and pharmacological skincare. Indoor/Outdoor pools and complete Fitness Center. The Terra Mar Restaurant boasts sweeping views of Long Island Sound and has seasonal outdoor dining. A founding member of the CT Farm to Chef Program the Terra Mar is a supporter of many local farms in The Connecticut River Valley. The on-site Marina like the Inn is recognized for it's environmental leadership. A past winner of "Marina of the Year" and an Atlantic Cruising Guide perennial 5 Bell Marina. Family Owned and Operated for 30 years. Saybrook Point Inn and Spa was among the first hotels in Connecticut to be certified as a Green Hotel by the State.

Rates: $199-$599, rates vary seasonally and on weekday and weekends. Number of Rooms: 80 Rooms

Cuisine: Modern American Cuisine with classical European and Asian influences. A proud founding member of The Connecticut Farm to Chef Program

Nearest Airport: Hartford, BDL, 50 miles, a little less than one hour away.

"The First State"

Famous for: Historic Brandywine Valley—Museums and Gardens, Du Pont Family Mansions, Beaches, Fishing, Wildlife, Farmland, Bird-watching, Nascar Races, and No-sales-tax Shopping.

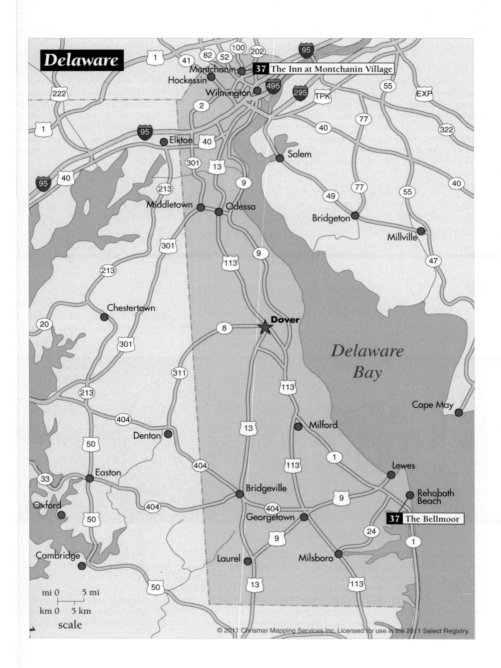

The Inn at Montchanin Village & Spa

www.montchanin.com
Route 100 & Kirk Road, P.O. Box 130, [GPS: 528 Montchanin Rd.
Wilmington, DE], Montchanin, DE 19710
800-269-2473 • 302-888-2133 • Fax 302-888-0389
inn@montchanin.com

Member Since 2002

General Manager Vera C. Palmatary

Listed on the National Historic Register, The Inn at Montchanin Village was once a part of the Winterthur Estate and was named for Alexandria de Montchanin, grandmother of the founder of the DuPont Company. One of the few remaining villages of its kind, the settlement was home to laborers who worked at the nearby DuPont powder mills. In eleven carefully restored buildings dating from 1799 to 1910, there are 28 richly furnished guest rooms/suites appointed with period and reproduction furniture, marble baths with all the amenities for the demanding and sophisticated traveler. Most rooms have beautifully manicured private courtyards and several have cozy fireplaces. The Spa at Montchanin is an innovative facility that offers facials, body treatments, and massages in a luxurious and peaceful environment. Nestled in the Brandywine Valley, 10 minutes NW of Wilmington and 25 minutes South of Philadelphia. Centrally located to all major museums – Winterthur, Longwood Gardens, Hagley Museum, Nemours Mansion, Brandywine River Museum, and Delaware Museum of Natural History.

Rates: Rooms: $192-$244; Suites: $290-$399. Free parking on site, European turndown, coffee maker, microwave, beverage area with icemaker, daily paper, free wireless internet, and fitness room. Please see website for package information. Number of Rooms: 28

Cuisine: Once the village blacksmith's shop, Krazy Kat's Restaurant is famous for it's fresh nouvelle cuisine and whimsical decor. They serve breakfast, lunch, Sunday brunch, and dinner. Our private dining room, The Crow's Nest, may accommodate up to 40 guests.

Nearest Airport: Philadelphia International (PHL) Airport: 20 milesNew Castle Airport: 10 milesBaltimore (BWI) Airport: 82.8 miles

The Bellmoor

www.thebellmoor.com
6 Christian Street, Rehoboth Beach, DE 19971
800-425-2355 • 302-227-5800 • Fax 302-227-0323
info@thebellmoor.com

Member Since 2004

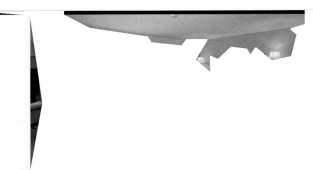

Proprietors Moore Family

Quiet moments in the garden. . .sunrise on the beach. . .the crackle of the fire in the Jefferson Library. . .a leisurely walk to unique boutique shopping and fine dining restaurants. . .a favorite book in the Sunroom. Our Day Spa offers over 30 services to restore and rejuvenate body and spirit. Whether you choose a seaweed wrap, hot stone pedicure or a soothing springtime facial, you can leave the world behind and experience refined relaxation and well-being. Additional complimentary services: concierge, bellman, high speed Internet access, wireless access, guest computer room, two pools, hot tub, and a fitness room. Enjoy complete relaxation in our beautifully appointed accommodations of unsurpassed comfort combining the warm, residential feel of a B&B with the efficient, professional service of a small European hotel. Enjoy the privacy and comfort of our newly renovated 4th floor Club Suites.

Rates: 55 rooms, $125/$465 B&B. 23 suites, $150/$695 B&B; suites include marble bath, fireplace, whirlpool, wet bar. Number of Rooms: 78

Cuisine: Full American breakfast served in the Garden Room or in the garden. Afternoon refreshments. 24 hour coffee service. Rehoboth Beach offers many fine dining options within walking distance of the Inn. Entire property non-smoking.

Nearest Airport: Philadelphia and Baltimore are both within a 2 hour drive.

"The Nation's Capital"

Famous for: The White House, the Capitol, Arlington Cemetery, Cherry Festival, the Smithsonian, Washington Monument.

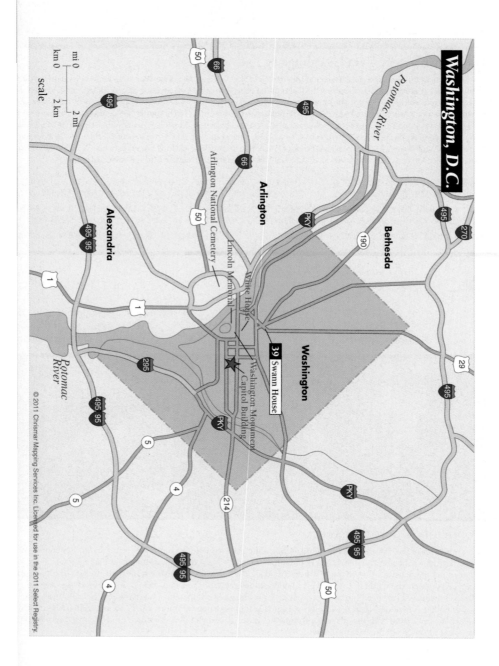

Swann House

www.swannhouse.com
1808 New Hampshire Ave. N.W., Washington, DC 20009
202-265-4414 • Fax 202-265-6755
stay@swannhouse.com

Member Since 2002

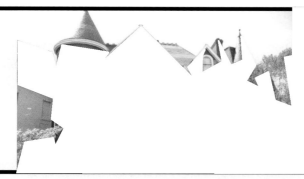

Innkeepers/Owners Richard & Mary Ross, Rick Verkler

Located on a tree-lined avenue in the heart of the Dupont Circle Historic District, Swann House welcomes you to the Nation's Capital and our 1883 Richardson Romanesque gem. Crystal chandeliers, elaborately carved fireplaces and original plaster moldings reflect just a portion of the nineteenth century craftsmanship that can be seen throughout our inn. Each individually decorated guestroom comes well appointed with sumptuous bathrobes, sateen sheets, down featherbeds and luxurious bath amenities. Select rooms include whirlpool baths, fireplaces and private decks for added luxury. Dozens of restaurants and cafes are just steps away allowing our guests to experience one of Washington's most vibrant and beautiful neighborhoods. Just 12 blocks from the White House and close proximity to several universities, galleries and conference venues, Swann House makes for a wonderful respite whether here for a romantic escape, business meeting or well-deserved getaway. "the Inn that launched 1,000 marriages" Frommer's "Fodor's Choice Gold Award" Fodor's Guide

Rates: 8 Rooms $169/$369; 4 Suites $269/$369. 6 w/ fireplace, 4 w/whirlpool. Swimming pool, WiFi, computer. Number of Rooms: 12

Cuisine: 2008 Silver Medalist Inn-Credible Breakfast Cookoff. Deluxe continental breakfast with home made granola and baked goods, seasonal fruit plus daily hot entree. Afternoon refreshments, evening sherry. Dozens of fine restaurants within walking distance.

Nearest Airport: Reagan National (DCA) 6 miles<n>Dulles International (IAD) 26 miles

---

DISTINGUISHED INNS OF NORTH AMERICA

Gift Certificates

The gift of an overnight stay or a weekend at an exceptional inn or B&B can be one of the most thoughtful and appreciated gifts you can give your parents, children, or dear friends. Employers are discovering that a gift certificate for a "getaway" is an excellent way of rewarding their employees, while at the same time giving them some much needed rest. A few ideas:

- **Weddings • Anniversaries •**
- **Holiday & Birthday gifts •**
- **Employee rewards/incentives • Retirement •**

Our gift certificates are valid at any of our more than 400 member properties. We process orders daily, packaging certificates with our complimentary Association guidebook and your personal message. Certificates may be ordered online or by phone, and expedited shipping is available at an additional cost. The next time you think about gift-giving, think about our Gift Certificate Program—the perfect gift for that special person, **1-800-344-5244** or online at **www.selectregistry.com/giftcertificates**.

"The Sunshine State"

Famous for: Disney World, Busch Gardens, St. Augustine (the oldest city in the U.S., founded 50 years before Plymouth), Florida Keys, Everglades, Space Shuttles, Beaches, Alligators, Oranges, Grapefruit, Wildlife.

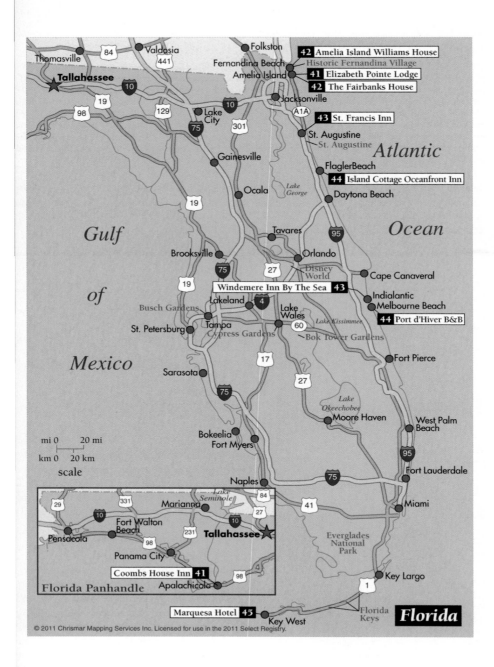

Coombs Inn

www.coombshouseinn.com
80 Sixth Street, Apalachicola, FL 32320
888-244-8320 • 850-653-9199 • Fax 850-653-2785
info@coombshouseinn.com

Member Since 2006

Owners Lynn Wilson and Bill Spohrer

The 1905 Coombs House Inn, located in Apalachicola on Florida's "Forgotten" Gulf Coast, occupies three elegant Victorian mansions in the historic district of this quaint seaside fishing village, adjacent to St. George Island with its white pristine beaches. Each of the 23 distinctively decorated rooms feature antique furniture and paintings, has its own full bath, cable TV, telephone and wireless internet access. Our seven luxury suites have romantic Jacuzzi tubs. Guests enjoy complimentary gourmet breakfasts, afternoon tea with home-baked cookies and weekend wine receptions. Camellia Hall, a spacious meeting room enhanced by gardens and a classic gazebo, provides the ideal setting for weddings and business meetings. Travel+Leisure Magazine recognized us as one of the "30 Great Inns." Discover this enchanting town, established in 1831 and rich with maritime history. Relax on the many verandas, enjoy a walk to charming restaurants, taste our delicious oysters, visit our museums and theatre, or go fishing and kayaking on the famous Apalachicola River.

Rates: 16 luxury rooms: $109 to $159. 7 jacuzzi suites: $139 to $269. Special "Wedding Romance Package" $999 includes: Ceremony, Bouquet and boutonnière, Wedding Cake, Champagne toast, Romantic Jacuzzi Suite, and Breakfast in Bed. Number of Rooms: 23

Cuisine: An elegant breakfast of culinary delights such as Eggs Benedict, homemade Quiche, biscuits, fresh fruit, juice and Starbucks' coffee.

Nearest Airport: Tallahassee & Panama City or private planes at Apalachicola Regional Airport.

Elizabeth Pointe Lodge

www.elizabethpointelodge.com
98 South Fletcher Avenue, Amelia Island, FL 32034
888-757-1910 • 904-277-4851 • Fax 904-277-6500
info@elizabethpointelodge.com

Member Since 1998

Innkeepers/Owners David and Susan Caples

Rated "One of the 12 Best Waterfront Inns" in America and Voted the #2 small hotel in the United States in the 2008 Conde Nast Traveler Reader's Choice Awards, the Pointe sits directly on the beach overlooking the Atlantic Ocean. Focusing upon individualized attention, the inn is Nantucket "shingle style" with an oversized soaking tub in each bath, USA Today and NY Times Digest delivered to your room daily, full seaside breakfast and a staff that wants to exceed your expectations. A selection of soups, salads, sandwiches, dessert, and room service available 24 hours. Complimentary WiFi DSL internet services available everywhere on the property. Only a short bike ride to the historic seaport of Fernandina. Concierge assistance available for 'day trips,' bicycle touring, horseback riding, tennis, golf, sailing, charter fishing, boat rentals, birding, kayak and Segway tours and Spa experiences. Custom packages may be developed for honeymoons, anniversary and birthday celebrations, golf instruction, 'all girl getaways' and small corporate meetings. AAA Three Diamond.

Rates: 20 Rooms, $225/$370; 4 Oceanhouse deluxe rooms $280/$485; 1 Cottage, $480/$530 B&B. Open year-round. Number of Rooms: 25

Cuisine: A complete and tended buffet breakfast in the Sunrise Room or outside on the deck overlooking the ocean. A light fare menu available 24 hours. Complimentary social hour each evening at 6 p.m. Our culinary staff welcomes special dietary requests.

Nearest Airport: Jacksonville International approximately 35 minutes away.

Fairbanks House

www.fairbankshouse.com
227 South 7th Street, Amelia Island, FL 32034
888-891-9880 • 904-277-0500
email@fairbankshouse.com

Member Since 1998

Innkeepers/Owners Bill & Theresa Hamilton

Featured in The Best Romantic Escapes in Florida and built in 1885, Fairbanks House is an 8000 sq. ft. Italianate villa rising above a quiet Victorian village on Amelia Island. Surrounded by soaring magnolias and live oaks with dripping Spanish moss, the mansion, its cottages and pool rest on a strikingly landscaped acre where guests enjoy a serene, smoke-free stay. Rooms are casually elegant with period antiques, romantic reproductions and comfortable seating. Numerous upscale amenities are designed for a carefree getaway, honeymoon or vacation. King beds, Jacuzzis, robes, bikes, beach gear and full concierge service are but a few examples of our attention to detail. Many of our rooms are quite spacious and give honeymooners and vacationers plenty of room to spread out. Walk to shops, restaurants, carriage and boat tours; bike to secluded beaches and a state park. Ask for details on seasonal specials, Romance Packages, Elopements, Major Holiday packages and Girls Just Wanna Have Fun Getaways. If you don't see it on the website, just ask. We're happy to accommodate.

Rates: 6 Rooms $175/$230, 3 Cottages $230/$365, 3 Suites, $265/$395 B&B. Open year-round. Number of Rooms: 12

Cuisine: Sumptuous gourmet breakfast served in our formal dining room, or on piazzas and patios amid our hidden gardens by the pool. Lively daily social hour with beverages, hot/cold hors d'oeuvres. 3 minute walk to cafes, taverns and fine-dining restaurants.

Nearest Airport: Jacksonville, FL

Amelia Island Williams House

www.williamshouse.com
103 South Ninth Street, Amelia Island, FL 32034
800-414-9258 • 904-277-2328
info@williamshouse.com

Member Since 2007

Innkeepers/Owners Byron & Deborah McCutchen

Come fall under the spell of this beautiful antebellum mansion, circa 1856 where romance, relaxation, and history combine to whisk you away to another place and time. Choose from ten elegantly decorated guest rooms with private baths and antique furnishings, some feature original working fireplaces w/hand carved mantels, whirlpool tubs, and a private hot tub. Sweeping verandas invite you to come and relax. Enjoy a delicious gourmet breakfast served in our beautiful dining room on antique china, crystal, and silver. Sip wine beneath our 500 year-old live oak tree in our flower lined courtyard. We are located in the historic seaside village of Fernandina Beach on Amelia Island, FL., just one block from downtown boutiques, bistros, antiques, art galleries,and world class restaurants. We offer complimentary bikes for exploring the island, beach equipment, wi-fi, and all the comforts of home. We offer packages for romance, birthdays, girls getaways, Christmas and other holidays. We are the perfect venue for Weddings, family gatherings, or business retreats.

Rates: 10 rooms $175–$265 weekend rates. Romantic getaway and spa packages available. Midweek discounts. Christmas and other hodliay packages. We are open year round. Number of Rooms: 10

Cuisine: Breakfast is served each morning in our dining room and consist of a fruit course followed by a savory or sweet dish with fresh ground coffee and juice. Each evening during our social hour we offer complimentary choice of wine and cheese.

Nearest Airport: Jacksonville, Florida

St. Francis Inn

www.stfrancisinn.com
279 St. George Street, St. Augustine, FL 32084
800-824-6062 • 904-824-6068 • Fax 904-810-5525
info@stfrancisinn.com

Member Since 2002

Innkeepers/Owners Joe & Margaret Finnegan

Guestrooms and suites with antiques, balconies with rocking chairs and swings, fireplaces and whirlpools add to the tranquil ambiance. Walk to everything from the Inn's Old City location. This historic inn overflows with hospitality, set in a lush tropical courtyard on brick paved streets with horse-drawn buggies passing by. A historic treasure, but modern comforts abound! Great value, with many guest amenities: swimming pool, gourmet Southern breakfasts, brunch on weekends and holidays, bicycles, social hour, evening sweets, DVD, wi-fi, health club privileges, private parking, free and discounted attractions tickets, coffee and inn-baked cookies, sherry and flowers in your room. Add inroom massages, gift baskets, inroom breakfasts, picnic baskets, flowers, champagne and other ala carte extras. Tropical setting provides endless outdoor activities, plus sightseeing, historic landmarks, cultural events and celebrations steps away. Many packages available to enhance your stay with added value and savings, themed for romance, history, and more.

Rates: 12 Rooms $149/$299; 4 Suites $229/$289; 2-BR Cottage $289/$349 for 4. Each with queen or king bed, private bath, central heat/air, wifi, cable tv, mp3/iPod connection. Several with fireplace, whirlpool, fridge. Great amenities! Number of Rooms: 17

Cuisine: Homemade breakfast entrees and more, enjoyed in our dining room, your room, on a private balcony or in the garden courtyard! Mimosas, Bloody Mary's at weekend breakfast. Appetizers & beverages at social hour; evening sweets; homemade cookies all day.

Nearest Airport: St. Johns County (SGJ); Jacksonville International (JAX)

Windemere Inn By The Sea

www.windemereinn.com
815 S. Miramar Avenue (A1A), Indialantic, FL 32903
800-224-6853 • 321-728-9334
stay@windemereinn.com

Member Since 2005

Innkeeper/Owner Elizabeth G. Fisher

Imagine ..a luxury, oceanfront bed and breakfast, only an hour east of Orlando. Guest rooms and suites are furnished with antiques and fine linens, most with ocean views, some with balconies, porches, whirlpool tubs or TVs. Start each morning with a full, gourmet breakfast, enjoy pastries and sherry at "tea time." Windemere is the ideal spot for your, small wedding, honeymoon or special getaway, corporate retreat, for watching a rocket launch form Kennedy Space Center, or witnessing sea turtles nest and hatch. The grounds have several gardens, including herbs for cooking. The central point is a koi pond alive with marine plants and animals. Sit on our Beach-side Pergola and watch dolphins and surfers play in the waves, or the sun or moon rise. The Inn has private beach access and provides beach gear. We are able to cater to most dietary needs upon request. Windemere is 45 minutes south of Kennedy Space Center, an hour east of Orlando and 10 minutes from Historic Downtown Melbourne with shopping, arts and entertainment and casual and fine dining. Visit www.windemereinn.com.

Rates: Guest rooms-7 $170 to $300. Two bedroom suites -2 $390 and $440. Weekly, AAA, & corporate discounts. Number of Rooms: 9

Cuisine: Start each day with sunrise over the Atlantic, and a full gourmet breakfast. A fruit course is followed by alternating daily sweet and savory dishes and freshly baked breads and muffins. Home made pastries and desserts are served at "tea time" daily.

Nearest Airport: Melbourne International Airport 15 minutes west, Orlando International Airport 1 hour west

Island Cottage Oceanfront Inn, Café & Spa

🍽️ 🍽️   🍷

www.islandcottagevillas.com
2316 S. Oceanshore Blvd., Flagler Beach, FL. 32136
87-ROMANCE-2 • 386-439-0092

Member Since 2007

Innkeepers/Owners Mark & Toni Treworgy

Tucked away in a tiny beach community along the Atlantic shoreline rests this quaint "Key West" styled jewel appreciated for its warmth, tranquility, spectacular ocean views, romantic ambiance & pampering. From the moment you enter the courtyard you'll want to kick off your shoes & relax in barefoot comfort as gentle music mentally transports you to a secluded tropical paradise. .... Plan to indulge in a couples massage or facial at the Inn's exclusive Spa or just sit back & enjoy the sparkling pool, the sounds of the surf & the scent of fresh sea air. .... Rooms feature dramatic ocean vistas, private decks, fireplaces & Jacuzzis for two, . . . & the on-site gift shop showcases original art of the innkeeper, scented soaps, candles & gift baskets. .... Guests are treated to "Afternoon Tea" each day plus a delicious & beautifully presented gourmet breakfast each morning served on elegantly set tables with pressed linens, shimmering silver, sparkling crystal & soft candlelight. Room service menu features fine wines, lighter fare salads & picnic baskets.

Rates: 3 rooms – $259 to $299/night ..... 1 Villa – $339/night ..... 2 Suites – $369/night. Same rate weekends/weekdays/holidays – minimums may apply. Inn is Open NOVEMBER through JUNE. ... Advanced Reservations are Required. Number of Rooms: 6

Cuisine: Gourmet hot breakfast includes fresh locally grown fruits, home grown herbs, coffee, tea, chilled juice & mimosas served by candlelight on individual tables. Afternoon Tea w/home baked cookies & fresh fruit. "Room Service" menu & fine wines available.

Nearest Airport: Daytona – 22 miles / Jacksonville & Sanford – 90 miles / Orlando – 100 miles

Port d'Hiver Bed & Breakfast

🍽️   🍷

www.portdhiver.com
201 Ocean Avenue, Melbourne Beach, FL 32951
866-621-7678 • 321-722-2727 • Fax 321-723-3221
info@portdhiver.com

Member Since 2008

Innkeepers/Owners Mike and Linda Rydson, Valerie Garofalo

Port d'Hiver Bed and Breakfast is old Florida luxury at its finest. A comfortable yet elegant retreat just 200 feet from the Atlantic Ocean, Port d'Hiver has ocean views, private porches, a bubbling spa pool & winding brick paths through a private compound of Island style buildings surrounded by lush tropical landscaping. Soak away the world in a large spa tub in one of our spacious new cabana rooms or watch the sunrise over the ocean from the deck of your beautifully restored historic room. Enjoy breakfast either on your porch or in our cheerfully inviting dining room. We also offer wine and refreshments at 5 o'clock in the main house, complimentary concierge services, wireless high speed internet inside and out, flat screen TVs, evening turn down service & the finest amenities. Fish, surf, dine, or watch the sea turtles. . . Melbourne Beach is a barrier island only .7 miles across from the ocean to the Indian River Lagoon. Port d'Hiver is a 2010 AAA ◆◆◆◆ property & in 2009 received TOP 10 MOST ROMANTIC INNS OF THE YEAR by American Historic Inns and iLoveInns.com.

Rates: $200/$525. Number of Rooms: 11

Cuisine: Casually elegant 3 course breakfast w/choice of entrees served individually in our dining room or on your private deck. Special vegetarian, lactose and gluten free diets are no problem. Wine & appetizers at 5 PM, cookies, coffee & snack room 24 hours.

Nearest Airport: Melbourne International – 7 miles, Orlando International – 69 miles

The Marquesa Hotel

www.marquesa.com
600 Fleming St., Key West, FL 33040
800-869-4631 Reservations Only • 305-292-1919 • Fax 305-294-2121
info@marquesa.com

Member Since 1991

Innkeeper/Owner Carol Wightman

In the heart of Key West's Historic District, The Marquesa Hotel and Cafe is a landmark 127-year-old home, restored to AAA four-diamond status. Floor-to-ceiling windows, exotic orchids, two shimmering pools and lush gardens are Marquesa trademarks. Rooms and suites are luxurious with private marble baths, bathrobes, flat screen televisions and fine furnishings. Located one block from Duval Street for shops, galleries, restaurants and nightlife. The Miami Herald rated it as one of Florida's top 10 Inns. Travel & Leisure Magazine's Reader Poll ranked The Marquesa in the "500 World's Best Hotels" and Conde Nast Traveller on their "Gold List." Zagat Survey members rated Cafe Marquesa as the highest rated restaurant in Key West. Off-site cottage rentals with private pools and kitchens are also available for family and group bookings. Explore nearby North-America's only living coral reef, go flats fishing, kayak, snorkel, deep sea fishing, para-sailing or relax by one of our two pools and do nothing! Our staff will help make the most of your stay.

Rates: 14 Rooms, $190/$395; 13 Suites, $300/$520. Open year-round. Special event minimum night stays apply. Number of Rooms: 27

Cuisine: Poolside or room service dining for breakfast; fine dining in Cafe Marquesa w/an innovative & delicious menu. Excellent wine list & full bar. Fresh local seafood, quality grilled meats. Named one of Key West's Top Five Romantic Restaurants by Key TV.

Nearest Airport: Key West International Airport — 3 miles

Gift Certificates

The gift of an overnight stay or a weekend at an exceptional inn or B&B can be one of the most thoughtful and appreciated gifts you can give your parents, children, or dear friends. Employers are discovering that a gift certificate for a "getaway" is an excellent way of rewarding their employees, while at the same time giving them some much needed rest. A few ideas:

- Weddings • Anniversaries •
- Holiday & Birthday gifts •
- Employee rewards/incentives • Retirement •

Our gift certificates are valid at any of our more than 400 member properties. We process orders daily, packaging certificates with our complimentary Association guidebook and your personal message. Certificates may be ordered online or by phone, and expedited shipping is available at an additional cost. The next time you think about gift-giving, think about our Gift Certificate Program—the perfect gift for that special person, **1-800-344-5244** or online at **www.selectregistry.com/giftcertificates.**

"The Peach State"

Famous for: Stone Mountain, Okefenokee Swamp, Live Oak Trees, Islands, Beaches, Peaches, Historic Savannah.

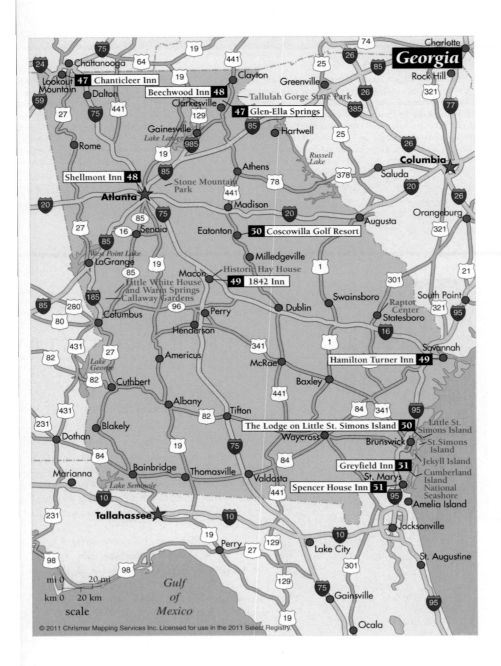

Chanticleer Inn Bed & Breakfast

www.stayatchanticleer.com
1300 Mockingbird Lane, Lookout Mountain, GA 30750
866-999-1015 • 706-820-2002 • Fax 706-820-7976
info@stayatchanticleer.com

Member Since 2003

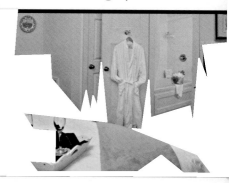

Innkeepers/Owners Robert & Audrey Hart

The Chanticleer Inn combines the ambiance of yesteryear with the comfort and amenities of today. Built in 1927, the Inn and the 17 English Cottage style guest rooms are nestled around the inn's courtyard and swimming pool. While the Mountain stone exterior retains it's original charm, the interior spaces have been completely renovated. Antique furnishings create a unique and inviting atmosphere in each guest room. Amenities include a patio, private bath, individual central heat and air, DVD player and flat screen TV with cable. Some rooms feature private patio, fireplace and/or whirlpool or steam shower. Located high atop historic Lookout Mountain & only 10 minutes from downtown Chattanooga, TN. The Inn is directly across the street from Rock City Gardens & two Banquet facilities all with spectacular views of the Chattanooga valley. Nearby are hiking trails with waterfalls, golf courses, restaurants, shopping, and many other attractions. Family owned and operated, the Inn serves a full home-made breakfast each morning. We'll make sure your stay is comfortable and memorable.

Rates: $135-$245/night rate includes full breakfast, evening cookies/desserts, bottled water, Coffee & Tea; Some rooms and suites offer Whirlpool, Steam Shower or Fireplace. All rooms have private baths, telephones and TV. WIFI Number of Rooms: 17

Cuisine: A complimentary breakfast is prepared by our chef each morning along with homemade cookies/desserts each evening. Made to order boxed lunches, cheese platters, antipasto, chocolate covered strawberries and more are available for an extra charge.

Nearest Airport: Chattanooga, 25 Minutes; Atlanta, 2 hours; Nashville, 2 hours; Birmingham, 2 hours

---

Glen-Ella Springs Inn

www.glenella.com
1789 Bear Gap Rd, Clarkesville, GA 30523
888-455-8786 • 706-754-7295 • Fax 706-754-1560
info@glenella.com

Member Since 1990

Innkeepers/Owners Ed and Luci Kivett

RELAX...RESTORE...REJUVENATE! Wander down a gravel road at the edge of the Blue Ridge Mountains and discover the peaceful setting of Glen-Ella Springs Inn and Meeting Place. Over a century old, the Inn features 16 rustic yet elegant rooms all with private baths and complete with amenities expected by today's discriminating traveler. The Inn's fine dining restaurant is open most evenings by reservation and has been named one of Georgia's Top Dining Destinations since 2004. Located on 17 acres, the property has a 12 acre meadow with extensive perennial herb and flower gardens as well as an open air swimming pool. If outdoor adventure peaks your interest, you will find numerous hiking trails and waterfalls close by. Tallulah Falls State Park and Black Rock Mountain State Park are within 30 minutes of the Inn offering some of the area's most beautiful vistas. Shopping enthusiasts will find art, pottery and antique galleries all around the region and guests can also plan to visit one of the many north Georgia wineries all within a short drive of the Inn.

Rates: 16 Rooms, $150/$275 B&B. Open year-round. Number of Rooms: 16

Cuisine: Freshly prepared full country breakfasts. Dinner is served every evening by reservation in our fine dining restaurant featuring American Continental cuisine prepared with a southern flare.

Nearest Airport: Greenville, SC or Atlanta, GA

Beechwood Inn

www.beechwoodinn.ws
220 Beechwood Dr, P.O. Box 429, Clayton, GA 30525
706-782-5485 • Fax 706-782-5485
info@beechwoodinn.ws

Member Since 2005

Innkeepers/Owners David & Gayle Darugh

Georgia's Premier Wine Country Inn offers luxury lodging in a rustic mountain setting. Nestled among 100 year-old terraced gardens overlooking Black Rock Mountain, it is a place where all elements add up to a culinary and wine-oriented journey. Come relax your mind, refresh your body, and rejuvenate your soul as we pamper you with affordable elegance. Each of our 8 guest room suites is individually decorated, most have fireplaces, private porches, mountain views and all have private baths. The inn's restaurant features a Wine Spectator Award of Excellence selection of vintages from its own wine cellar. The restaurant offers Saturday Prixe Fixe dining by advance reservation featuring fresh regional and Mediterranean-style meals using the best of local, organic and sustainable products from Georgia farms, vineyards and orchards. The beautifully landscaped 5 acre property is also perfect for weddings, receptions, and group functions. Travel Writer Becky Lamb says: "The Beechwood Inn is the closest thing to a Napa Valley Bed and Breakfast we have here in Georgia."

Rates: 7 guest suites, 1 cottage $159/$219. Private baths, fireplaces, porches, views, free WIFI, 600 thread count sheets, hair-dryers, complimentary soft drinks and itinerary planning. Complimentary wine-thirty daily. Number of Rooms: 8

Cuisine: Beechwood Bountiful Breakfast daily. Chef's Table dinners with local foods on Saturdays by advance reservation. Extensive wine list. Visit our website for information on gourmet wine events, cooking classes, wine tastings & special weekend packages.

Nearest Airport: Atlanta, GA and Asheville, NC each 90 minutes;Greenville SC 90 minutes

Shellmont Inn

www.shellmont.com
821 Piedmont Ave. N.E., Atlanta, GA 30308
404-872-9290 • Fax 404-872-5379
innkeeper@shellmont.com

Member Since 1994

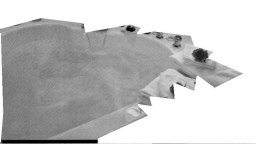

Innkeepers/Owners Ed and Debbie McCord

The Shellmont Inn is an award-winning premier Urban Inn offering all the luxurious amenities found in an upscale boutique hotel. Located in Atlanta's theater, restaurant and cultural district, this crowning jewel is an urban oasis just steps from Atlanta's Midtown Mile and bustling Peachtree Street. Business travelers find us technologically savvy, while leisure travelers find our Inn romantic and tranquil. Whether here on business or pleasure, Shellmont Inn offers outstanding personal service in a sophisticated, elegant atmosphere. Indulge in a sumptuous breakfast. Relax in a spa tub. Unwind on a wicker-laden veranda. When your travels bring you to Atlanta, Shellmont Inn will always exceed your expectations. THE EXPERIENCE IS UNFORGETTABLE!

Rates: Rooms $175/$200; Deluxe Whirlpool Suites $225/$275;Carriage House Cottage $245/$350. Open year-round Number of Rooms: 5

Cuisine: A Southern Regional inspired full gourmet breakfast features fresh local ingredients and herbs grown in our own garden. Complimentary beverages and delicious afternoon refreshments served daily. Evening turn-down service with treats,fresh fruit basket.

Nearest Airport: Hartsfield-Jackson Int'l — 8 miles South of Inn Location

1842 Inn
www.the1842inn.com
353 College Street, Macon, GA 31201
800-336-1842 • 478-741-1842 • Fax 478-741-1842
management@1842inn.com

Member Since 1994

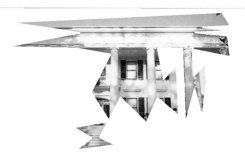

Owner Edmund E. Olson

The 1842 Inn boasts 19 luxurious rooms and public areas tastefully designed with fine English antiques, tapestries and paintings. A quaint garden courtyard and garden pool greet guests for cocktails or breakfast. Nightly turndowns and fresh flowers enhance many other gracious grand hotel amenities. Rooms available with whirlpool tubs and fireplaces. High level of service. Considered 'One of America's Top 100 Inns in the 20th Century' by the International Restaurant and Hospitality Rating Bureau.

Rates: 19 Guest Rooms, $189/$240 B&B. (Rates subject to change without notice.) Open year-round. Number of Rooms: 19

Cuisine: Full breakfast and hors d'oeuvres included. Full service attended cash bar.

Nearest Airport: Macon, Atlanta

Hamilton Turner
www.hamilton-turnerinn.com
330 Abercorn Street, Savannah, GA 31401
888-448-8849 • 912-233-1833 • Fax 912-233-0291
innkeeper@hamilton-turnerinn.com

Member Since 2003

Innkeepers/Owners Jim & Gay Dunlop

Experience the gracious Southern hospitality of Savannah at the elegant Hamilton-Turner Inn. The mansion, built in 1873 as a family residence for Samuel Hamilton, retains a 19th century grandeur infused with modern day sophisticated comforts and amenities. Nestled among the live oaks on beautiful Lafayette Square the inn is ideally situated in the center of the Historic District. Fine cuisine and other points of interest are within a short stroll. Our concierge staff is poised to offer recommendations and secure reservations for touring, restaurants and leisure activities. Choose from grand suites overlooking the moss-draped oaks in the park; luxuriously appointed rooms; garden-view courtyard rooms with private entrances; and three carriage house rooms with shared parlor. Some accommodations offer fireplace, whirlpool spa bath, and bay windows. Whether you are looking for a reunion with longtime friends, romantic honeymoon getaway, business travel retreat or golf vacation, the inn has a package to exceed your desires. Featured in Southern Living and Conde Nast Traveler.

Rates: 11 bedrooms, 6 suites from $189 to $369 per night, double occupancy. King, 2 queen, queen, and 2 twin beds available. Carriage house offers 3 guestrooms and parlor. ADA room and pet friendly rooms. Number of Rooms: 17

Cuisine: Complimentary cuisine features full southern mansion breakfast, afternoon iced-tea and sweets, evening wine and hors d'oeuvres, late evening port, turndown sweet.

Nearest Airport: Savannah/Hilton Head International SAV, 8 miles.

Lodge on Little St. Simons Island

www.LittleSSI.com
P.O. Box 21078, Little St. Simons Island, GA 31522-0578
888-733-5774 • 912-638-7472 • Fax 912-634-1811
Lodge@LittleStSimonsIsland.com

🍽 🍽 🍽 🍷

Member Since 1993

General Manager Joel Meyer

Nature prevails on this pristine Georgia island where 10,000 acres are shared with no more than 32 overnight guests at a time. Accessible only by boat, Little St. Simons Island unfolds its secrets to those eager to discover a bounty of natural wonders. Seven miles of shell-strewn, private beaches meet acres of legendary moss-draped live oaks, glistening tidal creeks, and shimmering salt marshes to provide an unparalleled setting for a host of activities and total relaxation. Guests enjoy guided interpretive tours, birding, canoeing, kayaking, fishing, hiking, and bicycling. Creature comforts include gracious accommodations, delicious regional cuisine, and warm Southern hospitality. The Lodge on Little St. Simons Island was recently voted #1 Resort in the Mainland US ~ Conde Nast Traveler's Readers' Choice Awards.

Rates: All-inclusive rates range from $600 – $775 per couple, per night. Full house and exclusive full island reservations available. Visit www.LittleSSI.com for special offers. Number of Rooms: 16

Cuisine: Delicious regional cuisine served family-style. Rate includes three meals daily, beverages, snacks, and a complimentary cocktail hour. Picnics are also available upon request. We gladly accommodate dietary restrictions.

Nearest Airport: Brunswick, GA (BQK), Savannah, GA (SAV), and Jacksonville, FL (JAX).

Cuscowilla Golf Resort on Lake Oconee

www.cuscowilla.com
126 Cuscowilla Drive, Eatonton, GA 31024
706-484-0050 • 706-923-2491 • Fax 706-484-0051
csmith@cuscowilla.com

Member Since 2010

Director of Operations Craig Smith

Cuscowilla Golf Resort on Lake Oconee is ideally nestled in the middle of Georgia's Lake Country, just 70 miles east of Atlanta on beautiful Lake Oconee. Award winning golf, water activities, boat rental, biking, and tennis are just a few of the amenities that you will enjoy. Rest assured, you and your family will reap the benefits of our friendly, attentive and well-trained staff, while experiencing a level of service far beyond compare. Highly ranked and regarded as #1 "Best Course You Can Play in Georgia" by Golfweek 2010. The Ben Crenshaw/Bill Coore designed golf course winds through rolling meadows and valleys of pine. Enjoy a tranquil and peaceful round of golf while walking this exceptional natural course with one of our well trained caddies, then settle in for dinner in either of our resort restaurants, the Golf House Grill or The Waterside Restaurant. We offer two tennis courts, walking trails, two swimming pools and lake access for boating activities, which can include boating, jet skiing, fishing, canoeing and kayaking.

Rates: Lodge Villas $150 – $225 Golf Cottages $150 – $625 Lake Villas $200 – $725 Number of Rooms: 89

Cuisine: Golf House Grill serving breakfast, lunch and dinner. Daily chef specials. Spectacular patio overlooking our award winning golf course. The Waterside Restaurant is available for groups and special events with spectacular views of Lake Oconee.

Nearest Airport: Atlanta Hartsfield Jackson International Airport 90 miles. Macon Airport 60 miles.

Greyfield Inn

www.greyfieldinn.com
P.O. Box 900, Fernandina Beach, FL 32035, Cumberland Island, GA 32035

Member Since 1982

888-243-9238 • 904-261-6408 • Fax 904-321-0666
seashore@greyfieldinn.com

Innkeepers/Owners The Ferguson Family

This turn-of-the-century Carnegie mansion is on Georgia's largest and southernmost coastal island. Miles of trails traverse the island's unique ecosystems along with a beautiful, undeveloped white sand beach for shelling, swimming, sunning and birding. Exceptional food, lovely original furnishings, and a peaceful, relaxing environment provide guests with a step back into another era. Overnight rate includes an island outing with our naturalist, bicycles and kayaks for exploring the island, round-trip boat passage on our private ferry, all meals and pantry snacks throughout the day, and all non-alcoholic beverages.

Rates: 16 Rooms, $395/$595 AP. Open year-round. Number of Rooms: 16

Cuisine: Hearty southern breakfast, delightful picnic lunch, gourmet dinner. All meals focus on local southern foods & traditions, including island grown produce & locally caught seafood. Full bar; wine, beer, liquor, cocktail hour with hors d'oeuvres.

Nearest Airport: Jacksonville, Florida

Spencer House Inn

www.spencerhouseinn.com
200 Osborne Street, St. Marys, GA 31558

912-882-1872 • 877-819-1872 • Fax Fax 912-882-9427

Member Since 2003

info@spencerhouseinn.com

Innkeepers/Owners Mike & Mary Neff

Spencer House Inn is located nine miles east of I-95 on the Georgia/Florida border by the St. Marys River. For your convenience, the Inn has an elevator and an outside ramp. Spencer House Inn, built in 1872, is in the heart of the St. Marys Historic District within walking distance to restaurants, shops, museums and the ferry to Cumberland Island National Seashore. We can assist you in making ferry reservations and also pack a picnic lunch for you as you head off for your day of adventure on a beautiful, undeveloped and pristine barrier island — the beach was voted "one of the best wild beaches" by National Geographic Traveler magazine — and we are on the Colonial Coast Birding Trail too. You will enjoy relaxing in the cypress rockers on the Inn's verandas. Take a leisurely stroll around the historic village to the waterfront park, fishing piers, boat ramp and marsh walk. There are golf courses nearby and outfitters available for a kayak trip. Okefenokee Wildlife Refuge is 45 minutes away. The beaches of Jekyll, St. Simons and Amelia Islands are a short drive.

Rates: $125/$235. Rates subject to change. All private baths. Elevator & outside ramp. Complimentary wireless access. Daily paper. HDTV with cable, HBO, ESPN & DVD player. Open year-round. Comp pick up from marina and St. Marys airport. Number of Rooms: 14

Cuisine: Full buffet breakfast with hot entree. Picnic lunches available. Walk to restaurants for lunch and dinner. Guest refrigerator. Afternoon iced tea, coffee and homemade treats.

Nearest Airport: Jacksonville, FL (JAX).

"The Prairie State"

Famous for: Hogs, Pigs, Cattle, Electronics, Chemicals, Manufacturing, Ancient Burial Mounds, Lake Michigan, Chicago "Windy City," Sears Tower, Wrigley Building.

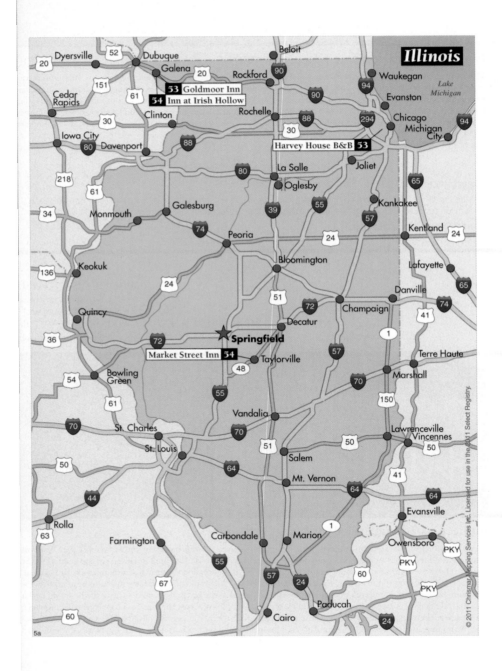

Goldmoor Inn

www.goldmoor.com
9001 W. Sand Hill Road, Galena, IL 61036
800-255-3925 • 815-777-3925 • Fax 815-777-3993
goldmoor@galenalink.com

Member Since 2001

Innkeepers/Owners Patricia Smith

Magnificent country inn overlooks the Mississippi River, 6 miles South of historic Galena. The Goldmoor with it's elite yet tranquil setting is the perfect venue for weddings, honeymoons, romantic getaways, anniversaries, family reunions and business retreats. All luxurious accommodations including suites, cottages and contemporary log cabins feature king size beds, two person whirlpools, fireplaces, galley kitchens, and private baths. Add to that, European terry robes, fine linens, heated towel bars, refrigerators stocked with complimentary beverages, satellite TV, stereo system, free wireless internet, and free long distance are just a few of the many ways you are pampered at the Goldmoor Inn. Runner-up in the 2007 Inn-Credible Egg Breakfast Cook-off and bronze winner in 2008, the Goldmoor provides our guests with a full, gourmet breakfast and free room service. Renew your mind, body and soul with a rejuvenating massage in the comfort of your accommodation, open air pavilion, or our soothing spa. The Goldmoor has been the top-rated ABBA inn in Illinois since 1993.

Rates: Seasonal: 12 Suites $155 — $335, 3 Cottages $185 — $335, 2 Cabins $155 — $275. Number of Rooms: 17

Cuisine: Breakfast served. Dining available for special occasions.

Nearest Airport: Dubuque, IA, 25 minute; Chicago, 2.45 hours.

Harvey House Bed & Breakfast

www.harveyhousebb.com
107 S. Scoville Ave., Oak Park, IL 60302
888-848-6810 • 708-848-6810
harveyhousebb@gmail.com

Member Since 2008

Innkeeper/Owner Beth Harvey

Selected as one of five for May issue of Chicago Magazine's Best Neighborhood Boutique Hotels/Inns! Chicago area's most luxurious romantic Inn featuring fireplaces and oversized luxury baths with Jacuzzi tubs, gourmet breakfast till noon, late checkouts.Combines the best of luxury hotels and boutique Inns.Perfect location with superb access to downtown and airports. WIFI, garage parking, great for romantic getaways, mini breaks, and also ideal for the discriminating business traveler that prefers great furnishings, great mattresses and great food. This upscale 6,000 sq. foot brick and limestone Victorian B&B in historical Oak Park consistently exceeds expectations. Oak Park is full of interesting shops, galleries and fine restaurants. Tour the internationally famous Frank Lloyd Wright Home and Studio. Visit Ernest Hemingway's birthplace. Listen to the Chicago Symphony Orchestra, the Lyric Opera, Chicago Jazz or Blues. Appreciate the magnificent Art Institute of Chicago, or take a trip to the top of the John Hancock Center or Sears Tower. The list goes on and on. . .

Rates: 5 suites all with private baths, 3 with fireplaces and jucuzzi tubs. Off Season: $165 — $325. In Season: $210 — $350. Number of Rooms: 5

Cuisine: Offering a friendly atmosphere in which to enjoy delicious food incorporating the best of what is freshest and in season. A full gourmet breakfast is served daily and we accommodate most dietary requests. Guest can choose what time they want breakfast.

Nearest Airport: Chicago, IL (ORD-O'Hare) 10 miles or Midway Airport also 10 miles.

Inn at Irish Hollow

🍽️ 🍽️ 🍽️ 🍷

www.irishhollow.com
2800 S. Irish Hollow Road, Galena, IL 61036
(815)777-6000
innkeeper@irishhollow.com

Member Since 2010

Owner/Innkeepers Bill Barrick, Tony Kemp, Matthew Carroll

Irish Hollow is the ultimate romantic, pampering and inspiring Inn, set in the magnificent rolling hills of the Galena countryside. Secluded on an amazing 500-acre Farm Estate, I.H. features Spectacular Cottages, Superb Amenities, Magical Meals, and the perfect background for your personal journey. Located near historic Galena, a stone's throw from the Mississippi River, down the valley from Downhill Skiing and surrounded by thousands of acres of Trail-carved Conservation Land, I.H. offers the ideal setting for everyone. Spend an awesome day on Snowshoes, Bikes, Woods-Wandering or just sitting by the Creek. WI-FI and IPod stations keep you connected.. . . while the roaring Wood-Burning Fireplaces, Private Candlelit Dinners in the Woods, Double Spa Tubs, Rain Showers for two, Horse-Drawn Buggy Rides and Couples Massage reconnect the two of you! I.H. specializes in All-Natural and Homegrown Cuisine, Outdoor Fitness, Special Diet accommodation, Great Wine and Personalized Service. . .all in a scrumptious setting. Our "CREATE YOUR OWN STAY" Menu lets you design your ultimate visit!

Rates: 5 Private Cottages and 3 Luxury Suites nightly $195-$450. Seasonal Packages (visit IrishHollow.com for details and rates), Full Country Gourmet Breakfast, Farmhouse Dinners, Organic Beds, Spa Tubs, Wood Fires, BodyWorks Treatments. Number of Rooms: 8

Cuisine: Internationally acclaimed All-Natural Cuisine. Country Gourmet Breakfast (with delivery option) 7-course Farmhouse Dinner, Luscious Picnic, Private Campfire in the Woods, Special Diets including Vegan, Gluten-Free, Hand-Crafted Bakery, Great Wine List.

Nearest Airport: Dubuque Regional Airport, 30 minutes. O'Hare International Airport, 2.5 hours.

Market Street Inn

🍽️　　　🍷

www.marketstreetinn.com
220 E. Market Street, Taylorville, IL 62568-2212
800-500-1466 • 217-824-7220 • Fax 217-824-7229
innkeeper@marketstreetinn.com

Member Since 2002

Innkeepers/Owners Joseph & Myrna Hauser

Rich in architectural detail, this romantic 1892 Queen Anne Victorian jewel boasts six original fireplaces, now with gas logs, and mantels, ornate woodwork, fretwork over pocket doors and beveled glass windows. Sit by the parlor fireplace and feast your eyes upon the antiques, semi-antiques and Oriental rugs to appreciate the blend of history, luxury, charm and hospitality. The grand oak staircase beckons one to unwind in one of the 8 guest rooms–each with delightfully different decor. Modern amenities include central air, private baths–most with double whirlpool tubs/showers, fireplaces, cable TV, and wireless DSL. Our Carriage House has two suites: the Hunt Club with two fireplaces, a wet bar, a double whirlpool and walk-in shower w/ body sprays, also an accessible suite. At day's end stroll through the perennial gardens to view over 200 hostas & then relax in a rocker in the gazebo of the Victorian wrap-around porch. Lincoln's Library, Museum, home & tomb are just 30 minutes away. Lincoln Prairie Bike Trail is six blocks away. FREE golfing–stay & play. Also skydiving.

Rates: 10 Rooms, $145-$275 most with double whirlpools & fireplaces. Accessible Suite in Carriage House. Queen Whirlpool Rooms $165, King Whirlpool Rooms $199. Standard Queen Room $145. Packages available on our website. Ask about pets. Number of Rooms: 10

Cuisine: Full hearty candlelight breakfast served daily. Social Hour: complimentary wine served daily and hors d'oeuvres. Complimentary soda & bottled water. Upscale dining 2 blocks away (www.oneeastmarket.com) & several other enjoyable dining choices.

Nearest Airport: Taylorville Municipal(TAZ) Springfield Airport (SPI) Bloomington (BMI) St. Louis International (STL)

"The Hoosier State"

Famous for: Farmlands, Cornfields, Wildflowers, Indiana Dunes National Lakeshore, Indianapolis 500.

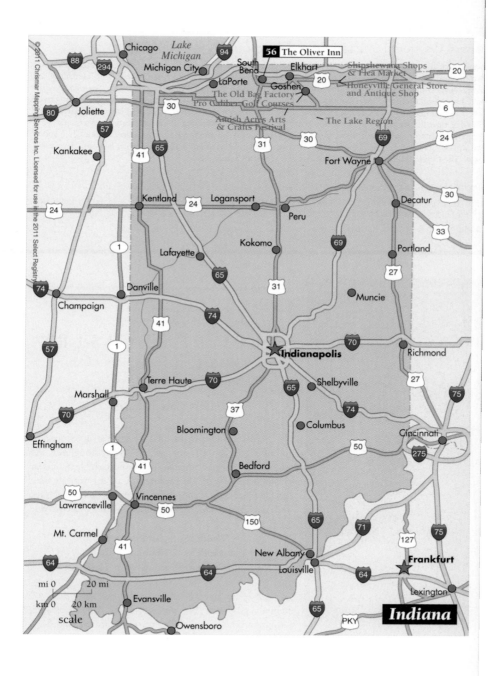

The Oliver Inn

www.oliverinn.com
630 W. Washington Street, South Bend, IN 46601
888-697-4466 • 574-232-4545 • Fax 574-288-9788
oliver@michiana.org

Member Since 2000

Innkeepers/Owners Tom and Alice Erlandson

Experience turn-of-the-century Victorian elegance at The Oliver Inn Bed & Breakfast. This historic 24 room mansion is surrounded by a lush acre of manicured gardens, with a gazebo, hammock, and lawn swings. The Oliver Inn features large, comfortable common areas, 11 fireplaces, nine beautiful guest rooms in the main house, private baths, two-person whirlpool tubs, A/C, CD players, sound machines, hairdryers, and luxurious robes. Enjoy a candlelit breakfast while listening to live piano music. Complimentary snacks, gourmet coffees and soft drinks available from the Butler's Pantry. Experience the ultimate in relaxation, luxury and serenity in our Carriage House Suite. This second floor suite features two queen bedrooms, two bathrooms, (jetted marble shower, double Jacuzzi tub), a living room with fireplace, a full kitchen and a screened in veranda. For dinner, stroll next door to Tippecanoe Place Restaurant in the Studebaker Mansion. Come discover why The Oliver Inn was voted the Michiana area's 'Best Bed & Breakfast.'

Rates: 8 Rooms plus 2, two-bedroom suites, $135/$339 — Rates higher for Special Events. Number of Rooms: 10

Cuisine: Full candlelight breakfast with live piano music. Complimentary drinks and snacks from Butler's Pantry. Dine at Tippecanoe Place Restaurant in the Studebaker Mansion right next door. Private lunches and dinners for groups of 8 or more.

Nearest Airport: South Bend (SBN) 90 Miles from Chicago, 140 Mi. from Indianapolis, 220 Mi. from Detroit.

SELECT REGISTRY
DISTINGUISHED INNS OF NORTH AMERICA

Gift Certificates

The gift of an overnight stay or a weekend at an exceptional inn or B&B can be one of the most thoughtful and appreciated gifts you can give your parents, children, or dear friends. Employers are discovering that a gift certificate for a "getaway" is an excellent way of rewarding their employees, while at the same time giving them some much needed rest. A few ideas:

• **Weddings** • **Anniversaries** •
• **Holiday & Birthday gifts** •
• **Employee rewards/incentives** • **Retirement** •

Our gift certificates are valid at any of our more than 400 member properties. We process orders daily, packaging certificates with our complimentary Association guidebook and your personal message. Certificates may be ordered online or by phone, and expedited shipping is available at an additional cost. The next time you think about gift-giving, think about our Gift Certificate Program—the perfect gift for that special person, **1-800-344-5244** or online at **www.selectregistry.com/giftcertificates**.

"The Bluegrass State"

Famous for: Horses, Kentucky Derby, Tobacco Farms, Fine Bourbon, Lakes, Hardwood Forests, Daniel Boone, Bluegrass music, "My Old Kentucky Home."

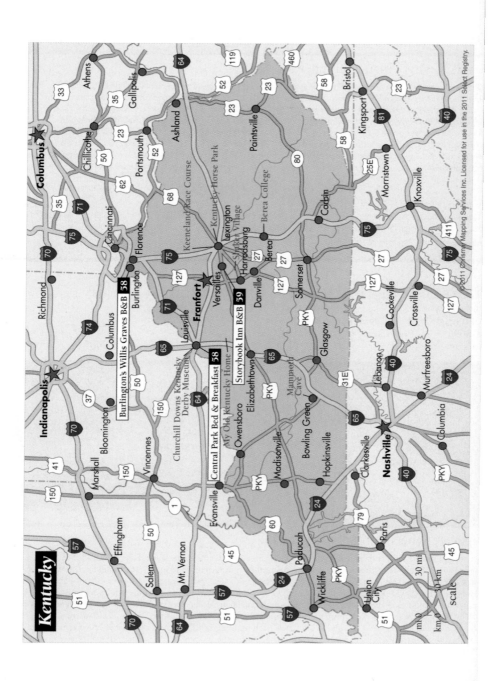

Central Park Bed & Breakfast

www.centralparkbandb.com
1353 South Fourth Street, Old Louisville Historic District, Louisville, KY 40208
877-922-1505 • 502-638-1505 • Fax 502-638-1525
centralpar@win.net

Member Since 2006

Proprietors Kevin & Nancy Hopper

Come and bask in the ambiance of a Gilded Age mansion facing Central Park. We are located in one of the largest Victorian neighborhoods in America. Relax and have a glass of wine on the veranda or sip a cup of tea by the 19th century grand piano in the parlor. We have created a bit of a Victorian dream for a romantic get away for any special couple wanting to soak in a tub for two or lounge in a king size bed dressed in luxury linens by the fireplace. It can be a romantic interlude or a corporate retreat. Whether you are a traveler searching for a luxurious respite or the business traveler looking for more than a hotel, we have the place for you. We prepare a delicious three course breakfast daily. Our coffees are specially blended for the inn and we always have specialty teas and treats. We have a wine and cheese reception each evening. We are centrally located close to downtown, the Expo Center, Churchill Downs, or the airport. All rooms have a private bathroom, a fireplace, television, comfortable sitting area, and internet access. The inn/antiques are of Victorian period.

Rates: Queens $125/$135; Kings/suites $165/$185; Carriage House (kid & pet friendly) $175.00 Corp. rates for single bus. travelers Call General Manager for Corp. Rates. Number of Rooms: 7

Cuisine: Creative 3-course breakfast served in dining room or on the veranda overlooking the courtyard. Fresh roasted coffee, teas, juices, & fresh baked pastries. Afternoon beverages & desserts. Fine & casual dining less than 2 blocks from inn.

Nearest Airport: Louisville International, 10-min.

Burlington's Willis Graves Bed & Breakfast Inn

www.burligrave.com
5825 North Jefferson Street, Burlington, KY 41005
888-226-5096 • 859-689-5096 • Fax 859-689-0528
inn@burligrave.com

Member Since 2007

Innkeepers/Owners Bob & Nancy Swartzel

Experience sophisticated charm and relaxed country living at this award-winning inn on the edge of a small town, just twenty minutes from Cincinnati. Choose between two masterfully restored early and mid-1800s buildings, the Willis Graves Federal brick homestead and William Rouse log cabin, furnished with appropriate antiques and reproductions. Attention to detail and luxurious touches are obvious everywhere. For your comfort and relaxation, we offer whirlpool baths, steam showers, plush robes and towels, fireplaces, triple sheeting with fine linens, down comforters, top quality mattresses, and fresh baked cookies. Guests may also enjoy in-room massage, wireless Internet, cable television, DVD and CD players, a comprehensive movie collection, and our inviting porches. Each morning, a full gourmet breakfast is served at individual tables set with white tablecloths, cloth napkins, and fine china. Suites offer in-room dining as an option. Gracious hospitality and beautiful surroundings create the perfect setting for your next romantic getaway, reunion, or business retreat.

Rates: $105-$225, special rates available. Number of Rooms: 5

Cuisine: A full gourmet breakfast is offered daily with a fresh fruit course to start. French roast coffee, assorted teas, juices, breads, and made from scratch entrees are served from our menu. Complimentary water and homemade cookies are in each room.

Nearest Airport: Cincinnati/Northern Kentucky International Airport

A Storybook Inn

www.storybook-inn.com

277 Rose Hill Avenue, Versailles, KY 40383

877-279-2563 • 859-879-9993 • Fax 859-873-0332

stay@storybook-inn.com

Member Since 2007

Innkeeper/Owner C. Elise Buckley

A delight to the senses! "Elegant," "A Real treasure!" Immaculate! are all words used by our discerning guests to describe beautiful, historic A Storybook Inn. Your search is over for a storybook destination that skillfully combines elegance with a gracious, tangible sense of calm. A Storybook Inn is not your "garden variety" Bed and Breakfast. It is more like a small European luxury hotel, say guests who have lived abroad. Every detail for our discerning guest's comfort has been considered; fantastic full breakfasts with premium fresh ground coffee and assorted teas, hand-selected furnishings and quality antiques, premium make-up mirrors, hi-thread count hand-pressed bedding, unique accessories and acres of beautifully landscaped grounds. Minutes from Keeneland Race Course, Midway [one of a kind fine dining and shops!], world class horse farms, Shaker Village, the Kentucky Horse Park, antiquing, Airport and downtown Lexington. Complimentary snacks and a glass of wine when you arrive. Always complimentary bottled water and soft drinks. Close to everything! Worlds apart!

Rates: Low Season Rates are: $199-$349 High Season rates range from $223 to $379. Ask us about our midweek discount. Discount for active military. Every room and suite is beautifully appointed. Number of Rooms: 5

Cuisine: We serve a full breakfast with fresh fruit, homemade bread, freshly prepared sweet or savory entree each morning. Fresh ground coffee, juice and filtered water. We serve breakfast in our newly added 50 ft. glass Conservatory overlooking the courtyard.

Nearest Airport: Lexington Bluegrass Field is a very convenient 10 minute from the inn. Louisville Airport is an hour from the inn.

"The Pine Tree State"

Famous for: Lobsters, Lighthouses, Rocky Coastlines, Potatoes, Pines, Ports, Paper.

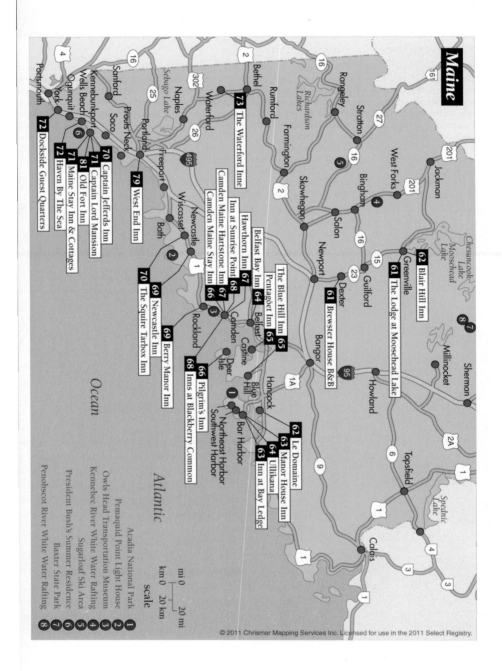

Member Since 2010

Scott & Ruth Thomas

Brewster House Bed & Breakfast is a comfortable and inviting 1888 Queen Anne Victorian home located among other historic homes, yet just steps from L.L. Bean and Freeport outlet shops. Built by a Mayflower descendant, Brewster House offers comfortable rooms with charming decor, gas fireplaces, bay windows and large private baths.Relax in your room, or in our cozy parlor, and enjoy our afternoon refreshments, after your visit to the Freeport shops and outlets, or your day trips to nearby lighthouses, coastal beaches and state parks, or a sail in Casco Bay on an antique wooden schooner. We'll provide maps, directions, and suggested itineraries to help you explore the Maine coast and find your way to lighthouses and lobster shacks.In addition to our 5 king or queen rooms, we have two 2-bedroom suites, for 3 or 4 guests. Three of our rooms have gas fireplaces, and all have fine linens, luxurious robes and slippers, coffee/tea service, clock radios with iPod/iPhone docks, air conditioning, and individual heat. There is complimentary WiFi throughout the house.

Rates: $159 – 199 king/queen rooms, $239 – 269 suites, seasonal rates, packages and specials. Open all year. Number of Rooms: 7

Cuisine: We serve a full, hot, gourmet breakfast daily. We begin with either a hot or cold fruit course, and alternate between sweet and savory main courses daily. Ruth loves to try new recipes, so you'll rarely have the same meal twice – even on return visits!

Nearest Airport: Portland, Maine (PWM) 25 minutes, Manchester, NH (MHT) 1:45 hours, Boston (BOS) 2 hours

Lodge at Moosehead Lake

www.lodgeatmooseheadlake.com
368 Lily Bay Road, P.O. Box 1167, Greenville, ME 04441
800-825-6977 • 207-695-4400 • Fax 207-695-2281
innkeeper@lodgeatmooseheadlake.com

Member Since 1995

Proprietors Dennis & Linda Bortis

Only The Lodge at Moosehead Lake captures the essence of the Maine North woods while pampering guests with luxurious amenities. Unspoiled vistas of Moosehead Lake against a mountain background provide the setting for this one of a kind country inn. Guests marvel at incredible sunsets from the dining room, pub, common areas, private decks and eight of the nine lodging rooms. Each room is individually decorated to reflect the natural surroundings of Moosehead Lake while providing the ultimate in luxury in every detail. You will enjoy a stone fireplace, one-of-a-kind hand carved beds, relics from the turn of the century logging era and twig furniture that defines the unique Moosehead Lake Region. A visit to the Lodge need never be the same twice! The travel and leisure industry has recognized the Lodge for its hospitality and uniqueness. This amazing spot is perfect for enjoying nature and incredible wildlife viewing. The goal is to make your visit as pleasant and stress free as possible. There are few places quite like this. Come see for yourself.

Rates: 5 Lodge Rooms, 4 Suites, $195 to $680. King or Queen luxurious beds. Open all year but April. Number of Rooms: 9

Cuisine: Hearty North woods breakfast included. Dinner features Up North Cuisine Friday-Sunday from Mid-June through Mid-October. Enjoy dining room with magnificent sunsets over Moosehead Lake. Winter suppers Friday and Saturday from January-March. Full bar.

Nearest Airport: Bangor, Maine; Portland, Maine; Manchester New Hampshire;

Blair Hill Inn

www.blairhill.com
351 Lily Bay Road, Greenville, ME 04441
207-695-0224 • Fax 207-695-4324
info@blairhill.com

Member Since 2005

Innkeepers/Owners Dan & Ruth McLaughlin

Like a country estate in the sky, Blair Hill Inn sits as the centerpiece of a former 2,000 acre hillside estate. Built in 1891 upon stately stone walls, the inn is blessed with commanding views of Moosehead Lake and the surrounding mountains for as far as the eye can see. This exclusive, 4-diamond country hotel is not your parent's B&B. Putting a fresh spin on tradition, Blair Hill Inn offers an escape in style. Each light-filled and spacious room has been meticulously restored and designed with current elegance. Guests love the refined simplicity that balances the grand architecture of the historic mansion. Countless windows open to cool evening breezes. A handsome cocktail lounge and lovely veranda provide perfect respites at day's end. Thoughtful luxuries & services abound and the welcoming hospitality is genuine. Everyone who travels up the winding drive to the top of Blair Hill, and stays or dines at this special place speaks of attaining an elusive experience that is both hard to find and to put into words. Come visit beautiful, welcoming Blair Hill Inn.

Rates: 7 Beautiful Guest Rooms and 1 two-bedroom suite $350/$495 double occupancy. Each is spacious, pristine, filled with fresh flowers, warmed by wood burning fireplaces, and features stunning views of Moosehead Lake. Number of Rooms: 8

Cuisine: Creative five-course menus feature the inn's own gardens & greenhouse and Maine's best farms and fishermen. An Aztec wood-burning grill adds summertime flavors; a hallmark of the inn's cuisine. Open weekends June-Oct. Breakfast is equally impressive.

Nearest Airport: Bangor International and Portland International

---

Le Domaine

www.ledomaine.com
P O 519, Hancock, ME 04640
800-554-8498 • 207-422-3395
info@ledomaine.com

Member Since 2002

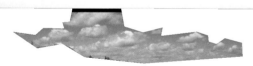

Manager Beth Clark

The colorful, sun-soaked atmosphere of Provence surrounds you when you step into Le Domaine. The scent of lavender and fresh flowers, French furnishings, cheerful prints, antiques and art create a truly unique atmosphere. There are many delights to savor. . . breakfast overlooking the garden, the elegant dining room, selecting from the delicious dinner offerings, studying our award-winning list of French wines, the waft of wonderful aromas, delectable desserts. However you choose to spend your days — at a concert, hiking in Acadia National Park or shopping for treasures in this lively area of Coastal Maine — Le Domaine makes any visit truly memorable.

Rates: 3 Rooms, 2 Suites $150./$225. June 20 to November 1. Number of Rooms: 5

Cuisine: Renowned French restaurant named 'One of the Best Restaurants in the World for Wine' by Wine Spectator. French provencal cooking using the finest Maine seafood, local produce and meats.

Nearest Airport: Bar Harbor/Trenton 20 minutes. Bangor 40 minutes.

Inn at Bay Ledge

www.innatbayledge.com
150 Sand Point Road, Bar Harbor, ME 04609
207-288-4204 • Fax 207-288-5573
info@bayledge.com

Member Since 2002

Innkeepers/Owners Jack & Jeani Ochtera

Amidst the towering pines, The Inn at Bay Ledge literally clings to the cliffs of Mt. Desert Island, which is locally and aptly referred to as "The Eden of New England." The veranda, appointed with comfy wicker, overlooks the spectacular coastline and is extremely inviting. Guests may enjoy a swim in our pool, relax in a hammock or take a stroll along our private beach. The elegant bedrooms compliment the style of the inn which was built in the 1900s and possesses an upscale country ambiance. Beautifully decorated with antiques, all rooms are unique with views of Frenchmen Bay. King and queen beds are covered with designer linens, down quilts and feather beds. The Summer Cottage sits just 25 feet from the cliff's edge, and every room has a bay view! Fireplace flanked by French doors with panoromic views of Frenchmen Bay. Air conditioned for your comfort! For your special holiday, the Summer Cottage will make it perfect.

Rates: 8 rooms, $125/$375 low season; high season $165/$475. 4 cottages $125/$375 low season; high season $175/$475. Number of Rooms: 12

Cuisine: Full gourmet breakfast served in the sunroom overlooking the bay. Afternoon tea & refreshments on the porch.

Nearest Airport: Bar Harbor 15 minutes, Bangor 1 hour, Portland 3 hours, Boston 5 hours

---

Manor House Inn

www.barharbormanorhouse.com
106 West Street, Bar Harbor, ME 04609
800-437-0088 • 207-288-3759 • Fax 207-288-2974
info@barharbormanorhouse.com

Member Since 1998

Innkeepers/Owners Ken & Stacey Smith

Manor House Inn was built in 1887 as the 22 room Cottage "Boscobel." It has been authentically restored to its original splendor and is listed on the National Historic Register. The Inn now includes the Victorian era Chauffeur's Cottage, 2 airy Garden Cottages and the Acadia Cottage. The moment you step into our front entry a romantic Victorian past becomes your present. Enjoy casual comfort, convenience, and privacy while staying within easy walking distance, on historic West Street, of Bar Harbor's fine shops, restaurants, and ocean activities. Wake each morning to the smell of sea air and a delicious home baked breakfast. After a day spent enjoying the natural beauty of Acadia National Park and exploring Mount Desert Island return to the Inn and take tea with us in the gardens and enjoy some sweets from the kitchen. Or simply relax on one of our many wicker filled porches surrounded by cool green ferns and the smell of fresh sea air. We look forward to welcoming you.

Rates: 18 Rooms/Suites $160/$275. Off-season $85/$200. We open in mid April and close in late October. Number of Rooms: 18

Cuisine: Each morning a full country breakfast is served buffet style from our Butler's Pantry. Afternoon tea and sweets are served each afternoon.

Nearest Airport: Hancock County Airport~20 minutes; Bangor International~1 Hour; Portland Jetport~3 Hours

Belfast Bay Inn

www.belfastbayinn.com
72 Main Street, Belfast, ME 04915
207-338-5600 • Fax 207-338-9100
info@belfastbayinn.com

Member Since 2009

Innkeeper/Owner Ed & Judy Hemmingsen

You are invited to Belfast's only AAA-◆◆◆◆ Award winning Boutique Hotel with upscale accommodations featuring luxuriously appointed 2-person guest suites. We are located in the heart of downtown Belfast, a quaint seaside city declared "Coolest Small Town" by Budget Traveler and ranked one of the top ten art communities in America. We are surrounded by shops, galleries, restaurants, and we are steps to the waterfront at the town pier. We fully restored these mid-1800 Greek Revival row houses to offer refined and sophisticated guest suites for discerning tastes. Each gracefully decorated suite has distinctive features including hardwood and stone floors, crown moldings, granite counter tops, classic original oil paintings, carefully chosen furniture and fine upholstery. Some suites have gas fireplaces, balconies and water views. Treat yourself to our many guest amenities by scheduling an in-suite massage. Enjoy breakfast delivered to your suite each morning. Select a movie from our gallery or browse our wine collection at our Molly Amber gift shop.

Rates: 6 Suites and 2 Rooms $198 — $378. Number of Rooms: 8

Cuisine: Hearty breakfast of homemade breads and sweets, fresh juices and fruits, granola and a changing menu of hot entrees. Evenings enjoy fresh baked cookies, coffee and tea.

Nearest Airport: Bangor International Airport

Ullikana & A Yellow House

www.ullikana.com
16 The Field, 15 TheField, Bar Harbor, ME 04609
207-288-9552 • Fax 207-288-3682
relax@ullikana.com

Member Since 2000

Innkeepers/Owners Helene Harton and Roy Kasindorf

Ullikana, a secluded, romantic haven, overlooking the harbor, and our sister inn, A Yellow House, only steps away, are two of the few remaining cottages from the 1800s in Bar Harbor. Only a minute walk from the center of town, our quiet location offers a haven of hospitality. Watch the lobster boats in the harbor from the garden or the patio, where sumptuous breakfasts are served. Relax in the casual elegance of these historic inns, where art is an important part of our decor. We invite you to share the history and hospitality of Ullikana and A Yellow House with us.

Rates: 16 Rooms, high season: $175/$330; low season: $150/$275. All our rooms have king or queen beds. All have private baths. Some have porches overlooking the harbor. Some rooms have fireplaces. Number of Rooms: 16

Cuisine: We serve a full breakfast on our patio, looking out on the water. Also we have afternoon refreshments on the patio.

Nearest Airport: Bangor and Bar Harbor

Pentagöet Inn
www.pentagoet.com
P.O. Box 4, Castine, ME 04421
800-845-1701 • 207-326-8616 • Fax 207-326-9382
stay@pentagoet.com

Member Since 2005

Innkeepers/Owners Jack Burke & Julie Van de Graaf

The Pentagöet has been welcoming guests since it was built as a steamboat era hotel in 1894 and continues a tradition of gracious hospitality. This authentic Queen Anne Victorian has a wraparound porch, three story turret, extensive perennial gardens and renowned window boxes. You will feel at home with the charming mix of antiques and collectibles, fine linens and amenities. Overlooking Penobscot Bay the vintage seaside village of Castine is on the National Historic Register. Our concierge can plan itineraries for kayaking, sailing, hiking, antiques and art galleries, there are guest bikes for a sunset pedal to the lighthouse. We are centrally located for day trips to Camden, Blue Hill, Deer Isle, Stonington, Acadia and Bar Harbor. We invite you to dinner in our nationally recognized restaurant. Enjoy our exceptional home cooking that honors the classics in its soulful simplicity, bowing to the seasons and our local farms. Have a nightcap in our cozy old world bar, the inn's "utterly fascinating Passports Pub," according to Andrew Harper's Hideaway Report.

Rates: 16 Rooms, all private baths, $125–$285. Open May-October. Seasonal packages and specials. Number of Rooms: 16

Cuisine: Full country breakfast, afternoon tea, evening hors d'oeuvres, guest coffee/tea bar. Dinner features local, organic produce, lobster, native fish and meats, New England specialties, fine desserts. Full bar and well stocked wine cellar.

Nearest Airport: Bangor (BGR) 1 hr, Bar Harbor (BHB) 50 min, Portland (PWM) 2.5 hrs

The Blue Hill Inn
www.bluehillinn.com
40 Union Street, P.O. Box 403, Blue Hill, ME 04614
800/826-7415 • 207/374-2844 • Fax 207/374-2829
sarah@bluehillinn.com

Member Since 1994

Innkeeper/Owner Sarah Pebworth

The coastal village of Blue Hill wraps around Blue Hill Bay and is centrally located for exploring Acadia National Park, Deer Isle, Castine, and the peninsula. This area offers rugged coastlines, blueberry fields, sea life, lighthouses, fine galleries, and small town charm. Stroll under evening skies brilliant with stars. The 1830 Federal inn, situated in the historic district, is a short walk to the bay, Kneisel Chamber Music Hall, and Blue Hill Mountain. The Blue Hill Inn retains many original features and was recognized as a 2010 Editors' Choice Best Classic B&B in Yankee Magazine's Travel Guide. After a day of hiking, boating, bird-watching, gallery hopping, or reading in the garden, you'll be pampered with afternoon treats, evening hors d'oeuvres, luxurious linens, air conditioned rooms, free wifi, and staff attentive to the every detail of your memorable stay. The inn offers a full bar and fine wines. Reserve a table in our candle-lit dining room for a meal designed with your pleasure in mind. The inn is proud to have been designated a Maine Environmental Leader.

Rates: 11 rooms, 2 pet-friendly suites with kitchens, all have private baths. In-season, our rates include our complimentary three-course breakfast, which features local produce, seafood, and meats as well as organic coffees and teas. Number of Rooms: 13

Cuisine: Enjoy a complimentary three-course breakfast with many choices, served in our sunny dining room. An elegant dinner is served at the inn Monday though Friday. Our varied menus feature locally grown produce and Maine seafood. Full bar and fine wines.

Nearest Airport: Hancock Co.-Bar Harbor (BHB) - 40 min., Bangor (BGR) -1 hour, Portland (PWM)-3 hours.

Pilgrim's Inn

www.pilgrimsinn.com
P.O. Box 69, 20 Main Street, Deer Isle, ME 04627
888-778-7505 • 207-348-6615 • Fax please call
innkeeper@pilgrimsinn.com

Member Since 1980

Innkeeper/Owner Tony Lawless & Tina Oddleifson

Overlooking Northwest Harbor and a tranquil pond, this 1793 colonial is surrounded by the unspoiled beauty of remote Deer Isle in Penobscot Bay. Glowing hearths, colonial colors, pumpkin pine floors and antique furnishings; combined with warm hospitality and flavorful meals in the cozy Whale's Rib Tavern have pleased many contented guests. Day trips to picturesque seaside villages and Acadia National Park make it an ideal location for an extended stay. The area is a kayaking, sailing and hiking paradise and is home to many artists, writers and the world renowned Haystack Mountain School of Crafts. The Inn is listed on the National Register of Historic Places; has been chosen as an Editors' Choice in Yankee Magazine's Travel Guide to New England; and as of one of the Country's Best B&Bs by Forbes.com. It has been designated as an Environmental Leader by the State of Maine and recently featured in the US edition of "1000 Places to See Before you Die." In addition to 12 rooms in the inn, three cottages on the property are perfect for families with children and pets.

Rates: 12 Rooms and 3 cottages; $89/$249, B&B. Most rooms have views of the pond or Northwest Harbor. All rooms have private baths. Open Mid-May through Mid-October. Number of Rooms: 15

Cuisine: Full country breakfast; refreshments available all day; and dinner at the Whale's Rib Tavern featuring American heritage cuisine and creative daily specials.

Nearest Airport: Bangor International Airport

Camden Maine Stay

www.camdenmainestay.com
22 High Street, Camden, ME 04843
207-236-9636 • Fax 207-236-0621
innkeeper@camdenmainestay.com

Member Since 1995

Innkeepers/Owners Roberta & Claudio Latanza

Relaxed, cozy, romantic and very friendly, the Maine Stay Inn is a grand old home located in the historic district of one of America's most beautiful seaside villages, known as the place "where the mountains meet the sea". It projects the true essence of New England, its history, its tradition. To visit the Maine Stay Inn is to literally step into a venerable piece of history. Built in 1802 by a direct descendant of John Alden, the striking main house, attached carriage house and four-story barn are an outstanding example of the progressive farm buildings common to 19th century Maine. Our three parlors are tastefully decorated with period furnishings and beautiful Italian paintings and ceramics. Winner of Karen Brown Reader's Choice Award 2009 for "Warmest Welcome in New England." Chosen by Frontgate as one of America's Finest Homes. In the words of Vacations Magazine, "Down east hospitality at its very best." Frommer's comments, "Camden's premier Bed and Breakfast", and Fodor's agrees, "Camden's best B&B." Welcome to the History and the Tradition of Maine!

Rates: From $115 to $270 per night. Each room has individual style and character. Many of them have original wide plank pine flooring and Vermont Castings stoves. All rooms are very romantic with private baths. Open year-round. Number of Rooms: 8

Cuisine: Gourmet breakfast, which may be enjoyed at our antique harvest table in the dining room or at a table for 2 on our sun porch. Tea and coffee served in the afternoon. Nearby restaurants offer fine dining and casual harbor settings. Lobster at its best.

Nearest Airport: Rockland (RKD); Bangor (BGR); Portland (PWM); Boston (BOS)

Camden Maine Hartstone Inn

www.hartstoneinn.com
41 Elm Street, Camden, ME 04843
800-788-4823 • 207-236-4259 • Fax 207-236-9575
info@hartstoneinn.com

Member Since 2002

Owners Mary Jo Brink and Michael Salmon

Steps from Camden Harbor! AAA 4 Diamond hideaway in the heart of Camden village that Fodor's considers "An elegant and sophisticated retreat and culinary destination," this Mansard style Victorian built in 1835 offers a unique experience in pampered luxury. "From luscious linens in the guest rooms to the world-class cuisine in the dining room and the collection of 400 orchids, Mary Jo and Michael Salmon get absolutely everything right," says the Maine Explorers Guide. Each air conditioned guestroom combines carefully chosen furnishings to create a mood of lavish comfort and romance. Luxurious amenities include: on site massage room, ipads, WiFi, fireplaces, Jacuzzi Tubs, soft robes, Flat Screen w/ dvd. The Cuisine at the Hartstone has been recognized by The American Culinary Federation with their Achievement of Excellence Award. For your vacation in Camden choose the Hartstone Inn and reward yourself with a sumptuous multi-course breakfast, join the fun at happy hour with specialty cocktails & complimentary hors d'oeuvres. Critics and Repeat Guest say "don't miss dinner!"

Rates: 6 rooms, 8 suites, $105/$280 B&B. Gourmet Getaway, Chef for a Day, Cooking Class and Spa packages available. Preview all of our packages www.hartstoneinn.com Number of Rooms: 14

Cuisine: Sumptuous multi-course breakfast, afternoon cookies and tea, happy hour w/specialty cocktails and complimentary hors d'oeuvres. Memorable five-course dinner is available nightly by reservation. Full bar and Wine Spectator award winning wine list.

Nearest Airport: Bangor or Portland

Hawthorn Inn

www.camdenhawthorn.com
9 High Street, Camden, ME 04843
866-381-3647 • 207-236-8842 • Fax N/A
info@camdenhawthorn.com

Member Since 2008

Owner/Innkeeper Maryanne Shanahan

The Hawthorn Inn is an elegant, 1894 Queen Anne-style Victorian mansion situated on 1.2 acres of lawn and beautiful gardens just north of Camden Village and steps from Camden Harbor. One of 66 homes listed in the National Register of Historical Places in the High Street Historic District, the inn offers spacious accommodations with beautiful decor, Jacuzzis, soaking tubs, gas fireplaces, private decks, seasonal views of the Harbor from most rooms. Guests experience the romance of this elegant retreat in pampered luxury. They love to savor the Inn's renowned gourmet breakfast on the terrace and decks in summer and in the sunny dining room or cozy library in winter. The Hawthorn has a reputation for its warm and welcoming atmosphere, offering the perfect balance in comfort and sophistication. Attention to detail in decor and guests needs is in abundance at the inn. With just a short walk to town and the Harbor steps away from the back gate, the Hawthorn offers a peaceful oasis close to the Village and a beautiful venue for weddings, reunions and retreats.

Rates: Suites and rooms, $100/289. Corporate retreats, weddings, commitment ceremonies. Open year-round. Packages and Specials. Number of Rooms: 10

Cuisine: Full, gourmet breakfast. Local and organic foods. Afternoon refreshments; happy hour with wine bar and complimentary hors d'oeuvres.

Nearest Airport: Knox Municipal (RKD), Bangor (BGR), Portland Jetport (PWM)

Inn at Sunrise Point

www.sunrisepoint.com
P.O. Box 1344, Camden, ME 04843
207-236-7716 • Fax 207-236-0820
info@sunrisepoint.com

Member Since 2005

Innkeeper/Owner Daina H. Hill

A pampering seaside haven, this Andrew Harper's Best Hideaways-recommended bed and breakfast inn offers spectacular ocean views and all the luxuries you can expect from a AAA Four-Diamond property. Set on five secluded acres, this oceanfront hideaway is five minutes from picturesque Camden. Sleep soundly in the wonderful sea air, comforted by the gentle murmur of waves outside your window. Awaken to extraordinary sunrises across Penobscot Bay before enjoying a sumptuous breakfast in the Inn's sunlit conservatory or ocean room. Later, relax in the cherry-paneled library with a glass of fine wine and watch the moonrise over the Bay. Stay in a beautifully furnished room in the main house – a wonderfully restored cedar shingled Maine summer "cottage," or in one of the romantic, luxury cottages at the water's edge.Or choose the spacious loft set high among the trees. A luxurious, romantic and elegant retreat for discerning travelers. Ocean views, private decks, fireplaces, free wireless and more in all accommodations.

Rates: 3 rooms $320-$415. 5 cottages $360-$625. Loft 2 rm suite $360-$610. Open Mid-April to Mid-November. Rates vary within range depending on dates. Number of Rooms: 9

Cuisine: Sumptuous three course breakfast in oceanfront conservatory, featuring Maine specialties and local produce; complimentary afternoon refreshments; full bar; fine dining and casual local seafood nearby for dinner.

Nearest Airport: Portland (PWM), Bangor (BGR), Rockland Municipal (RKD)

Inns at Blackberry Common

www.innsatblackberrycommon.com
82-84 Elm Street, Camden, ME 04843
800-388-6000 • 207-236-6060 • Fax 207-236-9032
innkeepers@blackberryinn.com

Member Since 2006

Innkeepers/Owners Jim & Cyndi Ostrowski

Just three blocks to the picturesque schooner filled harbor, our Inns are a quiet romantic oasis surrounded by over an acre of Maine gardens. Maine Explorer's Guide says "the prettiest interior in Camden." Three gracious parlors of the 1849 Victorian boast original tin ceilings and ornate moldings. Our extensive gardens, complete with a blackberry patch, are a quiet retreat after a day of sailing, hiking or kayaking. Choose an elegant guestroom in Maine's only recognized "Painted Lady" Victorian. Select a suite room in our restored Carriage House tucked amid the gardens. Or stay in a stately guestroom in our Federal Colonial or in the delightful Tinker's Cottage. Amenities include lavish featherbeds, fine linens, gas fireplaces, cable TV and soaking clawfoot or whirlpool tub for extra pampering. WiFi and A/C throughout. Create a special memory! Seasonal Dinner and Culinary packages. Fine selection of wines and spirits. Featured in "Gourmet Getaways: 50 Top Spots to Cook and Learn" 2009. Lighthouses and bicycling are our specialty.

Rates: $99/$289. Open all year. Fireplaces, whirlpools, WiFi & A/C. Seasonal lighthouse, dining and culinary packages. Number of Rooms: 18

Cuisine: Multi-course breakfast, local Maine specialties and our fresh garden herbs and berries served in our dining room or on the garden patio. Complimentary afternoon refreshments. Gourmet dinner service for guests. Excellent selction of wines daily!

Nearest Airport: Portland Jetport; Bangor International

Berry Manor Inn

www.berrymanorinn.com
81 Talbot Avenue, P.O. Box 1117, Rockland, ME 04841
800-774-5692 • 207-596-7696 • Fax 207-596-9958
info@berrymanorinn.com

Member Since 2007

Innkeepers/Owners Cheryl Michaelsen & Michael LaPosta, Jr.

Named by TripAdvisor as one of the "2008 Best Inns and B&Bs in the US." The Berry Manor Inn was built with all the grandeur of the Victorian age and remains one of the Rockland/Camden area's most stately homes. The spacious guest rooms are uniquely decorated in the colors and tones of the Victorian era with a pleasing balance of elegance and comfort without any pretentiousness. All guest rooms have private luxury baths including many with oversized whirlpool tubs and most have fireplaces. The inn prides itself on providing a range of guest services and amenities to enhance the comfort of our guests including the evening offering of homemade pie made by the MOMs! The inn is located in a quiet, residential neighborhood away from Rt.1, but within walking distance to Rockland's harbor, downtown shops, art galleries, Farnsworth Art Museum, Maine Lighthouse Museum, an array of great restaurants and just 6 miles from Camden. We invite you to enjoy our lobsters, nearby lighthouses, renowned museums and experience the Maine standard for B&B eco-hospitality and relaxed luxury

Rates: $175/$275 In season; $115/$185 Quiet season. Suite $400/$250. Open Year Round. Packages available. Number of Rooms: 12

Cuisine: Delicious multi-course breakfast featuring sweet or savory entrees that varies daily. Dietary restrictions accommodated with notice. Complimentary Guest Pantry area stocked w/soda, ice and our moms' homemade pies recently featured on the Food Network!

Nearest Airport: Rockland (RKD)5 min srv'd CapeAir/JetBlue @ Boston; Portland (PWM)1.5hrs; Bangor (BGR)2 hr

---

Newcastle Inn

www.newcastleinn.com
60 River Road, Newcastle, ME 04553
877-376-6111 • 207-563-5685
info@newcastleinn.com

Member Since 1990

Innkeeper/Owner Julie Bolthuis

Located in Maine's MidCoast, Newcastle Inn has been welcoming guests since 1911. All guestrooms have private bath and offer warmth and details such as gas fireplaces or stoves, four poster beds, Jacuzzi tubs or views of the Damariscotta River. There is complimentary WiFi and two rooms are dog friendly and your canine companion receives their own "goody bag." A delicious, made-from-scratch breakfast is served in the dining room, or weather permitting, outside on the deck which overlooks the gardens and the river. The common areas provide opportunity to mix and mingle with other guests, or if you prefer, there are spaces for you to find your own "private corner." Complimentary coffee, tea, cold beverages, snacks, and the "bottomless cookie jar" are available in the Guest Pantry. After a day exploring the area with its beaches, lighthouses, art galleries and antique shops, our pub is the perfect place to relax and enjoy a glass of wine or a Maine micro-brewed beer. The Newcastle Inn is centrally located for all you want to see and do on your trip to MidCoast Maine.

Rates: $180/$255 in season; $135/$195 off season. Corporate rates available. Two rooms accommodate a third guest for additional charge of $35.00/night. The dog fee is $30.00/night, limit one dog in the room. Number of Rooms: 14

Cuisine: A full breakfast is served each morning. You won't leave the table hungry! Dietary restrictions/allergies gladly accommodated.

Nearest Airport: Portland Jetport, Portland, ME — 1 hour

The Squire Tarbox Inn

www.squiretarboxinn.com
1181 Main Road, Westport Island/Wiscasset, ME 04578
800-818-0626 • 207-882-7693 • Fax 207-882-7107
innkeepers@squiretarboxinn.com

Member Since 1974

Innkeepers/Owners Roni and Mario De Pietro

Once upon a time, there was a Country Inn conspicuous from all others. After a restoration for your comfort, this colonial farm created an alternate luxury, amidst the splendor of nature. Set within fields, stone walls, and woods, and with kindness to all creatures great and small, pristine barns are filled with gentle animals. The Inn offers you peace and tranquility, away from tourist crowds, but convenient to coastal adventures. Relax with a drink on our screened in deck while watching the wild life or the beautiful sunsets. Dine leisurely and enjoy the ambiance in our 1763 dining room or on the deck with meals created by our Swiss/owner chef Mario, using all local organic vegetables from our own farm. Take a row or just daydream in the boat on the salt water marsh. Sleep with the luxury of down duvets and pillows and the comfort of Posturepedic mattresses. On the National Register of Historic Places.

Rates: $115/$199 double occupancy. Open mid April — Dec. 31. Number of Rooms: 11
Cuisine: A mouthwatering hot breakfast with eggs from our own chickens is served. Fresh goat cheese at the cocktail hour, chocolate chip cookies all day, and a full liquor license. A la carte dinner menu served daily.
Nearest Airport: Portland Jetport

Captain Jefferds Inn

www.captainjefferdsinn.com
P.O. Box 691, 5 Pearl Street, Kennebunkport, ME 04046
800-839-6844 • 207-967-2311 • Fax 207-967-0721
captjeff@captainjefferdsinn.com

Member Since 2008

Innkeepers/Owners Erik & Sarah Lindblom

On your next vacation to Maine, experience casual elegance in the heart of Kennebunkport. Enjoy our warm hospitality from the moment you step through the Inn's red front door. Our historic 1804 sea captain's home provides you with individually decorated guest rooms, extensive and comfortable shared spaces, and an exquisitely maintained landscape. Wake up to a 3-course candlelit breakfast in our Dining Room. Sit with a glass of wine on our Garden Terrace or in our four-season Sun Room. Stroll a few short blocks from our picturesque historic neighborhood to the center of the village where you'll find specialty boutiques, art galleries, and a full range of restaurants from casual to five diamond rated. Let our dedicated staff assist you with planning your vacation by scheduling a sail, a kayaking or biking tour, or a scenic driving trip. Whether you are looking for a romantic getaway, a relaxing spot to unplug, or someplace to experience an active and fun-filled vacation on the southern Maine seacoast, the Captain Jefferds Inn is "your very special place."

Rates: $149/$379 Seasonally adjusted. Open year-round. Number of Rooms: 15
Cuisine: Full served 3-course gourmet breakfast with fresh flowers, candlelight and fireplace in the cooler months. Afternoon tea with home baked goods and light hors d'oeuvres. Fine wines and champagne are available for purchase.
Nearest Airport: Portland, Me

Captain Lord Mansion

www.captainlord.com
6 Pleasant Street, P.O. Box 800, Kennebunkport, ME 04046-0800
800-522-3141 • 207-967-3141 • Fax 207-967-3172
innkeeper@captainlord.com

 *Member Since 1975*

Innkeepers/Owners Bev Davis and Rick Litchfield

Make enduring memories with us! Your comfort, serenity and relaxation are vitally important to us. We strive to provide warm hospitality and lots of personal service. Our central location, extensively landscaped grounds and large, beautifully-appointed guest rooms are dedicated to your complete satisfaction. Each guest-room offers such amenities as an oversize four-poster bed, cozy gas fireplace, flat screen TV and a heated marble bath floor. Several baths have multiple body-jet showers; 9 have double jacuzzi-style tubs. Find fresh flowers, freshly-prepared, family-style breakfasts, afternoon refreshments and lots of personal attention. New, on-premises romantic spa. The Inn's scenic location is situated at the head of a beautiful sloping green, overlooking the Kennebunk River. Our picturesque, quiet, yet convenient neighborhood affords you a terrific place from which to walk to explore the shops, restaurants and galleries in the historic village of Kennebunkport.

Rates: 15 Rooms, $179/$449 B&B; 1 Suite $349/$499 B&B. Open year-round. Number of Rooms: 16

Cuisine: Full 3-course breakfast. Also, casual afternoon tea, with available fresh fruit, cheese and crackers as well as freshly-baked sweets. The Inn also offers a selection of fine wines, chocolate-covered strawberries and fruit platters for purchase.

Nearest Airport: Portland, ME; 35 Miles north of inn.

Maine Stay Inn & Cottages

www.mainestayinn.com
34 Maine Street, P.O. Box 500A, Kennebunkport, ME 04046
800-950-2117 • 207-967-2117 • Fax 207-967-8757
innkeeper@mainestayinn.com

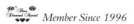 *Member Since 1996*

Innkeepers/Owners Judi and Walter Hauer

Experience relaxed sophistication at the Maine Stay Inn, where exceptional warmth and hospitality greet you at our door. Listed on the National Register of Historic Places, the Maine Stay is located steps from the quaint seaside village of Kennebunkport, known for its fine restaurants, shops, and galleries. And don't miss the area's incredible beaches, coves, and nature reserves! Enjoy afternoon tea and freshly baked cookies on our wrap-around porch or before the living room fire — a perfect opportunity to meet fellow guests and innkeepers. Or relax in your luxurious guest room with cable television, complimentary WiFi, fine linens, and many with whirlpool tubs and/or gas fireplaces. Choose a Victorian Inn Room/Suite, the intimacy of a Romantic Cottage Suite, or a stylish Contemporary Cottage Suite. Our Classic Cottage Suites offer spacious accommodations, perfect for families or friends traveling together. Cottage Suite guests often choose to have the gourmet breakfast delivered to their door — the ultimate in luxury! Enjoy classic elegance with modern comforts.

Rates: 4 Inn Rooms, $129/$269; 2 Inn Suites, $179/$329; 11 Cottage Rooms/Suites, $149/$349. Open year-round. Number of Rooms: 17

Cuisine: We strive to serve the freshest & most interesting breakfasts possible & offer guests different gourmet entrees daily. Enjoy summer fruit bruschetta w/candied nuts one day and savory french toast with baby greens the next. Afternoon refreshments daily.

Nearest Airport: Portland, ME

Haven By The Sea

www.havenbythesea.com
59 Church Street, Wells Beach, ME 04090
207-646-4194 • Fax 207-646-4194
jarvis@havenbythesea.com

Member Since 2006

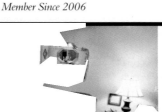

Innkeepers/Owners John & Susan Jarvis

The Grand Reopening Season, newly renovated and known as Wells Beach oceanside premier Inn. Find yourself just steps back from one of Maine's most beautiful beaches. Haven By The Sea is a place so charming, so welcoming, so relaxing, you will return time and time again. The Inn itself was once a seaside church located in a quiet residential neighborhood and uniquely restored as one of Southern Maine's destination spots. Enjoy breakfast in the multi-level dining room or terrace with its breeze from the ocean and surrounding marshlands. Enjoy a refreshment at "Temptations", the Inn's bar, for your added convenience and pleasure. Some guestrooms-suites have private decks and balcony waterviews. Original hardwood floors give the building a sense of history, warmth and old-world charm. Large common areas, all with fireplaces, offer a comfortable setting to relax and unwind. Historical colors and tasteful decor treat the eye. The Inn is conveniently located between the historic towns of Ogunquit and Kennebunkport with specialty shops and dining experiences .

Rates: 5 Rooms: $209/279 1 Suite: $299 King and Queen Beds; Private Baths, Cable TV, Wireless Internet, Central Air Conditioning Number of Rooms: 6

Cuisine: Full breakfast served in the Dining Room or Terrace. Full bar service available select hours (Monday — Saturday). Guest Services area offer a full-size refrigerator, bottled water and self-serve coffee/tea available during the day/evening hours.

Nearest Airport: Portland, ME 45 Min. Manchester, NH 1 Hr./15 Min. Logan, MA 1 Hr./30 Min.

Dockside Guest Quarters

www.docksidegq.com
22 Harris Island Rd., York, ME 03909
800-270-1977 • 207-363-2868 • Fax 207-363-1977
info@docksidegq.com

Member Since 1975

Innkeepers/Owners Eric & Carol Lusty

The Dockside is a special place that captures the essence of the Maine seacoast, with its natural beauty, gracious hospitality, abundant sights, recreation and activities. Uniquely situated on a private peninsula overlooking York Harbor and the Atlantic Ocean, each room has a panoramic water view. Accommodations are in the Maine House, a classic New England Cottage, furnished with antiques and marine art. The large wrap around porch, complete with wicker rocking chairs and iced tea, offers great views of the harbor activities. The multi-unit buildings at the water's edge offer several different room types, all with private decks and water views. Each room is tastefully and individually decorated. There is plenty to do on site and close by; pristine beaches, nature walk, golf, boat rentals, art galleries and antique shops. The Dockside Restaurant boasts a water view from every table. Our creatively diverse menu and extensive wine list will ensure a truly memorable dining experience. You can also, dine or enjoy your favorite beverage from the screened porch.

Rates: (19) water-view rooms $135-265, 6 suites $248-325. (1) 3 bedroom unit $2450 weekly. Off season rates & packages. Weekly discounts. Number of Rooms: 25

Cuisine: Our restaurant is a favorite with locals and visitors alike. Lunch or dinner on the porch, overlooking York Harbor is a special experience you are sure to enjoy. Our cozy bar or harbor view deck is great for a lite meal or beverages.

Nearest Airport: Manchester, NH 1 hr.; Boston, MA 1.5 hrs.; Portland, Maine 50 minutes.

The Waterford Inne
www.waterfordinne.com
Box 149, 258 Chadbourne Road, Waterford, ME 04088
207-583-4037 • 207-542-3630 • Fax 207-583-4037
inne@gwi.net

Member Since 1979

Innkeeper/Owner Barbara Vanderzanden

A 19th century farmhouse on a country lane amidst 25 acres of fields and woods, distinctively different, a true country inn offering special accommodations, a charming blend of three centuries — the warmth of early furnishings combined with contemporary comforts. An air of quiet simple elegance pervades the common rooms rich with antiques and art, pewter and primitives. An intimate library with an eclectic collection to appeal to all tastes–travel, nature, history. . . Step outside to explore the pleasures of country simplicity, to take a walk, to listen to the songbirds, to smell the freshness of a summer morning or perhaps the winter fragrance of a wood-burning fire. Wander through the gardens which provide a colorful array of flowers and a bounty of fresh fare for your dining table. Return inne-side to pamper your palate with country chic cuisine. The road to the Waterford Inne is traveled by hikers and cyclists, antiquers and skiers, discriminating travelers who seek charm, quiet and personal attention. Re-create your spirit with a peaceful journey back to the country.

Rates: 8 uniquely decorated guestrooms. 6 rooms with bath en suite $160-$200. 2 rooms with semi-private bath (excellent for families) $125 each. Open year round (with a few breaks between January and April.) Number of Rooms: 8

Cuisine: Full breakfast included. Fine dinners available with advance reservation. We do not offer a menu, but prepare a fine meal (with attention to guests' preferences and dietary restrictions.) $40 fixed price. Guests are invited to bring their own spirits.

Nearest Airport: Portland, ME The inn is approximately 60 miles NW of Portland.

"The Old Line State"

Famous for: Maryland Crabs, Chesapeake Bay, Ocean City, Atlantic Coast, River Valleys, Rolling Hills, Forests, Appalachian Mountains, Fort McHenry, Tobacco.

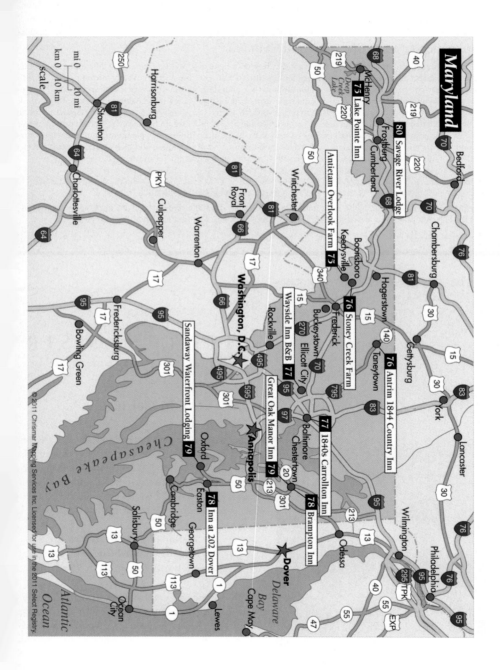

Lake Pointe Inn

www.deepcreekinns.com
174 Lake Pointe Drive, Deep Creek Lake, MD 21541
800-523-LAKE • 301-387-0111 • Fax 301-387-0190
relax@deepcreekinns.com

Member Since 2000

Innkeeper Ed Spak

The Lake Pointe Inn decorated in the Arts & Crafts style, embraces you with an exceptionally warm welcome when you enter the chestnut paneled Great Room with it's Mission Style furnishings. Nestled in the Lake Pointe Community in Western Maryland, the Inn is perched just 13 feet from water's edge. The wraparound porch invites you to relax in a rocking chair, read or watch the waterfowl frolic. It is easy to enjoy Garrett County's 4 season activities while staying at the Inn. Golf, skiing and snowboarding await you at the Wisp Resort, adjacent to the Lake Pointe Community. Tour the area using our complimentary canoes, kayaks and bicycles or hike in the 5 nearby State Parks. The outdoor fireplace, herb garden and hammock provide a perfect haven for private conversation or stargazing. Frank Lloyd Wright's Fallingwater and Kentuck Knob are nearby. Lake Pointe Inn is a perfect getaway in any season for any reason!

Rates: $232/$292; All have gas fireplaces, TV/DVD. Some rooms have:Spa Tub, Steam Shower, Balcony. Number of Rooms: 10

Cuisine: Full breakfast and light hors d'oeuvres included in daily rate; dinners served to Inn guests on 3-day holiday weekends.

Nearest Airport: Pittsburgh International PA Washington DC Baltimore MD

Antietam Overlook Farm

www.antietamoverlook.com
4812 Porterstown Rd., Keedysville, MD 21756
800-878-4241 • 301-432-4200 • Fax 301-432-5230
Reservations@antietamoverlook.com

Member Since 1992

Owner: Mark Svrcek Innkeeper: Michelle Krantz

Experience Antietam Overlook & 95-acres of mountaintop beauty. Elevation: 1000' at the edge of the Battlefield & 40 mile views of four states. The Inn is built of hand crafted timber frame, rough-cut pine and hardwood. Warm fireplaces & comfortable furnishings create an atmosphere that even the men appreciate. In the winter months, guests are invited to relax by the main fireplace where interesting conversation adds to the Antietam experience. The views are spectacular year round, but in the spring, summer & fall, the "Overlook" porch with its Western view for sunsets, is breathtaking. Spacious suites include fireplaces, comfy queen & king beds, soaking tubs, private baths and private screened porches. Enjoy the Hot Tub under the stars. While our seclusion and tranquility are unparalleled, guests also enjoy visiting The Antietam National battlefield, Harpers Ferry, Shepherdstown WV & Gettysburg. Antiquing? We have the route planned for you. Antietam's 150th Anniv. & special events are planned. Oh, Bring your horses and ride the 4200 acres of Battlefield. It is allowed.

Rates: 6 Suites, $145/$225 B&B. Generals Quarters $450. Open year-round. Attractions: Antietam National Battlefield, Harpers Ferry, antiquing, Charlestown horse races, Hollywood Casino, hiking, biking, horseback riding and relaxing. Number of Rooms: 6

Cuisine: 3 course gourmet breakfast is always included. Many dining experiences are nearby. Our House Chef is usually available to create your dream dining experience. Enjoy a Five Course Dinner with 5 wines for an added fee of $175.00 per person.

Nearest Airport: Reagan National, BWI & Dulles are 1 Hour. Hagerstown airport is 25 minutes away.

Stoney Creek Farm

www.stoneycreekfarm.com
19223 Manor Church Road, Boonsboro, MD 21713
301-432-6272
innkeeper@stoneycreekfarm.com

Member Since 2007

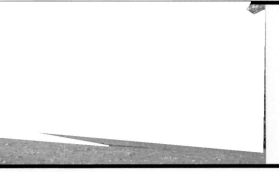

Innkeepers/Owners Denise Lawhead and David Kempton

Get away from the hustle and bustle, unwind at Stoney Creek Farm! Lovingly restored in 2005, our bed & breakfast spares no comfort and affords every modern amenity to eclectic travelers from near and far. Guests at the Inn enjoy our beautifully accommodated rooms, wonderful gardens and grounds, five miles of wooded trails for hiking or horse back riding as well as our delicious hot breakfast in the mornings and wine and cheese in the evenings. Delicious upscale dining and unique shopping, including many antique shops, are all around. We're just minutes from the beautiful C&O canal, Antietam Battlefield, and a twenty minute drive from historic Shepherdstown and a half hour from historic Gettysburg.Stoney Creek Farm is also a unique location for your special event including wedding ceremonies, receptions, civil unions or even your company retreat.Get away from the hustle and bustle, visit Stoney Creek Farm. (read less)Situated in the rolling hills of beautiful Washington County, Maryland, Stoney Creek Farm awaits your arrival and welcomes you home to our historic Inn

Rates: King Rooms $225 (Sunday through Thursday) $250 (Friday through Saturday)Queen Rooms $195 (Sunday through Thursday) $225 (Friday through Saturday) Number of Rooms: 4

Cuisine: Gourmet breakfast offered. Wine and cheese served nightly.

Nearest Airport: Baltimore, Washington Dulles

Antrim 1844 Country Inn

www.antrim1844.com
30 Trevanion Road, Taneytown, MD 21787
800-858-1844 • 410-756-6812 • Fax 410-756-2744
info@antrim1844.com

Member Since 1993

Proprietors: Dorothy and Richard Mollett

You are cordially invited to relive the elegance and hospitality of this National Historic Trust Antebellum Plantation. Antrim 1844 is located amidst 24 manicured acres of countryside accentuated by softly lit romantic walkways, rose gardens and bronze fountains. Embrace the comfort of one of our masterfully restored guestrooms adorned with lavish antique decor, fireplaces, jacuzzis, and WIFI. Savor our Modern French Six Course Pre-fixe fine dining experience in our award winning Smokehouse Restaurant or dine privately in The Wine Cellar which boasts over 20,000 bottles of an extrodinary wine collection. Wine Spectators "Best of Award of Excellence" for over a decade as well as a proud member of DiRoNA.

Rates: 40 Guest Rooms and Suites, $160/$400. Open year-round. Number of Rooms: 40

Cuisine: Afternoon tea. Evening hors d'ouevres. Elegant 6-course prix fixe dinner $68.50. Morning wake up tray at your door, plus full breakfast. Enjoy a drink in the Pickwick Pub or privately dine in the wine cellar which boasts over 20,000 bottles of wine.

Nearest Airport: Baltimore Washington International (BWI), Reagan Nationaland Dulles

1840s Carrollton Inn
www.1840scarrolltoninn.com
50 Albemarle Street, Baltimore, MD 21202
410-385-1840 • Fax 410-385-9080
info@1840scarrolltoninn.com

Member Since 2008

General Manager Timothy Kline

This boutique bed and breakfast comprised of a series of interconnected rowhomes, some dating back to the early 19th century, surrounds a central courtyard adjacent to the 1840s Plaza. The inn boasts historic quality antiques and decorator furnishings. Located at the center of historic Jonestown, the 1840s Carrollton Inn is within a short walk of Inner Harbor attractions, Little Italy's fine dining and the nightlife at Power Plant Live. The 1840s Carrollton Inn, next door to the historic Carroll Mansion, celebrates the life of Charles Carroll of Carrollton, the longest lived and only Catholic signer of the Declaration of Independence. Guests retreat to the comfort of overnight rooms with beds featuring handcrafted Kingsdown mattresses, large baths with whirlpool tubs and fireplaces topped with mantles of marble and oak. Business and leisure travelers alike enjoy the convenience of complimentary WI-FI access, flat-screen cable television, in-room telephone, refrigerator and microwave. Romance, spa, all-inclusive and elopement packages available as well as monthly specials!

Rates: Room rates range from $175 — $375 per night. Corporate, government and military rates available. Monthly and seasonal special rates, add-on and all-inclusive packages also available. Visit our website for details. Number of Rooms: 13

Cuisine: A full breakfast is served from a menu each morning, prepared to order, and included with overnight accommodations. Guests may enjoy dining in the charming garden courtyard, the historic first floor parlor or in the privacy of their room or suite.

Nearest Airport: Baltimore/Washington International Airport (BWI) is located just 10 miles from the Inn (a 20-minute drive).

Wayside Inn Bed & Breakfast
www.waysideinnmd.com
4344 Columbia Road, Ellicott City, MD 21042-5910
410-461-4636
bnbboy@verizon.net

Member Since 2008

Innkeepers/Owners David & Susan Balderson

Step back in time to a gentler way of living. Two hundred years of history await you at the Wayside Inn. Conveniently located in historic Ellicott City, Maryland, and within a short drive of either Baltimore or Washington, D.C., the Wayside Inn is the perfect place for you to escape into the past. Guests of the Inn enjoy outstanding, home-away-from-home hospitality. Your Room or Suite is filled with fine antiques or reproductions, the finest linens, and too many ammenities to list here. Your comfortable night's sleep in one of our exquisite rooms is followed by a full, gourmet breakfast, created fresh that morning by the innkeepers. Then spend the day exploring the area: shopping in Historic Ellicott City, antiquing in Frederick, touring our nation's capital, meandering through Annapolis, cruising on the Chesapeake Bay, or experiencing Baltimore's famous Inner Harbor. In the evening, treat yourself to a fabulous dinner at one of our area's many restaurants, wine bars or micro-breweries. Five of Baltimore Magazine's Top 50 restaurants within a five mile radius.

Rates: $159-$219. Number of Rooms: 6

Cuisine: A full, upscale breakfast is served each morning between 7:30 AM and 9:30 AM.

Nearest Airport: Baltimore/Washington International. Travelers also come into National and Dulles Airports.

Brampton Inn

www.bramptoninn.com
25227 Chestertown Road, Chestertown, MD 21620
866-305-1860 • 410-778-1860
innkeeper@bramptoninn.com

Member Since 2001

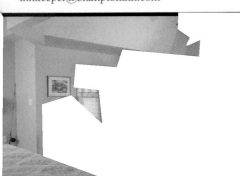

Innkeepers/Owners Michael & Danielle Hanscom, Rita Scardino

The award-winning Brampton Bed and Breakfast Inn is the Eastern Shore's romantic oasis. Located on 25 wooded and landscaped acres, one mile outside the charming waterfront town of Chestertown, Maryland. Brampton beautifully blends the grand elegance of a historical estate with the comfort and amenities today's travelers deserve. Ignite or rekindle romance in a spacious, private and well-appointed guest room, suite or cottage, offering wood-burning or gas fireplaces, whirlpool soaking tubs and glorious views. Enjoy a full a-la-carte breakfast graciously served at individual tables in Brampton's beautiful dining room or breakfast in bed delivered to the cottages upon request. Afternoon tea features delectable treats. Attention to detail, personal service, and friendly innkeepers will make your visit a memorable one. Chestertown is a colonial village with abundant outdoor activities, unique shops and great restaurants. It serves as a perfect base for exploring all that the Eastern Shore has to offer.

Rates: 13 rooms, suites and secluded cottages with private, en-suite bathrooms, featuring whirlpool tubs and/or showers. All our rooms have working wood or gas fireplaces. $199 — $419. Number of Rooms: 13

Cuisine: Our complimentary full breakfast includes: fresh seasonal fruit, just baked muffins or scones, choice of entree using local organic eggs, meat and vegetables. Daily afternoon tea. Beverages and home baked cookies 24/7. Visit bedandbreakfastfoodie.com

Nearest Airport: 90 min. to and from Baltimore (BWI) or Philadelphia (PHL)

Inn at 202 Dover

www.innat202dover.com
202 East Dover Street, Easton, MD 21601
866-450-7600 • 410 819-8007 • Fax 410 819-3368
info@innat202dover.com

Member Since 2009

Innkeepers/Owners Ron & Shelby Mitchell

Step through the elegant entry of this Victorian-era mansion for a sophisticated and relaxed stay in the heart of Chesapeake Bay country. Lovingly restored to its original grandeur, this inn offers luxurious accommodations for the discriminating traveler in historic downtown Easton. Walk to the historic Avalon Theatre, restaurants, boutique shops, the Historical Society Museum & Gardens, the Academy Art Museum, and art galleries. There are four suites -the French, English, Asian and Safari, each with a bedroom, sitting room and spacious bath with steam shower and jet tub, and one en suite Victorian guestroom. The Asian and Safari suites have fireplaces. All rooms are individually decorated with antiques, authentic reproduction pieces and special touches from family art & antiques, and feature Internet access, TV, DVD players, radios, and phones, imported linens, luxurious bathrobes and towels, and evening turn-down service. Voted among top ten romantic inns in the United States.

Rates: $279-$475. Number of Rooms: 5

Cuisine: Full breakfast. The Peacock Restaurant features classical and contemporary fresh regional cuisine. Voted among the top 11 romantic restaurants. Fine wines, beer and spirits served in the lounge and dining room. Thursday afternoon tea by reservation.

Nearest Airport: Easton Airport, Baltimore and Washington National airports 1 1/2 hours, Dulles 2 1/4 hours

Great Oak Manor

www.greatoak.com
10568 Cliff Road, Chestertown, MD 21620
800-504-3098 • 410-778-5943 • Fax 410-810-2517
innkeeper@greatoak.com

Member Since 2003

Innkeepers/Owners John & Cassandra Fedas

F. Scott Fitzgerald wrote of blue lawns and country houses such is Great Oak Manor. From the estate's walled garden bordered by 65-year old boxwoods and its circular drive on the estate side, to its magnificent view of the Chesapeake Bay and private beach on the water side, this country estate provides the appropriate setting for a relaxing getaway or a romantic weekend. Our guest and public rooms are spacious and beautifully furnished. Built at a time when grandeur was more important than cost, guests are swept away by the majesty of the house. This is a true Manor House with fine details, beautiful furnishings, Orientals, and an 850 volume library. We offer guest privileges at a private Country Club for 18-hole golf. The Manor has a reflection pool in the glass conservatory and a private beach. The Manor will meet your every need, with 1,200 ft. of waterfront lawn and towering trees on the Chesapeake Bay, and the most beautiful sunsets on the Eastern Shore of Maryland. Our Conservatory which overlooks the Bay, is popular for small business retreats or family reunions.

Rates: 9 rooms,$149/$315,3 suites,$249/$315.Elegant spacious rooms, fireplaces, massage therapy available. Number of Rooms: 12

Cuisine: Sumptuous Country Breakfast at private tables in the dining room on the patio overlooking the bay. Fresh baked goods cooked daily. Afternoon homemade sweets and refreshments, coffee,tea,water,and soda. Complimentary evening Port and Sherry.

Nearest Airport: BWI Baltimore MD.(90 min.), PHL (90 min.)

Sandaway Waterfront Lodging

www.sandaway.com
7 Miles From St. Michaels, 103 W. Strand Rd., Oxford, MD 21654
888-726-3292 • 888-SANDAWAY
info@sandaway.com

Member Since 1970

Innkeepers/Owners Ben Gibson — Innkeeper, Ken & Wendy Gibson — Active Owners

Sandaway is a Chesapeake Bay getaway with eighteen bed and breakfast style accommodations on 2.5 acres of waterfront property with a private beach. Our waterfront location in the colonial village of Oxford, Maryland makes us a unique destination. Guests can walk to restaurants, marinas, our museum, and some shops along brick sidewalks past charming homes with white picket fences. Overnight guests can choose between rooms in the circa 1875 Sandaway Lodge, or Sandaway's more modern River Rooms. Most rooms on the property have water views or porches, overlooking the Tred Avon River, Choptank River, and Chesapeake Bay beyond. Sandaway guests can take the car ferry across the river for a short-cut to St. Michaels, and also drive to the nearby towns of Easton, Tilghman, and Cambridge. At the end of the day, find yourself a beachfront seat at Sandaway. Sailboats entering the harbor at sunset and osprey flying by will create lasting memories. We are indeed "The Land of Pleasant Living."

Rates: Sandaway's room rates range from $169 to $299. Most rooms are waterfront with private porches. Number of Rooms: 18

Cuisine: 24 hour coffee, tea, and snacks. At breakfast time a "Lite Fare Breakfast" is delivered to your door in a basket. Walk to famous Oxford restaurants, or dine close by in St. Michaels, Trappe, Easton & Cambridge.

Nearest Airport: BWI & National — 1.5 hours. Dulles — 2 hrs. 15 min. Recommended directions at sandaway.com

Savage River Lodge

www.savageriverlodge.com
1600 Mt. Aetna Road, Frostburg, MD 21532
(301) 689-3200 • Fax (301) 689-2746
info@savageriverlodge.com

Member Since 2010

Innkeepers/Owners Jan Russell and Mike Dreisbach

The Savage River Lodge is situated on 42 acres in the center of a 750-acre state forest in Western Maryland. We offer 18 individual luxury cabins, a gourmet restaurant, fully-stocked bar and superior hospitality. Our outdoor recreation includes cross country skiing, snow shoeing, biking, fly fishing, geo-caching and miles of hiking trails. Other attractions in the area include Frank Lloyd Wright's Falling Water, kayaking, white water rafting, horseback riding, golf and downhill skiing. Our restaurant offers some of the most interesting food in the area such as bison, wild boar sausage and other wild game. The classic dishes such as meatloaf, steaks, chicken and seafood are also on our menu. We have in-cabin dining available for those who want a more private experience. Homemade muffins and juice are delivered to the cabins each morning. We were honored with the Maryland Small Business Award in 2009. We have been annually awarded the Wine Spectator Award of Excellence, the Wine Enthusiast Award of Distinction and SRL was a recipient of Travelocity's Local Secret Big Finds.

Rates: Our cabin rates begin at $230 per night for a double occupancy cabin. Includes the complimentary muffin basket. We are also pet friendly! Number of Rooms: 18

Cuisine: Our American classics menu changes seasonally. We are open for lunch and dinner daily, with breakfast on the weekends. We make every effort to accommodate any dietary needs; including vegetarian, vegan and gluten free diets.

Nearest Airport: 2 1/2 hours from Pittsburgh, Baltimore Washington International, and Dulles Airports.

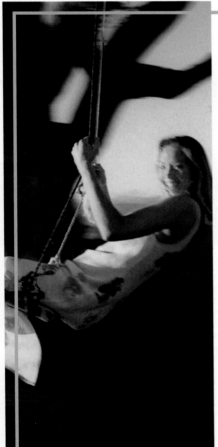

"The Bay State"

Famous for: Pilgrims, Thanksgiving, Salem Witch Trials, Boston Tea Party, Birth of the American Revolution, Minutemen, Freedom Trail, Swan Boats, Cape Cod, Education, Arts, Technology, and Medicine.

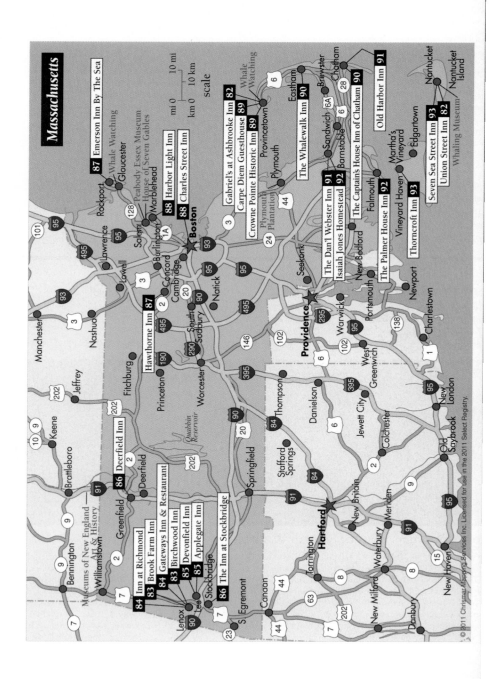

Gabriel's at Ashbrooke Inn

http://www.gabriels.com/
102 Bradford Street, Provincetown, MA United States 02657
508-487-3232
elizabethbrooke@me.com

Member Since 2011

Elizabeth & Elizabeth Brooke

Since 1979,û ôGabriel's at The Ashbrooke Inn has welcomed our family of friends to this unique and special inn. We welcome everyone including children and pets! We are located in the center of Provincetown bordering the Bas Relief Park. Once you arrive you will not need your car until you depart! Our beautifully appointed guest rooms all have Tempurpedic beds, Jacuzzi tubs, fireplaces, wet bars, TVs, DVD players, WiFi, amenity baskets and more. We offer an extensive free movie library, courtesy phone, bicycle storage and access to the Great Room/dining room anytime. Enjoy our lovely gardens, lounge on the sun decks, meet new friends in the Great Room at breakfast, or set out at twilight towards the bright lights of Commercial Street, or the last purple light of day fading over Herring Cove. You're certain to experience the unique character of Provincetown and the amazing hospitality of Gabriel's.

Rates: $150/$380 depending on the room and the season. We are open year round. Off season specials and packages are often available. Call Elizabeth directly for information 508-487-2779. Number of Rooms: 8

Cuisine: Gourmet chocolates in your room upon arrival. Homemade breakfast each morning, in season, in our Great Room. Our famous home baked cookies, tea, coffee, and organic drinks available anytime. Special dietary needs can be accommodated.

Nearest Airport: Provincetown Airport (PVC), Boston Logan Airport (BOS), Providence T.F. Green Airport (PVD)

Union Street Inn

www.unioninn.com
7 Union Street, Nantucket, MA 02554
888-517-0707 • 508-228-9222 • Fax 508-325-0848
info@unioninn.com

Member Since 2005

Innkeepers/Owners Ken & Deborah Withrow

Nantucket's boutique inn. "This mint 1770 house in the middle of town has more style than most–not a surprise, given the previous careers of proprietors Ken (ex-GM of the Royalton in New York City) and Deborah (a display manager at Henri Bendel). They've decorated the 12 rooms in impeccable New England-by-way-of-France style–Pierre Deux wallpaper, high-poster beds, polished original floorboards, and a few non-fusty antiques. Six also have fireplaces. Add to the mix delicious breakfasts served on the outside patio (try the challah-bread French toast with fresh berries), a concierge to score hard-to-get dinner reservations, and just-baked cookies served every afternoon, and you'll see why this place has return guests every summer."- Conde Nast Traveler. Rooms have private baths, flat screen TV's, Frette and Matouk bedding, bath amenities by Fresh, and complimentary Wi-Fi. Restaurants, shops, galleries, museums, and ferries are a short stroll. Walk or bicycle to Nantucket's beautiful beaches.

Rates: 12 Rooms. High Season: $299/$579; Shoulder Seasons: $159/$499. Closed November through March. Number of Rooms: 12

Cuisine: We are the only Nantucket B&B serving a Full Country Breakfast. Available in the Dining Room, Garden Patio or In Bed. Afternoon Treats include Home-Baked Cookies & Carrot Cake. Coffee, Tea, Bottled Spring Water always available

Nearest Airport: Nantucket Memorial Airport-10 minute taxi ride.

Birchwood Inn

www.birchwood-inn.com
7 Hubbard Street, P.O. Box 2020, Lenox, MA 01240
800-524-1646 • 413-637-2600 • Fax 413-637-4604
innkeeper@birchwood-inn.com

Member Since 2003

Innkeeper/Owner Ellen Gutman Chenaux

Imagine. . . a warm welcome to our Colonial Revival 1766 inn. . . the wag of a friendly tail. . . hot-from-the-oven chocolate chip cookies. . . Imagine. . . awakening to the aroma of freshly baked bread. . . savoring our sumptuous breakfasts, created by one of the "Eight Broads in the Kitchen". . . Imagine. . . New England stone-fenced gardens. . . a tranquil front porch, enjoying afternoon tea and the Berkshire breezes. . . curling up next to a crackling hearth with a good read and a steaming mug of mulled cider. . . Imagine. . . a hammock and spring blossoms. . . autumn's vibrant foliage. . . fireflies in the summer twilight. . . firesides when snowflakes fall. . . snow angels. . . Imagine. . . hiking, biking or snowshoeing on neighboring Kennedy Park's trails. . . a short walk to the shops, restaurants, and galleries of historic Lenox. . . picnicking at Tanglewood. . . exploring historic homes. . . indulging your passion for food with a "Fun for Foodies" experience. . . de-stressing in a yoga class. . .luxuriating in a spa day. . . all at our doorstep

Rates: $175/$335. Rates/minimum stays change seasonally. Comfortably elegant guestrooms, 6 w/ fireplaces. Number of Rooms: 11

Cuisine: Fireside "best breakfast in New England," featuring fruit dishes, local produce, homemade breads, & creative entrees served at individual tables. Afternoon tea w/homemade pastries, ice creams & sorbets. Freshly baked goodies for "sweet dreams."

Nearest Airport: One hour from both Albany and Hartford (Bradley) airports.

Brook Farm Inn

www.brookfarm.com
15 Hawthorne Street, Lenox, MA 01240
800-285-7638 (POET) • 413-637-3013 • Fax 413-637-4751
innkeeper@brookfarm.com

Member Since 2001

Innkeepers/Owners Phil & Linda Halpern

There is poetry here. . . This Victorian Berkshires treasure is nestled in a wooded glen, surrounded by award-winning gardens. Brook Farm Inn is just a short walk to historic Lenox village. Built in 1882, and furnished with antiques, the inn features a library filled with poetry, history and literature, where the sounds of classical music can be heard. The main building has 12 guest rooms, and the carriage house has luxury accommodations, including 2 handicap accessible rooms. Brook Farm Inn is close to Tanglewood and all cultural and outdoor attractions. Your friendly hosts offer gracious hospitality and assistance in planning a memorable Berkshires vacation. The sumptuous buffet breakfasts are unsurpassed. Afternoon tea and scones are served on weekends in the library. Seasonal activities are downhill and xc-skiing, hiking, biking, theater, concerts, antiquing and museum and historic home tours. The foliage season is spectacular, and special packages are offered. Attractions: Tanglewood, Berkshire Theatre Festival, Rockwell Museum, Shakespeare & Co., Hancock Shaker Village.

Rates: $149/$429 depending on season and room choice. Antiques, canopy beds. 9 rooms w/fireplaces, some w/whirlpool tubs. WIFI. Heated outdoor pool. Gardens. Open year-round. Number of Rooms: 15

Cuisine: Full buffet breakfast and afternoon tea with homemade scones. Well-stocked guest pantry with refrigerators, ice, tea, coffee, hot chocolate, and cookies.Breakfast is meatless.

Nearest Airport: 45 min. toAlbany, NY. One hour to Hartford, CT. 2 hours to Boston.

Gateways Inn

www.gatewaysinn.com
51 Walker Street, Lenox, MA 01240
888-492-9466 • 413-637-2532 • Fax 413-637-1432
innkeeper@gatewaysinn.com

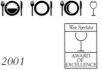

Member Since 2001

Innkeepers/Owners Fabrizio & Rosemary Chiariello

Gateways Inn is a stately neoclassical mansion, built by Mr. Procter of Procter & Gamble as a summer home in the picturesqe Berkshire Town of Lenox. The mansion later became an Inn. Today the Innkeepers & Staff welcome guests from the world over, providing gracious hospitality in a European Manor Home atmosphere. The 12 guest rooms are each unique in decor, all with private baths, as well as updated comforts & amenities. La Terrazza Restaurant showcases a Farm to Table seasonal Italian & Mediterranean menu. Open till midnight in season, serving all meals daily. Our award-winning Bar offers an impressively large collection of Single Malt Scotches and Grappas. Business travelers welcomed. Customized weddings, private parties & meetings are our specialty. Italian Cooking School events are scheduled throughout the year. Tanglewood, the summer home of the Boston Symphony Orchestra, is nearby. Our picnics are a unique experience! The Inn is a short stroll to Town Center with many fine shops and galleries. The nearby nature parks offer the best in outdoor activities.

Rates: 11 Rooms. 1 Suite, $150/$515, depending on season. Peak season minimum stays apply. Open year-round. Corporate Rates and packages available. Number of Rooms: 12

Cuisine: Full Breakfast served daily. The Restaurant offers all meals daily in summer, Afternoon Tea, and Late-Night Menu. Full bar service. Extensive wine list. Wine Spectator Award. Special menus for Holidays. Custom menus for weddings and private parties.

Nearest Airport: Albany, NY– 1 hour by car. Hartford, CT-1 1/2 hour by car. Boston, MA– 2 hours by car.

The Inn at Richmond

www.innatrichmond.com
802 State Road (Route 41), Richmond, MA 01254
888-968-4748 • 413-698-2566 • Fax 413-698-2100
innkeepers@innatrichmond.com

Member Since 2006

Owner – Carl M. Dunham, Jr./Innkeeper – Pam Knisley

Experience tranquility and comfort at The Inn at Richmond! Let this historic house be your home away from home as you explore all the Berkshires have to offer – spectacular theater, inspiring music and museums, outdoor activities for every interest. Nestled in the countryside near Pittsfield and Lenox, the Inn boasts acres of gardens and pastures; guests can enjoy a stroll through barns, spend quiet time on the terrace, cuddle by a roaring fire or play a game of pool in our game room. Conveniently situated, the Inn is a short drive to Berkshire attractions – Tanglewood, Barrington Stage, Norman Rockwell Museum, Jacob's Pillow and outdoor adventures – horseback riding lessons at Berkshire Equestrian Center, kayaking, hiking, biking, fishing, snow shoeing and skiing. The casual elegance of this historic home makes a perfect setting for your getaway, family celebration or intimate wedding. A pet-friendly cottage and stalls for guests to board horses during their visit are available. Be a part of the harmonious blend of scenic natural beauty and true New England hospitality.

Rates: 6 Rooms, Suites, some with fireplaces; 3 Cottages with kitchens. Rates: Nov - May $160/$270; June - Oct $210/$380. In room amenities include cable TV, phones, WI-FI in Main House. Weekly rates, special packages. Open all year. Number of Rooms: 9

Cuisine: Guests are treated to a delicious country breakfast - a freshly prepared hot entree featuring locally produced foods; fruits, breads, pastries, cereals, yogurt and the usual selection of breakfast beverages are offered.

Nearest Airport: Albany International Airport, Albany, NY - 50 minutes Bradley International Airport, Hartford, CT - 1.5 hours

Applegate Inn

www.applegateinn.com
279 West Park Street, Lee, MA 01238
800-691-9012 • 413-243-4451 • Fax 413-243-9832
info@applegateinn.com

Member Since 2002

Owners/Innkeepers Len & Gloria Friedman

Once inside the iron gate, the circular drive, lined with lilac bushes reveals this elegant 1920s white-pillared Georgian mansion. It is situated on a 6 acre country estate across the road from a golf and tennis club, half mile from the historic town of Lee and 3 miles from Stockbridge. The 11 upscale guest accommodations are uniquely decorated and luxuriously appointed. For your comfort, the inn is air conditioned and heated with individual room controls and provides wifi internet. From the screened porch look beyond the heated swimming pool to the lawns, towering trees and gardens. This is tranquility itself; a relaxing place to rejuvenate while pampered with attentive service, candlelit breakfasts, and wine and cheese served each afternoon. Explore Tanglewood, theater, dance, Norman Rockwell Museum, golf, tennis, hiking, swimming, boating, skiing, antiquing, shopping and other natural and cultural wonders of the Berkshires, or linger at the inn by a roaring fire, rest in a hammock for two under an old apple tree, or stroll the perennial gardens.

Rates: Rooms $150/$275; Suites $270/$395; Cottage $270/$375. AC, TV, VCR/DVD, CD, wifi, some with fireplace, jacuzzi, mini-fridge, balcony, patio and steam shower for two. All have robes, hair dryer, phone, flowers, brandy & chocolate. Number of Rooms: 11

Cuisine: Multi-course gourmet candlelit breakfast served on china & crystal. Wine & cheese served in the afternoon. Fruit bowl, cookie jar & guest pantry always available.

Nearest Airport: Albany & Bradley Airports

Devonfield Inn B & B

www.devonfield.com
85 Stockbridge Road., Lee, MA 01238
800-664-0880 • 413-243-3298 • Fax 413-243-1360
innkeeper@devonfield.com

Member Since 2003

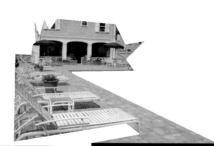

Innkeepers/Owners Bruce & Ronnie Singer

Centrally located, yet a world apart, Devonfield Inn is set on a 32 acre pastoral meadow shaded by graceful birch trees, with the rolling tapestry of the Berkshire Hills beyond. This 200 year old historic estate home has been graciously updated and is filled with fine antiques. It is sophisticated, yet comfortable and inviting. Devonfield's upscale suites and bedrooms are all beautifully appointed, spacious and offer modern private baths. Quilts, down comforters, plush sheets, towels, CD players and TV/DVDs enhance every room along with handmade chocolates and bottled water. Many have wood-burning fireplaces, Jacuzzis and fine terry robes. For your comfort, the Inn is completely air conditioned and provides wireless Internet. The guest pantry is always open and stocked with treats. There is a refrigerator and microwave as well. Follow breakfast with a stroll through the flower-filled gardens, play tennis, or take a dip in the heated pool, and then enjoy the best in cultural and recreational activities in all seasons. Or, just relax and enjoy the sights and sounds of nature.

Rates: 6 Rooms; 3 Suites; 1 Guest Cottage. Off Season: $180/$325. In Season: $225/$375 Number of Rooms: 10

Cuisine: A fireside (fall and winter) candlelit gourmet breakfast is served on fine china accompanied by classical music. Breakfast includes a buffet of fresh baked goods, fruits, granola, yogurt, juices and more, followed by a specially selected hot entree.

Nearest Airport: Bradley, CT (63 miles); Albany (45 miles)

The Inn at Stockbridge

www.stockbridgeinn.com
30 East St, PO Box 618, Stockbridge, MA 01262
888-466-7865 • 413-298-3337 • Fax 413-298-3406
innkeeper@stockbridgeinn.com

Member Since 1986

Innkeepers/Owners Len & Alice Schiller

Enjoy peaceful charm and elegance in a 1906 Georgian style mansion secluded on 12 acres in Stockbridge, a town described by Norman Rockwell as the best of New England and the best of America. Awaken to the aroma of fresh coffee, stroll the beautiful grounds, take a dip in the heated pool, exercise in the fitness room, relax on the wrap around porch and take time away from the cares of the world. Antiques, collectibles and luxury are very much at home here. Amenities and attention to detail found only in upscale properties for the discriminating traveler await you here. Fireplace and double whirlpool rooms with a private deck are available. Voted by the Discerning Traveler as one of the Most Romantic Inns. Centrally located to all Berkshire cultural attractions including the Norman Rockwell Museum and Tanglewood, theater, dance, golf, hiking, boating, skiing, antiquing, shopping. Enjoy the culture and the outdoors or just relax. The Schiller's have been inviting guests to enjoy the Berkshires for over 17 years.

Rates: Main house rooms $160/$295-8 Fireplace and/or Whirlpool Suites in the barn, cottage house and main house $265/$385. Rates vary by room and season. Number of Rooms: 16

Cuisine: Multi-course bountiful, gourmet candlelit breakfast featuring local products. Breakfast includes a buffet of freshly baked goods, fruit, granola, yogurt, and a specially selected entree. Wine and cheese served in the afternoon. Guest pantry with snacks and beverages always available.

Nearest Airport: Albany, NY — Hartford, CT

Deerfield Inn

www.deerfieldinn.com
81 Main Street, Deerfield, MA 01342-0305
800-926-3865 • 413-774-5587 • Fax 413-775-7221
frontdesk@deerfieldinn.com

Member Since 1996

Innkeepers Karl Sabo & Jane Howard

A traditional country inn, guests were first welcomed here in July 1884, as a plague of grasshoppers devoured its way across a drought-stricken county! Still the centerpiece of this National Historic Landmark village, the Deerfield Inn stands at the middle of the mile long village Main Street known as the loveliest in New England. We have 11 pleasing rooms in the main inn and 13 in the carriage house, all of individual size and style with organic amenities; cozy living rooms for reading and relaxing; an intimate porch for dining when the weather is fine; and a Relaxing Room for therapeutic massages. Champney's Restaurant & Tavern market-driven menus reflect our food philosophy of eating the view. A full bar, local draft beers, a martini menu, and a good wine list with many wines by the glass complement your experience. Deerfield is a perfect destination for those looking for the authentic, unspoiled New England. Enjoy Deerfield's museums, farms, attractions, country walks, area boutique shops, friendly folk, and beautiful scenery. We look forward to welcoming you here!

Rates: $160/$250 room. Kings, queens, double queens, twins, and a suite with gas fireplace. Complimentary afternoon tea & cookies, and a continental breakfast with house made granola, breakfast pastries, and eggs from happy chickens. Number of Rooms: 24

Cuisine: Champney's Restaurant & Tavern is open daily for breakfast, lunch, and dinner. Our market-driven menus make use of seasonal produce fresh from local farms, fields, and orchards, and everything is made from scratch. Full bar & local draft beers too.

Nearest Airport: Bradley Field, CT is 55 minutes away, and an easy drive up I-91N to exit 24.

Hawthorne Inn

www.concordmass.com
462 Lexington Road, Concord, MA 01742-3729
978-369-5610 • Fax 978-287-4949
Inn@ConcordMass.com

Member Since 1980

Innkeepers/Owners Gregory Burch and Marilyn Mudry

Relaxed Elegance—Just 30 minutes from Boston, three rivers wind through a Colonial landscape of Minutemens fields where moss-covered stonewalls embrace the homes of Hawthorne, Alcott, Thoreau and Emerson. Here you will find an intimate refuge, the Hawthorne Inn, filled with original artworks to delight your eyes, curios to excite the imagination, coverlets to snuggle on a crisp autumn eve and burnished antiques that speak of home and security. Seven vibrant Guestrooms, inspired by a refreshing mix of tradition and artistic expression, offer abundant comforts and modern amenities. Since 1976 the Inn has made welcome business-travelers, lovers, seekers, pilgrims and families to our historic 17th century village. As you amble in the footsteps of Patriots and Poets you will savor the Inn's unique location near the Authors Homes, Walden Pond, Minuteman National Park and Old North Bridge, where was fired, "the shot heard 'round the world." Many choose the Hawthorne as a base for day-trips to explore Boston, Cambridge, Sturbridge, Salem, Plymouth and the near by ocean beaches.

Rates: Graciously appointed rooms offering Canopy or Four-poster Bed, Refreshments at Check-in and Multi-course Breakfast. Rates vary by Seasonal Demand and length of stay. Nightly Accommodations from $159–$329. See website for Specials. Number of Rooms: 7

Cuisine: Guests enjoy a sumptuous Multi-course Breakfast around a convivial table. Changing Daily Specials: Inn's delectable Home-Made Granola, Award-Winning pear dish, Freshly-Baked Artisan Breads, Buttermilk Pancakes, Herb-Baked Frittata and Organic Coffee.

Nearest Airport: Boston Logan-30 min./ Manchester N.H.-50 min./ Private Planes at Hanscom Field- 10 min. See website for directions.

Emerson Inn By The Sea

www.EmersonInnByTheSea.com
One Cathedral Avenue, Pigeon Cove, Rockport, MA 01966
800-964-5550 • 978-546-6321 • Fax 978-546-7043
info@EmersonInnByTheSea.com

Member Since 1973

Innkeepers/Owners Bruce and Michele Coates

Ralph Waldo Emerson called the Inn "Thy proper summer home." Today's guests enjoy the relaxed 19th Century atmosphere from our broad oceanfront veranda, but can savor the 21st Century amenities of a heated outdoor pool, room phones, data ports, high speed wireless internet, air conditioning, cable television, private baths and spa tubs. Nearby are hiking trails along the oceanfront, tennis, golf, sea kayaking, scuba diving and the always popular whale watches. Halibut Point State Park features the history of the Rockport Quarries and downtown Rockport is famous for shops and art galleries. The historic Emerson is the ideal ocean front location for weddings, retreats and conferences. "Editors Pick," Yankee Travel Guide to New England. And as featured in 1000 Places To See in the USA Before You Die and in Zagat's 2005 & 2006 Top U.S. Hotels, Resorts, and Spas. Mobil Three Star, AAA ◆◆◆.

Rates: $99/$399 B&B; Two Seaside Cottages, each accommodates 8, available for a weekly rental. Open all year. Number of Rooms: 36

Cuisine: Award-winning Restaurant. 'Unparalleled ambiance' — The Boston Globe. Outdoor oceanfront dining and elegant turn-of-the-century dining room serving breakfast daily; dinner and live music schedules vary by season.

Nearest Airport: Boston Logan International Airport

Harbor Light Inn

www.harborlightinn.com
58 Washington Street, Marblehead, MA 01945
781–631–2186 • Fax 781-631-2216
info@harborlightinn.com

Member Since 1996

Innkeepers/Owners Peter & Suzanne Conway

Winner of numerous national awards for excellence, including Vacation magazine's "America's Best Romantic Inns." The Inn offers first-class accommodations and amenities found in the finest of lodging facilities. Elegant furnishings grace these two connected Federalist mansions. Formal parlors with fireplaces, dining room and bed chambers, double Jacuzzis, large HDTV's, WIFI, sundecks, patio, quiet garden and outdoor heated pool combine to ensure the finest in New England hospitality. Located in the heart of historic Harbor District of fine shops, art galleries and restaurants. Our intimate tavern is open nightly and offers fine wines, beers and cordials along with our bar menu of local favorites.◆◆◆

Rates: 20 Rooms, $155/$365; Suites, $195/$365 B&B. Open year-round. Number of Rooms: 20
Cuisine: Breakfast buffet featuring fresh homemade breads, fruit platters, yogurts, bagels, hot casseroles, salmon platter and daily specials. Wine, beer and cordials in new pub. Pub menu is available for lunch and dinner daily. 7 restaurants within 2 blocks.
Nearest Airport: Boston Logan International approximately 15 miles .

Charles Street Inn

www.charlesstreetinn.com
94 Charles St., Boston, MA 02114
877-772-8900 • 617-314-8900 • Fax 617-371-0009
info@charlesstreetinn.com

Member Since 2004

Innkeepers/Owners Sally Deane & Louise Venden

A luxury inn located in historic Beacon Hill within blocks of Boston's shopping, touring, and subway stops, the Charles Street Inn offers unique comfort and privacy in nine spacious rooms with elevator access. Each room features a private bath with whirlpool tubs, working marble fireplaces, fresh flowers, BOSE radio/CD player, Cable TV, VCR, DVD, AC controls, DSL and Wireless Internet, and Sub-Zero refrigerator. Authentic Victorian-era antiques, king & queen size canopy and sleigh beds, and rich imported linens complete each elegant setting. Relax in front of a fire or enjoy any of the fabulous restaurants that are literally steps from the inn. Recognized among Boston's Best by Travel + Leisure, Boston Magazine, and as one of the top 10 romantic inns in the US by America's Historic Inns. Concierge services available.

Rates: $250/$525 depending on room, season, and day of the week. Call for rates (US toll-free 877-772-8900) or visit "Reservations" on our web site. Number of Rooms: 9
Cuisine: Arrive to sweets, fresh fruit, snacks and refreshments in the lobby and in your room . Then, schedule your in-room breakfast with so many choices including quiche and eggs, delicious bowls of fresh fruit, a variety of pastries, cereals, and cheeses.
Nearest Airport: Boston

Carpe Diem Guesthouse & Spa

www.carpediemguesthouse.com
12 — 14 Johnson Street, Provincetown, MA 02657-2312
800-487-0132 • 508-487-4242
info@carpediemguesthouse.com

Member Since 2003

Innkeepers/Owners Rainer Horn, Jürgen Herzog, Hans van Costenoble

Carpe Diem — Seize the day — is not only the life motto of innkeepers Rainer, Jurgen and Hans, but for years a trademark for hospitality, luxury and friendliness on Cape Cod. Located in the heart of Provincetown, the Carpe Diem is an oasis of peace and tranquility close to the tasteful shops, gourmet restaurants and fun yet sophisticated nightlife Commercial Street has to offer. The secluded gardens and patios of the inn invite guests to rest, meet interesting people or simply enjoy life. The newly created spa is a year-round retreat where you can pamper yourselves with a rejuvenating massage, a relaxing steam bath, a stimulating hot sauna or some lazy time in the outdoor Jacuzzi. The guestrooms are decorated with exquisite taste, many feature fireplaces and whirlpool tubs. Breakfast is a social event when the varied guests gather all morning in the sun lit dining area. Food aficionados can start their day with a wonderful hot cup of Carpe Diem Coffee, homemade breads and pastry, egg dishes and specials like Belgian Waffles, French Crepes or Austrian Kaiserschmarm.

Rates: 18 rooms and suites, $95/$425. Open year round. Number of Rooms: 18

Cuisine: Jurgen's homemade German-style breakfast is famous. Out&About: "Imagine a cross between Martha Stewart cozy and cool European design. Similarly, the breakfasts are classic American gourmet meets German bounty." Afternoon wine & cheese and refreshments.

Nearest Airport: Boston & Providence

Wine Spectator
GRAND
AWARD
Member Since 2003

Crowne Pointe Historic Inn & Spa

www.crownepointe.com
82 Bradford Street, Provincetown, MA 02657
877-276-9631 • 508-487-6767 • Fax 508-487-5554
welcome@crownepointe.com

Innkeepers/Owners David M. Sanford & Thomas J. Walter

A prominent Sea Captain built this historic mansion, which has been fully restored to its 19th Century glory. The inn's stunning Victorian architecture includes two-story wrap around porches complete with turret and harbor views. The New York Daily News raves "Five Star Luxury Without the Cost." Revive at our full service on-site Shui Spa featuring many treatments and massage options. Shui Spa offers guests an intimate spa experience. Crowne Pointe is a AAA Four Diamond property located in the center of town, walk to everything. Our signature gourmet hot breakfast and afternoon wine and cheese social are included. Heated in-ground pool, two hot tubs, fireplaces and in-room whirlpools are offered. Spa packages are available. Our restaurant captures our guests with exquisite gourmet cuisine, and our hotel bar is a treasured place to socialize. The finest menu creations from our talented chefs, carefully selected labels from our wine cellar, and excellent service in a charming setting are waiting for you to indulge.

Rates: $99/$465 depending upon season. Minimum stay requirements may apply. Many special packages available, call for details. Number of Rooms: 40

Cuisine: The freshest regional ingredients arriving daily, our distinctive full hot breakfasts are unsurpassed. The main selections change daily and special dietary needs are accommodated.

Nearest Airport: Provincetown Airport (PVC) or Boston Logan Airport

The Whalewalk Inn and Spa

www.whalewalkinn.com
220 Bridge Road, Eastham, Cape Cod, MA 02642
800-440-1281 • 508-255-0617 • Fax 508-240-0017
reservations@whalewalkinn.com

Member Since 1993

Innkeepers/Owners Kevin & Elaine Conlin

Abandon every day life. Rekindle your romance and rejuvenate your body and mind. Relax at Cape Cod's most romantic country Inn and Spa. Secluded, but centrally located to all attractions which make Cape Cod so special. After a gourmet breakfast, walk the "Outer Cape" beaches while listening to the soothing sound of the waves lapping on Cape Cod Bay or crashing at the National Seashore. At the end of a day on the beach, riding the Rail Trail, kayaking, shopping or museum hopping, restore your inner balance and harmony at The Spa, a special place with your comfort and exercise regime in mind. Forget the weather; pamper your mind and body with a massage or facial; feel the heat of the dry sauna or workout in the indoor resistance pool or on cardiovascular machines. Have fun with Wii Sports and Fit. Stay in the luxurious Spa Penthouse or in one of 16 other beautiful accommodations. All are individually decorated having amenities such as air-conditioning, TV/DVD/CD, fireplace, refrigerator, and high speed WiFi. Come and enjoy our impeccable service and heartfelt hospitality.

Rates: $220/$420. Call for off-season rates. Open April to December. Number of Rooms: 17

Cuisine: Full-service gourmet breakfast with fresh home-baked delights and entrees: Waffle Sundaes, Eggs Benedict, Corn Pancakes with Dill Shallot Sauce and Salmon Rosettes, Grand Marnier Oatmeal Pie, Baked Omelet, and Granola Pizza. Evening hors d'oeuvres.

Nearest Airport: Boston, MA; Providence, RI

The Captain's House Inn

www.captainshouseinn.com
369-377 Old Harbor Rd, Chatham, MA 02633
800-315-0728 • 508-945-0127 • Fax 508-945-0866
info@captainshouseinn.com

Member Since 1989

Innkeepers/Owners James & Jill Meyer

Perhaps Cape Cod's finest small Inn, this historic 1839 sea captain's estate on two acres is the perfect choice for a romantic getaway or elegant retreat. Gourmet breakfasts, English afternoon teas, beautifully decorated rooms with king and queen size beds, fireplaces, seating areas, telephones, WI-FI capability and TV's with DVD players; some with whirlpool tubs. Enjoy uncompromising service from our enthusiastic international staff and enjoy the Inn's many gardens and fountains, heated outdoor pool, fitness center, and savor the scenic beauty of the historic seafaring village of Chatham with its 70 miles of spectacular shoreline. The Captain's House Inn of Chatham has been a AAA ◆◆◆◆ award winner since 1987.

Rates: 12 Rooms, $260/$350; 4 Suites, $260/$475 Summer $185/$250; $185/$315 Winter. Open year-round. Number of Rooms: 16

Cuisine: Breakfast, poolside lunches, afternoon tea, evening snacks.

Nearest Airport: Providence or Boston

Old Harbor Inn

www.chathamoldharborinn.com
22 Old Harbor Road, Chatham, MA 02633
800-942-4434 • 508 945-4434 • Fax 508 945-7665
info@chathamoldharborinn.com

Member Since 2004

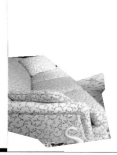

Innkeepers/Owners Ray & Judy Braz

Originally built by the local doctor in 1932, The Old Harbor Inn is now entering its fourth decade of providing distinctive lodging to the discriminating traveler. The Inn is ideally located just steps from the center of the historic seaside village of Chatham. Guests frequently tell us how enjoyable it is not to use their cars for several days as they explore all the attractions that Chatham has to offer. Designer appointed rooms with king or queen beds are just the start of a luxurious experience. WiFi throughout the Inn, as well as flat screen/DVD combos with an extensive DVD library, add to your in room enjoyment. The professionally designed and meticulously maintained gardens and Koi ponds are sure to please. Judy, Ray and their knowledgeable international staff are always available to help plan your days. Chatham serves as a centralized base for exploring all of Cape Cod and the Islands. Provincetown, Falmouth, Martha's Vineyard or Nantucket are all easily accessible. Whether you are planning a romantic getaway or an elegant retreat, every day you get our best.

Rates: Rates are: $199/$339 summer-$149/$259 spring and fall-$129/$209 winter. Peak season min. stays apply. Number of Rooms: 11

Cuisine: The full breakfast includes fresh juices, gourmet teas and coffees, seasonal fresh fruit, assorted breads and cereals, plus a fresh prepared entree and a fresh bakery specialty.

Nearest Airport: Boston or Providence

The Dan'l Webster Inn & Spa

www.DanlWebsterInn.com
149 Main St., Sandwich, MA 02563
800-444-3566 • 508-888-3622 • Fax 508-888-5156
info@DanlWebsterInn.com

Member Since 1994

Innkeeper/Owner Catania Family

This award-winning Inn set in the heart of Historic Sandwich, offers guests the romance of the past with today's conveniences. Canopy and four-poster beds, fireplaces, Keurig coffee makers and oversized whirlpool tubs await your arrival. Each guest room and suite has been individually appointed with exquisite period furnishings. The Beach Plum Spa at The Dan'l Webster offers the ultimate in luxury for Men and Women. . .from completely organic Body Treatments and relaxing Massages to soothing Facials, Hand and Foot Rituals and more, will pamper your mind, body and soul! Enjoy a romantic dinner with an emphasis on locally grown and organic ingredients. Savor delicious award-winning cuisine and creative chef's specials complemented by an acclaimed wine selection, or relax in a casual Tavern at the Inn and enjoy lighter fare and always a warm, friendly atmosphere. All suites are furnished with purifing e-showers, 300 ct. Pima cotton triple sheeting, selection of high quality pillows, photo-catalytic ionization air purifiers and silky micro fiber robes.

Rates: 35 Traditional/Deluxe/Superior Rooms, $109/$259; 13 Suites, $179/$399. Open year-round. Closed Xmas Number of Rooms: 48

Cuisine: Breakfast, lunch, dinner, and Sunday Brunch. Dining Al Fresco. Afternoon Tea. Tavern on premise. Fine and casual dining menus available serving contemporary and traditional American cuisine. Many organic, locally grown ingredients.

Nearest Airport: Logan Airport (Boston) or TF Green (Providence)

Isaiah Jones Homestead

www.isaiahjones.com
165 Main Street, Sandwich, MA 02563
800-526-1625 • 508-888-9115 • Fax 508-888-9648
info@isaiahjones.com

Member Since 1989

Innkeepers/Owners Don and Katherine Sanderson

Relax in pampered elegance in this 1849 Italianate Victorian Inn. The main house has five exquisitely appointed guest rooms with private baths featuring queen beds, antique furnishings, oriental carpets, all with fireplaces or glass-front stoves and two with oversize whirlpool tubs. The unique Carriage House includes two spacious junior suites each with a fireplace and whirlpool bath, one with a king bed. Located in the heart of Sandwich village, the inn is within easy walking distance of many shops, restaurants and attractions of Cape Cod's oldest town. Unwind by strolling the meandering garden paths around the goldfish pond, by sitting in comfortable Adirondack chairs placed around the well-manicured yard or by relaxing by the original antique-tiled fireplace in the gathering room. A full breakfast, served in our cherry-paneled dining room, sets a warm tone to start your day. Chosen Editors Choice, Cape Cod Travel Guide. Selected as "Insider Pick" for Romantic Getaways by Destination Insider. Featured in "Checking In," Boston Sunday Globe, April 6, 2008.

Rates: Seven rooms, $165/$300, including a full, three-course breakfast. Air conditioned. Open year-round. Number of Rooms: 7

Cuisine: Breakfast is served in our sunny, cherry paneled dining room or on the deck overlooking the garden. Enjoy a full three-course breakfast of fresh fruit, juices, creative hot entrees, home-baked scones and muffins, and our special blend of gourmet coffee

Nearest Airport: Logan Airport, Boston, MA; TF Green, Providence, RI

Palmer House Inn

www.palmerhouseinn.com
81 Palmer Avenue, Falmouth, MA 02540
800-472-2632 • 508-548-1230 • Fax 508-540-1878
innkeepers@palmerhouseinn.com

Member Since 2001

Innkeepers/Owners Bill & Pat O'Connell

On a tree-lined street in the heart of the Historic District, The Palmer House Inn is an elegant Victorian home. Stained glass windows, rich woodwork, gleaming hardwood floors and antique furnishings create an overall sense of warmth and harmony. Beautiful beaches, quaint shops, ferry shuttles, and excellent restaurants are only a short stroll away. The innkeepers pamper you with fresh flowers, extra pillows, fluffy robes, fine linens and meticulous housekeeping. The Palmer House Inn is the perfect place to stay, in splendid comfort and gracious care. Local activities include golf, swimming, cycling on the Shining Sea Bike Path on one of the Palmer House's bicycles, fishing, charter sailing, kayaking, hiking, bird watching and more.

Rates: 16 Rooms, $169/$269; 1 Cottage Suites, $245/$299. K, Q & DBL beds. 7 rooms w/ whirlpool tubs and 3 w/ fireplaces. Rooms have 600 thread count sheets, TV, phones, hair dryers, irons & boards, ice buckets, AC and WiFi. Open year-round Number of Rooms: 17

Cuisine: Full two to three course gourmet breakfast served with candlelight and classical music. Afternoon and evening refreshments. Early morning coffee.

Nearest Airport: TF Green (Providence), Logan (Boston)

Thorncroft Inn

www.thorncroft.com

460 Main St., P.O. Box 1022, Martha's Vineyard, MA 02568
800-332-1236 • 508-693-3333 • Fax 508-693-5419
innkeeper@thorncroft.com

Member Since 1994

Proprietors/Innkeepers Karl & Lynn Buder

Thorncroft Inn is situated in three restored buildings on 2 1/2 acres of quiet, treed grounds on the Island of Martha's Vineyard. It is secluded, exclusively couples-oriented and first-class. All rooms have phone, TV/VCR, high-speed wireless and wired internet access, air-conditioning, deluxe bathrobes and an array of amenities. Most rooms have working, wood-burning fireplaces and canopied beds. Some have two-person whirlpool bathtubs or private 250-gallon hot tubs. Several offer private exterior entrances or furnished private porches or balconies. Full country breakfast is served in our two dining rooms or breakfast is delivered to the room. Our concierge service is renowned and focuses on the specific needs of each couple. Thorncroft Inn is an ideal setting for honeymoons, anniversaries, engagements, birthdays or any romantic getaway for couples. AAA has awarded Thorncroft it's Four Diamond Award for 22 consecutive years. Voted best B&B on Martha's Vineyard-2011 by Martha's Vineyard Magazine.

Rates: 14 antique appointed rooms, $195 to $495 B&B per evening with seasonal variations. European Plan offered year 'round excludes breakfast at a $50 per night discount. Number of Rooms: 14

Cuisine: Full country breakfast served in two dining rooms at individual tables for two or an ample continental breakfast delivered to room; Traditional or healthful entrees.

Nearest Airport: Martha's Vineyard Airport (MVY) 5 miles; Logan Airport in Boston (BOS) 77 miles

---

Member Since 1996

Matthew Parker Innkeeper/Owner

Enjoy Seven Sea Street Inn, a truly charming Nantucket bed and breakfast Inn, where we pride ourselves on the attentive service and elegant accommodations that will make your stay with us a fond memory. Our Inn is distinguished by its beautiful red oak post and beam style, designed and constructed with an authentic Nantucket ambiance in mind. In addition to providing exceptional comfort and hospitality, we offer a stunning view of Nantucket Harbor from our Widow's Walk deck. All of our guest rooms are furnished with luxurious Stearns and Foster queen or king mattresses, the world's finest bedding. Each Main house guest room and suite is furnished with rainshower showerheads, ACs, high definition TV, high speed wireless connectivity and a bow box of Nantucket's famous chocolate covered cranberries. Our location, nestled on a quiet tree-lined side stteet and less than a five-minute walk from Main Street shopping, restaurants, museums and the beach, couldn't be better. Indulge yourself at our lovely Inn this year.

Rates: 13 Guest Rooms, $99/$349 B&B; 2 Suites, $159/$449 B&B. Seasonal rates. Number of Rooms: 15

Cuisine: Expanded Buffet Continental Breakfast served daily. Two seatings, 8 a.m. and 9 a.m. Gourmet coffee, tea, soda, bottled water and homemade cookies available anytime.

Nearest Airport: Nantucket Memorial Airport

"The Wolverine State"

Famous for: Great Lakes,(borders on four of the five Great Lakes),
Fishing, Swimming, Water Sports, Holland (Tulip Center of America),
Cherries, Farmland, Auto Manufacturing.

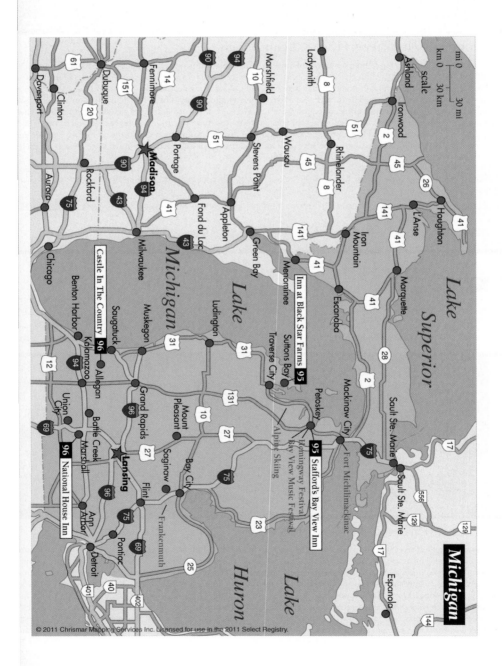

© 2011 Chrismar Mapping Services Inc. Licensed for use in the 2011 Select Registry.

Stafford's Bay View Inn

www.staffords.com
2011 US 31 N, P.O. Box 657, Petoskey, MI 49770
800-258-1886 • 231-347-2771 • Fax 231-347-3413
bayview@staffords.com

Member Since 1972

Proprietor Stafford Smith

Stafford's Bay View Inn was purchased by Stafford and Janice Smith in 1961. Stafford and his family has owned, operated, and lovingly restored, this grand Victorian Country Inn on the shores of Lake Michigan's Little Traverse Bay. Built as a rooming house in 1886 in the Historic Landmark District of Bay View, this Inn sets the standard in country Inn dining and gracious service. Each beautifully appointed guest room features a private bath, and individual climate controls. Visitors to the area enjoy summer Chautauqua programs, championship golf, paved bike paths just out our front door, fall color tours, winter ski packages, and sleigh rides around the Bay View cottage grounds. Petoskey's Historic Gaslight Shopping District and marina are located nearby. Our inn is an exquisite place to hold weddings, rehearsal dinners, receptions and reunions. Many quiet corners offer a wonderful environment for company meetings and conferences. Voted 'Michigan's Best Brunch' by Michigan Living. This Inn is the flagship property of Stafford's Hospitality.

Rates: 21 Victorian rooms $99/$195, 10 spa and fireplace Suites $135/$255. Number of Rooms: 31

Cuisine: Breakfast and Dinner: May-October and winter weekends. Lunch: Late May-October. Sunday Brunch: June-October and Holidays. Visit www.staffords.com for menus, dining schedules and info on full-service, year-round, innkeeper-owned properties nearby.

Nearest Airport: Pellston (PLN) — 17 miles, Traverse (TVC) — 65 miles

---

Inn at Black Star Farms

www.blackstarfarms.com
10844 E. Revold Rd., Suttons Bay, MI 49682
877-466-9463 • 231-944-1251 • Fax 231-944-1259
innkeeper@blackstarfarms.com

Member Since 2003

Proprietor Don Coe

Expect consistently exceptional experiences at our year-round Inn, nestled below a hillside of vineyards in the heart of Leelanau Peninsula wine country. Our nine contemporary guestrooms, each with private bath and some with fireplaces and spa tubs, have fine furniture, luxurious linens, and down comforters. Amenities include a bottle of our Red House wine, cozy robes, evening hospitality hour and complimentary tasting of our award-winning wines at our on-site tasting room. Massage services and sauna are available. A full gourmet breakfast is prepared for you daily using locally sourced products. While visiting our tasting room, sample artisanal raclette cheese from Leelanau Cheese Company. Casual and upscale dining is available seasonally at our Hearth and Vine cafe or in the Arcturos dining room, both featuring breads baked on site by 9 Bean Rows CSA. The farm also features boarding stables and wooded recreational trails that are great in any season. Meetings, reunions and receptions welcomed.

Rates: High season May 27,2011-Oct 29,2011: $295-$395/night. Low season Nov 1-May 27,2011: $225-$295/night rates subject to 6% sales tax and 5% destination fee Number of Rooms: 9

Cuisine: Our breakfasts feature fresh fruit and juices, homemade baked goods, a seasonal gourmet entree using local products, and coffee and tea.

Nearest Airport: Cherry Capitol Airport (TVC)

Castle in the Country

www.castleinthecountry.com
340 M-40 South, Allegan, MI 49010
888-673-8054 • 269-673-8054
info@castleinthecountry.com

Member Since 2008

Innkeepers/Owners Herb & Ruth Boven

Escape the ordinary at Castle in the Country. Walk hand in hand through our wooded forest trails, sip a glass of wine in the screened porch beside our private lake or close the door to your own romantic suite with a whirlpool tub for two, fireplace and gourmet breakfast. Schedule a side-by-side couple's massage in our secluded Royal Retreat Spa Area. Awarded "Most Romantic Hideaway in North America!" & Best Getaway in the Great Lakes. When you choose Castle in the Country, you choose a Michigan getaway with extraordinary decor, amenities, and service! Scenic countryside provides a peaceful pastoral and wooded setting for your getaway. We offer 10 individually decorated Rooms/Suites within the timeless beauty of our century-old Victorian Castle and in our contemporary country manor house, the Castle Keep. Whether you're looking for a romantic getaway for two to celebrate a birthday, anniversary or honeymoon or, the perfect venue for an elopement or a Destination Wedding and Reception, our Innkeepers will help you create an experience that will exceed every expectation.

Rates: 10 Rooms; 7 whirlpool/fireplace suites $199-$289 3 rooms fireplaces $139-$199 Midweek discounts; Spa & Dinner Packages; Wedding Packages; Business Retreats. Number of Rooms: 10

Cuisine: Full breakfasts are artfully presented and served daily at your own individual table for two in our dining rooms overlooking the pond. Picnic baskets filled with fresh baked bread, and creative Dinner Packages may be added by advanced reservation.

Nearest Airport: Kalamazoo/Battle Creek International

National House Inn

www.nationalhouseinn.com
102 S. Parkview, Marshall, MI 49068
269-781-7374
frontdesk@nationalhouseinn.com

Member Since 1978

Innkeeper/Owner Barbara Bradley

The only thing we overlook is the Fountain Circle in the middle of picturesque Marshall. Discover why the National Trust of Historic Preservation named our town as one of their "Dozen Distinctive Destinations" in the country! Enjoy every aspect of our inn with its heritage and tradition that has welcomed guests for 170 years. Just steps from the inn, you'll find shopping, museums, galleries, ghost tours, carriage rides, Schuler's Restaurant and more.

Rates: $105-$170 Number of Rooms: 17
Cuisine: Breakfast, afternoon tea, catered dinners for receptions.
Nearest Airport: Kalamazoo & Detroit

"The Magnolia State"

Famous for: Mississippi River, Fertile Soil, Cotton, River Boats, Catfish, Old South, Red Bluff, Civil War Sites, Antebellum Mansions.

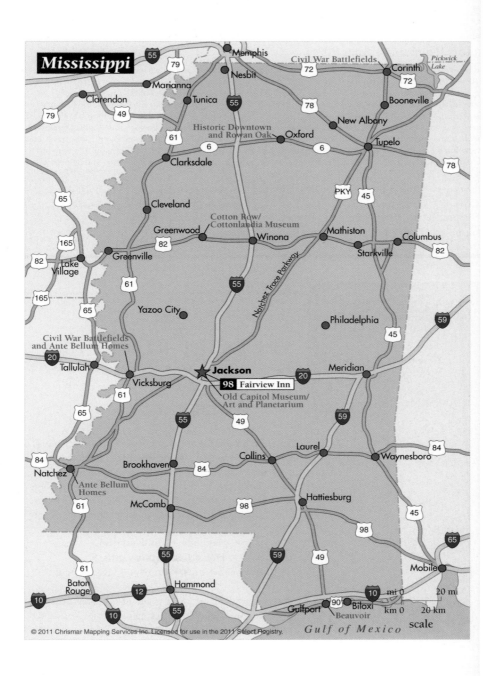

Fairview Inn

www.fairviewinn.com
734 Fairview Street, Jackson, MS 39202
888-948-1908 • 601-948-3429 • Fax 601-948-1203
innkeeper@fairviewinn.com

Member Since 1994

Proprietors Peter and Tamar Sharp

The Fairview Inn, Jackson's only AAA four-diamond small luxury hotel, invites you to experience this unique historic 1908 Colonial Revival mansion. This bed and breakfast Inn is one of the few architecturally designed homes of that period remaining, which exudes the rich history of Jackson, Mississippi. On the National Register of Historic Places and conveniently located in the Belhaven historic neighborhood adjacent to Millsaps and Belhaven Colleges, the Fairview Inn is minutes away from downtown Jackson's arts, theater, museums and shopping. Antique and boutique shops are also close by in the nearby Fondren District. More than a bed & breakfast, the Inn boasts 18 luxurious guest rooms, Sophia's restaurant serving lunch, dinner and Sunday brunch, nomiSpa for relaxation and rejuvenation, a game room and private guest lounge. The Fairview Inn is popular not only for leisure travelers seeking the history and culture of the South, but also with business travelers looking for unique, comfortable accommodations where they can entertain clients in a luxury and discreet setting.

Rates: 5 Rooms and 13 Suites, $139/$314 Luxury Inn. Open year-round. Rates Include Full Breakfast. Number of Rooms: 18

Cuisine: Full breakfast each morning for Inn guests. Fine Dining: Lunch Monday-Friday 11:00 a.m to 2:00 p.m. Dinner Tuesday-Saturday 5:30 p.m. to 9:30 p.m. Sunday Brunch 11:00 a.m. to 2:00 p.m. Full Bar and extensive wine list available.

Nearest Airport: Jackson International

SELECT REGISTRY
DISTINGUISHED INNS OF NORTH AMERICA

Gift Certificates

The gift of an overnight stay or a weekend at an exceptional inn or B&B can be one of the most thoughtful and appreciated gifts you can give your parents, children, or dear friends. Employers are discovering that a gift certificate for a "getaway" is an excellent way of rewarding their employees, while at the same time giving them some much needed rest. A few ideas:

- **Weddings • Anniversaries •**
- **Holiday & Birthday gifts •**
- **Employee rewards/incentives • Retirement •**

Our gift certificates are valid at any of our more than 400 member properties. We process orders daily, packaging certificates with our complimentary Association guidebook and your personal message. Certificates may be ordered online or by phone, and expedited shipping is available at an additional cost. The next time you think about gift-giving, think about our Gift Certificate Program—the perfect gift for that special person, **1-800-344-5244** or online at **www.selectregistry.com/giftcertificates**.

"The Show-Me State"

Famous for: Center of Continental United States, "Gateway to the West," Livestock, Ozark Plateau, Cottontail Rabbits, Dairy, Corn, Wheat, Cotton Lead, Zinc, Lime, Cement, Timber, Aircraft, Automobiles, Spacecraft.

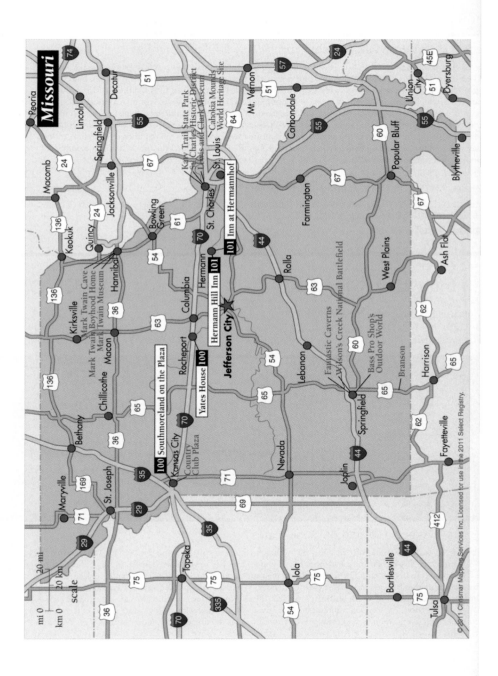

Southmoreland on the Plaza

www.southmoreland.com
116 East 46th St., Kansas City, MO 64112
816-531-7979 • Fax 816-531-2407
innkeeper@southmoreland.com

Member Since 1992

Innkeepers/Owners Mark Reichle and Nancy Miller Reichle

Southmoreland on the Plaza-an Urban Inn sets the standard for B & B hospitality and comfort. Located just one and one-half blocks off of the Country Club Plaza and two blocks from the Nelson Atkins Museum of Art, the Inn blends classic New England Bed and Breakfast ambiance with small hotel amenities. Twelve guestrooms and the Carriage House suite offer private baths, telephones, and off-street parking. Guests enjoy individually decorated rooms featuring decks, fireplaces or Jacuzzi baths. Business travelers find respite at Southmoreland. We are pleased to offer corporate rates and a rare mix of services conducive to business travel: in-room phones, Wi-Fi, fax, copier, voice mail, 24-hour access and switchboard, and guest privileges at a local full-service fitness center. Southmoreland on the Plaza is an Inn of national reputation, worthy of its Plaza locale; warm and accommodating like Kansas City itself. Featured on the Food Network's "Barbecue with Bobby Flay." Visit us at www.southmoreland.com.

Rates: 12 Rooms in Main House, $135/$200 Summer $130/$215 Winter $250 Carriage House (less $20 SGL.). Number of Rooms: 13

Cuisine: Gourmet breakfast served daily. Complimentary afternoon wine and hors d'oeuvres, with hot beverages and sweets served in the evening. Courtyard breakfast BBQ served Saturdays, Apr 15-Oct 15.

Nearest Airport: Kansas City International

Yates House Bed & Breakfast

www.yateshouse.com
305 Second Street, Rocheport, MO 65279
573-698-2129
info@yateshouse.com

Member Since 2005

Innkeepers/Owners Conrad & Dixie Yates

Midwest Living Magazine "2010 Best In the Midwest" Where to Stay category selection. Located in "One of America's Top Ten Coolest Small Towns" Frommers Budget Travel Guide. Everything you'll need for luxurious and relaxing lodging is provided. All rooms are large, beautifully furnished, and well equipped. King beds, jetted tubs, and fireplace are available. Wireless Internet and other business services are provided. Twenty-six seat dining/meeting room available and catering for small groups. Individual table or in-room breakfast provided. Famous for seasonal, gourmet breakfast menu and cooking classes. "Dixie can flat cook," observed Southern Living magazine. Within a block of most scenic section of Katy Trail State Park. Photogenic trails, bluffs, tunnels, and Missouri River within short walking distance. Vineyards, winery, shops and restaurants nearby. Voted "Favorite Day Trip" by readers of the Kansas City Star. Fortunately located midway between Kansas City and St. Louis and fifteen minutes from University of Missouri town of Columbia.

Rates: Five Rooms:$179–$289 One Suite:$269–$309 Number of Rooms: 6

Cuisine: Full, seasonally changing, gourmet breakfast menu with individual table or inroom service (Some rooms). Meal ingredients from local providers whenever possible. Afternoon cookies and beverage.

Nearest Airport: Columbia Regional Airport, 30 min. Delta/NWA nonstop connection to Memphis.

Hermann Hill Vineyard & Inn

www.hermannhill.com
P.O. Box 555, 711 Wein Street, Hermann, MO 65041
573-486-4455 • Fax 573-486-5373
info@hermannhill.com

Member Since 2005

Innkeepers/Owners Terry & Peggy Hammer

Enjoy the ultimate country inn experience at Missouri's most popular Bed and Breakfast. While both properties were built just for upscale lodging, you can choose the inn's traditional bed and breakfast amenities and service or opt for more privacy and even finer amenities at our Hermann Hill Village cottages. The inn's eight exquisitely appointed guest rooms offer you spectacular views from your own balcony or patio, luxurious private baths with Jacuzzi-style tubs for two, and the privacy and freedom to set your own pace. Sited on a bluff and surrounded by a vineyard, the inn rooms create the backdrop for your stay in an ever-changing panorama of Hermann and the Missouri River Valley. Our riverbluff cottages offer even higher amenities, including personal and private outdoor hot tubs overlooking the Missouri River, aromatherapy fireplaces, kitchens, outdoor gas grills, steam showers, and laundry facilities. We supply your cottage with breakfast entrees prior to your arrival, provide daily make up service and also samples of our Port Chocolate Raspberry sauce.

Rates: Suites range from $181/$407 for all eight Inn rooms and all 12 cottage rooms. Rates vary by season and day. Number of Rooms: 20

Cuisine: The Inn offers a full country breakfast with choice of entree served in the kitchen, dining room deck or brought to your room. The Cottages have your breakfast stocked in your refrigerator for your to warm at your leisure.

Nearest Airport: 70 miles west of St. Louis Lambert Airport

Inn at Hermannhof

www.theinnathermannhof.com
237 E. First Street, Hermann, MO 65041
888-268-1422 • 573-486-5199
theinn@hermannhof.com

Member Since 2008

Innkeepers James & Mary Dierberg

For a truly memorable experience, visit us in Hermann Missouri. The Inn at Hermannhof features spacious, historically decorated Suites with luxurious amenities and a full breakfast. The inn offers 8 Suites in the Festhalle and 6 Haus Wineries with 20 Suites. The inn is located in the heart of the historic district, placing you in the center of Hermann activities. Our Haus Wineries are located on East Hill and are former working wineries. Each Haus was thoughtfully reconstructed with attention to detail. Though no two Suites are alike, the highest standard of excellence is evident in all. Each Suite is designed with exquisite style to offer guests pencil post tiger maple beds, luxury linens, lustrous carpets over wood floors, wine cellars, sitting rooms, fireplaces, deep soaking and whirlpool tubs, oversized jetted and steam showers, Missouri River views and more. High speed Internet service and a flat screen cable TV make your stay convenient and relaxing. Everything has been selected with you, our guests, in mind. Hermann Lodging at it's best!

Rates: Rates vary by season and day, from $139 to $399. Number of Rooms: 28 Suites

Cuisine: Enjoy a complimentary full breakfast with locally made sausage or country ham, fresh eggs, biscuits, and other American and German favorites. We also offer lighter fare if requested.

Nearest Airport: Lambert St. Louis International Airport

"The Silver State"

Famous for: Casinos, Lake Tahoe, Lake Mead, Mount Charleston Wilderness, Golf, Art Festivals, Museums.

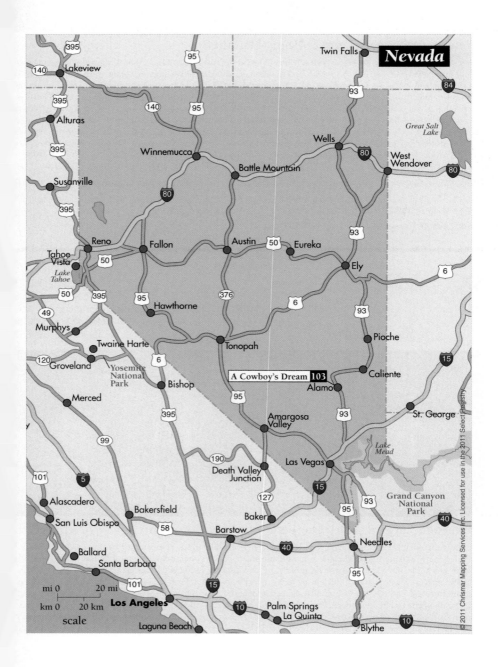

A Cowboy's Dream

www.cowboysdream.com
95 Hand Me Down Road, P.O.Box 357, Alamo, NV 89001
8778852236
info@cowboysdream.com

Member Since 2010

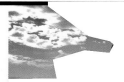

Owner Phyllis Covert Frias

When Phyllis Frias set out to create a memorial to her husband, the late Mr. Charlie Frias, it seemed only natural that it be brought about by the fulfillment of a dream they'd shared together — to create a destination rooted deep in the spirit of family and tradition. Set upon acres of uninterrupted desert landscape at the base of the picturesque Nevada Sierras, the 8 suite B&B is palatial and boasts every amenity conceivable, including custom bedding, natural rain showerheads, custom-crafted bath products, home-cooked meals and chartered excursions. Every one of its 18,997 square feet is nostalgically fashioned with a gentle nod to "the way the cowboys did it" while setting absolutely no indulgence aside. Unmarred views for miles around make for exceptional stargazing in the evenings -particularly enjoyed fireside. Indoors, hand crafted furniture beckons from every corner and every hallway, and the dedication to old west homage is evident in every photograph placed, every book shelved and every rug thrown. It is truly a sanctuary for the new American cowboy.

Rates: 8 Double Occupancy Suites starting at $499/night. Number of Rooms: 8

Cuisine: Bountiful homestyle country kitchen breakfast and dinner prepared by chef/owner. Round-the-clock cocktail lounge featuring a fine selection of spirits, wine and beer.

Nearest Airport: North Las Vegas Airport, McCarran International Airport

SELECT REGISTRY

DISTINGUISHED INNS OF NORTH AMERICA

Gift Certificates

The gift of an overnight stay or a weekend at an exceptional inn or B&B can be one of the most thoughtful and appreciated gifts you can give your parents, children, or dear friends. Employers are discovering that a gift certificate for a "getaway" is an excellent way of rewarding their employees, while at the same time giving them some much needed rest. A few ideas:

- **Weddings • Anniversaries •**
- **Holiday & Birthday gifts •**
- **Employee rewards/incentives • Retirement •**

Our gift certificates are valid at any of our more than 400 member properties. We process orders daily, packaging certificates with our complimentary Association guidebook and your personal message. Certificates may be ordered online or by phone, and expedited shipping is available at an additional cost. The next time you think about gift-giving, think about our Gift Certificate Program—the perfect gift for that special person, **1-800-344-5244** or online at **www.selectregistry.com/giftcertificates**.

"The Granite State"

Famous for: Granite, White Mountains, Lakes, Beaches, Prime Primary (the first state to hold presidential primary elections).

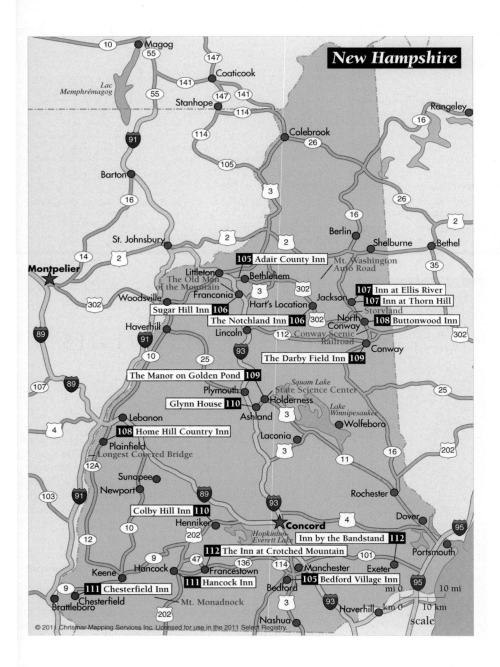

Bedford Village Inn

www.bedfordvillageinn.com
2 Olde Bedford Way, Bedford, NH 03110
603-472-2001 • 800-852-1166 • Fax 603-472-2379
jack@bedfordvillageinn.com

Member Since 2011

Jack Carnevale

The Bedford Village Inn was onnce the site of a working farm built in 1890. Through a multi-million dollar restoration, the original residence became the home of our nationally acclaimed AAA Four Diamond restaurant. The original barn was transformed into a luxury inn offering AAA Four Diamond lodging for the most discerning travelers from all over the world. Twin silos from the original property stand sentry to our magnificent Great Hall that soars three stories high and provides the most unique event site in New England. Its huge bay window overlooks an ever-changing seasonal courtyard garden. The inn rooms, also awarded Four Diamonds, were individually designed and decorated in the original barn and each one features a king-size four poster bed, sitting area with flat screen tv, free high speed internet access and elegant Italian marble baths with whirlpool tubs. The Federal architecture is elegantly complimented by miles of granite walkways throughout the estate and native rock walls that serve to highlight the manicured gardens filled with lush seasonal plantings

Rates: There are several choices. Luxury $195 520 sq. ft. Deluxe and Executive $325 750 sq. ft. Summit Suite $375 with fireplace and two bedrooms 1,100 sq. ft. The Woodbury House with 3,200 sq. ft. offers a wonderful historic stay. Number of Rooms: 14

Cuisine: The culinary offerings are diverse. The Dining Rooms serves Contemporary Regional New England cuisine in several individually decorated rooms. The Tavern is the spot for casual dining. Corks Wine bar is perfect for its own menu and great wine choices

Nearest Airport: The Manchester Boston Regional Airport is a short 5 minute drive and is served by our free Mercedes ML suittle.

Adair Country Inn & Restaurant

www.adairinn.com
80 Guider Lane, Bethlehem, NH 03574
888-444-2600 • 603-444-2600 • Fax 603-444-4823
innkeeper@adairinn.com

Member Since 1995

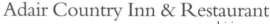

Owners Betsy and Nick Young / Innkeepers Ilja and Brad Chapman

"Adair Country Inn & Restaurant is everything you dreamed a New England country inn would be." - USA Today. Get away from it all and unwind at this peaceful country inn. Enter a woodland oasis via a long winding drive surrounded by stone walls, stately pines, ponds, gardens and 200 acres. The inn's scenic grounds were originally created by the Olmsted Brothers. This elegant inn sits atop a knoll and enjoys magnificent views of the Presidential Range and comfortably appointed guest rooms with fireplaces, antiques, reproductions and air conditioning. Adair serves as an intimate, romantic retreat for adults who enjoy observing wildlife, hiking, golfing, skiing and more in the nearby White Mountains. The inn's relaxing ambiance and casual dress belie uncompromising attention to detail, highly personalized, warm service and award-winning New England style cuisine. Adair is within a short drive of Franconia Notch, Mt. Washington, Mt. Lafayette, The Flume, superb hiking, numerous cross-country venues and major ski areas. Deliberately small. . . Naturally quiet!

Rates: $195/$325 B&B. Spacious rooms w/views and private baths, 7 w/fireplaces, 3 w/2-person tubs, Queen or King feather beds. Complimentary wireless internet. Number of rooms: 9 Number of Rooms: 9

Cuisine: Breakfast features fresh fruit, homemade granola, steaming popovers and a hot entree. Afternoon tea with homemade goodies. New England style cuisine Thursday thru Monday in a cozy fireside restaurant with seasonal patio seating. Full beverage service.

Nearest Airport: Manchester NH 95 miles, Boston MA 155 miles, Montreal 180 miles

Sugar Hill Inn

www.sugarhillinn.com
116 Route 117, Sugar Hill, NH 03586
800-548-4748 • 603-823-5621
info@sugarhillinn.com

Member Since 2001

Innkeeper/Owner Steven Allen

Nestled in New Hampshire's White Mountains, Sugar Hill Inn is a romantic getaway known for culinary adventure and warm, inviting guest rooms and cottages. You'll be immersed in country inn ambiance, New England hospitality and all the recreation of the Franconia region. Impeccably restored, this country inn ranges from charming and cozy to sophisticated and distinctive. This 1789 farmhouse is perched on a hillside on acres of woodlands, rolling lawns and gardens, enhanced by White Mountains view. All rooms have a/c, and many have fireplaces, whirlpool tubs, and private decks. The Dream Cottage with a cathedral ceiling, stone fireplace, whirlpool and sauna has been featured in "Everyday with Rachael Ray" magazine. Whether you seek a convenient base for the attractions and outdoor activities of Franconia Notch and the White Mountains or a special private hideaway to snuggle in front of a fireplace. . .come share the good life at the Sugar Hill Inn. . .your destination of choice. Yankee Magazine Editors' Choice. Distinguished Restaurants of North America (DiRoNA)'s award.

Rates: Classic Rooms: $155/$260; Cottages: $165/$410; Luxury Rooms: $190/$360. Open year-round. Number of Rooms: 14

Cuisine: Full breakfast and afternoon small bites and cocktails. Dinner Thursday–Monday by reservations. Relax in the Tavern with your favorite cocktail before dinner. Over 100 wines from around the world.

Nearest Airport: Manchester Airport - 100 miles.

The Notchland Inn

www.notchland.com
2 Morey Road, Hart's Location, NH 03812-4105
800-866-6131 • 603-374-6131 • Fax 603-374-6168
innkeepers@notchland.com

Member Since 1996

Innkeepers/Owners Les Schoof and Ed Butler

Get away from it all, relax and rejuvenate at our comfortable granite manor house, completed in 1862, within the White Mountain National Forest. Settle into one of our spacious guest rooms, individually appointed and each with a wood-burning fireplace and private bath. Children and pets are welcome in our newly completed mountain view cottages, ranging in size from 1 to 2 bedrooms and all with whirlpool baths. A wonderful 5-course dinner and full country breakfast are served in a fireplaced dining room overlooking the gardens. Nature's wonders abound at Notchland. We have Saco River frontage on our property and two of the area's best swimming holes! Top off an active day, in any season, with a soak in our wooden hot tub, which sits in a gazebo by the pond. Visit with Crawford and Felonie, our Bernese Mountain Dogs. Secluded, yet near to all the Mt. Washington Valley has to offer. Notchland. . .a magical location.

Rates: 8 Deluxe Rooms, 5 Suites, 2 Cottages $199/$385, B&B.Open year-round. Number of Rooms: 15

Cuisine: 5-course distinctive dinners Weds-Sun, hearty country breakfast daily. Fully licensed: wine/spirits/beer. Dinner is a leisurely affair, taking about 2 hours. $40 per person for in-house guests. $45 Wed, Thurs, Sun; $48 Fri, Sat & Holidays for others.

Nearest Airport: Manchester, NH, approx. 125 miles; Burlington, VT, approx. 130 miles

Member Since 1998

Inn at Thorn Hill
www.innatthornhill.com
Thorn Hill Road, P.O. Box A, Jackson Village, NH 03846
800–289–8990 • 603–383–4242 • Fax 603–383–8062
stay@innatthornhill.com

Innkeepers/Owners James and Ibby Cooper

Situated grandly on a knoll overlooking Jackson Village and the Presidential Mountains, the Inn offers 25 uniquely decorated guestrooms, suites, and cottages. The Main Inn features four suites and 12 luxury rooms, all with fireplaces, spa baths, and TV/DVDs, some with steam showers, wet bars, and mountain views. Common areas include a wrap-around porch; a lounge with a separate, casual menu; library; and spa level. Spa Facilities include an exercise room, sauna, yoga, and manicure/pedicure. Activities are available in all seasons at the Inn and throughout the White Mountains. Outdoor pool, year-round outdoor hot tub, cross-country skiing, and tobogganing at the Inn–hiking, golf, tennis, shopping, skiing, and sleigh rides are all nearby. Only AAA Four Diamond Inn and Restaurant in Mt. Washington Valley. Conde Nast Traveler's Gold List 2006. Travel & Leisure's World's Best Awards 2006.

Rates: Main Inn: 4 suites, 12 luxury rooms; Carriage House: 6 North Country rooms; 3 Cottages; Open year round. Breakfast, tea and three-course dinner included. $195/$430. Off Season Spa Packages. Number of Rooms: 25

Cuisine: New England Cuisine with Mediterranean influences and mountain views. Separate lounge menu. Well stocked bar with over thirty single malt scotches and the wine list has over 1300 selections.

Nearest Airport: Portland, ME

Inn at Ellis River
www.innatellisriver.com
P.O. Box 656, 17 Harriman Road, Jackson, NH 03846
800–233–8309 • 603–383–9339 • Fax 603–383–4142
stay@innatellisriver.com

Member Since 2009

Innkeepers/Owners Lyn Norris-Baker and Frank Baker

Nestled by a sparkling stream on several acres at the edge of picturesque Jackson village in the heart of the White Mountains, the inn's rooms and rustic cottage for two are appointed with period furnishings, many with two-person whirlpool tubs and/or balconies and most with fireplaces. Let the river's soothing sounds lull you to sleep, and awaken to clear mountain air and a bountiful homemade breakfast. Spend your days exploring waterfalls or enjoy scenic drives, hiking, golf, canoeing, fishing, mountain biking, or tax-free shopping. In summer, scale Mount Washington by road or cog railway, take a moose tour, or relax by our heated pool. In winter, cross-country ski, snowshoe, take a sleigh ride, or choose from one of five alpine ski centers nearby. Return each day to enjoy afternoon refreshments, a game of darts or billiards in our cozy gameroom/pub, the challenge of a Stave puzzle or board game in our sitting room, or the relaxing view of the river as you soak in our atrium-enclosed hot tub. Recipient of multiple Best of BedandBreakfast.com Awards, Mobil <S><S><S>.

Rates: Classic rooms $119/$199; Fireplace rooms $149/$219; 7 rooms & one cottage w/whirlpool tubs & fireplaces $199/$299. Number of Rooms: 21

Cuisine: Gourmet country breakfast with menu changing daily. Afternoon refreshments include home-baked sweets and seasonal beverages. Several restaurants within walking distance.

Nearest Airport: Portland, ME ~ 75 miles; Manchester, NH ~ 110 miles; Boston (Logan) ~ 140 miles.

The Buttonwood Inn on Mt. Surprise

www.buttonwoodinn.com

P.O. Box 1817, 64 Mount Surprise Road, North Conway, NH 03860-1817

800-258-2625 • 603-356-2625 • Fax 603-356-3140

innkeeper@buttonwoodinn.com

Member Since 1999

Innkeepers/Owners Bill and Paula Petrone

Awarded "THE MOST PERFECT STAY" by Arrington's Inn Traveler, an America's Favorite Inns Award winner, and Winner of 2010-2011 "Best of New England" and 2009-2010 "Best Food" on Bed and Breakfast. Com. Our inn is situated on more than five secluded acres of field and forests near the villages of North Conway and Jackson. Offering a peaceful, rural setting and the convenience of being close to area activities, the Inn was originally an 1820s farmhouse and retains a comfortable country atmosphere with wide pine floors, antiques, quilts, and stenciling. Unwind with afternoon tea and home baked treats in front of one of our wood burning fireplaces in either the spacious living room or the Mt. Surprise Room media and game room when days are cool. You can select a spot of sun or shade in our award-winning gardens, take a dip in our heated pool or soak in our open air hot tub with a view of the mountains and forest by day and stars by night. Watch outside for the appearance of deer, wild turkeys, moose, hawks and our active and entertaining hummingbirds.

Rates: Quiet Season: $99 – $205 April to Mid-June & November through Mid-December Inn Season: $125 – $235 Mid-June through Mid-September & Mid-December through March Peak Season: $170 – $299 Mid-September through Late October Number of Rooms: 10

Cuisine: A full gourmet breakfast with delicious starters and entrees is served daily. In addition, an afternoon beverage service with English teas and Paula's homemade baked treats is also offered.

Nearest Airport: Portland, ME – 65 miles; Manchester, NH – 100 miles;<n>Boston, MA – 139 miles

Home Hill Country Inn & Restaurant

www.homehillinn.com

703 River Road, Plainfield, NH 03781

(603) 675-6165 • Fax (603) 675-5220

inquiries@homehillinn.com

Member Since 2010

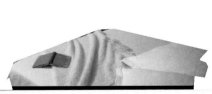

General Manager Paula Snow

Welcome to Home Hill Inn, a romantic, tranquil retreat set on 25 secluded acres in Plainfield, New Hampshire. Experience the luxury of our beautifully appointed rooms, inventive cuisine, pampering body massage treatments, and a boutique of local wares and crafts. Our seasonal packages include access to nearby golf courses and ski resorts. Breathtaking views, soul satisfying meals and attentive service make Home Hill Inn the ideal location for special functions, corporate retreats, family reunions or a romantic getaway. Bathed in light, Home Hill's dining room features dramatic floor-to-ceiling French doors, a decor awash in country reds and yellows and elegant furnishings accented by custom-designed chandeliers, an inviting atmosphere for unforgettable dining. Dinner is served Wednesday through Sunday from 5 pm until 9 pm. Brunch is served Sundays from 10 am until 2 pm.

Rates: Rates start at $100 off season mid week and up to $250 high season. Number of Rooms: 11

Cuisine: Farm to Table is Chef Paula Snow's passion and with so many farms on River Road alone that vision is realized in a tasty, creative and international style. Seasonal dining menu and tavern menu, Sunday Brunch and sumptuous breakfast are sure to please.

Nearest Airport: 10 minutes from the Lebanon Airport, 90 minutes from Manchester airport.

The Darby Field Inn

www.darbyfield.com
185 Chase Hill Road, Albany, NH 03818
800-426-4147 • 603-447-2181
marc@darbyfield.com

Member Since 1981

Innkeepers/Owners Marc & Maria Donaldson

Wander off the beaten path and discover the Darby Field Inn, a romantic country inn nestled on a quiet hill overlooking the White Mountains of New Hampshire. This inn is much more than a little bed and breakfast. It is a romantic getaway, offering deluxe rooms/suites with fireplaces and Jacuzzis, soothing spa services, and elopement, romance and wedding packages. It is an escape from the ordinary, offering candlelight dining, special weekend cookie and herb tour packages, and four seasons of local outdoor adventures! It is a relaxing mountain retreat that invites you to wander through on-site flower gardens, socialize with other guests in cozy Littlefield's Tavern, or swim in our outdoor heated pool. On-site wooded nature trails are the perfect way to work off breakfast, whether by snowshoe, foot, or x-country ski! The Inn is located only a few miles from local shopping and area attractions, and is only two hours North of Boston. No matter what initially brings you to the Darby Field Inn, we bet you'll find many reasons to return, year after year.

Rates: 7 standard rooms ranging from $140–$185 per night. 6 deluxe rooms/suites ranging from $210–$270 per night. All with private bath and WiFi. Rates are before 9% tax and 6% service. Number of Rooms: 13

Cuisine: Full country breakfast is included in room rates. Relaxed dining available most nights in either our mountain-view dining room, or Littlefield's Tavern. Enhance your meal with a bottle of wine from our international list.

Nearest Airport: (1) Portland, ME: 60 Mi. (2) Manchester, NH: 100 Mi. (3)Logan Airport (Boston), MA : 135 Mi.

The Manor on Golden Pond

www.manorongoldenpond.com
P.O. Box T Route 3, 31 Manor Drive, Holderness, NH 03245
800-545-2141 Reservations • 603-968-3348 • Fax 603-968-2116
info@manorongoldenpond.com

Member Since 1995

Innkeepers/Owners Brian and Mary Ellen Shields

It was the sheer romantic beauty of its mountain and lake view setting that inspired the building of The Manor on Golden Pond. And while the view still inspires, so does the hotel's cuisine and leisure facilities. The romantic story behind the resort began in 1904, when a wealthy Englishman fell in love with the mountain and lake view setting and built the Manor for his bride. In many senses, the idyll continues, inspiring the Oscar-winning Hepburn and Fonda film 'On Golden Pond.' Enjoy tea and dreamy end-of-day reveries in the library or alternatively retreat to the excellent restaurant. Guests awaken to our delectable Gourmet breakfasts each morning. The cuisine is the finest in the region, complemented by a celebrated cellar. Seasons Spa offers New Hampshire indigenous spa treatments to relax and soothe the most seasoned spa goers. Perhaps the best way to enjoy The Manor On Golden Pond is fireside after dinner, with a large Port and entertaining company. Fodor's 2010 Choice Hotel, Andrew Harper's "Hideaway Report" recommended. Zagat's Recommended. AAA Four Diamond rated.

Rates: 22 rooms & 2 Suites $220/$550 B&B for 2 ppl per night. Open year-round. Log-burning fireplaces, oversized jacuzzis & flat screen TV. Keurig coffee makers. Complimentary use of heated outdoor pool, clay tennis court & lawn games. Number of Rooms: 24

Cuisine: Our chefûÂã ̃ãÂs innovative creations showcase award-winning New England cuisine using the freshest local products & complemented by his wide-ranging culinary training. Experience our Van Horn Dining Room or "M" Bistro. Full gourmet breakfast each morning

Nearest Airport: Manchester, NH(MHT) (1 hour); Boston, MA (BOS)(2 hours); Portland, ME(PWM) (1.5 hour); Laconia, NH(LCI) (.5 hours)

The Glynn House Inn

www.glynnhouse.com
59 Highland Street, Ashland, NH 03217
866-686-4362 • 603-968-3775
innkeeper@glynnhouse.com

Member Since 2005

Innkeepers/Owners Pamela, Ingrid & Glenn Heidenreich

"New Hampshire's Finest Small Inn," this historic 1896 Victorian is the perfect choice for recreation, romance and relaxation. Delicious breakfasts are served at individual tables in the elegant Victorian dining room. Afternoon refreshments and complimentary wine & hors d'oeuvres are offered in the sitting room or outside on the wraparound porches. Tastefully decorated guest rooms include WiFi, fireplaces, A/C, satellite TV, DVD players and iPod radios. Eight suites, many with separate sitting rooms, also have double whirlpool baths. Venture away from the Inn and experience NH's spectacular lakes and mountains. Enjoy antiquing, art galleries, boating, fine dining, fishing, golf, hiking, historic sites, skiing, sleigh rides and snowmobiling. The innkeepers will make your visit an experience to remember by providing genuine hospitality and uncompromising service. Dogs are welcome in four pet friendly rooms.

Rates: Low season: $149–$279; High season: $159–$289; Peak season: $169–$299; Number of Rooms: 13; 5 bedrooms and 8 Suites

Cuisine: A gourmet breakfast with a choice of entrees is served each morning. Afternoon refreshments offered daily. Guests love our delicious cookies. In the evening, join other guests and the innkeepers for complimentary wine & appetizing hors d'oeuvres.

Nearest Airport: Manchester - 50 miles; Boston - 78 miles

Colby Hill Inn

www.colbyhillinn.com
33 The Oaks, P.O. Box 779, Henniker, NH 03242
800-531-0330 • 603-428-3281 • Fax 603-428-9218
innkeeper@colbyhillinn.com

Member Since 1993

Innkeepers/Owners Cyndi and Mason Cobb

Intimate and romantic country inn located in the charming unspoiled village of Henniker. Enjoy romantic touches including down comforters, plush bathrobes, two-person whirlpools, crackling fireplaces and luxurious linens. 14 romantic guest rooms including two intimate suites with period antiques. All guest rooms have private baths, phones and WiFi access. Award winning candlelight dining nightly overlooking lush gardens, antique barns and gazebo. "Exquisite and Romantic Dining. . ." says Getaways for Gourmets. Bountiful breakfasts and candlelight dinners. Genuine hospitality and central New England location make this an ideal getaway spot. Enjoy cooking classes and theme weekends including "Chocolate Lovers Weekend" and "WineFest Weekends." Outdoor pool, lawn chess, cross country and downhill skiing, hiking, biking, and tennis all nearby. Yankee Magazine Editor's Pick. Wine Spectator Award of Excellence. Featured in The Boston Globe and Ski Magazine. 90 Minutes North of Boston.

Rates: $140/$279 depending on season. Some guest rooms have two-person whirlpools/fireplaces. Gourmet breakfast included. Number of Rooms: 14

Cuisine: Full gourmet breakfast including specialties like pumpkin pancakes with warm maple cream. Afternoon cookies. Award-winning romantic candlelight dining with full service bar, fine wines and spirits. Dinner available nightly for inn guests and public.

Nearest Airport: Manchester

Chesterfield Inn
http://www.chesterfieldinn.com
20 Cross Road, West Chesterfield, NH 03466
800-365-5515 • 603-256-3211 • Fax 603-256-6131
info@chesterfieldinn.com

Member Since 1990

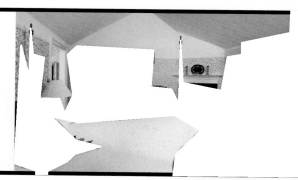

Innkeepers/Owners Phil and Judy Hueber

The Chesterfield Inn is a comfortable blend of new and old New Hampshire. The inn rests on a hill overlooking the Vermont Green Mountains and Connecticut River Valley. Originally built in 1787 as a farm, this luxurious country hotel is today a showpiece of elegance, style, and comfort. The inn has opulent guest rooms, stunning dining rooms, and beautifully landscaped grounds. Come and relax awhile at this elegant yet comfortable renovated farmhouse with its cathedral ceilings and rambling views of the Connecticut River Valley. Feel the stress of every day life disappear as you sit in front of the fire in the parlor of this small country hotel. Spend the day reading in one of the Adirondack chairs in the back yard or explore local villages and countryside. Return at dusk to a sumptuous dinner in our candlelit dining room. Privacy, delicious cuisine, and relaxation are yours at one of the most unique and accommodating inns in New England. This is a perfect place for a romantic getaway in the country!

Rates: 15 Rooms, $149/$344 B&B; 2 Suites, $269/$294 B&B. Open year-round except Christmas Eve and Christmas Day. Number of Rooms: 15

Cuisine: Full Country Breakfast cooked to order and served daily. Dinner is served Monday through Saturday in our candlelit dining room with sweeping views of the Green Mountains. Room service is available. Wine list and full bar available.

Nearest Airport: Hartford, CT is a one and a half hour drive and Boston is a two and a half hour drive.

The Hancock Inn
www.hancockinn.com
33 Main Street, P.O. Box 96, Hancock, NH 03449
800-525-1789 • 603-525-3318
innkeeper@hancockinn.com

Member Since 1971

 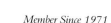

Innkeeper/Owner Robert Short

Since 1789, the first year of George Washington's presidency, the The Hancock Inn~1789~NH's Oldest Inn has hosted rumrunners and cattle drovers, aristocracy, and even a U.S. President. It's seen elegant balls, Concord Coaches, and the first rider of the railroad. Today, the Inn maintains its historic elegance combined with modern day amenities. The town of Hancock, located in the beautiful Monadnock Region of Southern New Hampshire, is considered by many to be one of the prettiest villages in New England, boasting a church with a Paul Revere Bell that rings in each hour, a friendly local general store and many homes that are listed on the National Historic Register. Year-round regional recreation opportunities include hiking, cross country/downhill skiing, swimming, boating and fishing. Visit in any season and find: spring daffodils and real maple sugaring; summer swimming and fishing at Hancock's town beach or music on the village square; fall colors and covered bridges; winter snow. . .and relaxing by our raging fireplace with a hot toddy!

Rates: 14 Rooms. $105/$260. Antiques, TV, phone, AC, WiFi, 10 with fireplaces, 4 with whirlpools. Number of Rooms: 14

Cuisine: Amidst the glow of candles and a flickering fireplace you will dine in Colonial splendor. The recipe for our signature dish, Shaker Cranberry Pot-roast, was requested by Bon Appetit. Full bar and Wine Spectator Award of Excellence.

Nearest Airport: Manchester Airport

The Inn at Crotched Mountain

www.innatcrotchedmt.com
534 Mountain Rd., Francestown, NH 03043
603-588-6840 • Fax 603-588-6623
innkeeper@innatcrotchedmt.com

Member Since 1981

Innkeepers/Owners John and Rose Perry

A quaint country Inn, offering 13 guestrooms, 8 with private bath, built in 1822, located on 65 acres, on the side of Crotched Mt. with spectacular views of the Piscatiqoug Valley. During the summer and fall, one may stroll among the vegetable, herb and flower gardens, sit, relax and enjoy the view by the swimming pool, or enjoy a game of tennis on one of the two clay tennis courts. For the more adventurous, take in the professional productions of The Peterborough Players, concerts and cultural events at The Old Meeting House of Francestown, hiking, or enjoying the many Antique shops. During the Winter, one can relax in front of the fireplace in one of the two sitting rooms, there is also downhill skiing within a mile from the Inn. Enjoy a full country breakfast. Light fare is served in The Winslow Tavern on Saturday nights. There are a wide variety of restaurants in the area for those evenings the inn does not serve. The Inn is a wonderful place to relax and unwind. John, Rose and their 3 English Cockers look forward to welcoming you to their comfortable and casual inn.

Rates: 13 Rooms, 3 with fireplaces, $75/$150 B&B. Open year round, except first two weeks in November. Number of Rooms: 13
Cuisine: Full breakfast daily. Light fare served in The Winslow Tavern on Saturday. Wine and liquor available.
Nearest Airport: Manchester, N.H.

Inn by the Bandstand

www.innbythebandstand.com
6 Front Street, Exeter, NH 03833
877-239-3837 • 603-772-6352
info@innbythebandstand.com

Member Since 2006

Innkeeper/Owner Jim Lane

The award-winning Inn by the Bandstand is the premier lodging establishment in Exeter, New Hampshire. This inn was originally an 1809 historic home. Only two blocks from the prestigious Phillips Exeter Academy, eight miles to the seacoast and beaches, and 20 minutes from Portsmouth. This charming boutique inn offers nine antique-furnished guest rooms, all with private baths and a delicious full breakfast. The inn is surrounded by quaint shops, museums and fine restaurants. You can explore the downtown bookstore, toy store, plus many fine gift and apparel boutiques. Stroll around the river walk near the Academy boat house. We also have the American Independence Museum, plus historical self-guided tours to broaden your knowledge and interest of this area and its importance in our nation's founding history. Our rooms are spacious, each with complimentary port wine, luxurious robes, WiFi, cozy seating areas, and most with fireplaces. Our beds are made with designer linens, and our bathrooms feature soft, plush towels. Two of our rooms have jacuzzi tubs.

Rates: $149/$259 double occupancy rooms. $219/$269 2-room family suites, up to 4 persons. Some weekends require a two-night minimum. Special academy weekends are priced higher. Number of Rooms: 9
Cuisine: Full, hot direct to the table breakfast next to the lit (fall/winter) dining room fireplace. Includes fresh seasonal fruit, homemade bakery products, and specially prepared breakfast entrees. In-suite served breakfast also available.
Nearest Airport: Manchester-Boston Regional Airport, Boston Logan Airport

"The Garden State"

Famous for: Princeton University, Battle of Trenton, Atlantic City, Atlantic Coastline, Industry, Menlo Park.

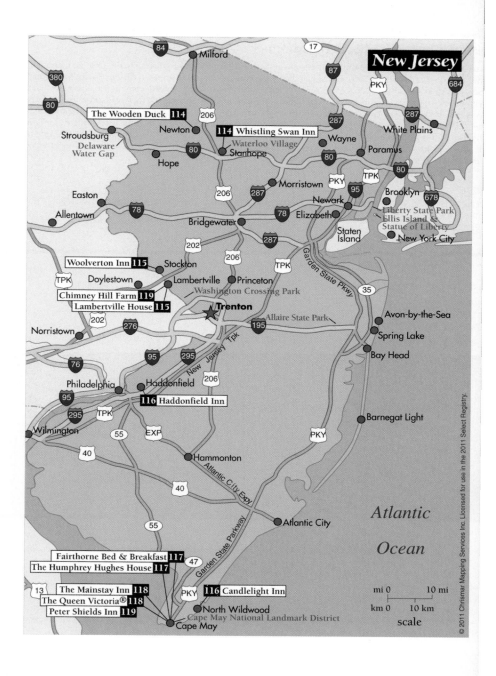

The Wooden Duck B&B

www.woodenduckinn.com
140 Goodale Road, Newton, NJ 07860
973-300-0395
woodenduckinn@aol.com

Member Since 2003

Innkeepers/Owners Karl & Beth Krummel

An oasis of country pleasures! This beautiful mini-estate is nestled on 10 wooded acres adjacent to the 1600-acre Kittatinny Valley State Park, abounding with wildlife and hiking trails. In-ground pool open all summer. All guestrooms have queen bed, private bath, clock radio, satellite TV/VCR, telephone, hair dryer, iron/ironing board, comfortable sitting area and a desk. Complimentary wireless Internet available throughout. Some rooms have soaking tub for two, 2-sided gas fireplace, DVD player and private balcony. Guests are welcome to use the game room with fireplace, TV/VCR, board games, and video library. The Guest Pantry with complimentary snacks, homemade cookies, soda, coffee, and tea is available 24/7. Nearby are many antique and craft shops, fine dining, winter and summer sports, horseback riding, hiking and fishing, mineral and mining museums, and numerous golf courses. Rated Mobil ☆☆☆. Less than an hour to the Crossings Outlet Mall in PA and only 55 miles to Times Square in Manhattan.

Rates: 10 rooms, $135-$299 per night/double. Corporate rates Sunday thru Thursday. Open all year. Number of Rooms: 10

Cuisine: Full country breakfast featuring a rotating menu of delicious baked French toast or egg casseroles, meat and fruit, with homebaked bread or coffee cake, juice, tea, and coffee. Trail mix, cookies, snacks, hot and cold beverages available 24/7.

Nearest Airport: Newark Airport, 45 Miles. Aeroflex private airport in walking distance.

Whistling Swan Inn

www.whistlingswaninn.com
110 Main St., Stanhope, NJ 07874
888-507-2337 • 973-347-6369 • Fax 973-347-6379
info@whistlingswaninn.com

Member Since 1992

Innkeeper Liz Armstrong

One of the Top Ten B&B's in the US says the Inn Traveler magazine. Set amidst a spectacular garden on a quiet, tree-lined street, the Whistling Swan Inn exudes romance and warmth. This 1905 Queen Anne Victorian features a gracious wraparound veranda where leisurely breakfasts are served on pleasant mornings. Each room embraces you with comfort and warmth with period antiques and modern conveniences; TV/VCR/DVD, A/C, wireless internet, plus refrigerators, gas fireplaces, and Jacuzzis in our suites. Whatever the season, a myriad of activities awaits you. After a busy day of hiking, biking, shopping or antiquing relax in a hammock or share pleasant conversations with new-found friends. Enjoy fine dining at one of the area gourmet restaurants, some within walking distance. At day's end, snuggle up with your special someone next to a crackling fire. Sink into your queen-sized feather bed and fall asleep to a movie from our video library.

Rates: 6 Rooms(all with private bath), $119-$169; 3 Suites(jacuzzi, fireplace), $189-$269. Corporate/Government/Single rates available. Number of Rooms: 9

Cuisine: Full country buffet breakfast, 24-hour complimentary guest snack bar. Special diets accommodated.

Nearest Airport: Newark — 45 minutes; Allentown, PA — 1 hour

Woolverton Inn

www.woolvertoninn.com
6 Woolverton Road, Stockton, NJ 08559
888-264-6648 • 609-397-0802 • Fax 609-397-0987
sheep@woolvertoninn.com

Member Since 2002

Innkeepers/Owners Carolyn McGavin and Bob Haas

Perched high above the Delaware River, surrounded by 300 acres of rolling farmland and forest, The Woolverton Inn provides the seclusion of a grand country estate, yet the activities of New Hope and Lambertville are just five minutes away. Enjoy the glorious setting and relaxed elegance of this 1792 stone manor, while feeling as comfortable as you would at your own home in the country. All guestrooms are unique and thoughtfully decorated; they feature bucolic views, fireplaces, whirlpool tubs and showers for two, private outdoor sitting areas, stocked refrigerators, and Bose CD Wave radios. Dogs are permitted in the Garden Cottage. As recommended by "1000 Places to See Before You Die in the USA and Canada" and National Geographic Traveler, among others.

Rates: 6 Rooms $150/$345; 2 Suites $285/$365; 5 Cottages $305/$435. Rooms offer featherbeds, fresh flowers, robes, luxury linens, CD Players, two person whirlpool tubs, two person showers, fireplaces. Number of Rooms: 13

Cuisine: Full gourmet breakfast served in our gardens or in bed. Signature Dishes include: homemade apple-cranberry turkey sausage, lemon-ricotta hotcakes, pina colada scones and fabulous cookies.

Nearest Airport: Philadelphia International and Newark

Lambertville House

www.lambertvillehouse.com
32 Bridge Street, Lambertville, NJ 08530
888-867-8859 • 609-397-0200 • Fax 609-397-0511
innkeeper@lambertvillehouse.com

 Member Since 2009

Proprietors Edric & Mary Ellen Mason

The Lambertville House has been a landmark in the Delaware Valley area since 1812 providing gracious hospitality to American presidents, business leaders, dignitaries, celebrities and discriminating guests from around the world. Proud recipients of the AAA ◆◆◆◆ for the past 12 years and listed on National Historic Register. Centrally located, yet a world apart this sophisticated boutique hotel offers amenities and attention to detail found only in the finest upscale properties. Each guest room features a private bath with whirlpool tub, fireplace, iPod docking radio, flat screen TV, Wireless Internet and exquisite ambiance. A short walk away is a complimentary health club, fabulous shops, antiques and award winning restaurants. A cozy hotel bar and European Continental breakfast. Uncompromising service and an experienced and knowledgeable staff is always available to assist you. An ideal choice for a romantic getaway for two, a business meeting designed to refresh people and ideas or, an all-inclusive event venue for a wedding, rehearsal dinner or special celebration.

Rates: Rates: 26 Rooms/Suites $190/$395. Beautifully appointed baths with large whirlpool tubs, complimentary bathrobes, exclusive Aveda amenities, Evening turndown service, daily paper, complimentary bottled water, coffee and tea. Number of Rooms: 26

Cuisine: Complimentary European Continental Breakfast. Hosting weddings, anniversary parties, rehearsal dinners. Unique space for business meetings, Executive Retreats with full catering service. Hotel bar on site. Outdoor patio seating.

Nearest Airport: Philadelphia International, Newark International

Haddonfield Inn

www.haddonfieldinn.com
44 West End Avenue, Haddonfield, NJ 08033
800-269-0014 • 856-428-2195 • Fax 856-354-1273
innkeeper@haddonfieldinn.com

Member Since 2005

Innkeepers/Owners Fred & Nancy Chorpita

This intimate, elegant hotel in historic Haddonfield is just minutes from Philadelphia and the Cooper and Delaware Rivers. The historic village of Haddonfield offers over 200 unique shops and restaurants. The surrounding areas include countless attractions from aquariums to zoos, museums, the Battleship New Jersey, art, concerts, history, sports and theater! Each of our lovely guest rooms has a private bath, (many with whirlpools), fireplace, Cable TV, phone with free local and long distance calls and wireless Internet access. Enjoy a full, gourmet breakfast served on individual tables adorned with candles and fine linens in our fire-lit breakfast room. In the warmer months, enjoy breakfast on the large, wrap-around porch in our beautiful residential neighborhood. Packages and extras include tickets for major sporting events and attractions in nearby Philadelphia, and fine dining. The High Speed line to Philadelphia is 3 blocks away giving you instant access to the city. The Inn offers special rates for the business traveler and can accommodate small to medium dogs.

Rates: Nine rooms all with private baths. Rates range from $139–$329, depending on the room and the day of the week. Number of Rooms: 9

Cuisine: Full, gourmet breakfast included. Complimentary coffee, tea, snacks and soft drinks available 24 hours. Many fine restaurants located within a short walk or drive.

Nearest Airport: Philadelphia International Airport & Atlantic City International Airport

---

Candlelight Inn

www.candlelight-inn.com
2310 Central Avenue, North Wildwood, NJ 08260
800-992-2632 • 609-522-6200 • Fax 609-522-6125
info@candlelight-inn.com

Member Since 2001

Innkeepers/Owners Bill and Nancy Moncrief and Eileen Burchsted

Let the Innkeepers of the Year be your host. Enjoy the quiet elegance reminiscent of another era. The Candlelight Inn is a beautifully restored Queen Anne Victorian home, offering rooms and suites with TV/DVD players, a decanter for a night-cap & specialty chocolates, fireplaces, private baths, some with double whirlpool tubs. Sit on our spacious veranda where cool ocean breezes delight you and watch fireworks Friday nights in the summer. Relax anytime of the year enjoying a starlit night in our outdoor hot tub, or during cool nights warm yourself by a fire in our inglenook. Minutes away are spacious, award winning beaches, water sports, lighthouses, antiquing, fine dining, nature activities, golfing, shopping, history, and a fun-filled boardwalk...something for everyone. Cape May County has islands with great Atlantic Ocean beaches, a Naval Air Station Museum, Historic Cold Spring Village, and Leaming's Gardens – the country's largest garden of annuals. Our inn is our small piece of the New Jersey Coast that we would like to share with you and your special someone.

Rates: 7 Rooms, $115/$205; 3 Suites, $135/$265. Some have double whirlpool tubs. All rooms have either queen or king beds, private baths, air conditioning, gas or electric fire places. Open year-round. Number of Rooms: 10

Cuisine: A 3-course, sit-down breakfast with a choice of entrees, afternoon refreshments, and complimentary soft-drinks, coffee & teas all day.

Nearest Airport: Atlantic City (ACY) – 40 minutes; Philadelphia Intern'l (PHL) – 90 minutes; Newark 'Liberty' Intern'l – 2 hours

The Fairthorne Cottage Bed & Breakfast

www.fairthorne.com
111 – 115 Ocean Street, Cape May, NJ 08204
800-438-8742 • 609-884-8791 • Fax 609-898-6129
fairthornebnb@aol.com

Member Since 2001

Innkeepers/Owners Ed & Diane Hutchinson

Innkeepers Diane and Ed Hutchinson warmly welcome you to their romantic old whaling captain's home. This 1892 Colonial Revival-style Inn features a gracious wraparound veranda where sumptuous breakfasts are served on pleasant mornings and stress-relieving rockers offer afternoon relaxation. The Fairthorne is beautifully decorated in period style without being too frilly or formal. Guestrooms are appointed with a seamless blend of fine antiques and contemporary comforts, including air conditioning, mini-fridges and TV&CD players plus gas log and electric fireplaces and whirlpool tubs in some rooms. Each day Diane and Ed invite you to gather for tasty snacks and fresh-baked cookies. Follow us on Facebook.

Rates: 9 Rooms, $145/$280, Antique furnishings, lace curtains,king or queen beds and TVs. All private baths. Number of Rooms: 9

Cuisine: Full breakfast and afternoon hot tea and coffee on cool days or iced tea and lemonade on summer days. Complimentary sherry. Excellent restaurants a short walk.

Nearest Airport: Philadelphia and Atlantic City

The Humphrey Hughes House

www.humphreyhugheshouse.com
29 Ocean Street, Cape May, NJ 08204
609-884-4428 • 800-582-3634
TheHumphreyHughes@comcast.net

Member Since 1999

Innkeepers/Owners Terry & Lorraine Schmidt

Nestled in the heart of Cape May's primary historic district, The Humphrey Hughes is one of the most spacious and gracious Inns. Expansive common rooms are filled with beautiful antiques. Relax on the large wraparound veranda filled with rockers and enjoy the ocean view and colorful gardens. Our large, comfortable guest rooms offer pleasant, clean accommodations. All rooms are air-conditioned with cable TV and Wireless Internet. Our location offers the visitor the opportunity to walk to the beach, restaurants, shops, theatre, concerts, nature trails. A full breakfast is served to all guests at 9:00 a.m. each day.

Rates: $145/$350 per night, Dbl. Weekday discounts Fall and Spring. All rooms and suites with queen or king Number of Rooms: 10

Cuisine: Delicious,and beautifully presented, Hot Breakfast is served in our Dining room each morning.When weather permits, is served on the front Veranada which provides both neighborhood and ocean views. Refreshments are available 24/7 on the sunporch.

Nearest Airport: Atlantic City International

The Mainstay Inn

www.mainstayinn.com
635 Columbia Ave., Cape May, NJ 08204
609-884-8690 • Fax 609-884-1498
mainstayinn@comcast.net

Member Since 1976

Innkeeper Diane Clark/Owners David and Susan Macrae

The Mainstay is a Landmark within a National Historic Town, and is but a short walk to restaurants, shops, theater, concerts, nature trails and beautiful beaches. All rooms are like stepping back in time and have queen, king and full beds. All are air-conditioned with cable TV and a private bath. Relax in the morning with our fresh brewed coffee or our afternoon Tea each day in our rockers on our wrap around veranda while enjoying the Gardens and Horse and Carriages as they go by. Beach chairs, towels, and small umbrellas are provided free of charge. We are listed in the book "1,000 Places to See Before You Die."

Rates: 9 Rooms, $165/360 B&B; 3 Suites, $195/$350 Opens April 1st closes January 1st, opens Valentines Wk Number of Rooms: 12

Cuisine: A Full Sit Down Breakfast served April to May, Hearty Buffet served June to September. All fresh baked Cakes and Fresh Seasonal Fruit Served Daily Fresh baked goodies with Savories served each day at our Afternoon Tea starting at 4 pm

Nearest Airport: Atlantic City International 45 minutes away.

The Queen Victoria

www.queenvictoria.com
102 Ocean Street, Cape May, NJ 08204-2320
609-884-8702
reservations@queenvictoria.com

Member Since 1992

Innkeepers/Owners Doug and Anna Marie McMain

A Cape May tradition since 1980, The Queen Victoria is one of America's most renowned bed & breakfast inns. Four impeccably restored 1880s homes are filled with fine antiques, handmade quilts, and many thoughtful extras. The hospitality is warm and the atmosphere is social. Choose from thirty-two inviting and spacious rooms and suites, all with private bath, AC, mini-refrigerator, and TV with DVD. Pamper yourself with a whirlpool tub or gas-log fireplace. For your Victorian enjoyment, rocking chairs fill porches and gardens. Wicker swings carry you back to a quieter time. Bicycles are provided free of charge, as are beach chairs and beach towels. The Queen Victoria is open all year and is located in the heart of the historic district, one block from the Atlantic Ocean, tours, shopping, and fine restaurants. Victorian Cape May offers tours, special events, and activities all year including the Spring Music Festival, the Jazz Festival, Victorian Week, and the Food & Wine Festival.

Rates: 25 Rooms: $120/$275. 9 Suites: $170/$505. Weekday discounts Fall, Winter and Spring. Always open. Number of Rooms: 34

Cuisine: Rates include generous buffet breakfast and afternoon tea with sweets and savories. Complimentary juices, soft drinks, bottled water, coffee and teas. Baked treats and fresh fruit always available. Fine dining nearby.

Nearest Airport: Atlantic City (ACY), Philadelphia (PHL)

Peter Shields Inn

www.petershieldsinn.com
1301 Beach Avenue, Cape May, NJ 08204
609-884-9090
petershieldsinn@comcast.net

Member Since 2008

Proprietors Cathy Pelaez & Jeff Gernitis

This 1907 Georgian revival mansion is an architectural masterpiece, directly across from the Atlantic Ocean in Cape May, New Jersey with golfing, fishing and Atlantic City all within reach. The Peter Shields Inn is the ideal choice for a relaxing getaway. Just a short stroll from Cape May's historic district, the inn offers a charming sanctuary. Enjoy easy access to our beautiful beaches in the summer season or sip a glass of wine next to a cozy fireplace in the fall and winter. We provide the perfect setting any time of year. Each of our nine guest rooms offers individual ambiance with private baths, most have Jacuzzi tubs and fireplaces, flat screen cable television, plush bedding, exclusive bath amenities, nightly turn down service, individual climate control for heat and air conditioning. The inn also specializes in both casual and elegant ocean front weddings and special events. With our inviting guest rooms, fine dining restaurant, beautiful location and an attentive and caring staff, your visit to the Peter Shields Inn is sure to be a memorable one.

Rates: $150-$425 Includes full breakfast daily, afternoon wine & cheese, 24 hour hospitality suite with complimentary soft drinks, & snacks, concierge service, free Wifi, private parking, beach chairs, towels, umbrellas and bicycles Number of Rooms: 9

Cuisine: Whether you're in the mood to dine indoors next to a warm fireplace or on our porch overlooking the sea, our award-winning, Zagat-rated restaurant offers Cape May's finest dining. The chef serves creative cuisine using the freshest local ingredients.

Nearest Airport: Atlantic City or Philadelphia International

Chimney Hill Farm Estate

www.chimneyhillinn.com
207 Goat Hill Road, Lambertville, NJ 08530
800-211-4667 • 609-397-1516 • Fax 609-397-9353
info@chimneyhillinn.com

Member Since 1998

Owners Terry Anne & Richard Anderson

On a country road up on the hill above the charming historic riverside towns of Lambertville and New Hope, Pa., resides Chimney Hill Estate Inn. This lovely fieldstone estate farm was built in 1820. In 1927, the Hunt family commissioned Margaret Spencer, the first woman architect and graduate from MIT to design and build an exceptional stone addition that made this home the elegant country estate it is today. The Estate home boasts eight spacious rooms with comfortable sitting areas and fireplaces to relax. A wonderful Stone Room and Living Room in which we host wine and cheese socials every weekend. Our renovated post and beam barn features 4 luxury and unique suites with whirlpool tubs for 2, fireplaces, private patios, and guest comfort pantries. The estate is surrounded by beautiful fields and gardens. How special is it that we also breed Alpacas and Llamas here at the Estate Farm. This you will never forget! Chimney Hill is 2 blocks from downtown Lambertville and New Hope. Both towns are known for their antiques, art galleries, fine and unique restaurants and museums.

Rates: Estate House M-Th $169/$225. Fri-Sun $225/325. Ol' Barn Suites M-Th $250/$325. Fri-Sun $325/$419. Number of Rooms: 13

Cuisine: Gourmet country breakfast served in Estate Dining Room daily, a guest butler pantry filled with cookies, beverages and sherry. Excellent Restaurants in Lambertville and New Hope.

Nearest Airport: Philadelphia 45 miles – Newark 42 miles

"The Land of Enchantment"

Famous for: Taos, Santa Fe, Pueblos, Adobe, Cliff Dwellings, Carlsbad Caverns (the largest in the world), White Sands, National Monument, Ghost Ranch, Ship Rock, Pecos National Historical Park, Pancho Villa State Park.

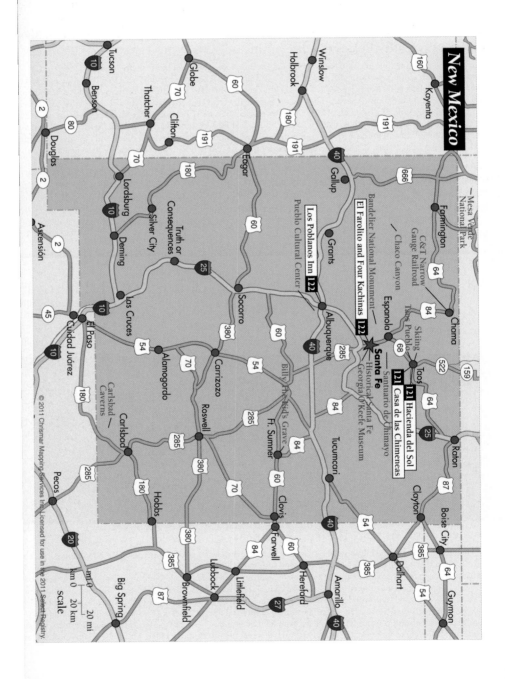

Casa de las Chimeneas

www.VisitTaos.com
405 Cordoba Road, 5303 NDCBU, Taos, NM 87571
877-758-4777 • 575-758-4777 • Fax 575-758-3976
casa@newmex.com

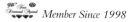

Member Since 1998

Innkeeper/Owner Susan Vernon

Guests to this AAA ◆◆◆◆ inn delight in offerings not often found at small properties. The Wellness Spa, complete with workout room, massage and spa treatment room, sauna and hot tub, entices guests to unwind. Dedicated staff see to every guest's need from a menu of possibilities as rich as Taos' multi-cultural history. Special seasonal activities bookable through the inn include hot air ballooning over and into the Rio Grande Gorge, white water rafting, golf, fly fishing, llama trekking, horseback riding, skiing and snowmobiling. A talented kitchen staff prepares two hearty and delicious meals a day, served casually. With three scenic byways in Taos County, guests often spend a day enjoying the same views that inspire the many artists that make Taos their home with a lunch packed in a custom backpack. Southwest gardens, to-die-for accommodations and a perfect location near the Historic Plaza complete the picture. The result: delighted guests who leave with refreshed and renewed spirits, eager to return to Taos' House of Chimneys.

Rates: 6 Rooms, $195/$290 MAP; 2 Suites, $325/$615 MAP. Open year-round. Number of Rooms: 8

Cuisine: Hearty breakfast with hot entree, light evening supper, complimentary in-room bars with juices, sodas, mineral waters and hot beverages. Optional custom picnics.

Nearest Airport: Albuquerque International Sunport

Hacienda del Sol

www.taoshaciendadelsol.com
P.O. Box 177, 109 Mabel Dodge Lane, Taos, NM 87571
866-333-4459 • 575-758-0287 • Fax 575-758-5895
sunhouse@newmex.com

Member Since 2003

Innkeeper/Owner Gerd and Luellen Hertel

Taos Mountain provides a magnificent backdrop to our Hacienda, which borders thousands of acres of panoramic and peaceful Indian Pueblo land. Enjoy a serene and beautiful view from the tranquil gardens or steaming jacuzzi as you stargaze in the stillness of our many clear nights. The original 1804 adobe once belonged to legendary art patroness Mabel Dodge Luhan. This historic inn has hosted guests such as D.H. Lawrence, Georgia O'Keefe, Frank Waters and Ansel Adams. Southwestern rooms enchant our guests with kiva fireplaces, viga and latilla ceilings, and handcrafted furniture. In the heat of summer, Taos elevation combined with the shade of towering cottonwoods, elms, willows and blue spruce on the property provide blissful conditions. Experience the culinary talents of award winning chef/owner Gerd Hertel every Thursday night for a fun cooking demonstration followed by a 4 course meal including wine. We also offer gourmet theme dinners for holidays and special occasions. Weddings can be arranged in either of our garden courtyards with full catering services provided.

Rates: 7 Rooms, $135/$325 B&B. 4 Suites, $190/$540 B&B. Open year round. Number of Rooms: 11

Cuisine: 2-course breakfast with hot entree. Gourmet Coffees and tea and hot cocoa available all day. Afternoon homemade snacks and sweets are available in the Dining room. Breakfast served on the patio in summer or by the open kiva fireplace in winter.

Nearest Airport: Santa Fe and Albuquerque Airport

El Farolito and Four Kachinas Inn

www.farolito.com and www.fourkachinas.com
514 Galisteo Street (El Farolito), 512 Webber Street (Four Kachinas) , Santa
Fe, NM 87501

888-634-8782 • 505-988-1631 • Fax 505-989-1323
innkeeper@farolito.com

Member Since 2001

Innkeepers/Owners Walt Wyss and Wayne Mainus

Surround yourself with the richness of Santa Fe's art, culture and history in two beautiful downtown properties – El Farolito Bed and Breakfast Inn (ELF) and the Four Kachinas Inn (4K). These inns, under the same ownership and management, offer you award-winning accommodations, showcasing exquisite original Southwestern art and handcrafted furnishings. The rooms are decorated in styles relevant to Santa Fe's rich cultural heritage of native American, Spanish and Anglo inhabitants. Modern amenities also abound including fine linens, rich fabrics, AC, private entrances, TVs, telephones and free Internet access. The two inns are conveniently located in the downtown historic district, a short pleasant walk to numerous galleries, shops, museums, world-class fine dining, and the central Plaza. Savor a leisurely breakfast on the back portal and relax on your garden patio. At ELF, enjoy a fireside breakfast in the brightly decorated dining room and the coziness of a fireplace in your room. At the 4K Inn, enjoy access to the cozy lounge and relax on one of our many garden patios.

Rates: 13 Rooms, $130/$240; 1 Suite, $210/$275. 7 rooms/1 suite at El Farolito and 6 rooms at Four Kachinas. Features: TV, phones, fine linens, AC, garden patios. Fireplaces, in-room coffee and refrigerators at ELF. Number of Rooms: 14

Cuisine: Complete healthy breakfast with quality home-baked goods, hot entree, fresh fruit, yogurts, and ample accompaniment. Complimentary afternoon light refreshments. Walking distance to numerous world-class fine dining restaurants.

Nearest Airport: Santa Fe and Albuquerque

Los Poblanos Inn

www.lospoblanos.com
4803 Rio Grande Blvd. NW, Los Ranchos de Albuquerque, NM 87107

866-344-9297 • 505-344-9297 • Fax 505-342-1302
info@lospoblanos.com

Member Since 2005

Innkeepers/Owners The Rembe Family

Set among 25 acres of lavender fields and lush formal gardens, Los Poblanos Inn is one of the most prestigious historic properties in the Southwest. The Inn was designed by the region's foremost architect, John Gaw Meem, the "Father of Santa Fe Style," and is listed on both the New Mexico and National Registers of Historic Places. Guest rooms are in a classic New Mexican style with kiva fireplaces, carved ceiling beams, hardwood floors, and antique New Mexican furnishings. Guests can relax around the Spanish hacienda-style courtyard or spend hours exploring the property's extensive gardens and organic farm. The buildings feature significant artwork commissioned during the WPA period by some of New Mexico's most prominent artists, including a fresco by Peter Hurd and carvings by Gustave Baumann. Detailed tours highlighting the property's cultural, political, agricultural and architectural history are available to every guest. "One could spend a lifetime at Los Poblanos and never fall out of love." – Su Casa Magazine

Rates: 20 Guest Rooms and Suites, seasonal rates from $145 to $300. Fireplaces, spa services upon request, wireless internet, flatscreen tvs, fitness center, free onsite parking. Open year-round. Number of Rooms: 20

Cuisine: Complimentary gourmet breakfast with fresh organic produce and ingredients from our farm. Add on options for guests include an in-room charcuterie and pantry, Field to Fork Dinners (bi-monthly) and cooking classes (monthly).

Nearest Airport: Albuquerque International Sunport

"The Empire State"

Famous for: Statue of Liberty, Ellis Island, Empire State Building, Times Square, Metropolitan Museum of Art, Central Park, Madison Square Garden, Madison Avenue, Wall Street, Brooklyn Bridge, Catskill Forest, Adirondack Mountains.

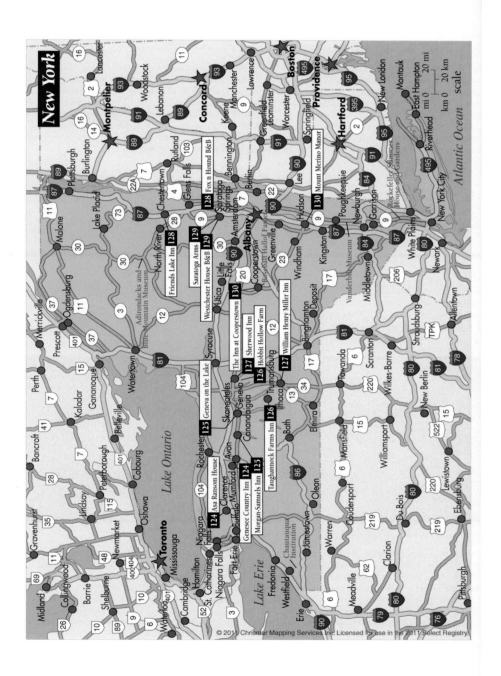

Asa Ransom House

www.asaransom.com
10529 Main St. Rt. 5, Clarence, NY 14031
800-841-2340 • 716-759-2315 • Fax 716-759-2791
innfo@asaransom.com

Member Since 1976

Innkeepers/Owners Robert Lenz and Abigail Lenz

On the site of the first gristmill built in Erie County (1803), where guests are romanced in the winter by the glowing fireplaces and spacious grounds full of herbs and flowers in the summer. Many rooms have porches or balconies to view the grounds or just relax. Experience world-class cuisine and full country breakfasts with delicious regional accents. Voted best food, service, hospitality, romantic setting and historical charm in Buffalo News readers survey. Often upon arrival you will find the aroma of fresh pies and breads lingering in the air! Clarence is known throughout the east for its antiques and treasures, along with unusual shops full of gifts, art and crafts. Explore the bike trails or visit the nearby Opera House, Erie Canal Cruises, Albright-Knox Art Gallery and Frank Lloyd Wright's Martin House Complex. Also Niagara wineries, Fort Niagara, Letchworth State Park and much more. Only 28 miles from Niagara Falls. AAA ◆◆◆

Rates: 10 Rooms, $120/$190 B&B; $190/$330 MAP. Full country breakfast included. Queen or king beds. Number of Rooms: 10
Cuisine: Fine country dining with regional specialties. Fully licensed — NYS Wine award. "Best Place to Take Out-of-Town Guests" award.
Nearest Airport: Buffalo/Niagara 9 miles, Amtrak 11 miles

Genesee Country Inn Bed and Breakfast

www.geneseecountryinn.com
948 George Street, P.O. Box 226, Mumford-Rochester, NY 14511
800-697-8297 • 585-538-2500 • Fax 585-538-9867
stay@geneseecountryinn.com

Member Since 1988

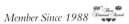

Innkeepers/Owners Deborah & Richard Stankevich

Step back to an era of simple elegance, fine hospitality and natural beauty. This historic Bed and Breakfast/Country Inn is situated on Spring Creek with mill ponds and a waterfall to enthrall any traveler. The Inn has wireless Internet, fax, and meeting facilities. Hike the grounds, the MacKay Wildlife Preserve, or the Genesee Country Village & Museum Nature Center. Enjoy the art of fly-fishing on our private Spring Creek, fish the famed Oatka Creek, and visit the historic NYS Fish Hatchery. The Inn, an 1833 plaster-paper mill, is situated on eight acres of natural setting, perfect for bird watching! The Inn's idyllic country ambiance is perfect for a secluded, romantic getaway, yet it is close enough to the arts, entertainment, Finger Lakes wineries, antique shops and over 70 golf courses. The Inn is a wonderful location for family reunions, corporate events, bridal or baby showers, and intimate weddings. Romance, spa and fly-fishing packages are available! Check our web site for additional special packages and getaway weekends. ◆◆◆

Rates: Six Old Mill Rooms-$120/$160; Three Garden Rooms-$160/$185; and One King Suite-$180/$200. Number of Rooms: 10
Cuisine: Full Country Breakfast daily. Refreshments available throughout the day.
Nearest Airport: Rochester International Airport (13 miles east); Buffalo International Airport (41 miles west)

Morgan–Samuels Inn

www.morgansamuelsinn.com
2920 Smith Rd., Canandaigua, NY 14424
585-394-9232 • 585-721-3383
MorSamBB@aol.com

 Member Since 1992

Innkeepers/Owners Julie & John Sullivan — Brad & Connie Smith

Travel the 2000 foot tree lined drive to this secluded and exquisite 1810 English style mansion. The Inn sits on a rise like a plantation surrounded by 46 acres. Four patios, trickling waterfall, tennis court, beautiful landscaped grounds canopied by 250 noble trees. Relax in a romantic atmosphere with soft music piped throughout the common areas. Enjoy an elegantly appointed common room with an open stone fireplace, baby grand piano and many museum quality oil paintings. Cozy library just off the common room. A sumptuous gourmet breakfast is served in three areas; the beamed dining room with a mural surrounding you, the tea room with floor to ceiling windows with garden views and the Victorian porch is glass enclosed with expansive views of the property and bird watching. There are five guest rooms and the Morgan Suite, 5 rooms with fireplaces, 3 rooms with double Jacuzzies, 3 rooms with French doors and balconies with the sound of trickling water over the rocks below. Recognized as one of the "12 Most Romantic Hideaways in the East" by Discerning Traveler Magazine.

Rates: 5 Rooms, $139/$249 B&B; 1 Suite, $229/$295 B&B; 3 Lake Villas $225/$395 B&B. Private bathrooms. Number of Rooms: 6

Cuisine: The candlelit gourmet breakfast featured in "Getaway for Gourmets" is the highlight. The signature fruit tray with a variety of 24 seasonal fruits starts the day followed by a verbalized menu which includes our renowned open faced omelets.

Nearest Airport: Rochester International

Geneva On The Lake

www.genevaonthelake.com
1001 Lochland Road, Route 14, Geneva, NY 14456
800-3-GENEVA • 315-789-7190 • Fax 315-789-0322
info@genevaonthelake.com

 Member Since 2003

General Manager William J. Schickel

Experience European elegance and friendly hospitality in the heart of Finger Lakes Wine Country. Amidst an ambiance of Italian Renaissance architecture, classical sculptures, luxurious suites and Stickley furnishings, guests from around the world enjoy vacation getaways, family gatherings, weddings and conferences. Rest, relax and surrender yourself to gracious service and breathtaking surroundings. Candlelight dining with live music. A complimentary bottle of wine and flowers are in your suite on arrival and The New York Times is at your door each morning. Complimentary high-speed wireless Internet is available. Glorious formal gardens for lawn games, a 70' outdoor pool, and a boat-house with dock and moorings. Adjacent are Geneva's charming Historic District and the campus of Hobart and William Smith Colleges, both replete with architectural gems. Enjoy magnificent scenic beauty on the Seneca Lake Wine Trail. Golf is nearby. "The food is extraordinarily good." — Bon Appetit. "One of the 10 most romantic inns in the United States." — American Historic Inns.

Rates: 29 Guest Suites (10 with 2 bedrooms). Open year-round. Many 4-Season Vacation Packages offered for a romantic getaway, honeymoon, gala New Year's and more. $217/$1245 per night. Number of Rooms: 29

Cuisine: Gourmet dinner is served with a smile in the warmth of candlelight and live music. Breakfast daily and Sunday Brunch. Lunch On The Terrace in summer.

Nearest Airport: Rochester International

Innkeepers/Owners Tom & Susan Sheridan

Relax and enjoy a bygone era at this Victorian country inn. Majestically situated above Cayuga's waters, the inn offers commanding views of the lake. This Finger Lake's wine region landmark, built in 1873, is known for its gracious hospitality, abundant American cuisine, and charming accommodations. In addition to the five rooms in the Main inn that are furnished with antiques, we also have four guesthouses for a total of 23 rooms. Our newest guesthouse, Edgewood, has 10 rooms with either covered balconies/patios that have outstanding views of Cayuga Lake, and 4 king units featuring jacuzzis. Savor a romantic dinner in the 150-seat fine dining restaurant overlooking the lake. The four-course meal features American cuisine and is complemented by wonderful Finger Lakes wines.

Rates: Main Inn rooms $90/$190. 3 Guesthouses $155/$210 per room. Full cottage $150/$490. Seasonal rates. Number of Rooms: 23

Cuisine: Expanded Continental breakfast of juice, coffee, fruit, breakfast pastries and at least one hot item. Dinner includes appetizer, salad or sorbet, entree, and dessert. Banquets available.

Nearest Airport: Tompkins County Airport

Hobbit Hollow Farm

www.hobbithollow.com
3061 West Lake Road, Skaneateles, NY 13152
800-374-3796 • 315-685-2791 • Fax 315-685-3426
innkeeper@hobbithollow.com

Member Since 1998

Proprietor William B. Eberhardt

Hobbit Hollow Farm has been carefully restored inside and out to recreate the casual comfort of an elegant country farmhouse. Hobbit Hollow serves a full, farm breakfast as part of the room price. Overlooking Skaneateles Lake, Hobbit Hollow Farm is situated on 320 acres of farmland with trails and ponds as well as private equestrian stables. Spend time contemplating the lake on our east veranda. Enjoy afternoon tea or coffee and watch the light play on the water in the soft wash of dusk. Rediscover what it means to be truly relaxed in a setting of tranquility. This is the perfect spot for a quiet, romantic getaway.

Rates: 5 Rooms, $100/$270, with master-crafted period furniture and antiques. 3 rooms include four-poster beds. Master Suite $250/$270; Lake View $200/$230; Chanticleer $175/$200; Meadow View $150/$170; Twin $100/$120. Open year-round. Number of Rooms: 5

Cuisine: Full gourmet country breakfast. Find excellent dinner and lunches at the Sherwood Inn, Blue Water Grill, and Kabuki.

Nearest Airport: Syracuse (Hancock International)

The Sherwood Inn

www.thesherwoodinn.com
26 West Genesee Street, Skaneateles, NY 13152
800-374-3796 • 315-685-3405 • Fax 315-685-8983
info@thesherwoodinn.com

Member Since 1979

Owner William B. Eberhardt

Built as a stagecoach stop in 1807, The Sherwood Inn has always been a favorite resting place for travelers. The handsome lobby with fireplace, gift shop, antiques and orientals offers a warm reception. Each room has been restored to the beauty of a bygone era to create a relaxing harmony away from everyday cares. Our newly renovated dining and banquet rooms are able to accommodate groups of all sizes. In addition to our dining rooms, many of our 25 guest rooms overlook beautiful Skaneateles Lake. Casual lakeside dining and The Sherwood are synonymous, and we have been recognized by the New York Times, Bon Appetit, Country Living, Harper's Bazaar and New Yorker magazines. Our extensive menu offers American cooking with a continental touch, accompanied by an impressive wine list which received the Wine Spectator "Award of Excellence."

Rates: 15 Suites and 10 Rooms, $150/$245. Suites have fireplaces/whirlpool baths. All have private baths, telephones and televisions. We are open year-round. Number of Rooms: 25

Cuisine: Our Tavern serves traditional American fare in a relaxed atmosphere. Our Dining Room offers candlelight dining in a lovely setting overlooking Skaneateles Lake. Serving Daily.

Nearest Airport: Syracuse (Hancock International)

William Henry Miller Inn

www.MillerInn.com
303 North Aurora Street, Ithaca, NY 14850
877-256-4553 • 607-256-4553 • Fax 607-256-0092
millerinn@aol.com

Member Since 2003

Innkeepers/Owners Lynnette Scofield & David Dier

We hope that The William Henry Miller Inn in the heart of downtown Ithaca will be your home as you experience the wonderful Finger Lakes. Designed and built by Cornell University's first architectural student in 1880, the Inn features all modern amenities but maintains the amazing details from its inception. Ithaca has been voted one of the country's Top Ten Small Foodie Cities and The Miller Inn is within walking distance of fifty restaurants. Theatre, shopping and movies are just steps away and Cornell, ten blocks. Ithaca College is less than ten minutes from the Inn. We strive to take care of all the details—from hand ironed linens to all homemade breads, English Muffins, bagels and homemade desserts every night. Come experience the Finger Lakes and experience all that Ithaca has to offer! The coffee pot is always on.

Rates: $165 to $250/night Full breakfast, evening dessert, beverages, wireless and parking included. Number of Rooms: 9

Cuisine: Breakfast with choice of two main dishes served during a two hour period. Homemade evening dessert and always available coffee and tea. Wonderful restaurants nearby including the world famous Moosewood, Just a Taste and Madeline's

Nearest Airport: Tompkins County (Ithaca) Airport is just ten minutes away. Syracus is seventy-five minutes.

Friends Lake Inn

www.friendslake.com
963 Friends Lake Road, Chestertown, NY 12817
518-494-4751 • Fax 518-494-4616
friends@friendslake.com

Member Since 1998

Innkeepers/Owners John and Trudy Phillips

Experience the comfort and intimate ambiance of this elegantly restored inn, surrounded by the natural beauty of the Adirondacks. Guest rooms feature antiques, fine fabrics, and featherbeds, most with lake views, Jacuzzis, steam showers and/or fireplaces. Nationally acclaimed cuisine is served daily in the candlelit Nineteenth Century dining room, complemented by gracious service and a Wine Spectator Grand Award-winning wine list for the tenth year. Swim in the lake or the pool, canoe, kayak or fish on Friends Lake. Ski, snowshoe or hike on 32 kilometers of trails. Many activities close by.

Rates: 17 Sumptuous guest rooms, all with private baths and lake or mountain views. Rooms with Jacuzzis or Adirondack Rooms with fireplaces available. Rooms range from $329/$479/couple. (MAP). Number of Rooms: 17

Cuisine: Full country breakfast and candlelight dinner served daily, lunch served on weekends. Inquire about conferences, rehearsal dinners, and weddings. Lighter Wine Bar Menu available. Extensive wine collection.

Nearest Airport: Albany

Fox 'n' Hound B&B

www.foxnhoundbandb.com
142 Lake Ave., Saratoga Springs, NY 12866
518-584-5959 • Fax 518-584-5959
Innkeeper@FoxnHoundBandB.com

Member Since 2004

Innkeeper/Owner Marlena Sacca

Visit the historic Fox 'n Hound Bed and Breakfast in Saratoga Springs, NY. Conveniently located within walking distance from downtown Saratoga shopping, dining, Saratoga Race Course, Skidmore College and Museums. A restored Victorian Mansion with colonial and Queen Ann architectural detail, the Fox 'n' Hound offers comfortable elegance with a cosmopolitan flair, European hospitality with the warmth of home, attention to detail found in the finest resorts, and the convenience of in-town location. Our amenities include luxurious rooms and suites (some with whirlpool tubs)private off street parking, free WiFi, gourmet breakfast, afternoon refreshments, high count linens, comfy robes, and more. Our motto is "Victorian elegance with a casual flair." Come and visit us soon.

Rates: 5 Rooms $169/$239, Racing Season $295/$400. Always check our Packages and Specials page. Number of Rooms: 5

Cuisine: Guests can expect to find seasonal fresh fruit, ethnic entrees, fresh fruit cobblers, fresh baked scones, strudels, muffins, fresh-brewed coffee, an assortment of specially blended teas, afternoon refreshment. Menu changes daily.

Nearest Airport: Albany International Airport

Westchester House

www.westchesterhousebandb.com
102 Lincoln Ave., P.O. Box 944, Saratoga Springs, NY 12866
800-579-8368 • 518-587-7613 • Fax 518-583-9562
innkeeper@westchesterhousebandb.com

Member Since 1996

Owners/Innkeepers Bob & Stephanie Melvin

Welcome to Westchester House Bed & Breakfast — Saratoga's hidden jewel. Nestled in a residential neighborhood of tree-lined streets and surrounded by exuberant gardens, this enticing Victorian confection combines gracious hospitality, old-world ambiance and up-to-date comforts. Lace curtains, oriental carpets, high ceilings, the rich luster of natural woods, king-or queen-sized beds, tiled baths and luxury linens provide elegance and comfort. The charm and excitement of Saratoga is at our doorstep. After a busy day sampling the delights of Saratoga, relax on the wraparound porch, in the gardens, or in the parlour, and enjoy a refreshing glass of lemonade. Walk to the thoroughbred race track, historic districts, downtown shopping, dining and entertainment, Spa State Park/SPAC. National Museums of Dance and Racing as well as Saratoga Automobile Museum and Skidmore College are less than a mile away. A short ride in the country to historic Saratoga Battlefield, turning point of the Revolutionary War.

Rates: Queen & King beds. Customary $140/$250, Special Events $195/$295, Racing Season (July 22 thru Labor Day, 2011) $295/$495. B&B Closed Dec. & Jan. Number of Rooms: 7

Cuisine: Full cold breakfast includes fresh fruit salad, platter of cold meat and cheeses, home made muffins, scones and breads. A wide variety of excellent restaurants within an easy walk of the Inn.

Nearest Airport: Albany (commercial), Saratoga County (private planes)

Saratoga Arms

www.SaratogaArms.com
497 Broadway, Saratoga Springs, NY 12866
518-584-1775 • Fax 518-581-4064
info@SaratogaArms.com

Member Since 2008

An award winning 1870 Second Empire brick concierge hotel located in the heart of Saratoga's downtown district. Walking distance to restaurants, museums, shopping, and colleges. Beautifully decorated rooms with high ceilings, fireplaces, double whirlpool tubs. State-of-the-art executive conference room. Individually appointed guest rooms blend nineteenth century ambiance and modern amenities for the best of both worlds including cable TV, WiFi, voice mail and personal climate control. Period antiques, family treasures and custom decor throughout the hotel carry on the genteel Saratoga style. The jewel of Saratoga Arms is the beautiful wraparound Saratoga porch that welcomes you as you approach the hotel and begs you to linger as you depart. It serves as a gathering place for guests and visitors. A collection of antique wicker extends an invitation to engage in lively conversation with other guests or to leisurely enjoy the passers-by.

Rates: $195-$375, Racing Season $350-$625. Cable TV with HBO. Individually controlled heat and air-conditioning WiFi. Number of Rooms: 31

Cuisine: Full Irish breakfast served each morning. Coffee and tea all day.

Nearest Airport: Albany, NY (ALB) 28 miles; Saratoga (private) 3 miles.

The Inn at Cooperstown

www.innatcooperstown.com
16 Chestnut Street, Cooperstown, NY 13326
607-547-5756 • Fax 607-547-8779
info@innatcooperstown.com

Member Since 1998

Innkeepers/Owners Marc and Sherrie Kingsley

A stay at The Inn at Cooperstown is a special treat. This award-winning historic hotel is ideally situated to enjoy all that Cooperstown offers. The Inn was built in 1874 and is thoughtfully improved upon every year. Spotless rooms are individually decorated with many charming touches. The new luxury suite is filled with upscale amenities. The relaxing atmosphere at the inn enables guests to escape the hectic pace of the modern world. After exploring the lovely village of Cooperstown, visitors unwind in rockers on The Inn's sweeping veranda or enjoy the fireplace in a cozy sitting room. The National Baseball Hall of Fame is just two blocks away. It is a brief trolley ride to experience another century at The Farmers' Museum, where exhibits, a recreated village and costumed staff depict life over 150 years ago. Nearby, the Fenimore Art Museum displays a premier collection of Native American Indian art, American paintings and folk art. The Glimmerglass Opera, beautiful Otsego Lake and many other treasures are located just beyond the village.

Rates: Guest rooms have private bath, A/C, CD/clock radio, hair dryer, iron, wireless internet. Televisions in sitting rooms and suites. Standard: $110/$199, Premium: $135/$235, Suites: $190/$305, $280/$495. Open year-round. Number of Rooms: 18

Cuisine: Expanded continental breakfast, afternoon refreshments, and fine restaurants within walking distance.

Nearest Airport: Albany, NY (ALB) or Syracuse, NY (SYR).

Mount Merino Manor

www.mountmerinomanor.com
4317 Route 23, Hudson, NY 12534
518-828-5583 • Fax 518-828-4292
info@mountmerinomanor.com

Member Since 2009

Innkeepers/Owners Patrick & Rita Birmingham

Enjoy the comforts of Mount Merino Manor, a luxury Bed & Breakfast in the historic Hudson Valley. Sitting on a lush hilltop surrounded by acres of shaded woodlands, this stately Victorian has magnificent views of the Catskill Mountains and Hudson River. Decorated with an eclectic mix of treasured furniture, period pieces and fine fabrics, each guest room has a distinct personality. All guest rooms have spacious private baths and many have mountain views, candle-lit fireplaces, whirlpool tubs, spa showers and king beds. Special amenities such as thick Egyptian cotton towels, luxury bed linens, spa robes, aromatherapy bath products, fresh flowers and bedside chocolates pamper every guest. This 1870's mansion also provides modern amenities such as complimentary wireless high-speed internet access, cable television and in-room climate control. Just outside the city of Hudson and a neighbor to Olana State Historic site, Mount Merino Manor is minutes to fine dining, shopping, art, antiques and all outdoor activities. An ideal location for intimate weddings and family reunions.

Rates: $175-$350. All private baths. Mid-week and seasonal rates/packages. 1 Room ADA compliant. Number of Rooms: 7

Cuisine: Breakfast is served in our light-filled dining room at intimate, individual tables. Fresh baked muffins and breads, seasonal fruit, and always a hot entree including gourmet coffee and teas. Locally grown produce and farm raised eggs when available.

Nearest Airport: Albany International Airport 45 miles. Columbia County Airport 10 miles.

"The Tar Heel State"

Famous for: Blue Ridge Mountains, Smoky Mountains, Outer Banks, Roanoke Island, Cape Hatteras, Kitty Hawk, Tobacco, Textiles, Furniture.

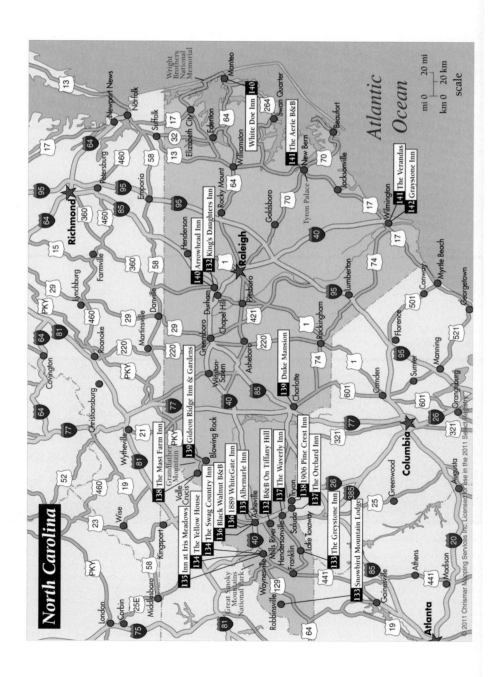

Bed & Breakfast on Tiffany Hill

www.BBonTiffanyHill.com
400 Ray Hill Rd , Mills River, NC 28759
828-290-6080
vacation@BBonTiffanyHill.com

Member Since 2010

Innkeeper/Owner Selena Einwechter

Casual Elegance filled with Southern Hospitality is what we strive for at the Bed & Breakfast on Tiffany Hill. Newly constructed in 2009, Tiffany Hill is situated on 6 acres of beautiful gardens nestled in the mountains of Western North Carolina. Conveniently located just south of Asheville, we are 10 minutes to the Asheville Regional Airport and 15 minutes to either Brevard or Hendersonville. On Tiffany Hill, each suite is specifically designed from one of our favorite southern towns. Suites include private baths, 7 layer beds, flat Screen TV/DVD players, wireless hi-speed internet access, piped-in music, luxurious robes, writing desks, keyless entry and 24 hour access to complimentary beverages and snacks. Second floor suites also have individual temperature controls. Your stay comes with a 3-course gourmet breakfast and lots of southern hospitality. Come do as much or as little as you like on Tiffany Hill.

Rates: Natchez Suite – $185; Madison Suite – $185; Seaside Suite – $215; Beaufort Suite – $215; Charlottesville Suite – $235 Number of Rooms: 5

Cuisine: Nearest Airport: Asheville Regional – 10 minutes

King's Daughters Inn

http://www.TheKingsDaughtersInn.com
204 N Buchanan Blvd., Durham, NC 27701
919-354-7000 • 877-534-8534 • Fax 866-489-2029
info@TheKingsDaughtersInn.com

Member Since 2011

Owner/Innkeepers Colin and Deanna Crossman

With funds donated by the Duke family in the 1920's, the King's Daughters of Durham built a grand building located in the heart of Trinity Park to care for single elderly women. The King's Daughters Home closed in 2006 and now this piece of Durham's history has been reborn as a 17 room Boutique Bed & Breakfast. Varied in their décor and well appointed with beautiful and unique furnishings, the rooms offer a breathtaking image of what it was like to be in the Opulent or Roaring Twenties. The King's Daughters Inn is a short walk to Duke University, Brightleaf Square, Ninth Street and minutes from the Durham Performing Arts Center, Research Triangle Park and Raleigh-Durham International Airport. Modern Amenities Include: • Mac Mini and wireless internet access • Plasma HDTV • Turn-down service with Port & Chocolate Truffles • Triple sheeting with Pillow Top Mattress • Luxurious Bathrobe & Slippers • In Room Massage Services • Full, Hot Complimentary Breakfast

Rates: Rates include a full hot breakfast, afternoon tea, and turn down service, as well as complimentary wireless internet and parking. Rates begin at $168.00. Number of Rooms: 17

Cuisine: The Inn serves a full, hot breakfast every morning. Focusing on fresh produce & homemade dishes, the Inn provides a hearty list of options. Alternatives include breakfast-to-go or in-room service. Afternoon Tea and evening spirits are also available.

Nearest Airport: Raleigh-Durham International Airport (RDU)

Snowbird Mountain Lodge

www.snowbirdlodge.com
4633 Santeetlah Rd., Robbinsville, NC 28771
800-941-9290 • 828-479-3433 • Fax 828-479-3473
innkeeper@snowbirdlodge.com

Member Since 1973

Innkeeper/Owner Robert Rankin

High up in Santeetlah Gap, on the Southern border of the Great Smoky Mountains National Park, lies this secluded, rustic yet elegant, historic lodge built of stone and huge chestnut logs. Offering the finest in modern convenience and traditional comfort, Snowbird is the perfect retreat from the pressures of a busy world. The view from the lovely mountaintop terrace is one of the best in the Smokies. An excellent library, huge stone fireplaces, tennis courts and hiking trails on 100 acres of forest with numerous "quiet getaway" spots, offer guests a rare chance to relax. Award-winning gourmet cuisine and a lovely fireside bar with an exceptionally well-stocked wine cellar will have you looking forward to your next meal. Whether it's fly-fishing, hiking, biking, or just relaxing in front of the fire, we can make your next trip to the mountains picture-perfect. It's no wonder that guests have been coming to Snowbird to relax and renew themselves for over 60 years.

Rates: 23 Rooms, $255-$365 FAP. In-room fireplaces, air conditioning, whirlpool tubs, steam showers and private hot tubs available. Number of Rooms: 23

Cuisine: Full gourmet breakfast, packed picnic lunch and four course gourmet dinner.

Nearest Airport: Knoxville, Atlanta

The Greystone Inn

www.greystoneinn.com
220 Greystone Lane, Lake Toxaway, NC 28747
800-587-5351 • 828-966-4700 • Fax 828-862-5689
info@greystoneinn.com

 *Member Since 1991*

Owner Reg Heinitsh, Jr.

All of the intimacies of a charming & historic inn are combined with the luxurious amenities of a full service resort at The Greystone Inn. Our AAA Four Diamond rated property is situated on the shores of North Carolina's largest private lake in the heart of the Blue Ridge Mountains, and is an ideal setting for those looking to truly get away from it all. Highlights include a pampering spa, lake activities, a new Kris Spence designed golf course, tennis, croquet, a fitness center, and more. Of course, our signature amenity is our daily Champagne cruise aboard our 26-passenger mahogany launch "Miss Lucy". Each guestroom is unique with amenities that include gas and wood fireplaces, private porches, lake views, Jacuzzi bathtubs, wet bars and more. We pride ourselves on attentive and personal service — our goal is to make folks feel like guests in our home. We hope to see you soon!

Rates: Rooms & Suites ranging from $380-$590. Rate includes MAP meals, tennis, croquet, canoes/kayaks, fitness center, and our daily Champagne cruise. Spa & Golf Packages are available. Number of Rooms: 31

Cuisine: A full breakfast, afternoon tea & treats, hors d'oeuvres, and a six-course dinner are included in our Modified American Plan (MAP) rates. A la carte lunch is available at the adjacent country club. We have a full bar and an extensive wine list.

Nearest Airport: Asheville (AVL)

The Swag Country Inn

www.theswag.com
2300 Swag Road, Waynesville, NC 28785
800-789-7672 • 828-926-0430 • Fax 828-926-2036
swaginnkeeper@earthlink.net

Member Since 1991

Innkeeper/Owner Dan & Deener Matthews

Where stress disappears . . . has an address . . . 30 miles west of Asheville. The Swag Country Inn is an intimate hideaway that invites you to discover the wonders of nature just steps from your bedroom. The Swag is where our favorite amenity, nature, meets the luxury resort. The Great Smoky Mountains National Park shares an old split rail fence boundary with our inn that stretches more than a mile. The spectacular beauty of our Appalachian high country is captured architecturally in the historic hand-hewn logs and local field stone design. The construction was inspired by the past while built for the future. The Swag's hidden and secluded mountain top setting opens to you treasures the crowds have yet to find. It all starts to unfold at the bottom of the mountain where the pavement stops, our gate opens, and your romantic adventure begins. The Swag – a small luxury resort as the Appalachians used to be.

Rates: 8 Rooms $490/$695; 6 Cabins/Suites $695/$785; AP. Open late April through mid-November. Number of Rooms: 14

Cuisine: A not-to-be-missed hors d'oeuvre hour precedes superb cuisine nightly. All 3 meals are included for two people in the room rate. We are in a dry county. Guests are welcome to bring their own spirits.

Nearest Airport: Asheville, NC; Knoxville, TN; and Greenville, SC

The Yellow House on Plott Creek Road

www.theyellowhouse.com
89 Oakview Drive, Waynesville, NC 28786
800-563-1236 • 828-452-0991 • Fax 828-452-1140
info@theyellowhouse.com

Member Since 1998

General Managers Don Cerise/Shawn Bresnahan

A European-style inn of casual elegance, the 19th century Yellow House accents fine service in a romantic, intimate setting. Located a mile from the lovely mountain community of Waynesville, NC, the inn sits atop a knoll 3,000 feet above sea level. Five beautifully landscaped acres of lawns and gardens feature two ponds, a waterfall, a footbridge and a deck. The Inn offers three rooms and seven suites, each with luxury linens, private bath, gas fireplace, coffee service, refrigerator and bathrobes; suites also have wet bar and 2-person jetted tub. Most accommodations include private balcony or patio. The Yellow House offers a quiet rural setting with exceptional views, soothing music, and complimentary wireless internet service for guests. Minutes from the Blue Ridge Parkway, Great Smoky Mountains National Park, Pisgah National Forest, Cherokee Indian Reservation, horseback riding and ski area, and Maggie Valley. Close to four mountain golf courses, Asheville and the spectacular Biltmore Estate. Picked by Lanierbb.com as BEST INN for changing of the leaves for 2011.

Rates: 3 Rooms, 7 Suites, $165-$275. Seasonal Rates and Packages Available. Entire Inn can be rented for weddings, reunions and business retreats. Number of Rooms: 10

Cuisine: Gourmet breakfast each morning served en suite, on private balcony, veranda or dining room depending on accommodation; sweets always and appetizers each evening. Picnics by request. Lunches, teas, and parties can be arranged with notice.

Nearest Airport: Asheville (AVL), Greenville/Spartanburg (GSP)

Inn at Iris Meadows

www.irismeadows.com
304 Love Lane, Waynesville, NC 28786
888-466-4747 • 828-456-3877 • Fax 828-456-3847
info@irismeadows.com

Member Since 2006

Innkeepers/Owners George & Becky Fain

Nestled high upon rolling meadows and iris gardens with commanding views of the picturesque town of Waynesville and the surrounding mountains, this stately inn is the perfect destination for romantic getaways, honeymoons, celebrations, and relaxing escapes. 7 lavishly appointed guest rooms, all with fireplaces, private designer baths, large jetted tubs, heavenly king/queen beds, fluffy robes, TV/VCR/DVDs, phones, WiFi, A/C, and intriguing antiques. A meticulously restored turn-of-the-century Greek Revival mansion in Waynesville's historic Love Lane neighborhood. Iris Meadows has spacious gathering areas including a library, music room, grand halls with leaded glass doors throughout, intricate woodwork, carved mantels, and wraparound porches. Chosen as "one of our new favorites" by the Atlanta Journal Constitution's "Go Guide" of southern retreats and one of the Palm Beach Daily Post's "Seven Southern Spots to Sit a Spell." Walking distance of 1/2 mile to area shops, galleries, and fine restaurants; 8 minutes to the Blue Ridge Parkway; 1/2 hr to Asheville's Biltmore Estate.

Rates: $225/$275 weeknights; $250/$300 weekends, holidays, and October. Corporate rates midweek. Number of Rooms: 7

Cuisine: Bountiful 3-course breakfast. Cookies/treats 4 pm. Complimentary beverages, fruits, coffee/tea service, guest refrigerator, microwave, 24 hr. a day in guest kitchen.

Nearest Airport: Asheville, NC; Greenville, SC

Albemarle Inn

www.albemarleinn.com
86 Edgemont Road, Asheville, NC 28801-1544
800-621-7435 • 828-255-0027 • Fax 828-236-3397
info@albemarleinn.com

Member Since 2002

Innkeepers/Owners Larry & Cathy Sklar

A classic turn-of-the-century Southern mansion on the National Register, the Albemarle Inn offers elegance in a warm atmosphere. The main parlor glows with restored oak wainscoting. An intricately carved staircase leads to period guest rooms, appointed with antiques, fresh flowers, cozy robes and fine linens. Morning begins with coffee or tea by the Arts & Crafts style marble fireplace and a gourmet breakfast served on the enclosed, plant-filled sunporch enhanced by candlelight, gleaming silver and soft music. In late afternoon guests relax on the massive stone veranda overlooking lush gardens enjoying refreshments and conversation. While minutes to downtown, the Biltmore Estate and the Blue Ridge Parkway, the Inn is set in a secluded period neighborhood. The perfect spot for romantic getaways and girlfriend escapes, the Inn offers in-room massage and a romance package complete with our hand dipped chocolate covered strawberries. Let us pamper you with a vacation you will never forget.

Rates: $100/$370. Elegantly appointed period rooms with claw-foot tubs, fine linens and fresh flowers. Number of Rooms: 11

Cuisine: Full multi-course gourmet breakfast served at private tables, late afternoon refreshments on the veranda or by the fire, complimentary chilled beverages and 24-hour coffee and tea.

Nearest Airport: Asheville/Hendersonvillle Airport (AVL)

1889 WhiteGate Inn and Cottage

www.whitegate.net
173 East Chestnut Street, Asheville, NC 28801
800-485-3045 • 828-253-2553 • Fax 828-281-1883
innkeeper@whitegate.net

Member Since 2005

Owners Ralph Coffey and Frank Salvo / General Manager Brenda Harris

Romance, elegance and tranquility describe the ambiance at the 1889 WhiteGate Inn & Cottage. A special place for special moments, the 1889 WhiteGate Inn & Cottage is listed on the National Register of Historic Places. The inn is nestled in the Blue Ridge Mountains, minutes from the Biltmore Estate and a short walk to downtown Asheville. A sumptuous 3 course breakfast begins each day. Then wander the stunning award winning gardens or stroll through the downtown shops, galleries and restaurant. Meet other guests while enjoying hors d'oeuvres and beverages served every evening in the garden. Treat yourself and loved one to the ultimate in luxury when staying in one of our Carriage House suites. King beds, two person Jacuzzi tubs, multi-headed showers and stone fireplaces set the tone for romance. Complete handicapped accessible suite available. 1 & 2 bedroom Bungalow suites offer ultimate privacy including a full kitchen. In room couples massage and spa treatments available by appointment. Our fitness room offers workout equipment and a dry sauna. Pet friendly units available.

Rates: $159/$379. Separate cottages with full kitchens, on site orchid greenhouse, gym, dry sauna. Some Pet Friendly rooms, complete ADA suite available. No Smoking Please Number of Rooms: 11

Cuisine: 3 Course Gourmet Breakfast, complimentary hors d'oeuvres & wine served each evening in garden, 24 hour cakes, cookies, fresh fruit, hot & cold beverages. 6 course Thanksgiving Dinner available by reservation. Picnic baskets & bag lunch by order.

Nearest Airport: Asheville

Black Walnut Bed & Breakfast

www.blackwalnut.com
288 Montford Avenue, Asheville, NC 28801
800-381-3878 • 828-254-3878
info@blackwalnut.com

Member Since 2007

Innkeepers/Owners Peter & Lori White

The perfect in-town location in the heart of the Historic District of Montford. Within walking distance to the shops, restaurants and galleries of the city. Surrounded by manicured gardens and waterfall Koi ponds. Relax in the rockers on the porch, or the terrace when the weather is fair, or enjoy a fire in one of the 11 fireplaces. All guest rooms are complete with private bath en-suite and King or Queen luxury kingsdown mattresses, most with working fireplaces. Fresh flowers, chocolates and luxury bedding compliment the antiques. Indulge in a gourmet 3-course breakfast with homemade pastries, fruit and hot entree. Your innkeepers have more than 50 years of experience as professional bakers and chefs! In the late afternoon, relax with complimentary fine wines and hors d'oeuvres with your hosts. We are always happy to help with suggestions, recommendations and reservations!

Rates: 6 rooms in the main house, 2 pet-friendly suites located in the carriage house. $185/$325. Full breakfast, complimentary beverages, WiFi, computer station, afternoon tea included. Off season rates available. Open all Year. Number of Rooms: 8

Cuisine: Decadent 3 course breakfasts. Afternoon tea with selection of fine wines and hot and cold hors d'oeuvres, homemade pastries. 24 hour complimentary beverages.

Nearest Airport: Asheville (AVL)

1898 Waverly Inn

www.waverlyinn.com
783 North Main Street, Hendersonville, NC 28792
800-537-8195 • 828-693-9193 • Fax 828-692-1010
register@waverlyinn.com

Member Since 1991

Innkeepers John & Diane Sheiry, Darla Olmstead & Debbie Jones

Located in the beautiful Blue Ridge Mountains of Western North Carolina, the inn is a short drive from the Biltmore Estate, Blue Ridge Parkway, Dupont State Forest, Chimney Rock Park, the Flat Rock Playhouse, and many other Western North Carolina attractions. Cited in national publications such as The New York Times and Southern Living, we received high praise in Vogue Magazine for our "southern breakfast". We use only the finest ingredients resulting in your choice of fresh fruit, omelets, french toast, pancakes with real maple syrup, grits, meats, farm fresh eggs and egg substitutes. Special touches like luxury sheets and towels, Shelbourne mattress pillowtops, robes, free wireless Internet, DVD players, and cable TV make our rates a real value. The inn is within walking distance of the Mast General Store, several fine restaurants, exceptional shopping, and antiquing. Two porches with rocking chairs await you. The New York Times suggests that you "arrive early enough to sit outside and enjoy the descending darkness." "Come experience hospitality as it was meant to be."

Rates: 14 Rooms & 1 Suite, $189/$219 B&B; Suite, $245/$285 B&B. Seasonal and promotional specials appear regularly on our website. Number of Rooms: 15

Cuisine: Full breakfast each morning using an abundance of fresh and local ingredients. A wide variety of beverages available 24/7. Darla's freshly baked delectables appear each afternoon. Evening social hour 5-6 PM. Guests welcome to bring their own spirits.

Nearest Airport: Asheville (AVL) 15 minutes; Greenville-Spartanburg, SC (GSP) 1 hour; Charlotte, NC (CLT) 1.75 hours

The Orchard Inn

www.orchardinn.com
Post Office Box 128, 100 Orchard Inn Lane, Saluda, NC 28773-0128
800-581-3800 • 828-749-5471
innkeeper@orchardinn.com

Member Since 1985

Innkeepers/Owners Marc & Marianne Blazar

No matter where you start, The Orchard Inn is a perfect destination. Situated on a 20-acre mountaintop with stunning views of the southern Blue Ridge Mountains, this national historic structure has long been a favorite retreat with its wraparound porches and large, inviting living room with stone fireplace. Guest quarters are furnished with period pieces and antiques. Private cottages feature fireplaces, whirlpools and private decks. Enjoy award-winning cuisine on the glass-enclosed dining porch overlooking the gardens and mountains. Hike nearby trails and waterfalls; fly fish native trout streams; paddle the nationally acclaimed Green River; schedule a massage or yoga class; watch over 50 species of native and migrating birds; visit the Biltmore Estate, Carl Sandburg's home or local craft galleries in historic Saluda; then, experience the peace and tranquility of this gracious inn. Picture the ideal setting for weddings and groups, or come to enjoy Shakespeare Weekend, Dickens Dinner, Gardening Weekend or the annual juried Sidewalk Art Show.

Rates: 9 Rooms, $125/$195 B&B; 5 Cottages, $175/$425 B&B. All rooms have private baths, some w/whirlpool & steam shower. Number of Rooms: 14

Cuisine: A full breakfast is included in room rate. Award-winning cuisine served by reservation Thurs-Sat evenings. Fine wines and beer available. Listed as a "Food Find" by Southern Living.

Nearest Airport: Asheville (AVL), Greenville (GSP), Charlotte (CLT)

1906 Pine Crest Inn & Restaurant

www.pinecrestinn.com
85 Pine Crest Lane, Tryon, NC 28782
800-633-3001 • 828-859-9135 • Fax 828-859-9136
select@pinecrestinn.com

Member Since 1991

Innkeeper/Owner Carl Caudle

Imagine 250-year old cabins so captivating they inspired literary greats F. Scott Fitzgerald & Ernest Hemingway. Or pamper yourself with a Jacuzzi tub, a massage, artisan cheese & a bottle of wine with a dozen roses. Tranquility & relaxation await you in any of our 32 romantic rooms, suites or private cottages on our beautifully landscaped 10-acre property. Art & antique shopping, golf, waterfall hikes & winery tours, white water rafting, drives along the Blue Ridge Parkway, The Biltmore Estate... these experiences & more can be found at our distinctive retreat just south of Asheville. Renowned for our "Best Breakfast in the Southeast," exceptional fine dining, & celebrity wine dinners. Our cellar has received the prestigious Wine Spectator 'Best of Award of Excellence'. Recognized in Southern Living, Fodor's, Our State Magazine, & on the National Historic Registry. Romance packages, destination weddings, reunions, or executive retreats in our conference center can all be managed with ease by our professional staff. Our guests create memories that will last a lifetime.

Rates: 20 Rooms $99-229; 8 Suites $179-279; 4 Cottages $189-599. Seasonal specials & packages available. Number of Rooms: 32
Cuisine: Sumptuous, made-to-order 3-course breakfast... that can be served in bed! Distinctive a la carte dinner menu with regional accents, organic ingredients & fresh herbs from our gardens. Afternoon tea, award-winning wine list, & evening port and sherry.
Nearest Airport: Asheville, NC (AVL), Greenville,SC (GSP), Charlotte, NC (CLT)

The Mast Farm Inn

www.MastFarmInn.com
2543 Broadstone Road, P.O. Box 704, Valle Crucis, NC 28691
888-963-5857 • 828-963-5857 • Fax 828-963-6404
stay@mastfarminn.com

Member Since 1988

Innkeepers/Owners Sandra Siano Danielle Deschamps

The Mast Farm Inn is more than a bed and breakfast, with inn rooms, private getaway cottages, fine dining and great wines, organic gardens, and unique gifts that complete our historic country appeal. The key to the Inn's success, however, lies in the exceptionally friendly and caring service offered to lodging and dinner guests alike. With inspired restoration and continuing care, the inn continues to welcome guests, as it did over 100 years ago. Choose from eight guest rooms in our 1880s farmhouse and seven cottages, some restored from original farm buildings. Cottages range in size from cozy ones suitable for a couple to large ones for up to six guests. All are unique spaces. The inn's restaurant is celebrated, enjoyed by lodging guests and locals. The service is attentive, yet relaxed and friendly. Enjoy fireside or terrace dining, depending on the season. The current innkeepers place special emphasis on the environment, creating a "green" inn where recycling, reducing waste, and buying organic produce locally are taken seriously.

Rates: 8 guest rooms: $145/$250. 7 private cottages: $225/$450. Number of Rooms: 15
Cuisine: Full 2-course gourmet breakfast included with lodging. Dinner features fresh, organic delightfully creative cuisine. Dining schedule varies seasonally. Fine wines and beer available. Private parties.
Nearest Airport: Greensboro (GSO) or Charlotte (CLT)

Gideon Ridge Inn

www.gideonridge.com
202 Gideon Ridge Rd., P.O. Box 1929, Blowing Rock, NC 28605
888-889-4036 • 828-295-3644 • Fax 828-295-4586
Innkeeper@gideonridge.com

Member Since 1990

Innkeepers/Owners Cindy & Cobb Milner

Gideon Ridge Inn is ten delightful guest rooms with mountain breezes, French doors and stone terraces. Ceiling fans and wicker chairs. Antiques and good books. Bedrooms with warm fireplaces and comfortable sitting areas. Crisp cotton bed linens and well-appointed bathrooms. Suites with whirlpool tubs and king beds. Fine breakfasts to linger over. Afternoon tea with fresh-baked shortbread to savor. Evening dining at Restaurant G, where guests and local residents enjoy farm to table fresh ingredients prepared by Chef Michael Foreman in the classic style. And in the library, a piano with a breathtaking view of the mountains. Really. . . . Guests enjoy hiking and walking the Blue Ridge Parkway. Golf at nearby clubs. Shopping and dining at Blowing Rock Village shops & restaurants. Biking in summer and skiing in winter. Or just sitting on our beautiful stone terrace and enjoying the cool mountain air.

Rates: 3 Deluxe Suites with king bed and separate sitting area. 3 Terrace Rooms with private stone terrace. 9 rooms have fireplaces. 4 have whirlpools. All rooms B&B. A/C $155/$325. Open year-round. Number of Rooms: 10

Cuisine: Full breakfast included, featuring our apple cornmeal pancakes, blueberry-stuffed French toast or other signature entrees. Afternoon tea with fresh-made shortbread cookies or scones. Dinner served Tues.-Sat. Cocktails and full wine list.

Nearest Airport: Charlotte, NC, 1.5 hours, (CLT); Greensboro, NC, 2 hours, (GSO)

The Duke Mansion

www.dukemansion.com
400 Hermitage Road, Charlotte, NC 28207
888-202-1009 • 704-714-4400 • Fax 704-714-4435
frontdesk@tlwf.org

Member Since 2005

General Manager Becky Farris

The Duke Mansion, built in 1915 and listed on the National Register of Historic Places, offers 20 unique guest rooms in true Southern splendor with a full breakfast. The rooms are residential in their decor, and appointed with beautiful artwork and furnishings, giving you a breathtaking image of what it was like to be a member of the prestigious Duke family who made The Mansion their home. All rooms have queen or king sized beds, private baths, exquisite linens, luxurious robes, and a gourmet goodnight treat. The Mansion is an integral part of Charlotte's most prestigious and beautiful neighborhood, and is situated on four and a half acres of beautiful grounds. Its professional culinary staff and beautiful public rooms can accommodate family or business celebrations of 10-300 guests. When you select The Duke Mansion, you are supporting a nonprofit where all of the proceeds are used to preserve and protect it.

Rates: 20 Rooms. $179-$279, including breakfast, plus tax. Special seasonal rates also available. Number of Rooms: 20

Cuisine: Full-time onsite professional culinary staff featuring New South cuisine. A deluxe, made to order breakfast is included with every guest room.

Nearest Airport: Charlotte-Douglas International Airport, 20 minutes

Arrowhead Inn

www.arrowheadinn.com
106 Mason Road, Durham, NC 27712
919-477-8430 • 800-528-2207 • Fax 919-471-9538
info@arrowheadinn.com

Member Since 2003

Innkeepers/Owners Phil & Gloria Teber

Relax in the quiet comfort of our 18th Century plantation home. The Arrowhead Inn rests on 6 acres of gardens and lawns amid venerable magnolia and pecan trees. Each of our elegant guest rooms, Carolina Log Cabin, and Garden Cottage provide a serene respite with the amenities of a fine hotel. The Arrowhead Inn, built circa 1775, has been carefully renovated retaining original moldings, mantelpieces, and heart-of-pine floors. Watch hummingbirds flutter on flowering hibiscus while relaxing with friends on our sun-warmed patio. Drift off for an afternoon nap next to your cozy fireplace. Unwind in your private whirlpool while enjoying fine wine & delicacies. Slip into your luxurious soft terry robe after refreshing yourself in a soothing steam shower. Awake to the delight of our abundant breakfast. Savour the cuisine of our fine dining, along with Durham's nationally famous chefs and restaurants. The Arrowhead Inn welcomes you for peaceful and romantic getaways, family gatherings, seminars, and business retreats. Our Tiffany Gazebo provides a lovely setting for small weddings.

Rates: Rooms and Suites in Manor House $135-$350 Garden Cottage and Log Cabin $265-$395. Business rates available. Check out Inn website for best rates and availability Number of Rooms: 9

Cuisine: Delicious homemade breakfasts: puffed souffles, blueberry french toast, fresh herbed frittatas, glazed scones, & baked fruits. Chef/owner prepares mouth-watering 5-course tasting dinners served in romantic settings or in the privacy of your suite.

Nearest Airport: Raleigh/Durham

White Doe Inn

www.whitedoeinn.com
319 Sir Walter Raleigh Street, Post Office Box 1029, Manteo, NC 27954
800-473-6091 • 252-473-9851 • Fax 252-473-4708
whitedoe@whitedoeinn.com

Member Since 2005

Proprietors Robert & Bebe Woody

The White Doe Inn is situated in the quaint coastal waterfront village of Manteo on Roanoke Island, which we believe is the best part of the Outer Banks of North Carolina. Luxury lodging, quality service, and a piece of the island life await you here. Centrally located, it's the perfect place to take advantage of all that the Outer Banks has to offer. Guests come from near and far to experience gracious hospitality in this lovely historic Victorian home. The inn offers a four course complimentary breakfast each morning, afternoon & evening refreshments, bicycles for our guests, concierge services, and much more. The Inn's staff is available to make reservations or to arrange the purchase of advance tickets to events and activities. The White Doe Inn is listed on the National Register of Historic Places and is noted for its historic and architectural significance. The inn is also a member of the North Carolina Bed & Breakfast Inns and the Professional Association of Innkeepers International.

Rates: Off: $175/$265, Mid: $199/$290, In: $232/335. Number of Rooms: 8

Cuisine: The White Doe Inn is pleased to provide outstanding service and a delicious full four-course seated and served breakfast that will delight your palate and be pleasing to the eye. Afternoon tea and pastries are set out daily as is evening sherry.

Nearest Airport: Norfolk International Airport, VA

The Aerie Bed & Breakfast

www.aeriebedandbreakfast.com
509 Pollock Street, New Bern, NC 28562
800-849-5553 • 252-636-5553 • Fax 252-514-2157
info@aeriebedandbreakfast.com

 *Member Since 2008*

Innkeepers/Owners Michael and Marty Gunhus

This stunning circa 1882 Late Victorian property is a favorite year-round Eastern Coastal North Carolina luxury accommodation. Experience the warmth and charm of historic New Bern by day and relax in The Aerie's comfort and elegance by night. An inviting welcome pervades the inn as the staff surrounds guests with detailed service, striking the perfect balance between personal attention and individual freedom. Recognized in "Our State" magazine, The Washington Post and featured on PBS, The Aerie's many awards and acclimations include repeatedly being voted as "Simply The Best B&B" by North Carolina's Sun Journal. A gourmet breakfast features a menu that changes daily and guests may choose between three delicious hot-entree selections. Seven delightfully distinctive guest rooms are ready to pamper with luxurious linens, exquisite furnishings and modern amenities. Suites offer whirlpool baths and king or queen beds. Period antiques complement modern conveniences such as Cable TV, DVD/CD players and WiFi Internet. En suite massage spa services available by our licensed staff.

Rates: Seven rooms including several whirlpool suites. Rooms $129-$159 Suites $169-$199. Number of Rooms: 7

Cuisine: Full breakfast included with an inspired menu that changes daily. Starter course and choice of three entrees. Evening wine and hors d'oeuvres. Coffee, tea and various cold beverages available 24 hrs.

Nearest Airport: New Bern (EWN), Raleigh (RDU)

The Verandas

www.verandas.com
202 Nun Street, Wilmington, NC 28401
910-251-2212 • Fax 910-251-8932
verandas4@aol.com

 *Member Since 2001*

Owners Dennis Madsen and Chuck Pennington

Towering above a quiet tree-lined street in the historic district stands this grand antebellum mansion. Built in 1854, the 13 year award-winning Inn is a blend of history, luxury, charm and hospitality. Guest space abounds with wonderful colors, original art, French and English antiques. Four verandas, garden terrace and cupola offer hideaways. Professionally decorated guestrooms have sitting areas, telephone, cable TV. Hand-ironed linens dress comfortable beds. Baths have soaking tubs, showers, marble floors, luxury amenities and robes. French pressed coffee with a gourmet breakfast. Complimentary beverages and snacks and social wine hour. Walking distance to the Riverwalk and restaurants and shopping. High speed wireless internet. Enjoy The Verandas — "An Inn Second to Nun!" ◆◆◆◆

Rates: 8 Corner Rooms $169/$269. Two-nights min. on weekends Dec.,Jan.,Feb.,special: 3 nights for two. Number of Rooms: 8

Cuisine: Included with the room rate is a full gourmet breakfast with French pressed coffee served in our beautiful dining room. Complimentary beverages and snacks are available and white wine is served in the evening.

Nearest Airport: Wilmington International

Graystone Inn

www.graystoneinn.com
100 South 3rd Street, Wilmington, NC 28401
888-763-4773 • 910-763-2000 • Fax 910-763-5555

Member Since 2005

Innkeepers/Owners Rich & Marcia Moore

The Graystone Inn, one of the most elegant historical structures in Wilmington, is located in the heart of the historic district and just three blocks from shopping, fine dining and the River Walk. The Graystone, originally the "Bridgers Mansion," was built as a private residence in 1905 by Elizabeth Haywood Bridgers and is an excellent representation of the neo-classical revival style. Each elegantly decorated bedroom has its own private bath, telephones with voice mail and data port, WiFi and cable TV. All rooms contain period furnishings, exquisite draperies and fine pima cotton linens, towels and robes. Intricately carved fireplaces grace seven of the nine bedrooms. The Graystone has frequently been used as a set for motion pictures and television and lists many notable personalities among its guests.

Rates: 6 rooms $159/$269. 3 Jr. suites $209/$369. Two night weekends. Open year round. Number of Rooms: 9
Cuisine: Full gourmet breakfast prepared by chef-owner. Early morning coffee bar. Complimentary beverages. Evening wine.
Nearest Airport: Wilmington International

SELECT REGISTRY
DISTINGUISHED INNS OF NORTH AMERICA

Gift Certificates

The gift of an overnight stay or a weekend at an exceptional inn or B&B can be one of the most thoughtful and appreciated gifts you can give your parents, children, or dear friends. Employers are discovering that a gift certificate for a "getaway" is an excellent way of rewarding their employees, while at the same time giving them some much needed rest. A few ideas:

- **Weddings** • **Anniversaries** •
- **Holiday & Birthday gifts** •
- **Employee rewards/incentives** • **Retirement** •

Our gift certificates are valid at any of our more than 400 member properties. We process orders daily, packaging certificates with our complimentary Association guidebook and your personal message. Certificates may be ordered online or by phone, and expedited shipping is available at an additional cost. The next time you think about gift-giving, think about our Gift Certificate Program—the perfect gift for that special person, **1-800-344-5244** or online at **www.selectregistry.com/giftcertificates**.

"The Buckeye State"

Famous for: Cincinnati Zoo, Cincinnati Union Terminal, Taft Museum, Neil Armstrong Air and Space Museum, Put-in-Bay Village and Perry Memorial (largest Doric column in the world), Rolling Hills, Farmlands, Burial Mounds.

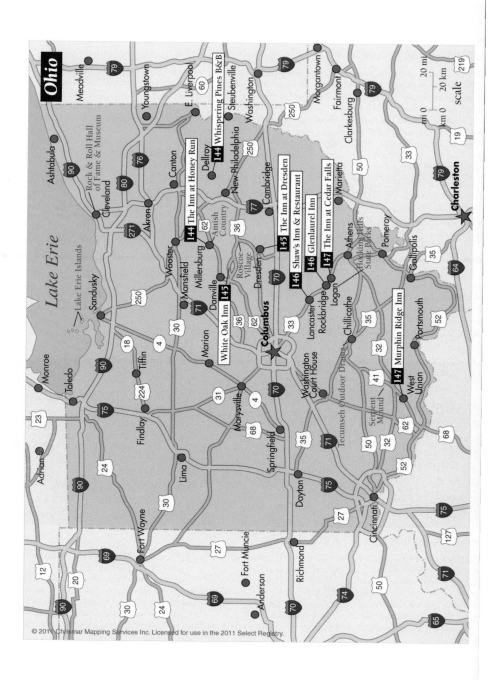

The Inn at Honey Run

www.innathoneyrun.com
6920 County Road 203, Millersburg, OH 44654
800-468-6639 • 330-674-0011 • Fax 330-674-2623
info@innathoneyrun.com

Member Since 1984

Proprietor Jason W. Nies

A full service boutique country inn located in the heart of Amish country in Holmes County, Ohio. The Inn at Honey Run provides a chance to refresh your soul. The inn offers privacy and serenity, in various accommodations. 24 uniquely decorated rooms in the Main Lodge; 12 earth-sheltered Honeycombs with stone fireplaces and patios; Guest Cottage with two bedrooms and a honeymoon/anniversary cottage with two person jacuzzi tub. Visit our Spa for massage therapy, body and facial treatments. Watch birds and nature from picture windows, read by blazing fireplaces, hike our many trails on our 50 acre property or explore the sights, sounds, and backroads of the countryside. Visit the Honey Run Gift Shop for unique items, or shop for furniture, quilts, cheese, Ohio wines, and local artisan wares in nearby villages. Enjoy seasonal educational symposiums, Sunday evening fireside presentations, hike our private trails or enjoy cocktails on one of our many patios. Packages available. Full Service Executive Conference Center for groups large and small.

Rates: Seasonal rates as low as $99.00 per night. Number of Rooms: 40

Cuisine: Rooms include continental breakfast served in restaurant. Upscale casual dining for lunch and dinner. Reservations are recommended. Fine wines, beers and spirits served.

Nearest Airport: Local airport (15 minutes) in Millersburg.<n>Akron/Canton 60 minutes.

Whispering Pines Bed & Breakfast

www.atwoodlake.com
1268 Magnolia Road, P.O. Box 340, Dellroy, OH 44620
866-4LAKEVU (452-5388) • 330-735-2824 • Fax 330-735-7006
whisperingpines@atwoodlake.com

Member Since 2006

Innkeepers/Owners Bill & Linda Horn

Whispering Pines is located in gently rolling hills overlooking beautiful Atwood Lake and its picturesque lush landscape. The lake views will take your breath away and the surroundings are indescribably tranquil. Enjoy a quiet conversation in an outdoor space — hammock, blanket on the hillside, or deck & gather around the warmth of the firepit in the evening roasting s'mores. Nine guest rooms with 2-person whirlpool tubs, wonderful views, Bose music system, exquisite authentic antiques, fireplace, private balcony and upscale amenities. Breakfast is served in our new very large sun-room overlooking the lake — the view is spectacular. We offer additional services such as an in-room massage, and other gift and seasonal packages. We can also accommodate small weddings. There are several restaurants in the area for dining. Endless activities with 28 miles of shoreline — a walk/hike in the park, kayak, pontoon, swimming, fishing, golf, museums, wineries, motorcycles and the Amish area. Whispering Pines — the perfect place for celebrating a special occasion or a brief getaway.

Rates: Inn-Season: $205 — $250, Quiet-Season: $185 — $240 Number of Rooms: 9

Cuisine: A delicious breakfast of seasonal fruit or cobblers, freshly baked breakfast sweets, & a variety of hot entrees served between 9-10:30 a.m., earlier upon request. Morning coffee delivered to your room. Afternoon cookies, tea, coffee, popcorn, s'mores.

Nearest Airport: Akron/Canton

The White Oak Inn

www.whiteoakinn.com
29683 Walhonding Rd (SR715), Danville, OH 43014
877-908-5923 • 740-599-6107
info@whiteoakinn.com

Member Since 1989

Innkeepers/Owners Ian & Yvonne Martin

Come and stay where a warm welcome awaits, the cookie jar is full of homemade treats and the resident black Labrador greets you with a wagging tail. Located in a wooded valley an hour from Columbus and close to Kenyon College, The White Oak Inn has ten comfortable guest rooms and two luxury log cabin cottages. It's the perfect location to explore Amish Country, enjoy outdoor activities, take a wine tour, or just sit on the front porch and watch the hummingbirds. Let us entertain you at a Murder Mystery, or just enjoy a pampering weekend with in-room massages and dinner delivered to your room. Innkeeper Yvonne, one of the Eight Broads of the bedandbreakfastfoodie.com blog, creates delicious breakfasts and dinner daily, using fresh local ingredients and herbs from the inn's gardens. Whether your visit is to celebrate something special or just recharge your batteries, The White Oak Inn has the perfect recipes for romance and relaxation. See our website for more information about our packages, including elopements, honeymoons and girlfriends' getaways.

Rates: Rooms $140 to $195 Luxury cottages $195 to $240. See our website for package rates and specials Number of Rooms: 12

Cuisine: Generous country breakfast daily. Evening meals available for inn guests, either as a delicious 4-course dinner in the dining room or a romantic dinner basket delivered to the room. Advance reservations requested. Lunches available for groups. BYOB

Nearest Airport: Columbus — 55 miles

The Inn at Dresden

www.theinnatdresden.com
209 Ames Drive, Dresden, OH 43821
800-373-7336 • 740-754-1122 • Fax 740-754-9856
info@theinnatdresden.com

Member Since 2000

Owner Thomas Lyall /Innkeeper James Madigan

Tucked away among the rolling hills of Southeastern Ohio, The Inn at Dresden provides the perfect setting for a relaxing getaway with family and friends, or a quiet weekend with someone special. Originally built by Dave Longaberger, founder of Longaberger Baskets, this elegant Tudor home offers guests a panoramic view of Dresden and the surrounding countryside. Guests at the inn enjoy a full gourmet breakfast, an evening social hour and optional fine dining. Individually decorated rooms feature CD/DVD players (350 movies available) and special amenities such as wraparound private decks, single and two person Jacuzzi tubs and gas-log fireplaces. In season there is access to a 10,000 sq.ft. pavilion for guest enjoyment.

Rates: 10 Rooms $115/$190 per night. Each room is individually decorated to depict the area. Number of Rooms: 10

Cuisine: The inn provides a full breakfast; an evening social hour of wine and cheese, followed by optional evening fine dining, by reservation for guests and their guests only.

Nearest Airport: Columbus Airport-60 min./ Akron Canton Airport-90 min.

Shaw's Restaurant & Inn

www.shawsinn.com
123 North Broad St., Lancaster, OH 43130
800-654-2477 • 740-654-1842 • Fax 740-654-7032
shaws@greenapple.com

Member Since 2005

Innkeepers/Owners Bruce & Nancy Cork, Susie Cork

Located on a tree-shaded square in historic downtown Lancaster, Shaw's has been described as "a unique blend of country freshness and well traveled sophistication." Just minutes from Hocking Hills, Shaw's Inn offers 25 individually decorated theme rooms. Ten have large in-room whirlpool tubs, in which some are called the Napa Valley, the Savannah, The Caribbean, and Louis XIV. Full breakfast in the restaurant is included with all rooms. Shaw's Restaurant has a reputation for New York Strip, Filet Mignon, Prime Rib, and Fresh Seafood. The Chef creates a daily changing menu with seasonal items–Spring Lamb, Soft Shell Crab, Fresh Walleye, 4-pound Lobster, and many others. Add to your Holiday Festivities with four weeks of Christmas Dinners. There are Cooking Classes every Saturday. Cork's Bar, serving every day, has a warm setting of dark wood and brass. Free High-Speed Wireless Internet access throughout. Nearby attractions include: the Sherman House, the Decorative Arts Center of Ohio, the Georgian, and the Ohio Glass Museum.

Rates: Whirlpool Rooms $152/$218, Deluxe Rooms $125/$145, Corporate Rooms $86/$96, Double Occupancy. Full Breakfast is Included in the Restaurant. Number of Rooms: 25

Cuisine: Known for Steaks, Prime Rib, and Seafood. Pasta, Small Plates. Changing Seasonal Menu–Holiday Dinners. Wine Spectator Award of Excellence.

Nearest Airport: Port Columbus Airport

Glenlaurel, Scottish Inn & Cottages

www.glenlaurel.com
14940 Mt. Olive Road, Hocking Hills, OH 43149-9736
800-809-REST • 740-385-4070 • Fax 740-385-9669
Info@glenlaurel.com

Member Since 1998

Innkeeper Greg Leonard

Sometimes at dinner, the story is told of how Glenlaurel was first imagined–300 years ago in the heart of the Scottish Highlands. Today, the heavily wooded 140-acre estate has the look of the old world, a veil of romance, and a pace of times gone by. Whether in the stately Manor House, the nearby Carriage House, or one of the crofts or cottages, luxury abounds with sumptuous fine dining, hot tub frolics, intimate fireside secrets, hiking through our Camusfearna Gorge, and a round of golf on our Scottish Links course as it was played 100 years ago! The old-world elegance of the Inn and the secluded, peaceful setting are ideal for romantic nights for two, peaceful getaways for one, intimate weddings, and small group events. Our Anniversary Club honors a successful marriage, year after year; so make Glenlaurel your anniversary destination.

Rates: 1 Garrett $159/$189, 2 Rooms $189/$229, 3 Suites $219/$269, 7 Crofts $249/$299, 6 Cottages $299/$349. Open year-round. Number of Rooms: 19

Cuisine: Dinner is "a private invitation to dine at an estate house in the country" with social time, greetings from your host, and a candlelit culinary adventure-in the European tradition.

Nearest Airport: Columbus, 55 minutes and onsite helipad.

Inn & Spa At Cedar Falls

www.innatcedarfalls.com
21190 State Route 374, Logan, OH 43138
800-653-2557 • 740-385-7489 • Fax 740-385-0820
info@innatcedarfalls.com

Member Since 1989

Innkeepers/Owners Ellen Grinsfelder & Terry Lingo

The restored and comfortably rustic 1840 log houses are an open kitchen-dining room, serving the most refined of American cuisine. Antique appointed guest rooms in a barn-like structure have rockers and writing desks and offer sweeping views of meadows, woods and wildlife. Quaint cottages are ideal for two, or secluded, fully-equipped 19th century log cabins accommodate up to six. Some dog friendly. Casual fine dining for lunch and dinner is served on the patio or the 1840's log cabins. Enjoy spirits in the tavern with a drink before dinner. Discover a new degree of relaxation as you escape into a sanctuary of natural beauty and personal discovery at the Spa At Cedar Falls. The Gathering Place, a state-of-the-art green meeting/wedding location is a perfect fit for all your needs. The rugged and beautiful Hocking Hills State Parks with glorious caves and waterfalls that flanks the Inn's 75 acres on three sides. Casual and avid hikers will enjoy Old Man's Cave, Cedar Falls and Ash Cave. A variety of cooking classes, wine tastings, and hikes are scheduled year round.

Rates: 9 Rooms, $129/$179 B&B; 12 Cottages, $179/$249 B&B; 5 Cabins, $199/$289 B&B and based on two people occupancy. Number of Rooms: 26

Cuisine: Watch meals being created in the open kitchen. Hearty country breakfasts, delectable lunches, sumptuous dinners. Picnic baskets for romantic dinners in your room. Brown bag lunches to take hiking. Patio dining in the warm months. Seasonal menus.

Nearest Airport: Columbus which is 50 miles.

Murphin Ridge Inn

www.murphinridgeinn.com
750 Murphin Ridge Rd., West Union, OH 45693
877-687-7446 • 937-544-2263 • Fax 937-544-8442
murphinn@bright.net

Member Since 1992

Innkeepers/Owners Sherry & Darryl McKenney

As one of National Geographic Traveler's top 54 inns in the U.S. and achieving a prestigious spot on its Geotourism MapGuide, this prize-winning inn welcomes you to 142 acres of year-round beauty. The Guest House has spacious rooms, some with fireplaces or porches, and romantic cabins with fireplace, two person whirlpool, luxurious shower and porch; all decorated with David T. Smith furniture. The 1828 farmhouse features dining rooms with original fireplaces and a gift shop. Dining is more than an amenity. Chef takes seriously the mandate to use the freshest, healthiest, regional and seasonal ingredients skillfully prepared to keep our award-winning reputation. Our full breakfast is the dessert of your stay. Fine wine, beer and liquors available every day, but Sunday. By night, view the Appalachian foothills by the firepit. By day, visit Amish Shops and the Great Serpent Mound or be pampered by an in-room massage. Murphin boasts an in-season pool, hiking, birding, tennis, and lawn games. Wi-fi makes us perfect for conferences. At Murphin Ridge, Innkeeping is in the details.

Rates: 10 Inn Rooms $135/$150 and 9 Cabins $220/$255. Call for business rates. Special rates Sunday through Thursday. Number of Rooms: 19

Cuisine: Chef Brad uses our, and our Amish neighbors' gardens, sourcing only the best for our "farm to table" cuisine. Bountiful breakfast daily. Boxed Lunches available. Seasonal Patio Dining. Pleasing our guests' palettes is our mission. No Sunday alcohol.

Nearest Airport: Cincinnati/Northern Kentucky International

"The Sooner State"

Famous for: Will Rogers Memorial, Alabaster Caverns, State Park, National Cowboy Hall of Fame, Pioneer Woman Statue, Cattle Ranching, Oral Roberts University, Oil, Plastics, Rubber, Cotton.

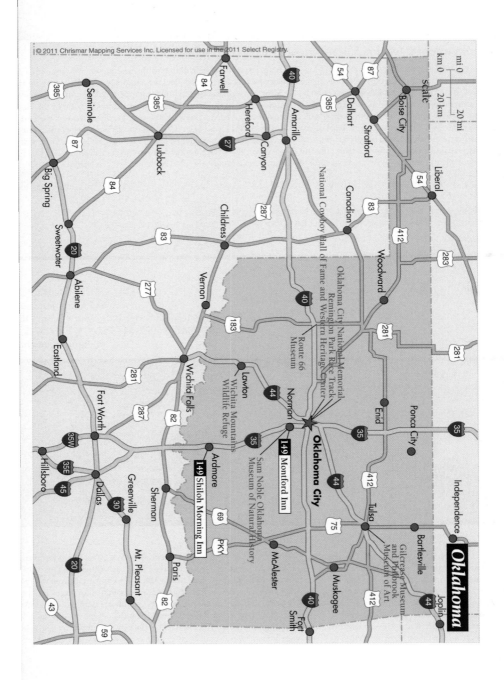

© 2011 Chrismar Mapping Services Inc. Licensed for use in the 2011 Select Registry.

Montford Inn & Cottages

www.montfordinn.com
322 W. Tonhawa, Norman, OK 73069
800-321-8969 • 405-321-2200 • Fax 405-321-8347
innkeeper@montfordinn.com

Member Since 1997

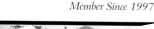

Innkeepers/Owners William & Ginger Murray, Phyllis & Ron Murray

Designed and built in 1994, the Murrays welcome you to the award-winning Montford Inn and Cottages. With its ten uniquely decorated rooms in the main house, and six incredible cottage suites, the Montford Inn has everything the discriminating inngoer is looking for in lodging. Located in the heart of Norman's Historic District, this Prairie-style inn envelops travelers in a relaxing atmosphere. Antiques, family heirlooms and Native American art accent the individually decorated guest rooms and suites. Awaken to rich coffees and a gourmet country breakfast served in the beautifully appointed dining room or in the more intimate setting of the suites. Relax in private hot tubs. Escape in luxurious whirlpool bathtubs. Unwind in elegant cottage suites. Stroll through beautiful gardens. Find your heart. . .at the Montford Inn and Cottages! Featured in Southern Living, Country, Holiday, Fodor's, and Oklahoma Today.

Rates: 10 Rooms,$99/$169; 6 Cottage Suites,$209/$239. Open year-round, possible restrictions for Christmas. Number of Rooms: 16

Cuisine: Full breakfast served in cottages and dining room. Complimentary wine and refreshments early evening.

Nearest Airport: Will Rogers World Airport in Oklahoma City

Shiloh Morning Inn & Cottages

www.shilohmorning.com
2179 Ponderosa Road, Ardmore, OK 73401
888-554-7674 • 580-223-9500
innkeepers@shilohmorning.com

Member Since 2004

Innkeepers/Owners David & Jessica Pfau

Shiloh Morning Inn is located on 73 wooded acres, just minutes off I-35, conveniently located half-way between Dallas and Oklahoma City. The suites and cottages offer large luxurious baths, king-size beds, fireplaces, TV/DVD, private hot tubs or jetted tubs for two, and a private balcony, patio, or deck. Guests choose from an extensive library of movies and books. The 73 acres include a large pond perfect for a picnic and/or fishing. Walking trails are dotted with hammocks and park benches. Wildlife abounds. With luxury and privacy as priorities, Shiloh Morning Inn is the perfect romantic getaway for couples seeking the quiet seclusion of a rural countryside.

Rates: 5 suites and 4 cottages; $159 to $299. Full breakfast included. Number of Rooms: 9

Cuisine: Three-course gourmet breakfast in dining room at tables for two. Dinner by reservation available for intimate in-room dining.

Nearest Airport: Dallas (DFW); Oklahoma City (OKC)

"The Beaver State"

Famous for: The Oregon Trail, Mount Hood, Flowers, Lumber, Wineries, Rose Festival, Crater Lake, Painted Hills National Monument, Columbia River, Gorge, Coast Range, Cascade Range, Redwoods.

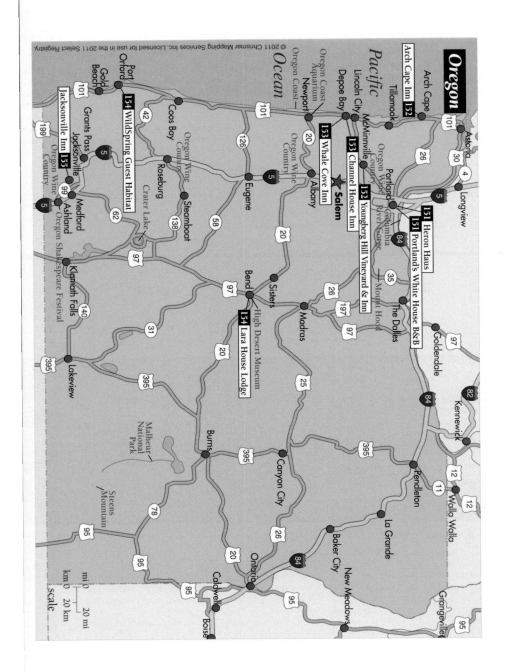

Portland's White House B&B

www.portlandswhitehouse.com
1914 NE 22nd Avenue, Portland, OR 97212
800-272-7131 • 503-287-7131 • Fax 503-249-1641
pdxwhi@portlandswhitehouse.com

Member Since 2004

Innkeeper/Owner Lanning Blanks

Situated in Portland's North East Historic Irvington District, Portland's White House was built as a summer home in 1911 by Robert Lytle, a wealthy lumber baron. The house was billed as the most expensive home built in the district for the period. This Greek Revival Mansion boasts a lifestyle of past years with 14 massive columns, circular drive and fountain to greet you. Summer days show impressive hanging baskets and wonderful flowers to warm your senses. Restored to its original splendor by Lanning with sparkling European Chandeliers, formal linened dining room, large parlor, grand staircase, magnificent leaded glass windows, gilt-gold ceilings, Trompe loeil and Grande Ballroom. Extensive collections of European and Continental Porcelains, 18th and 19th Century oil paintings. Guest rooms are appointed with period antiques, paintings, king or queen size feather beds and exquisite linens. Fresh local breakfast, utilizing SLOW FOODS when possible, served in the Main Dining room by candlelight. Romantic weddings, events, offered. "Top 10 City Inns" – Sunset Magazine

Rates: $135/$235. Molton Brown amenities all rooms. Secured wireless complimentary, flat screen cable TV. Number of Rooms: 8

Cuisine: Candlelight gourmet breakfast, always vegetarian, breakfast meat offered on the side. Housemade Bread Pudding French Toast, Crab Cake Eggs Benedict, Balsamic reduced Vegetable Fritatta, Oregon Blueberry Muffins, Pear Ginger Scones. Full Espresso bar.

Nearest Airport: Portland International Airport, 15 minutes. Located 2 blocks from public transportation.

Heron Haus

www.heronhaus.com
2545 NW Westover Road, Portland, OR 97210
503-274-1846 • Fax 503-248-4055
pam@heronhaus.com

Member Since 1994

Innkeepers/Owners Carl & Pam Walker

This elegant three-story 1904 English Tudor, designed by Joseph Jacobberger, is tucked into Northwest Portland, above Nob Hill. The inn offers a romantic getaway for couples, as well as quiet, comfortable accommodations for business travelers. Its six spacious guest suites, original oak parquet floors, mahogany library, sun room and delightful patio make it a gracious, but relaxing place to stay. All suites offer king- or queen-size bed, comfortable sitting area, work area, private bath, fireplace and wi-fi Internet access. Most have dramatic views of the city, Mt. Hood and Mount St. Helens. Off-street parking is provided. Within walking distance of the many outstanding restaurants and shops on 23rd Ave., the inn is ideally located for your Portland visit. Nearby attractions include the Japanese Garden, the Rose Garden and Hoyt Arboretum in Washington Park and the Chinese Garden in the Pearl District. Trail heads leading into Forest Park are a short walk from the inn. Forest Park is noted for its 4900 acres of forest, streams, canyons and hiking trails.

Rates: $155/$210 Double, $100/$150 Single. Six guest suites. Open year round. Low off-season rates. Number of Rooms: 6

Cuisine: A full gourmet breakfast is included. Breakfasts feature fresh ingredients always prepared in house with local farm produce, Oregon artisan cheeses and artisan breads. Inn favorites include savory brioche bread pudding, quiche, souffle and strata.

Nearest Airport: PDX -25 minute drive. (See web site for directions.) Public transportation: MAX lightrail.

Arch Cape Inn and Retreat

www.archcapeinn.com
31970 East Ocean Lane, Arch Cape, OR 97102
800-436-2848 • 503-436-2800 • Fax 503-436-1206
innkeeper@archcapeinn.com

Member Since 2009

Proprietors Stephen & Cynthia Malkowski

Step out of your vehicle and into a place with beauty so dramatic it quiets the mind and stirs the heart. Here, at Arch Cape Inn, nature takes center stage and the rigors of everyday life are washed away. With romantic architecture, our Inn offers pristine views of the Pacific Ocean and the lush Oregon Coast Mountains. The Inn will carry you away from the trials of everyday life. Our Oregon Coast getaway boasts many outdoor activities that lead to beaches, mountain overlooks and the historic Oregon Coast Trail. Old Growth forests give way to spectacular views of the Pacific Ocean and many creeks that meet it. Walks on the beach delight beachcombers as they skirt the waves while tide pools await their discovery. Nature lovers keep a watchful eye open for the many species of birds and wildlife that call Arch Cape home. For urban adventurers, the nearby town of Cannon Beach offers world-class shopping, art & cultural activities. Guests return to the Inn to find a warm fire, comfortable surroundings and delicious food & wine in a first class dining destination experience.

Rates: Seasonally adjusted average rates of $240 per night during the Low Season and $320 in our High Season. Number of Rooms: 10

Cuisine: Our Inn boasts 2 chefs, both of whom delight in preparing gastronomic delights for our guests in the morning, during our wine social hour and for guests and the public who dine in our evening Bistro. We are members of the James Beard Foundation.

Nearest Airport: The Portland Airport is a 2 hour drive of 105 miles.

Youngberg Hill Vineyards & Inn

www.youngberghill.com
10660 SW Youngberg Hill Road, McMinnville, OR 97128
888-657-8668 • 503-472-2727 • Fax 503-472-1313
info@youngberghill.com

Member Since 2008

Wine Spectator
AWARD OF EXCELLENCE

Innkeeper/Owner Nicolette Bailey

Oregon's premier wine country estate and one of Wine Spectator's favorite locations; set on a 50 acre hilltop surrounded by vineyard. We have an amazing 22 year old vineyard that is farmed organically. We are well known for producing award winning Pinot Noir and Pinot Gris wines. As passionate farmers and winemakers we are thrilled to share, educate, and talk wine. We respect the environment and believe that we can make a difference in how we treat the land and each other every day. We care for our wine and guests with this same respect and philosophy. Youngberg Hill will take your breath away with the most beautiful views, warm luxurious Inn, personal and impeccable service and exceptional estate wines. Youngberg Hill provides the perfect location for those seeking a quiet, romantic getaway and a great base for touring Oregon wine country. We are centrally located in the Willamette Valley and have over 100 wineries and tasting rooms within 20 minute drive.

Rates: $200-$350. Number of Rooms: 8

Cuisine: We create a 2 course gourmet breakfast each morning focusing on regional food and products. Our menu changes because of this regularly. Some of our guest favorites are sure to be around.* Cornished baked eggs * Salmon Hash * Pinot Poached Pears

Nearest Airport: Portland International (PDX)

Channel House Inn

www.channelhouse.com
35 Ellingson Street, P.O. Box 56, Depoe Bay, OR 97341
800-447-2140 • 541-765-2140 • Fax 541-765-2191
info@channelhouse.com

Member Since 1997

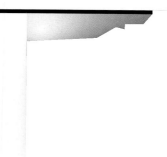

General Manager Sarah Jincks / Proprietors Carl & Vicki Finseth

Nestled in the Oregon Coast's magnificent scenery, Channel House combines the comforts of a first-class hotel with the congeniality of a small country Inn. Imagine fresh ocean breezes, sweeping panoramic views, powerful surf, truly unbelievable sunsets and whales within a stone's throw. Perched on an oceanfront bluff, guestrooms have an understated natural elegance and contemporary decor, including whirlpools on oceanfront decks and gas fireplaces. The friendly staff will attend to your every need. One of the West Coast's most renowned and romantic inns, it has been listed by Harry Shattuck among "a baker's dozen of world's (sic) most delectible hotels" and by Sunset Magazine as one of the 20 best Seaside Getaways on the West Coast.

Rates: 3 Oceanfront Rooms $230/$265; 14 Oceanfront Suites, $245/$330. Number of Rooms: 16

Cuisine: Buffet-style breakfast featuring fresh-baked goods is served in our oceanfront dining room. Enjoy a morning repast while having one of the best views on the coast. We have a significant wine selection available with many fine restaurants nearby.

Nearest Airport: Portland International (PDX) - 2.5 Hours

Whale Cove Inn

www.whalecoveinn.com
2345 S. Highway 101, P.O. Box 56, Depoe Bay, OR 97341
Reservations 800-628-3409 • 541-765-4300 • Fax 541-765-3409
info@whalecoveinn.com

 *Member Since 2009*

General Manager Sarah Jincks Proprietors Carl & Vicki Finseth

The Whale Cove Inn has eight luxury hotel suites perched above the pristine Whale Cove marine refuge on the Central Oregon Coast. Every amenity guarantees your stay will be the ultimate luxury experience - from king-sized Tempur-Pedic beds with down comforters to Jacuzzis on private decks. Each luxury suite is spacious, with cozy gas fireplaces, artisan-tiled showers with European water features, wet bars and flat-screen HDTVs. Every luxury suite offers panoramic views of Whale Cove and the Pacific Ocean - highlighted by orca whales in migration, bald eagles, and a front row seat for storm-watching, when the surf pounds the rocks at the mouth of the cove below. And there is no finer place to be for spectacular evening sunsets. As a quaint fishing village, Depoe Bay is home to many fine restaurants and a host of beach activities - from charter fishing for Chinook and Coho Salmon, Halibut, Albacore Tuna, Dungeness Crab, Rockfish and Ling Cod – to exploring tide pools, shopping or flying kites. Grey Whales can be seen 10 months of the year. ◆◆◆

Rates: 7 Signature Suites $395.00; 1 Owner's Suite $795.00 Other rates may apply for off season/holidays Number of Rooms: 8

Cuisine: Breakfast is included, with an assortment of oven-baked pastries, fresh seasonal fruit and juices, and fresh roasted coffee. Dinner is served in the oceanfront dining room with progressive new American cuisine of Restaurant Beck. restaurantbeck.com

Nearest Airport: Portland International Airport (PDX) 2.5 Hours

Lara House Lodge

ⓘ⦿⬩ ♀

www.larahouse.com
640 NW Congress St., Bend, OR 97701
800-766-4064 • 541-388-4064 • Fax 541-330-6272
innkeeper@larahouse.com

Member Since 2009

Innkeepers Peter & Lynda Clark

Lara House Lodge, a magnificent Craftsman on the National Register of Historic Places, in the heart of Bend, a quiet setting overlooking Drake Park and Mirror Pond. The inn is a few blocks from excellent restaurants, galleries, boutiques & day spas. The perfect setting for romance, relaxation and a base to enjoy year round recreation. Meticulously restored, the inn features exquisite original woodwork, antique furnishings and local art. Five Guest Rooms and One Suite exude warmth and coziness with down comforters, plush robes, exquisite linens, and contemporary conveniences; AC, private baths, cable TV, DVDs & WiFi. When searching for a romantic retreat or a place to call home after exploring all Bend and Central Oregon have to offer, you will be welcomed home to Lara House Lodge with attentive Pacific Northwest Hospitality. Best Places to Kiss in the Northwest "Simply Sublime", Fodor's Travel Guide's 2010 Choice Award, Recommended by Bend Living, Sunset and Seattle Magazines, Green Spot, Central Oregon Weddings, Lonely Planet and NW Best Places.

Rates: 6 Accommodations, 3 Kings/ 3 Queens. All Private Baths, Summer $249-$289, larahouse.com Specials and Northwest Romance Pkg.Roses/Wine/Chocolates $125. Luxurious rooms with comfortable sitting areas and exquisite bedding. Number of Rooms: Six

Cuisine: Coffee/tea 7:30-Full Gourmet breakfast 8:30-home baked treats, creative cuisine, fresh organic produce all served by candlelight. Enjoy Evening hors d'oeuvres and NW wine or local Microbrews in the Greatroom, Sunroom, on Cool Porch or on the Sunny Deck

Nearest Airport: Redmond International Airport Just 16 Miles from the Inn Portland International Airport is 159 miles from Inn

---

WildSpring Guest Habitat

ⓘ⦿⬩

www.wildspring.com
92978 Cemetery Loop, Box R, Port Orford, OR 97465
866-333-WILD • 541-332-0977 • Fax 541-332-0360
michelle@wildspring.com

Member Since 2006

Innkeepers/Owners Dean & Michelle Duarte

The great outdoors now comes with an equally great indoors. WildSpring Guest Habitat is a small, ecofriendly resort in Port Orford, overlooking Oregon's spectacular southern coast. On five acres of old Native American grounds, it offers luxurious accommodations in a naturally beautiful environment. Stay in elegant cabin suites built like small homes, filled with art and antiques, in a secluded forest. Relax in the Guest Hall, help yourself to hot chocolate, play a game or just gaze at the ocean on its lounging deck. Immerse in the open-air slate hot tub/spa and enjoy whale-watching by day or the Milky Way at night. Wander the walking labyrinth, find a hammock or secluded alcove and take a nap. Indulge in an in-cabin massage or pedicure. Make yourself popcorn, choose a movie (over 500 DVDs). Sleep to the sound of wind through the trees and wake up to deer outside your window. A short walk to an uncrowded beach for agates and driftwood, in a lovely small town with art galleries, hiking trails, birdwatching, historical sites and the most westerly lighthouse in the 48 states.

Rates: $198/$306 double, depending on the season and the cabin; $40/additional person. Open all year. Number of Rooms: 5

Cuisine: A breakfast buffet overlooking the ocean, including fresh fruit salad w/organic fruits, all sorts of treats & a special hot entree. We respond to dietary requests. Help yourself to refreshments, including fruit, juices, popcorn and chocolate any time.

Nearest Airport: United or Alaska Air connect to Crescent City CA, 1 hr S and North Bend OR, 1 hr N. Or Portland PDX, 4.5 hr drive.

Jacksonville Inn

www.jacksonvilleinn.com
P.O. Box 359, 175 E. California Street, Jacksonville, OR 97530
800-321-9344 • 541-899-1900 • Fax 541-899-1373
jvinn@mind.net

Member Since 2003

Innkeepers/Owners Jerry & Linda Evans

The inn offers its guests luxury and opulence, and its honeymoon cottages cater to romance and privacy of special occasions. Each has a king-sized canopy bed, whirlpool tub, steam shower, entertainment center, wet bar, fireplace, sitting room, computer with high-speed internet accessibility, WIFI, and private patio with lovely surrounding gardens and waterfall–perfect for intimate weddings, receptions, and private parties. Catering of these events, at the inn or off premise, is a specialty. Nestled in a National Historic Landmark town, the inn was featured on CNN and the Learning Channel's "Great Country Inns." Its restaurant is one of Oregon's most award-winning restaurants and features a connoisseur's Wine Cellar with over 2,000 selections. Dining in the Garden Patio is a summer treat. Five-star Diamond Academy Award of the Restaurant Industry. Recipient of "Readers" Choice Award–"Best Restaurant" by Medford's Mail Tribune newspaper five consecutive years. The inn has served three of the last four U. S. Presidents.

Rates: 8 Hotel Rooms: $159/$199 B&B; 4 Honeymoon Cottages: $290/$465 B&B. Number of Rooms: 12

Cuisine: Restaurant with International Cuisine; Feature fresh and in-season special menus.Both formal and Bistro dining; Sunday Brunch; Patio Dining; Catering–on and off premises; Wine and Gift Shop features over 2,000 wines that are available for dining also.

Nearest Airport: Medford International Airport (5 miles)

"The Keystone State"

Famous for: Liberty Bell, Declaration of Independence, Articles of Confederation, Constitution, Gettysburg Address, Valley Forge National Historical Park, Poconos, Hershey Chocolate World, Amish Homestead, Steel, Pumpkins, Glass.

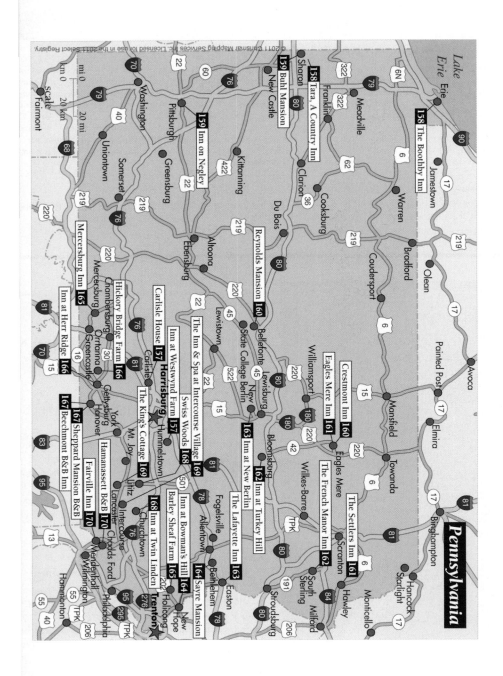

Inn at Westwynd Farm

www.westwyndfarminn.com
1620 Sand Beach Rd., Hummelstown, PA 17036
717-533-6764 • 877-937-8996 • Fax 717-835-0335
innkeeper@westwyndfarminn.com

Member Since 2011

Carolyn Troxell

Luxury Abounds Near the Sweetest Place on EarthThe Inn at Westwynd Farm invites you to step into a world of casual elegance and relaxation. Tucked away on our horse farm overlooking Hershey, the inn offers serenity found few other places. Enjoy carefully appointed rooms, beautiful gardens, lovely views, gourmet breakfasts and refreshments. Let us pamper you with comforting amenities accented by antiques, fireplaces, jacuzzis, and luxurious linens.The nuzzle of a horse, the soft purr of a sweet barn cat or perhaps a quiet glass of wine by the waterfall ensures any hint of care will drift away. Experience a bed and breakfast beyond your expectations midst rolling hills and horses, – just moments away from all that our region has to offer. Hersheypark, Chocolate World and the Giant Center, Hershey Theatre, Convention Center and Medical Center are minutes away. Amish Country, Civil War sites, antiquing, biking, canoeing, or shopping – whatever brings you here, the inn is situated to be the perfect base for your activities or a respite from a too hectic schedule.

Rates: Rates change seasonally and range from $109 to $295 reflecting room amenities. Number of Rooms: 10

Cuisine: American Gourmet featuring locally produced and farm fresh ingredients whenever possible. In addition to a full breakfast, complimentary beverages and refreshments are available throughout the day.

Nearest Airport: Harrisburg International – 15 miles away

Carlisle House

www.thecarlislehouse.com
148 South Hanover Street, Carlisle, PA 17013
717-249-0350 • Fax 717-249-0458
maryd@thecarlislehouse.com

Member Since 2011

Alan and Mary Faller Duxbury

Let us welcome you to the colonial frontier town of Carlisle, founded by the Penn family in 1751, and to the Carlisle House, c. 1826. Imagine the cannonballs of Confederate Colonel J.E.B. Stuart's artillery slamming into the Courthouse on the next block. Stroll around the Downtown Historic District and choose a relaxing dinner of Moroccan, Belgian, Thai, Japanese, English, French fusion, Italian, or American cuisine. Later in your room, do business with our free Internet and long-distance phone service, or relax with a DVD and a complimentary beverage from your in-room fridge. In the morning, enjoy a convivial breakfast before embarking on a day of antiquing, shopping, golfing, hiking on the Appalachian Trail, fly-fishing on two of the world's top streams (the Letort and the Yellow Breeches) or indulge in a sybaritic spa experience. Schedule your visit for a class at the Kitchen Shoppe's culinary school, an exhibit at the historical museum, or one of Carlisle's world-famous auto shows. Come enjoy hospitality with history!

Rates: Open year round featuring well-appointed rooms and suites from $129 to $239 (Double Occupancy). Private baths, several with whirlpools, soaking tubs, or jetted showers, individual A/C, HDTVs, luxurious linens, robes, and amenities. Number of Rooms: 10

Cuisine: Breakfasts are a social affair featuring our signature savory quiches, house-baked muffins or cake, fruit, cereals and juices, with freshly ground coffee and a selection of Twinings teas. Special needs accommodated. Walk to more than 20 restaurants.

Nearest Airport: Harrisburg 37 min; Balt/Washington 2hr; Philadelphia 2hr.20min; Washington Dulles 2hr; Washington Reagan 2hr.15min

The Boothby Inn

www.theboothbyinn.com
311 West Sixth Street, Erie, PA 16507
866-266-8429 • 814-456-1888 • Fax 814-456-1887
info@theboothbyinn.com

Member Since 2005

Innkeepers/Owners Wally & Gloria Knox

Swing open the door of this Victorian era home and thrill to the rich oak paneled hallway with its impressive stairway. Notice the three stained glass windows that grab the sunlight and shine on the portrait of Gloria Boothby, namesake of the inn. Settle down in the living room awash with natural light and pale yellow walls, or sit in front of a fireplace in the adjoining library filled with old and treasured family books. Enjoy the large dollhouse built as an exact replica of a family home in Springfield, Illinois, or curl up with a book in the Shakespeare room, so called because of the tiles around the fireplace of different Shakespeare plays. Outside on warm mornings, you may have breakfast served to you in the garden patio with a fountain's quiet soothing sounds, or stroll through the perennial garden. You may also sit on the comfortable front porch and watch the world go by! This is a sanctuary for the vacationer and business traveler. New this year we are offering the inn for small intimate weddings of 25 or less. AAA Three Diamond rated.

Rates: $120/$170 with Midweek and corporate discounts of $20 per room and AAA 10% discounts on the full rates. Some rooms have a gas-log fireplace or a Jacuzzi tub. Number of Rooms: 4

Cuisine: A full gourmet breakfast is included. A guest galley at the end of the hall is stocked with refreshments and snacks all free to guests.

Nearest Airport: Erie International Airport is only 20 minutes away.

Tara – A Country Inn

www.Tara-Inn.com
2844 Lake Road, Clark, PA 16113
800-782-2803 • 724-962-3535 • Fax 724-962-3250
Info@Tara-Inn.com

Member Since 1986

Owner: Donna Winner / General Manager: Deborah DeCapua

Celebrating 25 years of hospitality. Inspired by the greatest movie of our time, Gone With the Wind, Tara is in essence an embodiment of the Old South. Tara, although located in the "North," offers you a lasting impression of Southern Hospitality and a chance to enjoy the luxuries of days gone by. Tara is a virtual museum of Civil War and Gone With the Wind memorabilia and antiques. Indulge in our magnificent guest rooms complete with fireplaces and Jacuzzis and enjoy the finest in gourmet or casual dining. Tara offers an extensive wine list and an expertly stocked lounge. Afternoon Tea is a daily opportunity for houseguests to mingle and enjoy. Take a leisurely swim in either our indoor or outdoor heated pools, or stroll through formal gardens overlooking the beautiful 450-acre Shenango Lake. Guests may enjoy massages in-house or pamper themselves at nearby Buhl Mansion Spa. Celebrating 25 years of award-winning dining and overnight accommodations, Tara is the ultimate in World Class Country Inns, devoted to guests who expect the exceptional and appreciate the best.

Rates: Gone With The Wind Getaway Packages (MAP) $350–425. (B&B) $200–350. Corporate rates available. Number of Rooms: 27

Cuisine: Ashley's Gourmet Dining Room offers the finest in 7-course white-glove and candlelight service while Stonewall's Tavern boasts a casual atmosphere with a wide array of hearty dinner selections.

Nearest Airport: Pittsburgh, PA; Cleveland, OH

Buhl Mansion Guesthouse & Spa

www.BuhlMansion.com
422 East State Street, Sharon, PA 16146
866-345-2845 • 724-346-3046 • Fax 724-346-1702
Info@BuhlMansion.com

Member Since 2002

Owner: Donna Winner / General Manager: Laura Ackley

Buhl Mansion Guesthouse & Spa, rated one of America's Top 10 Most Romantic Inns, offers the ultimate in luxury, pampering and unsurpassed hospitality. Listed on the National Register of Historic Places, this 1890 Romanesque castle is steeped in history and romance. After years of neglect and abuse, the opulent home of Steel Baron Frank Buhl is now lovingly restored and offers grand memories of a lifetime as guests experience the life of America's royalty in our lavishly appointed guestrooms with fireplaces and Jacuzzis. The full-service spa offers the epitome of indulgence with over 100 options of services from which to choose. The Spa Romance Package is the most popular, offering couples massages, facials, manicures, lunch and a bottle of champagne. Guests have complimentary access to the spa's sauna, steam room and monsoon showers. Indulge each morning with breakfast in bed or dine in the picturesque sunroom. The limo takes guests to Tara for gourmet or casual dining. Perfect for romantic getaways, indulgent spa escapes, exclusive executive retreats and castle weddings.

Rates: Castle Escape Packages: $350 King & Queen Rooms; $450 Royal Grand Rooms; $50 off 2nd night. "Castle for a Day" packages available for weddings, spa, golf or executive retreats. Number of Rooms: 10

Cuisine: Champagne & Welcome Tray in each room. Afternoon Tea served daily, Champagne Reception served Fri & Sat. Rates include 25% discount at Ashley's Gourmet Dining Room or Stonewall's Tavern both at Tara-A Country Inn (Limo provided on weekends).

Nearest Airport: Pittsburgh, PA; Cleveland, OH

The Inn on Negley

www.innonnegley.com
703 South Negley, Pittsburgh, PA 15232
412-661-0631 • Fax 412-661-7525
info@innonnegly.com

Member Since 2006

Proprietor Elizabeth Sullivan

The Inn on Negley is a beautifully restored period home located in the heart of Pittsburgh's charming and historic Shadyside area. Each of our eight guest rooms are custom designed with period furnishings, elegant bathrooms, exquisite linens, and a careful attention to detail. To enhance the experience, every guest is gifted L' Occitane bath products upon arrival as well as at turndown. The Inn is just one block from Walnut Street and Ellsworth Avenue, which offers the finest and most unique shopping, dining, and entertainment experiences in Pittsburgh. Guests can linger and enjoy the tranquil atmosphere over refreshments while the innkeepers assist with plans to enjoy Pittsburgh. Additionally, our lovely Fernwood Tea room accepts appointments for English High Tea service offered each afternoon. Whether guests plan a full day of activities, business meetings, or an afternoon enjoying a splendid high tea service, The Inn on Negley can accommodate every preference.

Rates: King Suites: $205/$240. Queen Suites: $180/$190. Suites are beautifully appointed with private baths, luxurious linens, fireplaces, jacuzzi tubs, robes, slippers, high speed Internet, cable television & private phones w/ voicemail. Number of Rooms: 8

Cuisine: Room rate includes gourmet breakfast for two. Breakfast: onsite chef prepared baked goods, hot, sweet and savory gourmet entrees, fresh fruit, yogurt, homemade cereals and granola. Also includes afternoon pastires, iced tea, and evening wine.

Nearest Airport: Pittsburgh International (20 miles)

Reynolds Mansion

reynoldsmansion.com
101 West Linn St., Bellefonte, PA 16823
814-353-8407 • 800-899-3929 • Fax 814-353-1530
innkeeper@reynoldsmansion.com

Member Since 2001

Innkeepers/Owners Mike and Tricia Andriaccio

Located in the heart of Bellefonte's National Register Historic District, the Reynolds Mansion Bed and Breakfast boasts breathtaking woodwork and spectacular architectural detail. In our three-story historical mansion, you will find six spacious guest rooms. These rooms will fill your expectations of luxurious accommodations. The Reynolds Mansion is conveniently located near State College, home of Penn State University, and is the perfect base to explore beautiful State Parks, Amish Country, and famous trout streams. At our B&B, you will be minutes from Nittany Lion football at Beaver Stadium, world-class entertainment at the Bryce Jordan Center, Penns Caves, Spikes minor league baseball games, museums, golf, the Arboretum at Penn State and more. The Reynolds Mansion is only miles off of Route 80 and is walking distance to the many esoteric shops and other Victorian mansions in charming downtown Bellefonte, PA. Ideally situated, travelers find us to be a great half-way destination between points west and the east coast.

Rates: M-Th $135/$155,F-S $185/$205,Sun $145/$155,PSU Football/Graduation $285/$325 Number of Rooms: 6

Cuisine: A full gourmet breakfast is served daily in the dining room. We prepare our menus to meet your food preferences, whether you choose a 3-course gourmet, heart-healthy, gluten free, vegetarian or vegan. All chef-prepared, onsite.

Nearest Airport: University Park (SCE) 8 Miles

Crestmont Inn

www.crestmont-inn.com
Crestmont Dr, Eagles Mere, PA 17731
800-522-8767 • 570-525-3519 • Fax 570-525-3534
crestmnt@epix.net

Member Since 1989

Innkeepers/Owners Fred & Elna Mulford

The Crestmont Inn is nestled in the woods on the highest point in Eagles Mere, a quiet historic mountaintop town surrounded by a pristine lake, State Parks and State Forests. Our restaurant is well known for delicious cuisine, romantic fireplaces, original art and warm hospitality. Our suites include king or queen beds, large private baths with clawfoot tubs, whirlpool tubs, spacious sitting areas with cable TV/HBO, fireplaces and refrigerators. Our family suites can accommodate four to six people. Enjoy nature walks, hiking, biking, tennis, lake activities, cross country skiing, ice skating, antiquing, shopping or simply relax. Crestmont Inn "Romance and Nature at its Best"!

Rates: $110/$240 per night Bed & Breakfast. MAP Rates are available. Economy Rooms, Suites, Whirlpool Suites, and Family Suites each with private bath, Cable TV/HBO and telephone. Number of Rooms: 15

Cuisine: Traditional country breakfast included. Fine dining and casual dinners available weekends in off season and 6 nights per week in season. Cocktail lounge with fine selection of spirits, wine and beer.

Nearest Airport: Williamsport, PA

Innkeeper/Chef Toby Diltz

Eagles Mere, 'the last unspoiled resort,' sits on a mountain with a pristine lake surrounded by giant hemlock, rhododendron, and mountain laurel. Restored in 2000, we are the last full service historic inn remaining from the 1800s. Incredible waterfalls, sunsets, hiking trails, birding, covered bridges, fishing, golf, tennis and swimming. Featured by numerous travel writers. Guests enjoy genuine hospitality and personal attention. We loan our bikes, XC skis and canoe. If you want a quiet, relaxing place to spend time together while enjoying warm hospitality and gourmet meals, visit our web site or call for reservations. "The LAST UNSPOILED RESORT" now waits for you!

Rates: 16 rooms/3 suites $169/$259 includes five course Gourmet Dinner and Breakfast for two. Number of Rooms: 19

Cuisine: Selected as a "Top Ten" Pennsylvania Inn, we continue the tradition of offering first-class cuisine while utilizing local products as much as possible. We serve a five-course meal which is included in the room rate, as well as a full country breakfast.

Nearest Airport: Williamsport Regional Airport (IPT)

Member Since 1992

The Settlers Inn at Bingham Park

www.thesettlersinn.com
4 Main Avenue, Hawley, PA 18428
800-833-8527 • 570-226-2993 • Fax 570-226-1874
settler@thesettlersinn.com

Innkeepers/Owners Grant & Jeanne Genzlinger

The Settlers Inn is a place to gather. relax, play and rejuvenate at this carefully restored arts and crafts inn. Stroll the extensive grounds and discover colorful flower and herb gardens, a quiet reflecting pond, or sit along the banks of the meandering Lackawaxen River. Guestrooms are thoughtfully and simply appointed with your comfort in mind. Luxurious European linens, featherbeds, whirlpool tubs and fireplaces invite travelers to pamper themselves. High speed wireless Internet, available at no additional cost, provides the flexibility to stay connected. The cornerstone of the inn is the award winning farm-to-table restaurant highlighting artisan breads and menus influenced by the seasons. The Dining Room and Chestnut Tavern reflect the style of William Morris which is carried throughout the building. After a day of hiking or cross-country skiing, bask in the warmth of the bluestone fireplace. Summer offers dining alfresco on the terrace overlooking the grounds as well as the Potting Shed, a gift shop in the garden.

Rates: 21 Rooms and Suites, $165/$260 B&B. Open year-round. Number of Rooms: 21

Cuisine: Our award winning restaurant, rated AAA 4 Diamond, has a 20+ year tradition of working with local farmers and producers. It offers a comfortable and casual atmosphere for a romantic dinner for two or gathering place for friends and family.

Nearest Airport: Scranton (AVP), Allentown (ABE)

The French Manor Inn and Spa

www.thefrenchmanor.com
P.O. Box 39, 50 Huntingdon Drive, South Sterling, PA 18460
877-720-6090 • 570-676-3244 • Fax 570-676-8573
info@thefrenchmanor.com

Member Since 1991

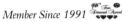

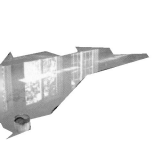

Innkeepers/Owners The Logan Family

An enchanting storybook stone chateau, the French Manor Inn and Spa is nestled on 45 acres overlooking the beautiful Pocono Mountains. Old world charm and elegant furnishings are seamlessly joined with all the modern conveniences. Guests can enjoy luxurious suites with fireplace, Jacuzzi, and private balconies. Every guest is welcomed with complimentary sherry, cheese and fruit plate, and pampered with turndown service with Godiva chocolates. Our fine French restaurant features authentic and Nouvelle French cuisine served in our "Great Hall" where a wonderful vaulted ceiling and magnificent twin fireplaces create a romantic setting. Travelers can also enjoy a cocktail or a casual meal in Hanna's Cafe. Enjoy miles of trails for hiking, mountain biking, picnicking, snowshoeing, and cross-country skiing. NEW — Le Spa Foret at the French Manor is a Green Spa offering all natural spa services, indoor salt water pool, hot tub, fitness room, couples massage suite with fireplace, and five luxurious suites all with Fireplace, Jacuzzi, and balcony views. AAA ◆◆◆◆

Rates: 5 Rooms, $190/$285 B&B; 14 Suites, $265/$375 B&B. Most suites FP, whirlpool tub & balcony view. Number of Rooms: 19

Cuisine: Gourmet breakfast. Room service available. Nouvelle and authentic French cuisine for dinner. Spa Cuisine Lunch and picnic basket lunches available upon request. Cafe and Bar onsite. An extensive wine list is available and top-shelf liquors.

Nearest Airport: Scranton/Wilkes-Barre (AVP), Lehigh Valley International Airport (LVIA)

The Inn at Turkey Hill

www.innatturkeyhill.com
991 Central Road, Bloomsburg, PA 17815
570-387-1500 • Fax 570-784-3718
info@innatturkeyhill.com

Member Since 2002

Innkeeper/Owner Andrew B. Pruden

From romantic couples seeking a weekend diversion, corporate travelers looking for a tranquil place to rest, the inn is a casually elegant and comfortably appointed escape of charm and class. Among the rolling hills and farmlands of rural eastern Pennsylvania, The Inn at Turkey Hill is considered "an oasis along the interstate." Conveniently located just off Interstate 80, guests are treated to a hospitable atmosphere of towering trees and friendly, resident ducks waddling about the courtyard complete with a gazebo and pond. Rejuvenate yourself in one of our guest rooms attractively furnished with reproduction pieces or give in to the allure of a whirlpool bath and fireplace. An award winning restaurant located in the main house features creative, world class cuisine and acclaimed wine list. Also on the property is a renovated 1839 bank barn transformed into a brewpub and casual dining establishment. The Turkey Hill Brewing Company Pub and Grille features house-brewed beer in a unique and diverse environment.

Rates: 14 Traditional rooms $126/$141; 2 Inn rooms $131/$145; 5 Stable Rooms $165/$198; Deluxe King $180/$220; King Supreme $187/$240. Number of Rooms: 23

Cuisine: Complimentary continental breakfast including hot entree. Afternoon refreshments. American-Continental cuisine featured nightly. Full service tavern.

Nearest Airport: Wilkes-Barre

The Inn at New Berlin

www.innatnewberlin.com

321 Market Street, P.O. Box 390, New Berlin, PA 17855

800-797-2350 • 570-966-0321 • Fax 570-966-9557

stay@innatnewberlin.com

Member Since 1997

Innkeepers/Owners Nancy & Robert Schanck

The Philadelphia Inquirer purports, "A luxurious base for indulging in a clutch of quiet pleasures." A visit to central Pennsylvania wouldn't be complete without a stay at The Inn at New Berlin. In the heart of the pastoral Susquehanna Valley, this romantic getaway offers an abundance of life's gentle pursuits. Bike country roads and covered bridges less traveled; explore charming downtowns and mountain hiking trails; shop antique coops, and artists' galleries. Meanwhile, back at the inn, Innkeepers Nancy and Robert Schanck invite guests to relax on The Inn's front porch, stroll the gardens, savor an exquisite meal and a glass of fine wine, and rediscover the nourishing aspects of simple joys and time together. The inn offers gracious accommodations in two restored historic homes, fine dining at Gabriel's Restaurant, lighter fare at the Salutation Tavern, and Swedish massages in our Carriage House Spa. Wednesday evenings, all bottled wines are half price. Friday evenings enjoy live piano music. Guests state they depart feeling nurtured, relaxed, and most of all inspired.

Rates: 11 rooms in 2 historic buildings, $149/$239 B&B. Whirlpool, fireplace, and suite rooms available. Number of Rooms: 11

Cuisine: Gabriel's Restaurant & Salutation Tavern: dinner Wednesday through Sunday evenings 5:00–8:00, Sunday brunch 10–2. Contemporary American cuisine. Enjoy fresh fruit, vegetables and herbs from Gabriel's gardens. Wine Spectator Award of Excellence

Nearest Airport: Harrisburg

The Lafayette Inn

www.lafayetteinn.com

525 W. Monroe St., Easton, PA 18042

800-509-6990 • 610-253-4500 • Fax 610-253-4635

info@lafayetteinn.com

Member Since 2000

Innkeepers/Owners Paul and Laura Di Liello

Our elegant mansion, built in 1895, is situated in a beautiful historic neighborhood near Lafayette College. Eighteen antique filled guest rooms welcome travelers visiting the Lehigh Valley's many attractions. The suites feature fireplaces and whirlpool tubs for that special getaway. The inviting parlor, wrap-around porch and tiered patio call out to those longing to relax with a cup of coffee and a good book. A bountiful breakfast is served at individual tables in our bright sunroom or on the porch. Complimentary soft drinks, coffee, fresh baked goods and fruit are available all day. The entire inn has wireless high-speed internet access and a loaner laptop is available. Whether visiting the colors of the Crayola Factory with the kids, riding the historic, mule-drawn canal boats, hot air ballooning above the countryside, exploring underwater diving excitement, visiting area colleges or just lounging and rejuvenating, The Lafayette Inn makes a great base for your getaway. Welcome to our inn!

Rates: 18 Rooms/Suites $125/$250. Antique-filled rooms, private baths, TV/DVD, phones, WiFi. Number of Rooms: 18

Cuisine: Full breakfast daily, complimentary soft drinks, coffee, fruit, and pastries available all day. Excellent restaurants within walking distance. No liquor license.

Nearest Airport: Lehigh Valley International, Newark, Philadelphia

Sayre Mansion

www.sayremansion.com
250 Wyandotte Street, Bethlehem, PA 18015
877-345-9019 • 610-882-2100 • Fax 610-882-1223
innkeeper@sayremansion.com

Member Since 2003

Proprietors Grant & Jeanne Genzlinger and Carrie Ohlandt

Timeless Elegance in a Distinguished Gothic Revival Mansion. The Inn offers luxury and comfort in nineteen guest rooms each preserving the architectural details of the Main House. In addition to the Main House, our classically restored Carriage House offers guests a home away from home atmosphere in their choice of three suites. Each suite provides a separate living room and bedroom allowing guests ultimate privacy. Amenities include: fine linens, private baths, high-speed wireless internet access, featherbeds, jacuzzi bathtubs, and flat screen TV's. Robert Sayre's Wine Cellar offers guests an opportunity to sample a selection of wine. Personal Service is the cornerstone of the guest experience. The Asa Packer Room, our unique conference center, is ideal for business meetings. Gatherings and special events are held in a pair of elegant parlors, each with its own fireplace. Century old trees adorn the two acres of picturesque grounds which provide a beautiful setting for weddings or large gatherings under our 30' x 60' tent.

Rates: 22 rooms and suites, $160/$325 B&B. Open Year-Round. Number of Rooms: 22

Cuisine: Breakfast highlights artisan breads, home made pastries, house specialties including belgian waffles, quiche, and omelets. Excellent restaurants serving lunch and dinner are located within one mile of the Inn.

Nearest Airport: Lehigh Valley International Airport is a five minute drive.

The Inn at Bowman's Hill

www.themostbeautifulinn.com
518 Lurgan Road, New Hope, PA 18938
215-862-8090 • Fax 215-862-9362
reservations@theinnatbowmanshill.com

Member Since 2006

Proprietor Michael Amery

Award-winning luxury, romance and privacy on a manicured 5-acre gated estate adjacent to the 100-acre Bowman's Hill Wildflower Preserve . . . and yet just minutes from the "action" in downtown New Hope. The Inn is the only AAA Four-Diamond property in the county and in just the past 3 years has been named one of the Top 10 Bed & Breakfast Inns in the Nation by four different organizations including Forbes Traveler (2009) and Trip Advisor (2010)! This exclusive retreat offers just 4 rooms and 2 flagship suites . . . the Regal Tower and English Manor Suites . . . all with 2-person heated whirlpool tubs, fireplaces, King-size featherbeds and more. In-suite spa services, custom romance and engagement packages. Visit our website for last minute specials and packages updated daily. Sign up for our Newsletter for additional special offers. Beautiful grounds, heated swimming pool, hot tub and a stunning boardroom . . . a perfect environment for creative brainstorming, strategic planning or high-level client interactions. Corporate jet access is just 15 minutes away. Exceptional! (Breakfast)

Rates: Rooms $375/$475. Suites $475/$575. 2-night min. on weekends. Rates vary by season and day of the week and may change without notice. Holiday rates may apply. Check our website for prevailing rates, last-minute specials & packages. Number of Rooms: 6

Cuisine: 3-course breakfast including the choice of our "Signature" full English breakfast or gourmet breakfast entrées that change daily. All selections cooked to order by resident chef. Seasonally appropriate afternoon snacks. 24-hour tea & coffee service.

Nearest Airport: Trenton Mercer (private aviation) or Philadelphia International (commercial)

The Inn at Barley Sheaf Farm
www.barleysheaf.com
5281 York Road (Rte 202), Holicong, Bucks County, PA 18928
215-794-5104 • Fax 215-794-5332
info@barleysheaf.com

Member Since 1982

Innkeeper/Owner Christine Figueroa

Recommended by National Geographic Traveler and Fodor's Travel Guide, The Inn at Barley Sheaf Farm is the only historic Select Registry property in Buck's County. One of the most important historic properties in the region, thanks to its native American, colonial, and Alogonquin Round Table histories, the grand estate dates back to 1740 and inlcudes The Manor House, Guest Cottage, and Stone Bank Barn. Complimentary wine and cheese served everyday, extensive brunch and full afternoon high tea are all included in your stay. All rooms feature flat screen TVs, Bose Stereos, Pratesi linens, Frette towels, and robes, featherbeds. Many offer fireplaces, whirlpool tubs, steam showers with body sprays, wet bars, sunrooms and private terraces. Two hundred acre views, fire pit, junior size olympic size swiming pool, putting green, spa, work out facility. Croquet, volleyball, walking trails, miniature horses on property. 24 hour room service and laundry/dry cleaning services. Available for weddings and conferences with event planners on site.

Rates: 16 luxurious suites, $275/$525 Open year round. Activities: Spa, New Hope shops, antiquing, museums, art galleries, Delaware River outdoor activities. Number of Rooms: 16

Cuisine: Full gourmet brunch, afternoon snack, dinners Friday and Saturday evenings, other nights by request. Wine and cheese in our Conservatory Dining Room from 4-6 PM.

Nearest Airport: Philadelphia Airport (PA) and Newark Airport (NJ)

Mercersburg Inn
www.mercersburginn.com
405 South Main St., Mercersburg, PA 17236
866-MBURG-01 • 717-328-5231 • Fax 717-328-3403
Lisa@mercersburginn.com

Member Since 1998

Owners Jim & Lisa McCoy

In 1909, Ione and Harry Byron had a magnificent dream, to build a home that brought comfort and entertainment to those that entered. From that dream, the 24,000 sq. ft. Prospect, with 11 ft. ceilings throughout, was born. The mahogany-paneled dining room and the sun-filled enclosed porch invite our guests to a culinary experience that will not be soon forgotten. Large enough to ensure your privacy but still able to maintain the intimacy and service of a country inn. The double-curving staircases lead you to our luxuriously appointed guest rooms. Draw yourself a nice warm bath in one of our antique soaking tubs, dry off with the softest of towels, slip on a fine robe, and drift away to sleep on your feather-bed. Awake in the morning to the smell of fresh baked morning goods, and our delicious 3-course breakfast. If the season permits, stroll through the flower and herb gardens that appoint the 5.5 acre property. If golfing, hiking, swimming, fly-fishing, or skiing are on your to-do-list, let our staff make the arrangements for you. We look forward to having you in our home.

Rates: $140/$395 B&B. 3 w/fireplaces, 1 w/clawfoot whirlpool tub, 2 w/Jacuzzi and TV, 3 w/antique baths. Kings and Queens. Open year round except Christmas Eve and Christmas Day. Number of Rooms: 17

Cuisine: Enjoy our full gourmet breakfast. Fine dining and wines at Byron's, our fine dining restaurant. Seating from 5:30 till 8:30 p.m. Thurs. Fri. and Sat. and 5:00 till 8:00 p.m. on Sunday. Reservations are recommended. Full bar service

Nearest Airport: BWI, Dulles, Hagerstown Regional

Hickory Bridge Farm

www.hickorybridgefarm.com
96 Hickory Bridge Road, Orrtanna, PA 17353
717-642-5261 • Fax 717-642-6419
info@hickorybridgefarm.com

Member Since 1976

Innkeepers/Owners Robert and Mary Lynn Martin

A quaint country retreat offering 5-bedroom farmhouse (circa 1750's) accommodations (some with whirlpool baths), and four private cottages with wood burning fireplaces along a mountain stream. Dinner is served in a beautiful restored Pennsylvania barn decorated with hundreds of antiques. All meals are farm-fresh and bountiful. Full breakfast is offered to overnight guests at the farmhouse and is taken to their room on Sunday morning. The farm is located 9 miles west of Gettysburg, Pennsylvania, on 75 beautiful acres-a wonderful place to relax while visiting Gettysburg or antiquing in the nearby area. Featured in Taste of Home magazine and National Geographic Traveler. Family owned and operated since 1977.

Rates: 9 Rooms, Cottages and Farmhouse, $110.00/$165 B&B. Open year-round. Number of Rooms: 9

Cuisine: Fine country dining in a beautiful restored Pennsylvania barn. Friday, Saturday, and Sunday. banquets and parties served daily. No spirits are served; you may bring your own. Reservations Suggested!

Nearest Airport: Harrisburg

Inn at Herr Ridge

www.herrtavern.com
900 Chambersburg Rd., Gettysburg, PA 17325
800-362-9849 • 717-334-4332 • Fax 717-334-3332
info@herrtavern.com

Member Since 2004

Innkeeper/Owner Steven Wolf

The enchanting atmosphere of the Inn at Herr Ridge is unforgettable. Built in 1815 and nestled between the historic battlefields of Gettysburg and one of Pennsylvania's wooded treasures, Caledonia State Park on historic Rt 30. The Inn offers a rare experience to every guest who crosses the threshold, and is only minutes from town. Tastefully decorated, charmingly unique rooms await. Enjoy our roof top patio overlooking Seminary Ridge or step into your private Jacuzzi bath. Hungry? Relax while our chef creates a fabulous meal soon not to be forgotten. And don't forget the wine. Our Wine Spectator award winning wine list offers over 1000 selections, many of which are stored in our exquisite, windowed wine cellar. Our full-service bar also offers premium spirits. The main house of the Inn became the first Confederate hospital during the battle of Gettysburg. It is beautifully restored and listed in the National Register of Historic Places. If you are searching for a relaxing and romantic getaway, look no further. The fireplace is glowing & the wine is chilled. Come visit us!

Rates: $169/$359. Open year-round. All rooms have private baths, spa robes, pillowtop featherbeds, and gas fireplaces. Most rooms with two person jacuzzi tubs. Number of Rooms: 16

Cuisine: Bountiful breakfast consisting of daily baked muffins & cinnamon buns. House made granola and a hot breakfast created by the chefs. Fabulous innovative and seasonal influenced lunch and dinner menus. Private Dining and Banquet facilities.

Nearest Airport: Harrisburg (MDT), Baltimore (BWI)

The Beechmont Bed & Breakfast Inn

www.thebeechmont.com
315 Broadway, Hanover, PA 17331
800-553-7009 • 717-632-3013 • Fax 717-632-2769
innkeeper@thebeechmont.com

Member Since 2003

Innkeepers/Owners Thomas & Kathryn White

Recognized as Pennsylvania's 2009 Innkeeper of the Year, the Whites consider hospitality one of The Beechmont's most important offerings. Breakfast is a close second, as Kathryn is part of Eight Broads in the Kitchen, a group of imaginative innkeepers who share recipes and local insights (www.bedandbreakfastfoodie.com). Located on a tree-lined street of stately historic homes in a town just 14 miles east of Gettysburg, The Beechmont welcomes business and leisure travelers with thoughtful extras designed to meet their needs. A well-stocked library, gardens and patio offer a backdrop for relaxed conversation, while well-appointed guest rooms assure a comfortable stay and sweet dreams. Experience the 150th anniversary of the Civil War at the Gettysburg Battlefield and museum. Explore President Eisenhower's farm. Search for bargains in antique malls, bicycle back country roads, savor fresh vegetables and fruits from farmers markets, tour wineries, watch Harley Davidson manufacture motorcycles or Utz make chips, enjoy a great dinner, or get married in our gardens.

Rates: $174 – $129. Corporate rates Mon-Thur. A/C, WIFI, guest internet station, cable TV, fireplaces, jetted showers. Number of Rooms: 7

Cuisine: Sumptuous breakfast served at the time you select. Start with freshly brewed coffee from Mukilteo Coffee roasters, then a made-from-scratch breakfast featuring locally grown produce and goods. Afternoon sweet treat. Excellent restaurants nearby.

Nearest Airport: Baltimore Washington International (BWI), Harrisburg, National and Dulles.

The Sheppard Mansion

www.sheppardmansion.com
117 Frederick St., Hanover, PA 17331
877-762-6746 • 717-633-8075 • Fax 717-633-8074
reservations@sheppardmansion.com

Member Since 2002

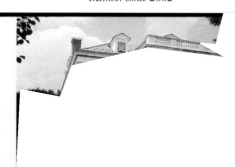 

Innkeeper/Owner Kathryn Sheppard Hoar

Nestled in the heart of Hanover's Historic District stands a grand 3-story brick and marble Mansion surrounded by lush gardens. Built in 1913 by Mr. and Mrs. H.D. Sheppard, co-founder of The Hanover Shoe, the Mansion now operates as an elegant full service Inn and event facility. Full of the original furnishings and restored with modern amenities, the Mansion features bedrooms and suites with over-sized soaking tubs in the private marble baths—all for our guests' enjoyment. Days can be spent exploring nearby Gettysburg, antique hunting or touring Lancaster, Baltimore, Washington, DC. Want to relax instead? Have a massage and lounge around the house. Complete your pampered experience with an exquisite meal in our Dining Room, serving seasonal refined American cuisine Wednesday through Saturday nights. Check our website for lodging and dining packages. Our entire staff eagerly awaits the opportunity to be of service; whether for business or pleasure, the Sheppard Mansion is sure to be an unforgettable experience.

Rates: 6 rooms and suites, King, Queen Beds, $140/$350 per night. 2 BR Guest Cottage on property available weekly. Corporate rates available. All rooms have private baths, A/C, WiFi, TV, Telephones and in-room coffee. Number of Rooms: 6

Cuisine: Full gourmet breakfast included. Fine dining offered Wed. thru Sat. nights features local produce in an ever-changing seasonal menu of refined American cuisine.

Nearest Airport: BWI – 1 hour, MDT – 1 hour

Inn at Twin Linden

www.InnAtTwinLinden.com
2092 Main St., Churchtown, PA 17555
866-445-7614 • 717-445-7619
info@InnAtTwinLinden.com

Member Since 2011

Norm and Sue Kuestner

Imagine the luxurious ambience of a restored 1840's country estate - a gracious manor surrounded by beautiful gardens and stately trees. Farm-dotted valleys stretch as far as the eye can see while the "clip-clop" of horse-drawn buggies is heard echoing down the main street. These pleasures await you at the Inn at Twin Linden where discriminating guests are welcomed with exceptional accommodations and the finest cuisine. Guest rooms feature canopy beds, fireplaces and whirlpool tubs. Deluxe suites offer the ultimate in privacy with a refined contemporary decor. The inn is surrounded by two acres of splendid gardens overlooking scenic Amish and Mennonite farm valleys, yet is conveniently located to a wide range of activities - from farm tours, country auctions, and antiquing to wineries, museums, theatre, state parks and outlet shopping. Relax at day's end by wandering through moonlit gardens or sip sherry by the fire - then retire to turned-down beds with Belgian chocolates and a cordial at bedside.

Rates: 6 rooms $130-$180, 2 suites with grand view of scenic countryside $245–$275. Private Baths, Fireplaces, Whirlpool Tubs, Bath Robes, Crabtree & Evelyn Amenities, Cable TV, Free WIFI. Number of Rooms: 8

Cuisine: A full-course breakfast served in our garden-view dining room by candlelight. Refreshments available 24/7. Fine dining offered on Saturday evenings by reservation - prix-fix menu with alternate entree choice. Dietary restrictions accommodated.

Nearest Airport: Lancaster (LNS) 18 mi., Philadelphia (PHL) 41 mi., Harrisburg (MDT) 43 mi., Lehigh Valley (ABE) 46 mi.

Swiss Woods

www.swisswoods.com
500 Blantz Road, Lititz, PA 17543
800-594-8018 • 717-627-3358 • Fax 517-338-1939
innkeeper@swisswoods.com

Member Since 1993

Innkeepers/Owners Werner and Debrah Mosimann

Surrounded by meadows, gardens and woods Swiss Woods is a quiet retreat on 35 acres in Lancaster's Amish country. Perfect for those who love quiet and all things nature. Our rooms feature patios or balconies, some with lake views, and are decorated with the natural wood furnishings typical of Switzerland. Fabulous breakfasts, complemented by our own blend of coffee and a wide assortment of quality teas, are served in a sunlit common room. Afternoons feature pastry and biscotti. Convenient to Lancaster's Amish community, famous farmers markets, greenhouses and quilt shops, Hershey is also just a short drive. After a day of antiquing, shopping or touring enjoy views of extraordinary gardens, landscaped with a wide variety of annuals and perennials. Take a relaxing hike through the woods, watch the huge variety of birds, or enjoy a drink on the garden swing with a good book and a sweet treat from our kitchen. Canoes are available at the lake from April through November. In winter settle in to read next to the inn's handsome sandstone fireplace. German spoken.

Rates: 6 Rooms (2 with Jacuzzi, balconies, and high open beamed ceilings), all with patios or balconies. $165-225 1 suite $205/$255 Number of Rooms: 7

Cuisine: Inn breakfast specialties may include garden fritatta, freshly-baked breads from old world recipes, all created by one of the 8 Broads in the Kitchen. The afternoon boasts sweets on the sideboard such as caramel apple cake or fresh fig cake

Nearest Airport: Harrisburg and Philadelphia. Lancaster Airport has is close and has connection with BWI

The King's Cottage
www.kingscottagebb.com
1049 East King Street, Lancaster, PA 17602-3231
800-747-8717 • 717-397-1017 • Fax 717-397-3447
info@kingscottagebb.com

Member Since 1995

Innkeepers/Owners Janis Kutterer and Ann Willets

Feel yourself unwind as you travel through Lancaster county's tranquil back roads in Amish Country. Enjoy world-class entertainment, savor Pennsylvania Dutch cooking, visit historic sites, stroll art galleries, enjoy intimate gourmet restaurants — all within minutes of the King's Cottage — your home away from home. Come enjoy our wonderful Lancaster Bed and Breakfast. Elegant, luxurious guest rooms with cozy fireplaces enhance relaxation and romance! Let us pamper you with our gourmet breakfast, afternoon goodies and even a massage that melts your cares away. Or immerse yourself in a decadent rose petal bath while you nibble on chocolate-covered strawberries. The possibilities for celebrating a special occasion or just plain spoiling yourself are endless at the King's Cottage. Our location offers the best of both worlds — being a mile and a half away from a buzzing art scene and fabulous restaurants, while just a few minutes from Amish Country! And we have not forgotten our business traveler with 24-hour check-in, early breakfast, fax service & complimentary WiFi.

Rates: 7 rooms (2 with whirlpool tub), 1 Honeymoon Cottage with whirlpool tub: $160/$295. Fireplaces, DVD, WIFI, Business rates available. Number of Rooms: 8

Cuisine: Gourmet breakfast, afternoon refreshments. Dietary restrictions accommodated with advance notice. Close to casual and fine dining. 24 hr. guest kitchen with ice, bottled water, snacks, hot beverages.

Nearest Airport: Harrisburg (MDT) 40 min, Philadelphia (PHL) 90 min, Baltimore (BWI) 120 min

---

The Inn & Spa at Intercourse Village
www.inn-spa.com
3542 Old Philadelphia Pike — POB 598, Intercourse, PA 17534
800-664-0949 • 717-768-2626
innkeeper@inn-spa.com

Member Since 2005

Innkeeper Ruthann Thomas

Winner of the "Top Ten Romantic Inns" Award. Enjoy elegance in a quiet village setting that entreats you to a place of peace, beauty and comfort. Travel through time as you enter the 1909 Victorian Inn filled with period furnishings and antique treasures. Its refinement and sophistication deliver high-class accoutrements for those of discerning tastes. If upscale country is more your style, then reserve one of our Country Homestead suites with private entrance and over 400 sq. ft. of space to relax in and forget the world around you. Our suites include queen pillowtop beds, private bath, jetted tub, steam shower, separate sitting area with love seat, gas-log fireplace, flat panel TV, wet bar and many other special treats. For divine romance and relaxation, find yourself engulfed in sumptuous grandeur in our Grand Suites complete with Jacuzzi for two, King pillowtop bed, flat panel TV, gas-log fireplace. Arise to a full five course candlelit breakfast and indulge yourself in a delightful diversion at our on site Spa, then relax and stroll thru the Historic Village.

Rates: Grand Suites w/King pillowtop bed, flat panel TV, fireplace, Jacuzzi for two-$269-$399, Homestead Suites w/Queen pillowtop bed, flat panel TV, fireplace, $169-$239, Victorian Rooms w/Queen pillowtop bed. flat panel TV, $149-$199.AAA 3 Diamond Rated Number of Rooms: 9

Cuisine: Enjoy a nice 5 course candlelit breakfast, prepared by our chef and served on fine English china in our Victorian dining room. Walk to the village for lunch. Enjoy sodas, coffee, fruit & pretzels — provided all day

Nearest Airport: Harrisburg International 1 hr, Philadelphia International 1 1/2 hrs, Baltimore 1 1/2 hrs.

Hamanassett Bed & Breakfast

🍽️   🍷

www.hamanassett.com
725 Darlington Road, P.O. Box 366, Chadds Ford, PA 19017
877-836-8212 • 610-459-3000
stay@hamanassett.com

Member Since 2005

Innkeepers/Owners Glenn & Ashley Mon

A worthy destination in the Brandywine Valley, Hamanassett is a grand 1856 English country house on 7 acres where Southern hospitality and personal service is emphasized. Seven spacious bedrooms and suites, featuring en suite baths, hardwood floors, antique furniture, queen or king beds, TV/DVD with free movies, free WIFI & guest computer, robes. Enjoy the billiards room, living room, and light-filled sun room, terrace or porch overlooking the koi pond with waterfall. Two private two story 2 bedroom cottages for those traveling with small children or for those who just want extra privacy. Dog friendly, Cooking classes. Near Longwood Gardens, Winterthur, Wyeth Museum, Barnes museum, Nemours, and Philadelphia. Only 20 minutes to Wilmington, De. and one hour from Amish Country. Recommended by major publications, The New York Times "The elaborate breakfasts are a highlight." "Sets the standard for luxury in the Branywine area" David Langlieb from his book "Philadelphia, Brandywine Valley & Bucks Co." Enjoy our user friendly front porch!

Rates: Rooms: $165/$265. Carriage House: $350/$500/nt. Cottage: $325.00/nt. Weekly/monthly rates available. Number of Rooms: 9

Cuisine: Full gourmet candlelight breakfast. Special diets accommodated if notified in advance. Guest pantry stocked with complimentary soft drinks and snacks, microwave oven, ice maker, refrigerator and home baked cookies available 24 hours.

Nearest Airport: Philadelphia International 17 miles, Baltimore Washington International 94 miles. See web site for directions.

Fairville Inn

🍽️   🍷

www.fairvilleinn.com
506 Kennett Pike (Rte. 52), Chadds Ford, PA 19317
877-285-7772 • 610-388-5900 • Fax 610-388-5902
info@fairvilleinn.com

Member Since 1995

Innkeepers/Owners Richard and Laura Carro

The Fairville Inn, located in the heart of the Brandywine Valley and listed on the National Register of Historic Places, echoes the pastoral scenes of Wyeth Family paintings. The allure of the Brandywine Valley, which reaches in all directions from Chadds Ford, comes from the enchanting landscape. World famous Longwood Gardens and distinguished museums, such as Winterthur, Hagley, and the Brandywine River ("Wyeth") Museum, are just minutes away. Leisurely travel the Brandywine Valley Wine Trail and sample the latest vintages of local wineries. Accented with barn wood, beams, and the occasional cathedral ceiling, the Inn is the embodiment of elegant comfort. Most rooms feature decks overlooking the gardens or the meadow rolling toward a serene pond. Each room in the Main House (ca. 1826), Carriage House, and Springhouse has a private bath, satellite TV, telephone (with voice mail and complimentary local and long-distance service), wireless Internet, and individually controlled heating/air conditioning. Most rooms have a canopy bed and many have fireplaces (seasonal).

Rates: 11 Rooms ($170 – $225), 2 Deluxe Rooms ($265), and 2 Spacious Suites ($295). Open every day. (Rates are subject to change modestly.) Please visit our website for seasonal and other specials. Number of Rooms: 15

Cuisine: Full breakfast (Mon-Fri 7-9 am; weekends and holidays 8-10 am) of refreshing beverages, cereal, fresh fruit, yogurt, Inn-baked goods and a choice of three hot entrees. Afternoon tea served daily with cheese, crackers, fresh fruit, and Inn-baked goods.

Nearest Airport: Philadelphia International, about 28 miles.

"Little Rhody"

Famous for: Jazz Festivals, Seaside Victorian Mansions, "Mile of History." Cliff Walks, Beaches, Sailing.

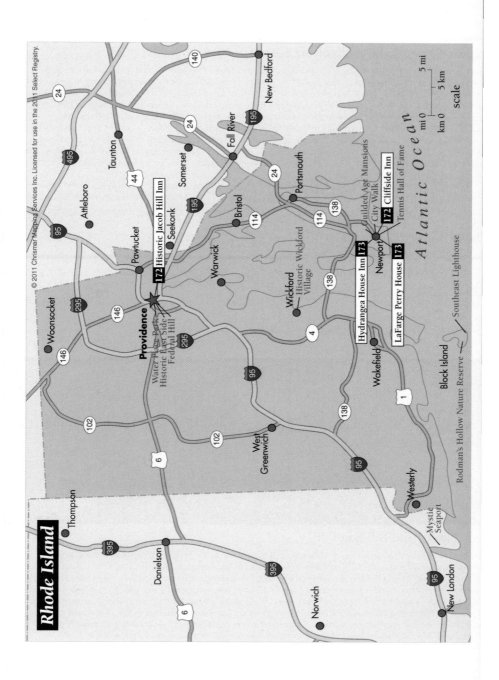

Historic Jacob Hill Inn

www.Jacobhill.com
P.O. Box 41326, Providence, RI 02940
888-336-9165 • 508-336-9165
host@jacobhill.com

Member Since 2000

Innkeepers/Owners Bill & Eleonora Rezek

Located on a peaceful country estate, just a 10 minute drive from downtown Providence, the Rhode Island Convention Center, Brown University and the Historic East Side. Built in 1722, Jacob Hill has a long history of hosting America's most prominent families, including the Vanderbilts. Recently updated rooms are spacious, all with private bathrooms; most have Jacuzzi tubs. King-and queen-sized canopied beds blend with hand-picked antiques, period wall coverings and Oriental rugs. The gleaming wood floors mirror the romantic flames from the original fireplaces. The elegant surroundings are complemented by the genuine warm hospitality that will make you feel at home. Awarded "Top 10 Most Romantic Inns," ZAGAT "Top U.S. Hotels, Resorts & Spas," TripAdvisor.com "Travelers' Choice Award," Inn Traveler "Best Guest accommodations," "Ten best Urban Inns" Forbes.com, "Room of the Year" North American Inns Magazine. AAA Four Diamond Award. Featured by the New York Times, Country Living Magazine, USA Today and many others.

Rates: 12 unique guestrooms, w/private bathrooms $199/$459. Phones, TV, AC, Internet Access. Open year-round. Pool, tennis, ping pong, billiard room w/large plasma TV, meeting room, & gazebo to view the beautiful sunsets. Spa services. Number of Rooms: 12

Cuisine: Award-winning breakfast, complimentary beverages, chocolate chip cookies and cheese plate. Many fine restaurants nearby for lunch and dinner.

Nearest Airport: Providence T F Green

Cliffside Inn

www.cliffsideinn.com
2 Seaview Avenue, Newport, RI 02840
800-845-1811 • 401-847-1811 • Fax 401-848-5850
reservations@cliffsideinn.com

Member Since 1997

Owners, Nancy and Bill Bagwill

The celebrated Cliffside Inn, formerly the site of St. George's School and home of legendary artist Beatrice Turner, has earned a worldwide reputation as one of New England's most distinguished Bed and Breakfast luxury inns. Known for seamlessly blending today's finest deluxe amenities – whirlpools, steam baths, fireplaces, grand beds, fine Italian linens, iPod sound systems, wifi – with Victorian elegance and antiques, refined design, and stunning artwork. The Cliffside Inn is a magical hideaway. The grand Victorian Manor House and "coastal chic" Seaview Cottage are peacefully perched above the Atlantic Ocean and Newport's dramatic Cliff Walk. Whether you are looking for a relaxing escape or romantic getaway, guests enjoy warm hospitality and attentive service with a number of Cliffside special touches and epicurean delights. The regional wine bar features the best of the nearby vineyards, and signature in-room spa services are available.

Rates: 7 Deluxe Suites/State Rooms $300/$500; 5 Deluxe Rooms $250/$425; 4 Classic Rooms $200/$400. Number of Rooms: 16

Cuisine: Multi-course breakfast. Afternoon tea featuring a seasonal menu of tea sandwiches, scones, tarts, and other sweets & savories is offered twice weekly. A manager's wine tasting reception on other days. Our signature Fondeles at turndown.

Nearest Airport: Providence, Boston

Hydrangea House Inn

www.hydrangeahouse.com
16 Bellevue Avenue, Newport, RI 02840
800-945-4667 • 401-846-4435 • Fax 401-846-6602
hydrangeahouseinn@cox.net

Member Since 2005

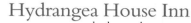

Innkeepers/Owners Grant Edmondson & Dennis Blair

Enter a world of grace, elegance and style where the intimate charm of Hydrangea House is complemented by its prestigious Bellevue Avenue address where once lived the Vanderbilt's, the Astors and the Dukes. Its proximity to the magical gilded mansions, recreational harbor, historic sites, fine dining, and extraordinary shopping means you can walk to almost everything. All nine rooms and suites are individually decorated with a dramatic use of color, sumptuous fabrics and trims and elegant furnishings. Suites have the added luxury of a two-person spa tub, marble shower and steam bath and flat screen "mirror" television. All rooms offer plush robes, triple sheeting, high speed Internet, long distance and local calling, CD players and iPod hook-ups. Complimentary wine and cheese is served daily in the parlor or one of Hydrangea House's expansive porches, and don't miss a home-made cookie to make the night complete. AAA Four diamond award. Named "Top 10 Most Romantic Inn" in 2008 by American Historic Inns and ILoveInns.com. Winner of Yankee Magazine "Editors Choice" 2006 award.

Rates: $265/$475 year round. Year round packages available. Number of Rooms: 10

Cuisine: Expect to find more than the usual continental breakfast. We will serve you our own special blend of fresh ground House Coffee, home-baked breads & granola—as well as our incredible raspberry pancakes perhaps or seasoned scrambled eggs in puff pastry.

Nearest Airport: Providence Airport (PVD) 30 minutes.

La Farge Perry House

www.lafargeperry.com
24 Kay Street, Newport, RI 02840
877-736-1100 • 401-847-2223 • Fax 401-847-1967
reservations@lafargeperry.com

Member Since 2006

Owner Jeanie Shufelt

La Farge Perry House is a Victorian-era luxury inn located on a quiet street within walking distance to major attractions in Newport. The inn is named after the famed artist John La Farge, who lived in the house in the 1860's. Each of the inn's six distinctive rooms honor La Farge, his family, and ancestors. Four guestrooms feature queen-sized beds and two feature king beds. All rooms are adorned with luxurious private bathrooms, luxury bedding and amenities, and feature fresh flowers from the award winning gardens. Many rooms also feature Jacuzzi tubs, fireplaces, and large sitting areas. Common areas include a formal living room, French Provencal kitchen with sitting area and a fireplace, dining room with hand-painted panoramic murals of Newport, secluded balcony on the third floor, front porch with white wicker furniture, and Adirondack chairs in the award-winning backyard gardens. Innkeeper, Midge Knerr, former award-winning executive chef from Manhattan, is available to ensure that each guest turns La Farge Perry House into their home away from home.

Rates: Summer Rates range from $249 to $349 on weekdays and from $289 to $499 on weekends. Winter Rates range from $139 to $169 on weekdays and from $189 to $289 on weekends. Number of Rooms: 6

Cuisine: Breakfasts are cooked to order by our innkeeper with many choices, including Eggs Benedict on Sundays. The table is set daily with homemade jams, pastries, fresh fruit, and more. Seasonal afternoon refreshments are offered with our famous macaroons.

Nearest Airport: Providence/TF Green, RI

"The Palmetto State"

Famous for: Congaree Swamp National Monument, Hilton Head Island, Myrtle Beach, Plantations, Charleston, Blue Ridge Mountains, Fort Sumter, Tobacco, Corn, Peaches, Cotton, Textiles.

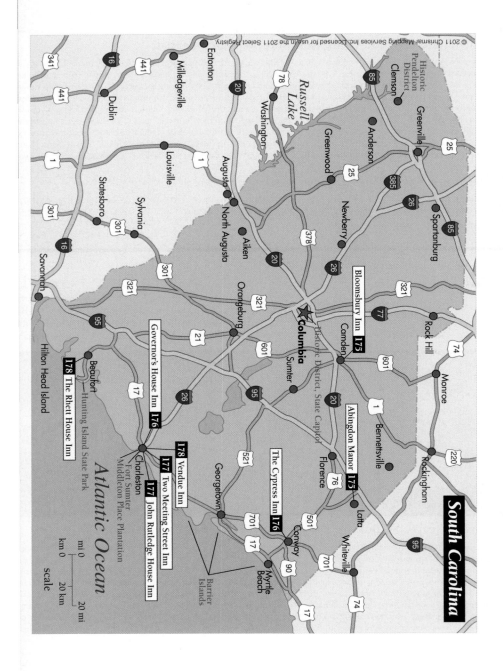

Bloomsbury Inn

www.bloomsburyinn.com
1707 Lyttleton Street, Camden, South Carolina United States 29020
803-432-5858 • Fax 803-432-5858
info@bloomsburyinn.com

Member Since 2010

Bruce A. and Katherine L. Brown

Bloomsbury is known for Southern hospitality, gourmet breakfasts and complimentary socials which include a walk through history with the innkeepers. Located in the historic district, 3 miles off I-20, near fine shops/arts and great restaurants, this award winning property, circa 1849, awaits your arrival. Significant notoriety is derived from the writings of the famous diarist, Mary Boykin Chesnut, author of A Diary from Dixie, and of the diaries used by Dr. C. Vann Woodward to write his Pulitzer Prize winning book, Mary Chesnut's Civil War. From the outside in, this beautifully appointed property is old world charm with modern comforts. Sitting on two acres of manicured grounds, several garden sitting areas and the veranda offer peace and tranquility from the everyday stresses of life. Inside the lovingly restored antebellum home, with uncompromising attention to detail, the Browns have created a warm and welcoming environment for all who traverse the leaded glass doorway. With luxurious amenities and thoughtful touches, Bloomsbury will well-surpass your expectations.

Rates: Enjoy gracious, oversized guest bed chambers, king and queen, with Italian tile private baths, featuring luxury amenities. $159.00 – $215.00 (inclusive rate: full gourmet breakfast, 5:30 pm social, wifi, top amenities, all taxes). Number of Rooms: 4

Cuisine: Delicious gourmet breakfasts, using local products...farm fresh eggs, homemade breads, real butter, aged cheeses, custom-blended coffee. Dining room or veranda; diet restrictions considered. Complimentary social: tea/wine and light hors d'oeuvres.

Nearest Airport: Columbia SC or Charlotte NC are very easy drives. I20, exit 93, N Hwy 521, right @ Chesnut St, left @ Lyttleton St

---

Abingdon Manor

www.abingdonmanor.com
307 Church Street, Latta, SC 29565
888-752-5090 • 843-752-5090
abingdon@bellsouth.net

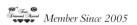 *Member Since 2005*

Innkeepers/Owners Chef Patty & Michael Griffey

The only establishment offering luxury accommodations and fine dining in the Carolinas and Georgia close to I-95, Abingdon Manor is the overnight destination for travelers on the East Coast. Halfway between NYC and Palm Beach, the Inn offers superior lodging, extraordinary cuisine and impeccable service. One of only a select few properties in South Carolina to be awarded a AAA 4-diamond rating annually for both the Inn and Restaurant, Abingdon Manor offers the amenities of a small luxury hotel in an opulent National Register mansion. Located in a quaint, quiet and safe turn of the century village, the Inn features 3 acres of landscaped grounds. For destination travelers, the inn offers a variety of activities including cooking school weekends, historic touring, antiquing, nature-based activities and private country club golf. Food writers and critics consistently rank "The Dining Room at Abingdon Manor" as one of the best restaurants in the Carolinas. Abingdon Manor offers a refined, yet comfortable, atmosphere for the discriminating traveler. Abingdon Manor is a AAA Four Diamond and Mobil Three Star Inn and Restaurant.

Rates: $180/$215. All guestrooms offer ensuite bathrooms, cable TV, working fireplaces, individual temperature controls and wifi. Number of Rooms: 7

Cuisine: The award winning restaurant offers exceptional fine dining nightly. The one seating, pre-fixe meal is crafted daily using the freshest ingredients available and begins with cocktails at 7:00. A full breakfast is offered from 7:45 to 9:00 am.

Nearest Airport: Florence, Myrtle Beach

The Cypress Inn

www.acypressinn.com
16 Elm Street, Conway, SC 29526
800-575-5307 • 843-248-8199 • Fax 843-248-0329
info@acypressinn.com

Member Since 2001

Innkeepers/Owners Hugh & Carol Archer and George & Anne Bullock

Overlooking the Waccamaw River, tucked away in the historic town of Conway, this luxury Inn is near, but distinctly apart from the golf mecca of Myrtle Beach. Located 2 blocks from the downtown area of Conway, the inn is within walking distance of charming shops, restaurants, art galleries and stately live oak trees. Eleven unique guestrooms offer comforts such as en-suite private baths with Jacuzzis, plush robes, individual heat/air, high speed internet (Wi-Fi). We also have an on-site massage therapist. The Inn offers the privacy of a hotel with the personal service of a bed and breakfast. Enjoy the pristine beaches of the South Carolina coast or the peacefulness of an ancient river; an outstanding sculpture garden, or live theater shows. Many extras such as fresh flowers, chocolates and strawberries and a selection of fine wines are available. In addition to being a charming destination, the inn is great for those traveling north or south along the east coast and for the business traveler seeking a relaxing atmosphere. Meeting and banquet facilities are also available.

Rates: $130/$240 B&B. Open year-round. Corporate Rates. Number of Rooms: 12

Cuisine: A wonderful hot breakfast is served each morning. There are fine restaurants within walking distance. A small guest refrigerator is stocked with lemonade, sodas, bottled water. Complimentary wine and beer, cookies and other treats.

Nearest Airport: Myrtle Beach

Governor's House Inn

www.governorshouse.com
117 Broad Street, Charleston, SC 29401
800-720-9812 • 843-720-2070 • Fax 843-805-6549
governorshouse@aol.com

Member Since 2000

General Manager Mary Kittrell/Owners Janice Gardner, Sue and Kevin Shibilski

Governor's House is a magnificent National Historic Landmark (circa 1760) reflecting the Old South's civility and grandeur. Praised by one national publication as "Charleston's most glamorous and sophisticated inn," the former Governor's mansion is the perfect blend of historic splendor and romantic elegance. The mansion's original living rooms, dining room, nine fireplaces, Irish crystal chandeliers, and sweeping southern porches delight guests from around the globe. Harmonize these aristocratic pleasures with luxuries like whirlpool baths, wetbars, high speed Internet and individually controlled room environments, and the result is refined gentility. During the American Revolution, Governor's House was the home of Edward Rutledge, youngest signer of the Declaration of Independence. Today, the inn has been acclaimed as "a flawless urban hideaway" by Southern Living. Visit us online at: www.governorshouse.com

Rates: Governor's House offers 11 guest rooms and suites. Rates are $195-$560, depending on season, and include Southern breakfast, afternoon tea, wine and cheese, evening sherry, bicycles, WiFi, concierge services, and private parking. Number of Rooms: 11

Cuisine: Gourmet breakfast, Low-country afternoon tea. Wine and cheese is also served during the tea hour. Premiere restaurants nearby.

Nearest Airport: Charleston

John Rutledge House Inn

www.johnrutledgehouseinn.com
116 Broad Street, Charleston, SC 29401
800-476-9741 • 843-723-7999 • Fax 843-720-2615
kleslie@charminginns.com

Member Since 1992

Owner Richard Widman

John Rutledge, one of the 55 signers of the U.S. Constitution, built his home in 1763. Now exquisitely restored, it is one of only fifteen homes belonging to those signers to survive and the only one to now accommodate overnight guests. One may choose between the classic elegance of rooms and spacious suites in the grand residence or its two carriage houses. The inn is located in the heart of the Historic District where you are just a few steps away from the famed "South of Broad" neighborhood. Antique and boutique shopping, museums and many other local attractions are just around the corner. Spa services and dinner reservations at acclaimed Circa 1886 Restaurant available nearby to our guests. Afternoon tea, port and sherry and evening brandy are offered in the Signers ballroom where patriots, statesmen and presidents have met. Wireless internet access, nightly turn-down service and breakfast included with your room. A charter member of Historic Hotels of America, designated a National Historic Landmark. AAA◆◆◆◆

Rates: 16 Rooms, $199/$355 and 3 Suites, $299/$435.Open year-round. Daily parking fee. 19 total rooms. Number of Rooms: 19

Cuisine: Breakfast with daily hot item and expanded continental included. Afternoon tea and refreshments. Guests have a choice of having breakfast served in their room, in the courtyard or the Signers Ballroom.

Nearest Airport: Charleston International

Two Meeting Street Inn

www.twomeetingstreet.com
2 Meeting Street, Charleston, SC 29401
888-723-7322 • 843-723-7322
innkeeper2meetst@bellsouth.net

Member Since 1992

Innkeepers/Owners Pete and Jean Spell, Karen Spell Shaw

No other place is like Charleston, and in Charleston, no place is quite like Two Meeting Street Inn- the jewel in the crown of the city's historic inns. From the Inn's gracious Southern veranda- one of the most photographed porches in the South- guests enjoy layers of natural beauty. The Queen Anne Mansion was given as a wedding gift by a bride's loving father in 1890. The inn features a carved English oak stairwell and Tiffany windows, as well as the Spell's collection of antiques and silver. Immediately surrounded by century-old live oaks amid lush gardens with a finely manicured lawn and cherry red azaleas, the Inn overlooks Charleston's historic harbor, tip of the Battery; a few blocks away, world-class dining, modern boutiques, antique shops, art galleries, and historic museum houses await. Guests enjoy a hot Southern breakfast in the oval dining room and gracious afternoon tea on the veranda. Here, the pace slows and the mind rests. The Inn invites you to discard your stress and relish the exquisite civility and romance of Charleston. We await your arrival.

Rates: 9 Unique guest rooms with private baths. Tariffs $225 to $519. Besides breakfast and afternoon tea, our complimentary package includes concierge services, daily newspapers, hi-def cable television, wireless internet and parking. Number of Rooms: 9

Cuisine: Begin your day with Southern pecan coffee and a full, hot breakfast. Be rejuvenated with Lowcountry afternoon tea. Indulge in an enticing array of Key Lime Pound Cake, Plantation Brownies and Benne Wafers. An evening cream sherry ends your day.

Nearest Airport: Charleston International Airport 12 miles from downtown.

Vendue Inn

www.vendueinn.com
19 Vendue Range, Charleston, SC 29401
800-845-7900 • 843-577-7970 • Fax 843-577-2913
info@vendueinn.com

Member Since 2002

General Manager Susie Ridder

Imagine a place where the genteel comfort of a bygone era has been perfectly preserved. Where the style is more sophisticated, the service, more gracious. A place that offers every convenience in an intimate setting that exceeds every expectation. You've found someplace very special at Charleston's Vendue Inn where comfort, cobblestone streets and genteel Southern hospitality await. Charleston, South Carolina is known for its warm hospitality, gracious living, vibrant history, and Southern charm. Experience it all at The Vendue Inn. In the heart of Charleston's Historic District, one block from the harbor and Waterfront Park, the Vendue Inn is nestled in what is known as the French Quarter. Guests consistently remark on the attentive personal service they receive; our staff's hospitality is warm even by Southern standards! The Vendue Inn is a luxury historic small hotel. Our friendly, caring, and experienced staff awaits your arrival.

Rates: 66 Rooms, $129/$379; 15 Suites, $259/$699. Sixty-six beautifully appointed guest rooms and suites. Number of Rooms: 66

Cuisine: Complimentary Southern Family Breakfast. The Rooftop Bar and Restaurant serves lunch and dinner 7 days and features nightly live entertainment. The Library Restaurant is open Tuesday through Saturday from 5:00 PM until 10:00 PM.

Nearest Airport: Charleston

The Rhett House Inn

www.rhetthouseinn.com
1009 Craven Street, Beaufort, SC 29902
888-480-9530 • 843-524-9030 • Fax 843-524-1310
info@rhetthouseinn.com

Member Since 1991

Owners Steve & Marianne Harrison

Located in historic Beaufort. The Rhett House Inn is a beautifully restored 1820s plantation house, furnished with English and American antiques, oriental rugs, fresh orchids, fireplaces and spacious verandas. Lush gardens provide the perfect setting for weddings and parties. Our town was the film site for "Forrest Gump," "Prince of Tides," "The Big Chill" and "White Squal." History-laden Beaufort, Charleston and Savannah offer rich exploring.

Rates: 17 Rooms $175/$315, 8 with fireplaces and whirlpool baths. Open year-round. Number of Rooms: 17

Cuisine: Breakfast, afternoon tea, evening hors d'oeuvres, picnic baskets, desserts.

Nearest Airport: Savannah/Hilton Head International Airport

"The Volunteer State"

Famous for: Cumberland Gap National Historic Park, Cumberland
Caverns, Fall Creek Falls, Grand Ole Opry House, Great Smokey
Mountains, Graceland, Guinness World Research Museum, Country
Music Hall of Fame, Tennessee Valley.

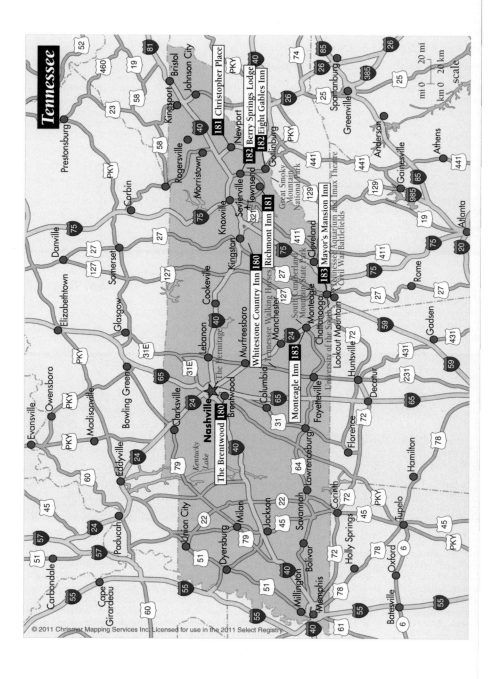

The Brentwood, A Bed & Breakfast

www.brentwoodbandb.com
6304 Murray Lane, Brentwood, TN 37027-6210
800-332-4640 • 615-373-4627 • Fax 615-221-9666
info@brentwoodbandb.com

Member Since 2003

Innkeeper/Owner Bud & Lisa Rusche

The luxurious Brentwood estate is located in one of the finest sections of greater Nashville. The drive over the stream, through the trees and up to the white columns welcomes you to our "Classic Hospitality." The casual elegance of the interior and eclectic combination of traditional furnishings, family and European antiques and objects d'arte creates an atmosphere of quiet relaxation. Private decks overlook the rolling hillside and fireplaces warm the cool evenings. Tours of Civil War sites, Grand Ole Opry, Country Music Hall of Fame, The Ryman, The Hermitage and Antebellum mansions can be arranged. Close to fine dining, country music spots, shopping and downtown Nashville. Only 10 minutes to historic Franklin, golf courses, hiking and nature trails.

Rates: Rooms $135/$175, Suites $210/$250. All suites have custom Jacuzzi tubs, some with fireplace and decks. Number of Rooms: 7

Cuisine: Full breakfast and afternoon refreshments. Special dietary menus with notice. Minutes from fine dining and the historic attractions of Nashville, Belle Meade and Franklin.

Nearest Airport: Nashville International — 20 Minutes

Whitestone Country Inn

www.whitestoneinn.com
1200 Paint Rock Rd., Kingston, TN 37763
888-247-2464 • 865-376-0113 • Fax 865-376-4454
info@whitestoneinn.com

Member Since 2000

Innkeepers/Owners Paul & Jean Cowell

A spectacular 360 acre Country Estate with views of the Smoky Mountains provides you with a serene combination of natural woods and landscaped gardens. Whitestone's rolling hillsides and peaceful surroundings are guaranteed to soothe your soul and calm your spirit. We serve three lavish meals a day and you can nibble on home baked cookies and other delectable treats anytime. Many of our rooms are equipped with the sensuous delight of waterfall-spa showers and private decks. You will be surrounded by 5,400 acres of wildlife-waterfowl refuge and 39,000 acre Watts Bar Lake with opportunities for birding, fishing, kayaking, canoeing, paddle-boating or just rocking on our many porches and swinging in our hammocks. This is the perfect place for vacations, retreats, meetings, weddings or honeymoons. Whitestone Country Inn is one of only seven AAA, four-diamond properties in Tennessee, and was named one of the '10 Most Romantic Inns in America!' Discover a Sanctuary for your Soul.

Rates: 22 Rooms/Suites, $165/$325 per night. Each room and suite has fireplace, king bed, spa tub, TV/DVD, free Wi-Fi, and refrigerator. Number of Rooms: 22

Cuisine: The very best classic cuisine. Enjoy elegant meals in one of our three dining rooms, two overlooking the lake. For between-meal snacks, sample from the cookie jars in our kitchen.

Nearest Airport: Knoxville, Mcghee/Tyson airport

The Richmont Inn of the Great Smokies

www.richmontinn.com
220 Winterberry Lane, Townsend, TN 37882
866-267-7086 • 865-448-6751 • Fax 865-448-6480
innkeeper@richmontinn.com

Member Since 1997

Innkeepers/Owners Jim & Susan Hind

Escape to the Great Smoky Mountains and refresh your body and soul. Relax in an Appalachian cantilevered barn, with 18th century English antiques and French paintings. The secluded mountain top setting provides breathtaking views, privacy and quietness with relaxing amenities such as spa tubs, private balconies, and wood-burning fireplaces, candlelight desserts, and a gourmet breakfast. New Chalet with luxurious suites, ideally suited for small business groups, family socials or a romantic rendezvous. Open air Chapel-in-the-Woods and wedding services for small groups, private and memorable. Rated "Top Inn" by Country Inns and awarded grand prize by Gourmet Magazine for our signature dessert. ". . .may be the most romantic place in the Smokies" –Southern Living. "A wonderful place to recharge your batteries" –Country Magazine "Romantic getaway" –HGTV Richmont Inn

Rates: 9 Rooms, $170/$200, 1 Luxury Suite $200/$220, Chalet Luxury Suites $350/$400; King beds/spa tubs/fireplace/balconies/fridge Number of Rooms: 14

Cuisine: Full French and Swiss style breakfasts. Also complimentary gourmet desserts, flavored coffees by candlelight and afternoon tea. Classic four course Swiss fondue dinners by reservation. Fine Champagnes, wines, and imported beers.

Nearest Airport: Only 30 mins. from McGhee Tyson (Metro Knoxville) airport.

Christopher Place

www.christopherplace.com
1500 Pinnacles Way, Newport, TN 37821
800-595-9441 • 423-623-6555
stay@christopherplace.com

 *Member Since 2000*

Innkeeper/Owner Marston Price

Secluded in the scenic Smoky Mountains on a 200-acre private estate, Christopher Place, an Intimate Resort, is the ideal inn for a romantic, relaxing getaway. An elegant setting is coupled with friendly, unpretentious service and unspoiled, panoramic views. The hosts know your name and greet you with a warm smile. You can fill your days with activities, or with none at all, as the inn is centrally located to most of the sights and attractions of the Smokies and offers many resort amenities of its own. Rooms and Suites are spacious and romantically appointed. Casual fine dining with an extensive wine list completes your romantic retreat. Special requests are encouraged. Voted the area's Best B&B. Named one of the 10 most romantic inns in America; one of the 12 best locations for a fantasy B&B wedding; and a winner of BedandBreakfast.com's Best of the South! We invite you to sit back, enjoy, and overlook nothing but the Smoky's.

Rates: 4 Rooms, $175; 4 Suites, $275/$330. Suites offer double whirlpools, woodburning fireplaces, private dinning, cable TV, and scenic views. Number of Rooms: 9

Cuisine: Hearty mountain breakfast served at your leisure. Picnics and back-pack lunches. Intimate 4-course candlelit dinners by reservation at tables set for two in our exquisite dining room overlooking the mountains.

Nearest Airport: Knoxville

Eight Gables Inn

www.eightgables.com
219 North Mountain Trail, Gatlinburg, TN 37738
800-279-5716 • 865-430-3344 • Fax 865-430-8767
eightgablesinn@aol.com

Member Since 2002

Owners Lee Bennett & Guy Jacobs

Eight Gables Inn, The Smoky Mountains' Premier Country Inn, offers 21 luxurious rooms and suites. All rooms have private baths, cable TV, feather top beds, plush bathrobes, telephones, personal amenities and several feature the warmth of fireplaces and whirlpool tubs. Our rates include a full served breakfast, and evening dessert. Conveniently located on the drive between Gatlinburg and Pigeon Forge, our peaceful setting lends itself to a casual elegance and relaxing charm. Eight Gables is easily accessible to all the area attractions including the Smoky Mountain National Park. Knoxville and the airport is just 30 miles away. We are also on the trolley route. AAA Four Diamond rated.

Rates: 10 Rooms $125/145; 9 Deluxe Suites $150/175. Diamond Suites $175/205, TV/VCR/CD, complementary designer coffees, teas, sodas and bottled water, bath robes, most with King beds, fireplaces, Jacuzzi . Number of Rooms: 21

Cuisine: Full seated service breakfast, and evening dessert.

Nearest Airport: Knoxville TN, McGee Tyson

Berry Springs Lodge

www.berrysprings.com
2149 Seaton Springs Road, Sevierville, TN 37862
888-760-8297 • 865-908-7935
stay@berrysprings.com

Member Since 2005

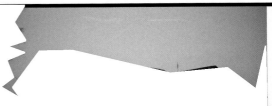

Innkeeper/Owner Patrick & Sue Eisert

Perched on a 33 acre secluded scenic ridge top in the Great Smoky Mountains, this lodge offers the perfect picture of solitude and romance. Take a leisurely walk down to the bass or catfish ponds and try your luck. Ride bikes, play horseshoes, relax in a hammock or just sit back and enjoy the beautiful views of the Smoky Mountains from your rocking chair on the main deck of the lodge. With this remote setting, one would not guess the lodge is within a 15-minute drive of most area destinations, including Gatlinburg, Pigeon Forge, Sevierville and the "Great Smoky Mountain National Park" Awards and Accolades 2007 Trip Advisor: "Top-Rated B&B in TN" 2006 USA Today: "10 great places to settle into for fall viewing" 2005 Blue Ridge Country: "Tennessee's Berry Springs Lodge Gives the Gift of Trees" 2004 Arrington's Inn Traveler: "Best Scenic Mount View" 2003 Arrington's Inn Traveler: "Best Inn for Rest and Relaxation" 2001 Better Bed and Breakfasts: "Enjoy the Best of Both Worlds at Berry Springs Lodge"

Rates: 9 rooms. $169/$229, 2 Suites $229/$269. Includes breakfast and evening desserts. Open year-round. Number of Rooms: 11

Cuisine: Country gourmet breakfast. Lunch and dinner picnic baskets are available upon advanced request. Local restaurants within 15 minutes. Nightly signature desserts.

Nearest Airport: Knoxville

Monteagle Inn & Retreat Center

www.monteagleinn.com
204 West Main Street, P.O. Box 39, Monteagle, TN 37356
888-480-3245 • 931-924-3869 • Fax 931-924-3867
suites@monteagleinn.com

Member Since 2006

Innkeeper/Owner Jim Harmon

Monteagle Inn is located atop the Cumberland Plateau just minutes away from The University of the South, with hiking trails, antique shops and superb restaurants. The Living areas are outfitted with overstuffed furnishings graced with special antiques, which invite you to relax and experience the mountaintop. The inn's large living room with 4 distinct sitting areas encourages you to curl up on one of the oversized sofas with a good book. A welcoming fire in the cool months adds to the total relaxation. Picturesque balconies, a spacious front porch and garden courtyards provide private outdoor relaxation hide-a-ways. Crisp white linens welcome you to relax and enjoy your bedroom with hot cookies and flavored teas. The spacious dining room is filled with light and color from windows on 3 sides while Provencal linens grace the windows and tables. Brightly-patterned Italian urns, bowls and dishes serve as a backdrop for your gourmet breakfast specialties. Monteagle Inn is the perfect place for your getaway and business retreats, family reunions and wedding functions.

Rates: All of the rooms have spacious private baths and are furnished with luxurious white bed and bath linens including coverlets; fluffy towels, the most comfortable pillows. Wireless DSL is available throughout the Inn. $160/$265. Number of Rooms: 13

Cuisine: Extensive herb & vegetable gardens help create acclaimed "mountain gourmet" breakfast.New Orleans Praline French Toast, Mays Eggs Bearnaise, Garden Fresh Frittatas & Herb Roasted Sweet Potato Fries are just a few bountiful items prepared each morning.

Nearest Airport: Chattanooga-45 miles<n>Nashville-85 miles

Mayor's Mansion Inn

www.mayorsmansioninn.com
801 Vine Street, Chattanooga, TN 37403
423-265-5000 • Fax 423-265-5555
info@mayorsmansioninn.com

 *Member Since 1996*

Innkeepers/OwnersMC LADD Hospitality LLC

Chattanooga, Tennessee's only AAA 4-Diamond Bed and Breakfast Inn, where luxury meets privacy in a timeless setting.The Mayor's Mansion Inn built in 1889, is conveniently located a mile away from the Tennessee Aquarium and many other popular Chattanooga attractions, many within walking distance from the Inn. Boasting 11 beautiful guest rooms and suites, the Mayor's Mansion Inn offers peaceful outdoor spaces, delicious breakfasts, weekend appetizer hour and a level of service unlike any other. Allow our friendly staff to recommend a special restaurant, local event or attraction during your stay. Named "one of the best inns in the South" by National Geographic Traveler Magazine, this historic Victorian Romanesque-style inn offers Southern charm blended with the luxury of modern amenities. Our unique and elegant spaces are also available for weddings, private dinners, corporate retreats and meetings. The Mayor's Mansion Inn has been honored by the National Trust for Historic Preservation and located in the Fort Wood Historic Neighborhood.

Rates: $130-$295.Seasonal, Corporate, Group rates available. Number of Rooms: 11

Cuisine: Start your morning with a 3-course breakfast served in our elegant Tiffany Dining Room or "en suite". Hors d'ouerves Friday & Saturday evenings. Find more than 60 restaurants in a 2 mile radius of the the Inn or order from over 20 restaurants nearby.

Nearest Airport: Chattanooga Metro Airport-13 miles, Nashville Intl-135 miles, Atlanta Intl-125 miles

"The Lone Star State"

Famous for: The Alamo, San Antonio Missions National Historic Park, Enchanted Rock, Big Bend National Park, Padre Island National Seashore, Marfa Lights, Guadalupe Mountains National Park, Lyndon B. Johnson Space Center.

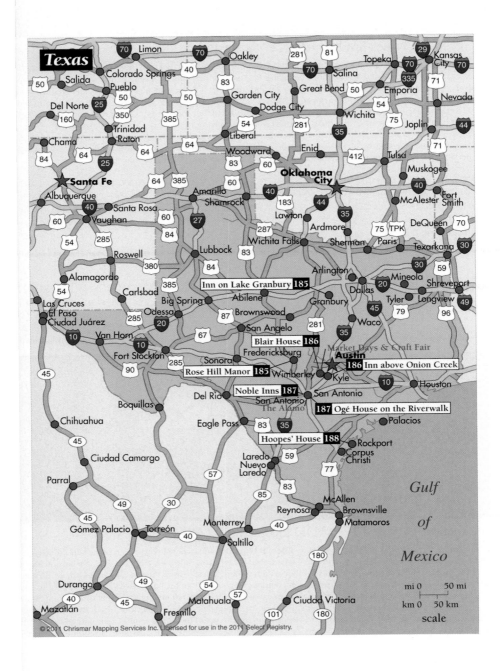

Inn on Lake Granbury

www.innonlakegranbury.com
205 West Doyle Street, Granbury, TX 76048
877-573-0046 • 817-573-0046
info@innonlakegranbury.com

Member Since 2006

Innkeepers/Owners Cathy Casey and Jim Leitch

The Inn has 13 upscale guestrooms and suites on almost three acres directly on Lake Granbury. Each room has an oversized king bed, fabulous guest robes, private shower (some with steam showers and heated bathroom floors), some with jetted tubs, some with lake views, and all with wireless Internet access. Experience our flagstone encased pool with tanning ledge and waterfall or sit on the swing under 200 year old oak trees for a spectacular view of the lake. Walk less than three blocks to the historic square for shopping and fine dining. Complimentary appetizers and beverages are served every afternoon along with a full breakfast each morning.

Rates: $215/$285 Sunday-Thursday and $235/$335 Friday and Saturday. Number of Rooms: 13

Cuisine: Rates include a full gourmet breakfast and appetizers and beverages each afternoon. Lunch and dinner for group stays upon request.

Nearest Airport: Dallas Fort Worth Airport

Rose Hill Manor

www.rose-hill.com
2614 Upper Albert Road, Near Fredericksburg, TX 78671
877-767-3445 • 830-644-2247
rosehill@ktc.com

 *Member Since 2006*

Innkeepers/Owners Robert & Patricia VanderLyn

Rose Hill Manor is the only place in Texas where you can stay at a AAA Four Diamond inn with a fine dining restaurant and walk to a winery and tasting room. Our graciously appointed and spacious accommodations offer all the amenities required by the Four Diamond standard. Enjoy the celebrated cuisine of the on-site gourmet restaurant, where great meals are creatively prepared and wines are poured from a thoughtfully chosen cellar highlighted by fine vintages from around the world and premium liquor. Nestled in the heart of the Texas wine country, Rose Hill is located only fifteen minutes from the historical town of Fredericksburg, Texas and serves as an excellent base for exploring the region's best wineries, historical architecture, shopping and museums. Rose Hill has received critical acclaim for both the lodging and restaurant in Gourmet Magazine, Wine Spectator, Victoria Magazine, The Dallas Morning News, and Texas Highways. Come escape to an oasis of tranquility, Texas hill country style!

Rates: 1 Queen Suites, $155/$249. 3 King Suites, $155/$249. 8 King Cottages, $155/$249. Number of Rooms: 12

Cuisine: Complimentary multiple-course breakfast to overnite guests at private tables. On-Site upscale gourmet restaurant with outstanding wine list, each Wednesday through Sunday night – open to both our guests and the general public.

Nearest Airport: Either the San Antonio or Austin airport ~ 1 hour away. Airport for small planes in Fredericksburg – 15 minutes.

Blair House Inn

www.blairhouseinn.com
100 W. Spoke Hill Drive, Wimberley, TX 78676
877-549-5450 • 512-847-1111
info@blairhouseinn.com

Member Since 1998

Innkeepers/Owners Mike and Vickie Schneider

Conveniently located just minutes from the Wimberley Square, Blair House Inn is situated on 22 peaceful acres featuring breathtaking hill country vistas. Meticulous service, warm hospitality, delectable food and luxury amenities provide the ultimate in comfort. This inviting inn is light and airy and features one of the best art galleries in Wimberley. A pool and whirlpool spa set in the hillside allows for spectacular views while relaxing. Blair House also provides spacious and attractive common areas including a living room with a fireplace, a television/game room, a library, plus a front porch with beautiful sunset views and a patio by the herb garden. Guests can enjoy a massage, use the sauna, hike the grounds, venture out on one of the bicycles or just nap in a hammock. Rated third nationwide as "Best Evening Cuisine" and "Best B&B for Relaxing and Unwinding," by Inn Traveler Magazine and the "Best Breakfast in Texas" – Southern Living.

Rates: 3 Rooms, Main House, $150/$170. 5 Suites, $215/$248. 4 Individual Cottages, $289/$345. Open year-round. Number of Rooms: 12

Cuisine: Full 3-course gourmet breakfast, evening dessert, 5-course fixed menu gourmet dinner on Saturday evenings. Complimentary beverages.

Nearest Airport: Austin/San Antonio

The Inn Above Onion Creek

www.innaboveonioncreek.com
4444 W FM 150, Kyle, TX 78640
800-579-7686 • 512-268-1617 • Fax 512-268-1090
info@innaboveonioncreek.com

Member Since 2003

Innkeeper Amy Dolan

Tucked away on 88 acres at the end of our mile-long driveway, the Inn Above Onion Creek awaits you with 15-mile hill country views. While you may feel a million miles away from everything, the Inn is conveniently located near great wineries on the Texas Wine Trail, excellent shopping, and many popular hill country attractions. Each night's stay includes a three-course dinner and full hot breakfast, fresh flowers in your room from our garden and all the homemade cookies you can eat! Each of the twelve rooms features classic antique pieces, luxurious linens, fireplace, wireless internet, flat panel television and DVD player. Relaxing by the pool, sitting on a porch to read your favorite book, or taking a hike on our miles of hiking trails are appealing ways to enjoy a day at the Inn. Our Spa offers relaxing massages, body and skin treatments for those looking for a more pampering stay. Come see why the Inn Above Onion Creek has 100's of glowing reviews. We're destined to become your favorite getaway.

Rates: 12 rooms, incl. 2 suites, 2 cottages: $199/$499. All w/fireplace & porch, 6 w/whirlpool bath. Number of Rooms: 12

Cuisine: 3-course dinner served at 6:00 each evening. Full hot breakfast served from 8:30-10:00 each morning. Complimentary coffee, tea, cold drinks, homemade cookies and fruit available 24 hours a day.

Nearest Airport: Austin Bergstrom

Noble Inns

www.nobleinns.com
107 Madison Street, San Antonio, TX 78204
800-242-2770 • 210-223-2353 • Fax 210-226-5812
stay@nobleinns.com

Member Since 2001

Owners Don & Liesl Noble

Don and Liesl Noble, sixth-generation San Antonians, invite guests to experience the rich history and ambiance of San Antonio. Noble Inns comprise The Jackson House (JH) and Aaron Pancoast Carriage House (PCH), two 1890s-era historic landmarks, located four houses apart in the King William Historic District. Both provide Victorian elegance with modern luxuries and superior amenities for the discerning business or leisure traveler, and are just off the Riverwalk near all downtown sites, including the Alamo, convention center and Alamodome. All rooms include private marble bath, gas fireplace with antique mantel, antique furnishings and elegant fabrics, complimentary high-speed internet (wired and/or wireless), color cable TV, private phone w/voice mail, custom guest robes, and central air conditioning. Gardens feature two pools and heated spa. Two-person whirlpool tub in bath, canopy bed, DVD player w/complimentary DVD library are available in certain suites and rooms. Complete your experience by booking transportation in our classic 1960 Rolls Royce Silver Cloud II.

Rates: 7 Rooms, $179/269; 2 Suites, $239/299. Inquire about special group and corporate rates, discounts, and last minute specials. Number of Rooms: 9

Cuisine: The Jackson House features a delicious full breakfast, afternoon refreshments, evening sherry and port. Aaron Pancoast Carriage House features full breakfast for adult groups at the Oge House and expanded continental breakfast for groups w/ children.

Nearest Airport: San Antonio International — 9 mi./13 min. via expressway to downtown.

The Ogé Inn on the Riverwalk

www.nobleinns.com
209 Washington St, San Antonio, TX 78204
800-242-2770 • 210-223-2353 • Fax 210-226-5812
stay@nobleinns.com

Member Since 1994

Owners Don & Liesl Noble

Boasting 1.5 landscaped acres directly on the famous RiverWalk in the King William Historic District, this 1857 Antebellum Mansion is one of Texas' historic architectural gems. With its grand verandas and spacious rooms, it is known for its elegance, quiet comfort and luxury. Furnished in European and American antiques, all rooms have been recently redecorated and feature a king or queen bed w/down featherbed, private bath w/tub and shower, flat-panel TV w/cable and DVD player, DVD library access, phone, custom robes and guest refrigerator. Delicious full breakfast served at private tables in the dining room or on front veranda. Most rooms have fireplace and/or porch. All suites feature luxurious granite baths with double Jacuzzi tub and separate shower, multi-room stereo system w/CD player, fireplace and porch (one w/private Riverwalk balcony). Conveniently located downtown near the Alamo, convention center, Alamodome, shopping, dining and entertainment. Amenities for business travelers include complimentary high-speed Internet, in-room desk, and flexible breakfast options

Rates: 7 Rooms and 3 Suites on 3 floors, $229/$449. Inquire about special corporate and group rates, as well as specials and last minute discounts. San Antonio's only 4 diamond inn. Number of Rooms: 10

Cuisine: Delicious full breakfast, afternoon refreshments including home-made cookies, evening sherry and port.

Nearest Airport: San Antonio International – 9 mi./13 min. via expressway to downtown.

Hoopes' House

www.hoopeshouse.com
417 N. Broadway, Rockport, TX 78382
800-924-1008 • Fax 361-790-9288
hoopeshouse@sbcglobal.net

Member Since 2010

General Manager Paula Sargent

Built in the 1890's, the historic Hoopes' House in Rockport, Texas has been meticulously renovated and restored to its original splendor. The sunny yellow inn commands a panoramic view of Rockport Harbor and is within walking distance of museums, shops, galleries and restaurants. The main house consists of four charming guest rooms, each with a private bath. For those wanting a more private experience, a new wing houses four additional guest rooms, each beautifully appointed. The grounds feature a pool, a hot tub and a gazebo. Elegant but casual, the Hoopes' House combines modern luxury with old world charm. Hardwood floors, 12 foot ceilings, intricately carved fireplaces, crown molding, fine art and antiques recall another time. . . another era. Relax with a good book in the parlor. Enjoy the Gulf breeze under the gazebo. Linger over morning coffee in the sun-room. Listen to the call of the gulls on the porch. Delight in the pleasures of a slower time.

Rates: $175 B&B, full facility available for $1,400/night. Closed Christmas week. No pets allowed. Number of Rooms: 8

Cuisine: Breakfast is served each morning from 9 am to 10 am in either the formal dining room, gazebo or sun-room. Breakfast fare includes pineapple casserole, fresh fruit, blueberry pancakes and cream cheese bread pudding for starters.

Nearest Airport: Located 35 miles north of Corpus Christi

"The Green Mountain State"

Famous for: Maple Syrup, Dairies, Lakes, Forests, Mountains, and Skiing.

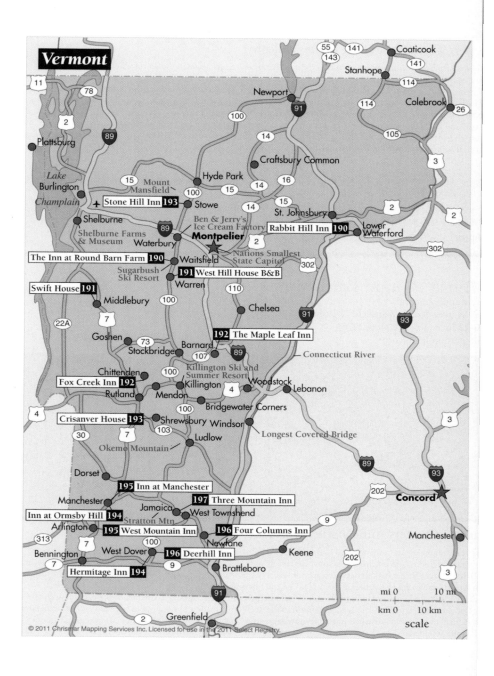

Rabbit Hill Inn

www.rabbithillinn.com
48 Lower Waterford Rd., PO Box 55, Lower Waterford, VT 05848
800-76-BUNNY • 802-748-5168 • Fax 802-748-8342
info@rabbithillinn.com

Member Since 1990

Innkeepers/Owners Brian & Leslie Mulcahy

Even in these fast-paced, continuously connected times, there are still a few places in the world where one can escape to unwind and spend some special time with that special someone. Named One of the World's Top 100 Hotels by Travel+Leisure Magazine, Rabbit Hill Inn offers all the luxuries that one would come to expect — fireplaces, double spa tubs, fine bath amenities, and more; yet what sets Rabbit Hill apart from just any nice place to stay is the warmth, comfort, and personal caring provided by its long-time hands-on innkeepers and wonderful staff. Dining at the inn is truly outstanding. Sophisticated, locally sourced food at an intimate, candlelit table adds to a most romantic evening — comfortable and always unpretentious. In-room massage, free wi-fi, and a myriad of seasonal activities. Zagat Guide said it best: "...this just might be the most romantic place on the planet...!"

Rates: Classic Rms: $199/$239 B&B; Superior Rms w/fireplace: $259/$299 B&B; Luxury Rms w/whirlpool & fireplace: $335/$399 B&B
Number of Rooms: 19

Cuisine: Full country breakfast and afternoon tea and pastries included. Locally sourced, yet sophisticated multi-course dinner by our very talented chef team, in our romantic and intimate dining room. Beer, wine, and spirits available in our Snooty Fox Pub.

Nearest Airport: Manchester, NH (MHT)-2 hours; Burlington, VT (BTV)-2 hours; Logan Int'l (BOS)-3 hrs.

The Inn at Round Barn Farm

www.theroundbarn.com
1661 East Warren Road, Waitsfield, VT 05673
802-496-2276 • Fax 802-496-2276
lodging@theroundbarn.com

Member Since 2000

Innkeepers/Owners AnneMarie DeFreest & Tim L. Piper

We invite you to our elegant, romantic Bed & Breakfast Inn, located amidst 245 acres of lush green hills, flower-covered meadows, graceful ponds, and extensive perennial gardens in Vermont's Green Mountains. This four season retreat in the Sugarbush/Mad River Valley has offered an escape for lovers of the arts, history, and the outdoors since 1987. The interior of the Inn is memorable; the restoration impeccable. The Inn offers wireless throughout. The Inn's 12 guest rooms are individually decorated while maintaining refurbished wide-board pine floors covered in oriental rugs, beautiful wallpapers in a palette of rich tones, decorative accents and attention to the details that matter. In winter, our meadows and woodlands are covered in a blanket of snow. Snowshoe trails and snowshoes are available for our guests to experience the magic of our Vermont winter wonderland. In the summer enjoy concerts, theater, our very own three week opera festival in June and a variety of outdoor activities. Our Innkeepers (and freshly baked cookies) await your arrival at the Inn.

Rates: Rates $175/$335. Tempur-Pedic beds, down comforters, whirlpool tubs, steam showers, green products, gas fireplaces, individual heat and A/C. Number of Rooms: 12

Cuisine: As founding members of the Vermont Fresh Network and having our own certified organic garden, our breakfasts and hors d'oeuvres are prepared with seasonal/local ingredients. Dinner is enjoyed at one of 15 area restaurants.

Nearest Airport: 43 Minutes from the Burlington International Airport (BTV)

Swift House Inn

www.swifthouseinn.com
25 Stewart Lane, Middlebury, VT 05753
866-388-9925 • 802-388-9925 • Fax 802-388-9927
info@swifthouseinn.com

Member Since 2005

Innkeepers/Owners Dan & Michele Brown

A historic 20-room former governor's mansion, the Swift House Inn is Middlebury's only in-town Country Inn, and offers the essence of New England warmth. Large, comfortable rooms provide modern amenities in period decor. The Inn's three buildings are on five acres with extensive lawns and gardens. Enjoy a casual dinner in the bar, on the deck, or in Jessica's Restaurant. Relax, sip a glass of wine by the fireplace, or ponder your favorite book. Every window frames a picture of country tranquility, yet shops, museums, and Middlebury College are a short walk away. The Town Hall Theater and College bring numerous world class performing artists to the area with performances most weekends. Enjoy hiking the Trail Around Middlebury or in the nearby Green Mountains. Bike the Champlain Valley, fly fish our numerous rivers and creeks, or participate in water activities on nearby lakes Champlain and Dunmore. Downhill and cross country ski areas are just a short drive. Bring your bike, golf clubs, fly rod or just come to relax. After a busy day enjoy the sauna or steam shower.

Rates: 20 Rooms in three buildings $129/$299. Many with fireplaces and two person whirlpool tubs. Individual heat and A/C controls, satellite TV Number of Rooms: 20

Cuisine: Full Breakfast from 7:30 to 9:30. Dinner in Jessica's is served 4 nights a week winter/spring and 5 nights summer/fall; changing menu prepared with many local Vermont products. Full bar service and extensive wine list, Wine Spectator Award

Nearest Airport: Burlington International Airport, 35 miles Albany Airport 112 miles

---

West Hill House Bed & Breakfast

www.westhillbb.com
1496 West Hill Road, Warren, VT 05674
800-209-1049 • 802-496-7162
innkeepers@westhillbb.com

Member Since 2009

Innkeepers/Owners Peter & Susan MacLaren

Nestled in the serene setting of the Green Mountains, this beautiful 1850s home on a quiet country road and surrounded by gorgeous perennial gardens offers a peaceful retreat from the rush of everyday life. Just minutes away, the shops, artisans and marvelous restaurants of Warren and Waitsfield await you. A four seasons destination, the B&B is located just 1 mile from Sugarbush's ski and golf resort — adjacent to its Robert Trent Jones, Sr. championship golf course, and 7 miles from Mad River Glen, America's only cooperatively owned major ski area. The Catamount Ski Trail crosses our property and we are just a short distance from hiking on the famous Vermont Long Trail. An excellent base for enjoying the many attractions and activities of central Vermont, our classic Vermont B&B offers comfort, hospitality and delicious breakfasts. The guest rooms have gas fireplaces, A/C, free phone calls and WiFi and large ensuite bathrooms with Jacuzzis and/or steam showers. An ideal spot for elopements, weddings up to 80 guests, business retreats, and most especially a place to relax.

Rates: Open year round. $140-$250 per night double occupancy. 2-night minimum stay preferred. Queen or king beds. Self-Catering apartment available weekly. Number of Rooms: 8

Cuisine: Our sumptuous breakfast starts with fruit juice, home made bread or muffins & a fruit dish. A tantalizing hot entree gives your taste buds a morning treat. Hot beverages, home-made cookies and honor bar are always available. Single Malt bar in evening.

Nearest Airport: Burlington International (BTV) is a beautiful 45 mile drive from the B&B.

The Maple Leaf Inn

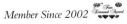

www.mapleleafinn.com
PO Box 273, 5890 Vermont Route 12, Barnard, VT 05031
800-516-2753 • 802-234-5342 • Fax 802-234-6456
innkeeper@mapleleafinn.com

Member Since 2002

Innkeepers/Owners Mike & Nancy Boyle

We welcome you to refresh your spirit and restore your soul in this pastoral corner of Vermont where it is nestled snugly within sixteen acres of maple and birch trees. Enjoy hiking, biking, golfing, cross-country skiing, and snow-shoeing on the trails nearby, or go fishing, canoeing and kayaking at nearby Silver Lake. Fantastic restaurants are a short drive away. Each luxurious, light-filled guest room has its own personality and charm with crisp linens, comfy duvets and handmade quilts. Individually controlled central heating/air-conditioning, heated bathroom tile floors and a pillow library all add to your personal comfort. Wood-burning fireplaces are set daily for your convenience and a collection of romantic videos awaits your viewing. Snacks, sodas, coffee, tea and bottled water are available at any time. Complementary wine and beer are served every day. Memorable gourmet breakfasts are prepared fresh each morning and served at candlelit tables for two. Our inn has been awarded the AAA Four Diamond award for 14 years

Rates: $140/$290 B&B. Spacious guest rooms with king beds, luxurious private baths w/whirlpools, WIFI. Number of Rooms: 7

Cuisine: A gourmet three-course breakfast is served at candlelit tables, and light afternoon refreshments are served in the parlor at check-in. Complimentary coffee, tea, sodas and snacks. Dinners available upon request. Beer and wine available.

Nearest Airport: Burlington, VT; Manchester, NH; Boston, MA

Fox Creek Inn

www.foxcreekinn.com
49 Dam Road, Chittenden, VT 05737
800-707-0017 • 802-483-6213 • Fax 802-483-2623
innkeeper@foxcreekinn.com

Member Since 1998

Innkeepers/Owners Jim and Sandy Robertson

Just the way you have always pictured a Country Inn. Here is the Vermont you have been searching for. There are a myriad of activities: hiking, biking and water sports in summer and downhill alpine and cross country skiing in winter. Relaxing in front of a fireplace or sitting on the front porch with a glass of wine, these are the times when memories are made. Once the home of William Barstow, you can easily imagine the family entertaining their friends, the Fords, Firestones, and his partner, Thomas Edison. We strive to keep the tradition of entertaining alive. Fox Creek is an inn full of charm and casual elegance and with a gentle pace that permits you to relax and enjoy the moment.

Rates: 8 Rooms, all with private baths most with fireplaces and spa tubs. B&B $175-285/$215-325 high season. Number of Rooms: 8

Cuisine: Enjoy a full Vermont country breakfast. A four course dinner, by advance reservation, featuring the freshest local ingredients. Select a wine from our wine list with many older vintages. Enjoy our quaint pub that features single malt scotch.

Nearest Airport: Rutland and Burlington

Crisanver House

www.crisanver.com
1434 Crown Point Road, Shrewsbury, VT 05738
800-492-8089 • 802-492-3589 • Fax 802-492-3480
info@crisanver.com

Member Since 2005

Innkeepers/Owners B. Michael & Carol Calotta

"It is a truth, universally acknowledged, that a man or woman in need of repose in beautiful countryside with most elegant surroundings and food fit for the gods, should repair immediately to Crisanver House where they will be superbly looked after." A painstakingly restored 200 year old farmhouse, amid 120 acres at 2000 feet, commands an exquisite mountain panorama in Central Vermont, minutes off the highway. Unscale decor features original woodboard floors graced by Oriental rugs and an eclectic mix of antiques, paintings, sculpture and a splendid new conservatory. Wood burning fireplaced living room with a baby grand piano. Pool, tennis, bocce, shuffleboard, hiking, pond, snowshoeing on site. Shopping, museums, golf, cheese and microbrewery trails nearby. "Listed "1000 Places to See in US and Canada"

Rates: 4 Deluxe Rooms Main House $145-$265, 2 Suites Main House $245-395, 3 Cottage Deluxe Rooms $205-375. Number of Rooms: 9

Cuisine: Epicurean dining featuring the freshest of local offerings and our garden harvest. Complimentary served full country breakfast. Afternoon tea. Prix fixe candlelight dinner by reservation. Fine European wines. Many restaurants nearby.

Nearest Airport: Rutland Regional – 10 minutes; Albany, Hartford, Burlington International – each 2 hours

---

Stone Hill Inn

www.stonehillinn.com
89 Houston Farm Road, Stowe, VT 05672
802-253-6282 • Fax 802-253-7415
stay@stonehillinn.com

Member Since 2002

Owner Amy Jordan/Innkeepers Skip & Sharon Peckham

This inn was created to be a peaceful, romantic, one-of-a-kind getaway. Relax in your bubbling, fireside Jacuzzi for two—every room has one—along with many other thoughtful touches & indulgent amenities. All rooms offer WiFi, iPod docks, LCD TV w/DVD, luxury linens, robes, and more. Schedule a massage by the fireplace in the privacy of your room, or outside in our summer perennial gardens. In winter, glide down the hill on the toboggan, borrow snowshoes and explore the woods, or enjoy the hot tub under the stars. Stowe is known as the 'Ski Capital of the East,' but this scenic mountain village offers much to do year-round. After dinner at one of 40 local restaurants, return to the Inn for billiards, games, and puzzles by the huge stone fireplace, or select a movie from our library (popcorn provided!). Stone Hill Inn is proud to have received a perfect score in Select Registry's rigorous quality inspection. Chosen one of the Twelve Best B&Bs in North America, Forbes.com. Recommended by the New York Times, Boston Globe, Montreal Gazette, Washington Post, and USA Today.

Rates: $330-$425 (varies by season). Visit Stone Hill Inn.com for exact seasonal rates and seasonal packages. Number of Rooms: 9

Cuisine: A full country breakfast is served daily in the window-walled breakfast room at tables set for two. An evening hors d'oeuvre is offered at 5 PM. Coffee, tea and soft drinks are complimentary and available in our 24-hour guest pantry. BYOB if you wish.

Nearest Airport: Burlington, VT (45 min). Morrisville (10 min) has a small airport for private aircraft.

Hermitage Inn

🍴🍴🍴 ♀

www.hermitageinn.com
25 Handle Road, PO Box 2210, West Dover, VT 05356
(877) 464-3511 • (802) 464-3511 • Fax 802)464-3575
info@hermitageinn.com

Member Since 2010

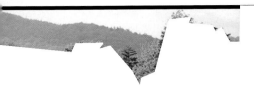

General Manager Steven O'Hern

Welcome to an exquisite retreat where traditional Vermont hospitality meets 21st century luxury, both formal and casual. Upon arrival, guests enter an elegant 18th century Vermont farmhouse with soft music and lights, enchanting art at every turn, a warm fireplace, and an equally warm staff that addresses you by name. With the rustic delights of southern Vermont at your doorstep, you'll feel at home the way home should be. Spring, summer and fall activities include fly-fishing in our stocked trout pond, hiking and bicycling miles of trails through and beyond our own trails, and garden tours. Off-site activities include the Clay Shooting School, golf courses, and water activities. In winter, at the inn, our guests can enjoy cross-country skiing, snowshoeing, ice-skating, tubing, a sauna and hot tubs, and downhill skiing at Mount Snow. We also have a full fitness room, spa facilities, and a game room. We host special culinary events in our exhibition wine cellar. We warmly welcome you to enjoy the epitome of Vermont country luxury, a sublime escape from everyday life.

Rates: Superior: $195-$245 Deluxe: $245-$295 Queen: $295-$345 King: $320-$370 Carriage House: $345-$395 Number of Rooms: 15

Cuisine: The Hermitage is a culinary experience to relish, featuring fresh Vermont ingredients in innovative fare. Enjoy fine dining in our Main Dining Room or lite fare in our pub and tavern. Extensive wine list. Full Vermont breakfast included with your stay.

Nearest Airport: Albany, NY: 1 hour 45 minutes Hartford, CT: 2 hours

---

The Inn at Ormsby Hill

🍴 ♀

www.ormsbyhill.com
1842 Main Street, Historic Route 7A, Manchester , VT 05255
802-362-1163 • 800-670-2841 • Fax 802-362-5176
stay@ormsbyhill.com

Member Since 1996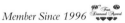

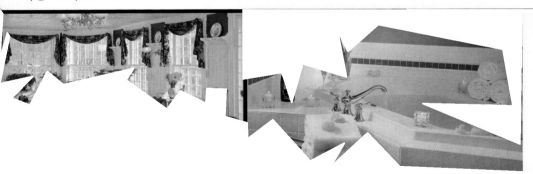

Innkeepers/Owners Ted and Chris Sprague

Experience the romance of the past, in the luxury of the present. Steal away to a magical bed and breakfast, rich with history (c. 1764), and nestled in the Green Mountains. ". . .arguably one of the most welcoming inns in all of New England." Lonely Planet. Renowned for comfort, heartfelt hospitality, and profound attention to detail. Be pampered in bed chambers with canopies, fireplaces, air-conditioning, digital flat-screen televisions, and endless amenities. Luxurious bathrooms with Jacuzzis for two; some with two-person steam saunas and views of the fireplace. ". . .the elegance of the bed chambers and public rooms is matched by the sumptuousness of the inn's breakfast offerings." Three times an Editors' Pick — Yankee Magazine. If our lavish rooms and nationally-acclaimed breakfasts aren't enough to take your breath away, our spectacular views of the Taconic and Green Mountains will. Proud recipients of the AAA Four Diamond Award for the past twelve years – a Manchester inn exclusive. One enchanting evening with us and you'll understand why.

Rates: 8 Rooms and 2 suites, all with fireplace and Jacuzzi for two, $205/$425 B&B. Open year-round. Number of Rooms: 10

Cuisine: "Expect truly memorable and bountiful breakfasts!" – Andrew Harper's Hideaway Report. ". . .a breakfast that'll knock your socks off. . ." – Yankee Magazine's Travel Guide. ". . .perhaps the best breakfasts in Vermont," says New England Travel.

Nearest Airport: Albany, New York (1 hour 15 minutes). Hartford, Connecticut (2 hours 15 minutes).

The Inn at Manchester

www.innatmanchester.com
3967 Main Street, P.O. Box 41, Manchester , VT 05254
802-362-1793 • 800-273-1793 • Fax 802-362-3218
innkeeper@innatmanchester.com

Member Since 2008

Innkeepers/Owners Frank & Julie Hanes

Unforgettable personality and unlimited possibilities await you at one of Vermont's most inviting getaways, The Inn at Manchester. Tucked away in the breathtaking landscape of the Taconic and Green Mountains in Vermont's cultural haven, Manchester — where there's something for everyone year round. Golf, skiing, hiking, fishing, shopping, theatre or art, Manchester and the Mountains has something for every taste. As always, there is no rule you ever have to leave the inn! Unwind beside the hearth in the living room, or over a game of chess in the cozy den. Maybe take a stroll around our beautiful grounds, a dip in the pool, or just relax in a rocker on the porch. Then drop in for a cocktail in the Nineteenth Room, our fully licensed pub — one of the places where guests gather to relax and socialize. We look forward to welcoming you to the Inn at Manchester, a Gem in the Green Mountains.

Rates: Our rates run from $155 to $295. Number of Rooms: 18

Cuisine: We pride ourselves on a full traditional breakfast that is guaranteed to start your day off in the right way! Try our famous cottage cakes with hot apricot sauce or a savory omelet. Also, sneak into our guest pantry and help yourself to refreshments.

Nearest Airport: Albany, New York (Approximate time: 1 1/2 hours)

West Mountain Inn

www.WestMountainInn.com
144 West Mountain Inn Road, Arlington, VT 05250
802-375-6516 • Fax 802-375-6553
info@WestMountainInn.com

Member Since 1984

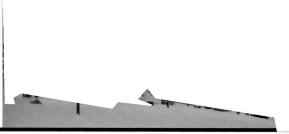

Innkeepers/Owners The Carlson Family

A Vermont country retreat you can call your own! Luxurious rooms, splendid meals, refreshing outdoor pursuits, relaxing afternoons and convivial evenings — that is what a visit to the West Mountain Inn is. Set high on a mountainside overlooking the historic village of Arlington and Green Mountains beyond, the century-old West Mountain Inn has welcomed guests for over thirty years. Visitors to the Inn are surrounded by fantastic views & 150 acres of gardens, lawns, woodlands and meadows. Without having to leave the Inn's property, guests can hike or snowshoe on miles of trails, flyfish, swim or canoe in the famous Battenkill River and relax in the Adirondack chairs on the front lawn. The Inn's wood-paneled dining room provides a perfect setting for the lavish country breakfasts and sumptuous 5-course dinners created daily by our award-winning chef. The Inn also offers private dining rooms & a wonderful antique barn for the unique celebration of weddings, birthdays, anniversaries, reunions or business retreats. Mobil ☆☆☆, Fodor's "Choice," Frommers "Highly Recommended".

Rates: 12 Rooms, 3 Suites, 3 Townhouses $155/$340 B&B, $255/$420 MAP. Service charges included in all rates. Number of Rooms: 20

Cuisine: A lavish country breakfast and splendid 5-course dinner are prepared daily. Seasonal menus focus on local VT products and organic produce. Weddings and rehearsal dinners a specialty. Full bar, premium beers and exceptional wine list.

Nearest Airport: Albany, NY — 1 Hour. Hartford, CT/Manchester, NH/Burlington, VT — all 2 1/2 hours.

Four Columns Inn

www.fourcolumnsinn.com
P.O. Box 278, 21 West Street, Newfane, VT 05345
800-787-6633 • 802-365-7713 • Fax 802-365-0022
innkeeper@fourcolumnsinn.com

Member Since 2000

Innkeepers/Owners Bruce & Debbie Pfander

The Four Columns Inn was lovingly built in 1832 by Pardon Kimball to replicate the childhood home of his southern wife. Today that home is an elegant country inn with 15 delightfully refurbished guest rooms, each featuring a queen or king-sized bed, private bath, individual heat-a/c, period antiques, high-speed wireless internet, complimentary phones, and afternoon treats. Gas fireplaces are the focal point in 11 rooms, and the deluxe, grand, and luxury rooms deliver extra large bathrooms with spa tubs and separate showers. Select rooms also offer TV/DVD players plus a huge library of complimentary dvd's. A hearty country breakfast is included for all house guests. Evening dining by reservation. Situated on the historic Newfane Village Green, unchanged since the 1830s, the property includes an inviting stream, ponds and exquisite gardens, all nestled at the base of its own private mountain. Guests enjoy a lovely outdoor pool, or nearby hiking, biking, horseback riding in summer, plus world-class skiing, snowshoeing, or snowmobiling in winter. . .all only a short drive away.

Rates: $175-325 Sun-Thu; $200-375 Fri-Sat; $225-400 Holidays/Foliage. 2 night minimum stay weekends, holidays, foliage. All rates per night with full breakfast included. Seasonal specials & packages available online. www.fourcolumnsinn.com Number of Rooms: 15

Cuisine: Named in Boson Magazine's "Top 20 Destination Restaurants in New England" (April 2011), Chef Greg Parks and team deliver on their well-earned reputation for creative regional cuisine. Wood-burning fireplace in winter. Reservations. Full bar, wine list.

Nearest Airport: Bradley-Hartford CT, 1.5 hours Logan-Boston MA, 2.5 hours JFK-New York NY, 3.5-4 hours

---

Deerhill Inn

www.deerhill.com
14 Valley View Road, P.O. Box 136, West Dover, VT 05356
800-993-3379 • 802-464-3100
innkeeper@deerhill.com

Member Since 1999

Innkeepers Michael Allen, Stan Gresens, Ariane Burgess

Relearn to relax at Deerhill Inn – where the old fashioned art of hospitality and personal service have not been forgotten. Indulge yourself in comfortable, but unpretentious surroundings. Enjoy the seasonal Modern American cuisine in our romantic candlelit dining room. Savor a glass of wine from the award winning wine list. Wake up to a made to order breakfast with fresh squeezed orange juice, custom blended coffee and premium loose teas brewed just for you. Three suites and ten guest rooms feature fireplaces, porches, whirlpool tubs as well as microfiber robes and French toiletries. Wi-Fi is available throughout the inn and internet access is available at the dedicated guest computer. Comfortable sitting rooms, art gallery, gift shop, secluded "grotto" pool, lush gardens complete the experience. Perfectly located in the middle of Southern Vermont, Deerhill Inn has access to the best of Vermont and the Berkshires of Massachusetts: museums, theaters, antiquing, shopping, hiking, boating, and of course skiing at nearby Mt Snow. Only four hours from New York, and three hours from Boston.

Rates: 3 suites & 10 rooms from $160-$325 (Summer weekend rate). Special packages & off-season discounts. Number of Rooms: 13

Cuisine: Enjoy the full, made to order, Country breakfast; Seasonal American Cuisine in a romantic setting; and a Wine Spectator awarded wine list. Full liquor license.

Nearest Airport: Albany, NY – 1.5 hours; Hartford, CT – 2 hours

Wine Spectator
AWARD OF EXCELLENCE

Four Diamond Award *Member Since 1982*

Three Mountain Inn

www.threemountaininn.com
3732 Main Street Route 30/100, P.O. Box 180, Jamaica, VT 05343
800-532-9399 • 802-874-4140
stay@threemtn.com

Innkeepers/Owners Ed & Jennifer Dorta-Duque

The Three Mountain Inn, located in the small, unspoiled village of Jamaica, Vermont is a perfect choice to spend a few days of rest and relaxation. Peacefully set among Vermont's Green Mountains, the Inn overlooks the woodlands and trails of the Jamaica State Park and is just minutes away from Stratton, Bromley and Magic Mountain Ski areas and the shopping mecca of Manchester. Our individually decorated rooms — named after nearby towns — feature luxurious linens, relaxing robes, period pieces, fabulous queen or king featherbeds, private baths, air conditioning and WiFi. Most have fireplaces while some have private decks, whirlpool tubs and TV/DVDs. With its wide-planked pine walls and multiple fireplaces, the Three Mountain Inn has an abundance of history and a sense of luxury. Whether you enjoy a romantic dinner in our AAA ◆◆◆◆ rated Dining Room, relax by one of the many fireplaces, indulge in our incredible three-course breakfast, or explore the various outdoor possibilities; the Three Mountain Inn will revive your senses.

Rates: $165 to $360 Seasonal Packages available. Visit www.threemountainn.com. Number of Rooms: 15

Cuisine: Southern Vermont's only AAA Four Diamond restaurant offers an elegant dining experience, showcasing contemporary Vermont Fresh Cuisine.

Nearest Airport: Hartford, CT (1.5 hours); Albany, NY (1.5 hours)

"The Old Dominion"

Famous for: Blue Ridge Mountains, Mount Vernon, Monticello, Arlington National Cemetery, Skyline Drive, Manassas National Battlefield Park, Colonial Williamsburg, Jamestown Settlement, Virginia Beach, Yorktown, Chesapeake Bay.

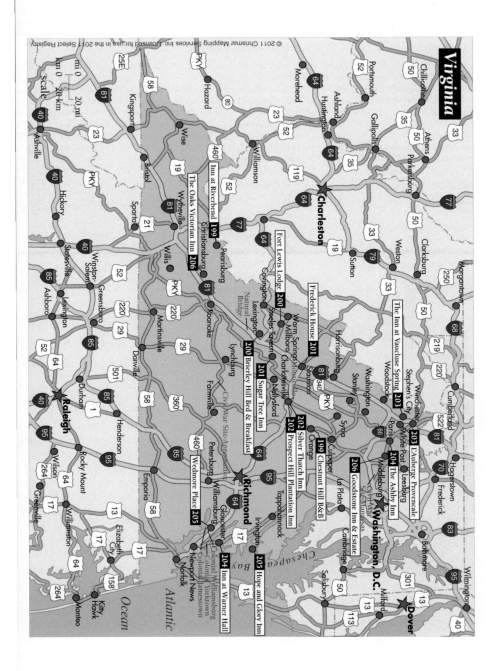

Chestnut Hill Bed & Breakfast

www.chestnuthillbnb.com
236 Caroline Street, Orange, VA U.S.A. 22960
888-315-3511 • 540-661-0430 • Fax 540-661-4212
info@chestnuthillbnb.com

Member Since 2010

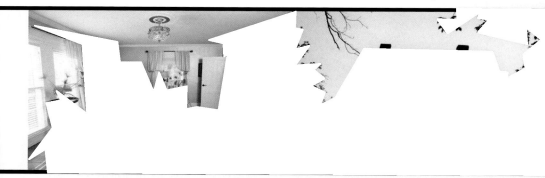

Kathleen Ayers

Built in 1860, the award-winning Chestnut Hill is located in the center of Virginia's wine country and has been skillfully renovated to preserve the master craftsmanship of this renowned historic home. As a result of the extensive six-year renovation combined with being professionally decorated, Chestnut Hill provides guests with an opportunity to appreciate the past while enjoying the luxuries and comforts of the present. Each room offers a private bath with hairdryers, quality toiletries, pillow-top beds dressed in triple-sheeted superior quality cotton linens, lush cozy spa robes, HD flat-screen televisions, and Wi-Fi Internet access. Two guestrooms, Alexander Daley's Master Suite and Ask Anna, feature hot tubs. Extra special touches may include fresh-cut flowers, bottled flat or sparkling water, and homemade tea-time treats & confections. Our savory fusion breakfast, evening wine & cheese tasting, all-day complimentary beverages, access to our outdoor cinema, and unparalleled customer service are always standard offerings during your stay at Chestnut Hill.

Rates: Six luxurious guest rooms with private baths. Fireplaces and hot tubs available. Prices include a full two-course gourmet breakfast served each morning and wine & cheese tasting each afternoon. Prices range from $179 – $295. Number of Rooms: 6

Cuisine: Our two-course fusion breakfast varies from sweet one day to savory the next, sometimes a combination of each. We are always prepared to accommodate special dietary needs. Join us for a glass of Virginia wine during our afternoon wine & cheese tasting.

Nearest Airport: Richmond International Airport, Washington Dulles Airport & Reagan National Airport.

Inn at Riverbend

www.innatriverbend.com
125 River Ridge Drive, Pearisburg, VA 24134-2391
540-921-5211 • Fax 540-921-2720
stay@innatriverbend.com

Member Since 2005

Innkeepers/Owners Janet & Jimm Burton

Newly constructed in 2003, the Inn at Riverbend sits on 13 acres overlooking the New River, the oldest river in the United States. Designed for the panoramic views of the mountains and river from the Great room, TV room and each guestroom; spacious decks and terraces provide plenty of space to enjoy panoramic views, bird watch and even spot deer in the lower meadow. The distant sound of the train sets the tone for a restful sleep. Perfect for romantic getaways, outdoor enthusiasts, retreats & family gatherings, and small intimate weddings. All rooms feature private baths, Comphy microfiber sheets, robes, satellite TV, WiFi, DVD and CD Players w/MP3 connections & thoughtful amenities. Enjoy afternoon refreshments, freshly baked cookies, and a sumptuous breakfast each day. Casual dinners are available Fridays & 3-course dinners available on Mondays, both with 48 hour notice. We are located two miles from the Appalachian Trail. Let us help plan a guided wine tour, a hike, a trip down the river, or pack a picnic for the Cascades Waterfalls!

Rates: $179/$259. Two night min. for all weekends and holidays. Corp and military rate available. Number of Rooms: 7

Cuisine: Full plated breakfast included with Riverbend roasted coffee, teas and juices. Complimentary 24 hour beverage bar. Friday and Monday dinner w/advance reservation.

Nearest Airport: Roanoke-ROA

Brierley Hill Bed & Breakfast

www.brierleyhill.com
985 Borden Road, Lexington, VA 24450
800-422-4925 • 540-464-8421 • Fax 540-464-8925
relax@brierleyhill.com

Member Since 2007

Innkeepers/Owners Ken & Joyce Hawkins

Brierley Hill offers the best of both worlds...spectacular views of the Shenandoah Valley and Blue Ridge Mountains and only minutes from the center of historic downtown Lexington, Virginia. Our individually decorated rooms – named for the Pati Bannister print that graces each – feature private baths, fireplaces (gas or electric), 350+ count linens, TV/DVD combinations, wireless Internet access and CD/MP3/radio alarm clocks. The suites additionally offer whirlpool tubs with bathrobes, refrigerators and separate sitting areas. Both the main house and Magnolias cottage feature central air conditioning/heat for our guests' comfort. The common area consists of two rooms where you can meet other guests or just curl up with a good book. These rooms have a television, snack area, 24-hour hot beverage machine, refrigerator and a guest computer with high-speed Internet access. Guests are welcome to stroll through the award-winning gardens and enjoy our panoramic views of the Shenandoah Valley.

Rates: $139 / $329 (Dec 1 – Mar 31), $189 / $379 (Apr 1 – Nov 30), open year round. Number of Rooms: 6
Cuisine: Full 3-course country breakfast, snacks available in common area. Excellent restaurants in downtown Lexington.
Nearest Airport: Roanoke (1 hr.)

Fort Lewis Lodge

www.fortlewislodge.com
603 Old Plantation Way, Millboro, VA 24460
540-925-2314 • Fax 540-925-2352
info@fortlewislodge.com

Member Since 1990

Innkeepers/Owners John and Caryl Cowden

Centuries old, wonderfully wild, uncommonly comfortable. A country inn at the heart of a 3200-acre mountain estate. Outdoor activities abound with miles of river trout and bass fishing, swimming, extensive hiking trails, mountain biking, and magnificent vistas. Fort Lewis is a rare combination of unpretentious elegance and unique architecture offering a variety of lodging choices where every room has a view. Three "in the round" silo bedrooms, three hand-hewn log cabins with stone fireplaces, and Riverside House are perfect for a true country getaway. Evenings are highlighted by contemporary American-style cuisine served in the historic Lewis Gristmill. Like most country inns, we trade in a change of pace, romance and exceptional fare. But over the years, we've come to understand that Fort Lewis has an asset that very few others have. Our wilderness — the mountains, forests, fields and streams and all the creatures that call this their home.

Rates: 13 Rooms, $215/$230 MAP; 3 Family Suites, $230 MAP; 4 Log Cabins, $270/$310 MAP. Open April-mid Nov. Number of Rooms: 20
Cuisine: Dinner and breakfast included in the daily room rate. Evening meals offer a vibrant mix of fresh tastes, just plucked vegetables and interesting menus. The aroma of hickory smoke rising from the grills will leave you yearning to hear the dinner bell.
Nearest Airport: Roanoke, VA (1.5 hrs.); Charlottesville, VA (1.75 hrs.)

Sugar Tree Inn

www.sugartreeinn.com
145 Lodge Trail, Vesuvius, VA 24483
800-377-2197 • 540-377-2197
innkeeper@sugartreeinn.com

Member Since 1998

Innkeepers/Owners Jeff & Becky Chanter

Recently featured as one of Washingtonian Magazine's "Most Romantic Inns" and called "Mountain Magic" by Hampton Roads Magazine! High above the Shenandoah Valley in the Blue Ridge Mountains (but only 6 miles from I-81) and less than a mile from the Blue Ridge Parkway, is our haven of natural beauty. Set on twenty-eight wooded acres at 2800 feet, Virginia's Mountain Inn is a place of rustic elegance, peace, and tranquility. Enjoy our 40-mile views, which are complemented by spring wildflowers, cool summer nights and brilliant fall colors. Each elegantly rustic room has a wood-burning fireplace, incredibly comfortable bed, private bath, coffee maker, CD player, and is decorated with a colorful country quilt. A full breakfast is served in our glass-walled dining room and you can savor our fine evening dining by reservation.

Rates: 1 Luxury Cabin, $248; 9 Rooms, $148/$198; 2 Suites, $178 & $198; Creek House w/2 bedrooms, bath & full kitchen, $178. Number of Rooms: 13

Cuisine: A full country breakfast is served daily. Nicely prepared three course dinners with a choice of entrees available Friday and Saturday. Casual fare most busy weekdays.

Nearest Airport: Roanoke, Charlottesville

Frederick House

www.frederickhouse.com
28 North New Street, Staunton, VA 24401
800-334-5575 • 540-885-4220 • Fax 540-885-5180
stay@frederickhouse.com

 Member Since 1997

Innkeepers/Owners Joe and Evy Harman

Frederick House is a small, full service, historic, bed and breakfast hotel in seven separate buildings across from Mary Baldwin College in downtown historic Staunton, the Shenandoah Valley's oldest city. Five historic guest houses contain twenty three guest rooms or suites accommodating up to fifty seven guests and conference facilities for groups up to twenty five. Two furnished apartments are available for overnight or extended stays. Reception and Chumley's, the breakfast room at Frederick House open each morning from 7:30-10:00, are located in a vine covered building adjacent to one of three Frederick House parking lots. Breakfast includes a choice of beverages, hot or cold cereals, homemade granola and yogurt, whole grain waffles with real maple syrup, apple raisin quiche, ham and cheese pie, and strata. Special dietary requests can be met when requested. The restaurant at Frederick House, Ailoli, in an historic building adjacent to reception, serves contemporary Mediterranean cuisine.

Rates: 12 Rooms, $109/$189; 11 Suites, $153/$279. Ask about our many packages.Open year-round. Number of Rooms: 25

Cuisine: 15 Restaurants available within walking distance; Fine Dining, Seafood, Steaks, Pizza American, Italian, Mexican, Ribs, Gourmet Deli, Southern Home Cooking, Indian, Coffee Shops, Homemade Ice Cream.

Nearest Airport: Shenandoah Valley Regional Airport or Charlottesville Albemarle

Prospect Hill Plantation Inn

www.prospecthill.com
Box 6909, 2889 Poindexter, Louisa Co, VA, Charlottesville, VA 23093
800-277-0844 • 540-967-0844 • Fax 540-967-0102
Info@prospecthill.com

Member Since 1979

Innkeeper/Owner The Sheehan family since 1977

Award-winning country inn on historic 1732 plantation complex located just 15 miles East of Charlottesville, VA. Romantic candlelight dining daily with 12 rooms, suites and cottages featuring breakfast-in-bed, working fireplaces, double Jacuzzi baths (in 8 rooms), outdoor swimming pool, and gazebo on over 40 acres of beautiful grounds in the serenity of the countryside near Jefferson's "Monticello". Nearby are many excellent wineries and other historic sites. B&B rates from $195 and also offering weekend dinners at $49 pp that includes pre-dinner wine reception and candlelight dining at private table for two. Guests have the choice breakfast-in-bed served on a tray to their room or in our dining room. Corporate, meeting, MAP package and other special rates available. Go to www.prospecthill.com for descriptions, rates, virtual tours of all rooms, sample menus to get an idea why so many romantics choose Prospect Hill for their getaway. Selected many times over the past 33 years as one of America's most romantic getaways. Uncle Ben's "10 Best Country Inns" award three times.

Rates: 12 rooms/suites from $195 – $350 B&B. Number of Rooms: 12

Cuisine: Elegant Continental-American four course price-fixe dining by candlelight Fri & Sat evenings at 8 pm for $49pp. Wine and snacks in room on arrival, predinner wine reception, full country breakfast-in-bed (or served in dining room).

Nearest Airport: Charlottesville-Albemarle or Richmond International

---

Silver Thatch Inn

www.silverthatch.com
3001 Hollymead Drive, Charlottesville, VA 22911
800-261-0720 • 434-978-4686 • Fax 434-973-6156
info@silverthatch.com

Member Since 1986

GRAND AWARD

Innkeepers/Owners Jim and Terri Petrovits

This historic inn began its life as a barracks built in 1780 by Hessian soldiers captured during the Revolutionary War. As wings were added in 1812 and 1937, it served as a boys' school, a tobacco plantation, and a melon farm. It has been providing gracious lodging in antique-filled guest rooms and elegant candlelit dining since the 1970s. Relax and unwind in our intimate pub. Enjoy contemporary cuisine from our menu and wines from a list which has consistently won the Wine Spectator Award of Excellence, the Wine Enthusiast Award of Unique Distinction, and the inaugural Virginia Cellar Master 5 Stem award.

Rates: $175/$210 B&B. Open year-round. Number of Rooms: 7

Cuisine: Breakfast for house guests; Dinner served Wednesday — Sunday, specializing in contemporary cuisine, featuring local produce when available and eclectic sauces. Open to the public. Great English Pub, outstanding selection of wine and spirits.

Nearest Airport: Charlottesville/Albemarle Regional Airport, 2 miles.

The Inn at Vaucluse Spring

www.vauclusespring.com
231 Vaucluse Spring Lane, Stephens City, VA 22655
800–869–0525 • 540–869–0200 • Fax 540–869–9546
mail@vauclusespring.com

Member Since 2000

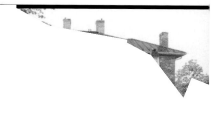

Innkeepers/Owners Barry & Neil Myers

Your place in the country. Set amidst 100 scenic acres in the rolling orchard country of the Shenandoah Valley, this collection of six guest houses is the perfect country retreat. Experience the elegance of the gracious 200 year old Manor House or the charm of an 1850s log home. For the ultimate in peace and privacy, stay in the Mill House Studio at the water's edge, the Gallery Guest House with views of the meadow, or the Cabin by the Pond. Relax beside Vaucluse Spring's cool, crystal clear waters. Savor the region's bounty at the delicious breakfasts and weekend dinners. Enjoy the pool in summertime or roam the pasture and woods year round. Ideally located between the historic sites of Winchester and the outdoor activities near Front Royal and the Shenandoah National Park's Skyline Drive. Acclaimed by guests for warm hospitality and fabulous food, the Inn has received TripAdvisor.com's Travelers Choice Award for Top 10 Best Inns and B&B's in the U.S.

Rates: 12 Rooms/Suites: $165/$260 B&B. 3 Private cottages: $280/$320. Beautifully furnished, queen or king beds, all have fireplaces, 14 with Jacuzzis, most have water, mountain, or meadow views. Number of Rooms: 15

Cuisine: Full 3-course breakfast served daily. A 3-course 'Gourmet Southern Comfort' Friday night supper and a romantic 5-course Saturday dinner are available by advance reservation. Wine and beer available.

Nearest Airport: Dulles International and Winchester Regional

L'Auberge Provencale

www.laubergeprovencale.com
13630 Lord Fairfax Highway, Boyce, VA 22620
800–638–1702 • 540–837–1375 • Fax 540–837–2004
celebrate@laubergeprovencale.com

Member Since 1988

 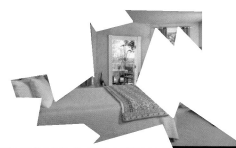

Innkeepers/Owners Chef Alain & Celeste Borel

Experience a touch of Provence in the Shenandoah Valley. L'Auberge Provencale is a destination for the discerning traveler & gourmand. Zagat and USA Today rated L'Auberge Provencale as one of the top 100 hotel dining rooms in the country. Indulge yourself in one of the guest rooms or suites at our quintessential French Country Inn. We feature cheerful yet elegant decor with faux walls, French fabrics and antiques to create an atmosphere of a true "Auberge," blending French country comfort with modern luxury. Dine evenings at the main manor house at Mt. Airy (circa 1753) in one of the three intimate dining rooms. Orchards, flower, vegetable and herb gardens supply the best and freshest for our cuisine. The inn is designated "Green" by the state of Virginia & supports sustainable local farming. Our Villa La Campagnette offers a swimming pool, luxury suites and privacy. The two inns offer a special experience for discerning guests with exquisite food and courteous, attentive service. If you can't go to France, visit L'Auberge Provencale.

Rates: 8 Charming Rooms, $165/$275; 6 Romantic Suites, $295/$325. Fireplaces, Aroma Therapy Steam Showers, Flatscreens, Wireless Internet, Jacuzzi Tubs, Virginia Garden Tour Gardens and Majestic Views. Number of Rooms: 14

Cuisine: Enjoy elegant, romantic dinners with Provencale flair. Featuring fresh, local produce, meats, fruits and herbs. Dinner served six days, closed Tuesdays. Multi-course breakfast of one's dreams, gourmet picnics. Wine Spectator Award of Excellence.

Nearest Airport: Washington Dulles, National, and Winchester Regional

The Ashby Inn & Restaurant

www.ashbyinn.com
692 Federal Street, Paris, VA 20130
866-336-0099 • 540-592-3900 • Fax 540-592-3781
info@ashbyinn.com

Member Since 1988

Owners Jackie and Chuck Leopold/Innkeepers Star and Neal Wavra

This 1829 inn finds its character in the historic village of Paris and its heart in the kitchen. The menu is guided by the seasonal offerings of its local farmers and vendors with great attention paid to seasonal foods like asparagus, shad roe, softshell crab and game. Much of the produce, herbs and flowers come from its own gardens. Guest rooms furnished in period pieces, half with fireplaces and balconies, offer bountiful views stretching beyond the formal perennial gardens to the hills of the Blue Ridge. The four dining rooms are as intimate as they are distinct – from an enclosed porch, to a converted kitchen with walnut beams and fireplace, to a cozy room with booths set against faux painted walls and striking paintings. Summer dining on the covered terrace overlooking the lawn attracts a wide Washington following. Located in the heart of Virginia's wine country, guests have a variety of activities to choose from. Within just minutes from the inn, one will find over half a dozen wineries, ample hiking at Sky Meadows State Park and boutique shopping in Middleburg.

Rates: 6 rooms at the Main Inn, $155-225 & 4 rooms at the School House, $275-295. Includes full breakfast. Number of Rooms: 10

Cuisine: A full farmstead breakfast is included for our inn guests. Lunch and Dinner are available Wednesday-Sunday offering modern farm fare. Brunch on Sunday. Wine list and full bar available.

Nearest Airport: Winchester Regional Airport (16 miles, Washington/Dulles International Airport (36 miles)

Inn at Warner Hall

www.warnerhall.com
4750 Warner Hall Road, Gloucester, VA 23061
800-331-2720 • 804-695-9565 • Fax 695-9566
info@warnerhall.com

Member Since 2006

Innkeepers /Owners Troy & Theresa Stavens

Old world charm and new world amenities create the perfect balance between luxury and history in this beautifully restored romantic waterfront retreat. Established in 1642 by George Washington's great, great grandfather, Warner Hall beckons guests to relax and enjoy. Comfortable elegance, fabulous food and attentive, friendly service are the essence of Warner Hall. Spacious guest rooms combine sumptuous antiques, fabrics and art with modern conveniences. Many rooms offer fireplaces, Jacuzzis or steam showers – all have spectacular views. Experience Chef Eric Garcia's delicious cuisine paired with a bottle of fine wine. Explore the historic triangle of Williamsburg, Yorktown and Gloucester, or simply relax at the Inn's charming boathouse. Ideally situated at the head of the Severn River surrounded by 500 acres of fields and forest, Warner Hall resonates with tranquility and southern hospitality. National Register of Historic Places. Recommended by Travel + Leisure, Hampton Roads Magazine, Virginian Pilot and Free Lance Star.

Rates: $190/$250 Mon.-Thurs. $210/$275 Fri-Sun. Number of Rooms: 11

Cuisine: Extraordinary breakfasts included. Chef's Tasting Dinners Fri./ Sat., or by special reservation. Cocktail and wine bar. Gourmet supper baskets Sunday-Thursday. Box lunches daily.

Nearest Airport: Nearest Airports Richmond/Norfolk

Hope and Glory Inn

www.hopeandglory.com
65 Tavern Road, P.O. Box 425, Irvington, VA 22480
800-497-8228 • 804-438-6053 • Fax 804-438-5362
inquiries@hopeandglory.com

Member Since 2008

Innkeepers/Owners Dudley & Peggy Patteson

TOP 100 IN THE WORLD – Twice "TOP 10 IN THE U.S." – Four times. Frommer's, Fodor's and Moon Travel Guides have awarded the Hope and Glory Inn their highest rating. The only inn in Virginia with this honor. An historic (1890) and very mega stylish schoolhouse, eclectically styled and hopelessly romantic, with quaint Garden Cottages surrounded by flowers rarely seen in Virginia gardens today. Unique in so many ways – a moon garden, which only blooms in the evening; and, an outdoor garden shower (Breakers Hotel circa 1940) with a claw foot tub in a most private setting. Additional accommodations can be found within walking distance in the Hope and Glory's Vineyard. Four Carpenter Gothic cottages called "tents" modeled after Oak Bluffs on Martha's Vineyard. Retreats are delightfully held here with today's technology in a creative environment and totally wireless. The inn also offers fine dining in its Dining Hall, cruises aboard its vessel; a hip pool; massage treatments in our special spa space; tennis courts; golf and chic shops in a classy Chesapeake Bay waterfront town.

Rates: Schoolhouse Rooms – $175-$290; Garden Cottages – $255-$345; Vineyard Tents – $310-$695. Number of Rooms: 25

Cuisine: We offer the best of fine dining in our Dining Hall. Our dinners are four courses and prix fixe. The menu changes daily and with the seasons. We have America's only Crab Cruise; and, offer wine tastings in the Hope and Glory's vineyard.

Nearest Airport: Newport News/Williamsburg (PHF) 55 min.; Richmond (RIC) 65 min; Norfolk (ORF) 90 min.; Dulles (IAD) 3 hrs

Wedmore Place

www.wedmoreplace.com
5810 Wessex Hundred, Williamsburg, VA 23185
866-WEDMORE • 757-941-0310 • Fax 757-941-0318
info@wedmoreplace.com

Member Since 2007

Founders & Managers – The Duffeler Family

Wedmore Place is an elegant European Country Hotel, in the midst of a 300-acre winery farm located just 3 miles from Colonial Williamsburg. Whether for business or pleasure, the hotel offers a highly luxurious and relaxing atmosphere. The decor of each room is inspired by the culture and traditions of 28 different European provinces. Each is furnished and decorated in the style of the province after which it is named; all rooms have wood burning fireplaces. In the hotel's delightful cobblestone courtyard you'll find an impressive stone fountain imported from France. Exquisite dining is available in the Cafe Provencal, where fine Mediterranean cuisine is served daily. The dining room overlooks the pool terrace, offering guests a romantic and relaxed setting. Guests at the hotel can also make use of the massage facilities, fitness room, British Club style Library and wine cellar. No stay is complete without a walk next door to The Williamsburg Winery for a tour and wine tasting and shopping in the retail store. See what our guests are saying on Trip Advisor.

Rates: Traditional Rooms-$165-$205,Classic Rooms-$190-$245, Superior Rooms-$235-$345, 3 Suites: from $300-$625Weekend rates – Friday and Saturday Holiday Rates may apply Number of Rooms: 28

Cuisine: Fine Mediterranean Cuisine. European-Style dining.Chef Tim feels that presentation and atmosphere of the restaurant are important, but without a Chef who creates the experience into a special event, they become nothing more than curiosities.

Nearest Airport: Newport News/Wmbg Airport (PHF), 26 Miles; Richmond, VA (RIC), 50 Miles; Norfolk, VA (ORF), 65 Miles

Goodstone Inn & Estate

www.goodstone.com
36205 Snake Hill Road, Middleburg, VA 20117
877-219-4663 • 540-687-4645 • Fax 540-687-6115
information@goodstone.com

Member Since 2008

General Manager Mark Betts

Goodstone Inn & Estate, a luxurious country retreat in Middleburg, VA, is situated in the heart of Hunt & Wine Country 45 minutes from Washington, DC. The historic property features elegant lodging in six distinctive dwellings: the charmingly converted Carriage House, The Dutch Cottage, The Manor House, The French Farm Cottage, The Spring House and The Bull Barn. Goodstone provides superb cuisine, an impressive wine cellar featuring an extensive selection from Virginia and around the world, an elegant afternoon English Tea, breakfast, and facilities for corporate and social events. Wireless Internet access is available throughout the property. Recreational opportunities abound including use of an outdoor pool nestled within Wisteria-covered ruins of the estate's original mansion, an all-season Jacuzzi, walking trails, mountain biking, stables for boarding guests' horses, canoeing, spa treatments, and superb shopping in Middleburg. Goodstone is a member of Andrew Harper's Select Registry and won "Most Excellent Inn" by Conde Nast Johansens for 2011.

Rates: Guest room rates range between $275-$740 and include a full farmstead breakfast, afternoon tea service and a variety of activities on the 265 acre estate. Number of Rooms: 18

Cuisine: Executive Chef William Walden varies the menu to use fresh ingredients from our gardens and local farms. Your dining experience will be enhanced by his expertise. Enjoy wine selected by our sommelier to complement each course.

Nearest Airport: Dulles International Airport is a 40 minute drive.

The Oaks Victorian Inn

www.theoaksvictorianinn.com
311 East Main St., Christiansburg, VA 24073
800-336-6257 • 540-381-1500
stay@theoaksvictorianinn.com

Member Since 1993

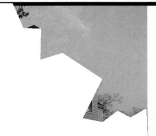

Owners and Hosts Linda and Bernie Wurtzburger

Listed on the National Register of Historic Places; The Oaks is the only B&B In the Mid-Atlantic Region to receive the prestigious Four Diamond AAA award for 16 consecutive years. This Queen Anne Victorian is located in the small town of Christiansburg, near Roanoke just 2 miles off I-81; 3 miles from Blacksburg, home of Virginia Tech and Radford University. Whether you are planning to elope, a "romantic getaway," a reunion, a historic trip to the New River, Roanoke and Shenandoah Valleys or the majestic Blue Ridge Parkway or Virginia wineries, come and enjoy the glorious setting in relaxed elegance. Fireplaces and beautiful private baths with Jacuzzis for romantics. Each room has wireless Internet, cable TV, DVD players and stocked refrigerators. Beautiful surroundings, luxurious guest rooms, a dedication to detail, warm hospitality and memorable breakfasts are the hallmark of The Oaks. The region provides the best in bike trails, hiking, antiques, live music, boating and golf. . .or just relax on the world class wrap-around porch.

Rates: 5 Rooms, 1 Cottage, $139-$229; Corp. rates Sun. through Thurs., Sgl. Only. Open year-round. Number of Rooms: 6

Cuisine: Full breakfast by candlelight, excellent restaurants for dinner nearby.

Nearest Airport: Roanoke, 30 miles

"The Evergreen State"

Famous for: Mount St. Helens, Redwoods, Olympic National Park, Grand Coulee Dam, Space Needle, Pike Place Market, Puget Sound, San Juan Islands, Mount Rainier, Kettle Falls, Cascade Mountains, Apples, Jets, Hi-Tech.

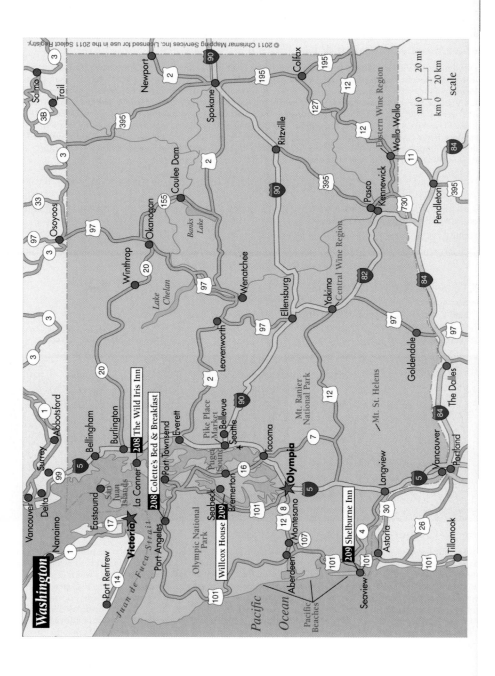

The Wild Iris Inn

www.wildiris.com
121 Maple Avenue, P.O. Box 696, LaConner, WA 98257
800-477-1400 • 360-466-1400
info@wildiris.com

Member Since 2003

Innkeepers/Owners Stephen & Lori Farnell

The award-winning Wild Iris Inn is located in the charming artist community of La Conner, Washington. La Conner is a short drive from Seattle and Vancouver, British Columbia, but "miles away". The Inn's convenient location is perfect for your exploration of the Pacific Northwest; located just 20 minutes from the ferry terminals in Anacortes that lead to the San Juan Islands, Victoria, BC and points beyond. Each season brings wonderful changes to La Conner. In winter, swans and snow geese cover the fields in a sea of white. The farmlands are brightly colored with daffodils in March, world famous tulips in April, iris in May, and dahlias in August. In summer, whale watching cruises leave Anacortes each day and follow magnificent orcas in the North Puget Sound. The highlight of your stay will be the hospitality, service and amenities of The Wild Iris Inn. Guest suites feature spa tubs, fireplaces and decks facing the Cascade Mountains, as well as all of the other amenities you would expect from a Select Registry property.

Rates: 12 Guest Suites w/King beds $159/$209 B&B. 6 Casual Guest Rooms 4 w/King beds, 1 Queen bed and 1 Twin bedded room-$119/$139 B&B. Open Year Round. Number of Rooms: 18

Cuisine: A full breakfast including fresh baked goods, homemade granola, hot entrees and fresh fruits is served each morning at tables for two. In-room and early departure breakfast options.

Nearest Airport: Seattle & Vancouver, BC

Colette's Bed & Breakfast

www.colettes.com
339 Finn Hall Road, Port Angeles, WA 98362
877-457-9777 • 360-457-9197 • Fax 360-452-0711
colettes@colettes.com

Member Since 2003

Innkeepers/Owners Richard & Karen Fields

Colette's is a breathtaking 10 acre oceanfront estate nestled between the majestic Olympic Range and the picturesque Strait of Juan de Fuca. This unique area is the gateway to Olympic National Park, a world of stunning coastline with booming surf, wave-manicured beaches, and sweeping vistas in every direction. Each perfect day at Colette's starts with a gourmet multi-course breakfast.Luxurious King Suites with magnificent oceanfront views, romantic fireplaces, and indulgent Jacuzzi spas for two rejuvenate guests at the end of the day. Stroll through Colette's 10 acre outdoor sanctuary which includes enchanting gardens, towering cedars and lush evergreen forest.Fodor's Pacific Northwest – "Top Choice" for the Olympic Peninsula – considered the very best. Karen Brown's Guide Pacific Northwest- "Top Pick". Best Places to Kiss Pacific Northwest "Utopian Oceanfront Hideaway". Voted "Greatest Value" Award by Karen Brown's Pacific Northwest Exceptional Places to Stay. Selected as one of the "Top 10 Romantic Inns" by I Love Inns. Fine Gardening Magazine/June 2011 – "Front Cover"

Rates: Luxury King Suites $195/$395. Number of Rooms: 5

Cuisine: Our chef has created an exciting variety of culinary delights. Enjoy your multi-course, gourmet breakfast served with a panoramic view of the Strait of Juan de Fuca and the San Juan Islands.

Nearest Airport: Seattle and Port Angeles

♀

Willcox House Country Inn

www.willcoxhouse.com
2390 Tekiu Rd. NW, Seabeck, WA 98380
800-725-9477 • 360-830-4492
willcoxhouse@silverlink.net

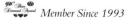
Member Since 1993

Innkeepers/Owners Cecilia and Phillip Hughes

The Willcox House Country Inn is surrounded by the forest and overlooks the sparkling waters of Hood Canal. Located between Seattle and the Olympic mountains, this 1930's mansion offers guests peace and tranquility. From your private table in the dining room enjoy the spectacular view of the water and the Olympic Peninsula. The inn is furnished with antiques and period pieces for relaxation and comfort. Relax by the fire in the great room, play a game of pool in the game room or watch a movie in the theater. The terrace and the library are great places to enjoy a glass of wine in the afternoon. Five guest rooms, all with private baths, overlook the water and the Olympic mountains. Beautiful gardens host a champion Japanese maple tree and two fish ponds. Walk the oyster laden saltwater beach looking for driftwood and wildlife. Golfing, birding, and hiking are nearby. The combination of Native American, Scandinavian, Military, and world class garden attractions make Kitsap County an easy-to-tour destination rich in history and diversity.

Rates: Guest rooms have different amenities (fireplace $259, double spa tub $239, balcony $229) $169/$259 B&B. Open year-round. Number of Rooms: 5

Cuisine: Breakfast, afternoon wine and cheese included. The three course dinner is available by reservation only. All dining is private table. Extensive wine list. Beer is available. Complimentary hot beverages.

Nearest Airport: Seattle (SEA) Interstate 5 south to Tacoma; Hwy 16 to Bremerton; web site for specific mileage to inn 1&1/2 hours

---

 ♀

Shelburne Inn & China Beach Retreat

www.shelburneinn.com or www.chinabeachretreat.com
P.O. Box 250, 4415 Pacific Hwy, Seaview, WA 98644
800-INN-1896 • 360-642-2442 • Fax 360-642-8904
innkeeper@shelburneinn.com

Member Since 1988

Innkeepers/Owners David Campiche and Laurie Anderson

An unspoiled 28-mile stretch of wild Pacific seacoast is just a short walk through rolling sand dunes from this inviting Country Inn, built in 1896. Art Nouveau stained glass windows and period antiques highlight the decor. A sumptuous gourmet breakfast featuring the best of the Northwest is complimentary. In the restaurant and pub musical entertainment is scheduled at various times throughout the year. Innovative cuisine and a discriminating wine list have brought international recognition to the restaurant and pub. Wireless Internet. Outdoor activities abound, including The Discovery Trail which parallels the majestic Pacific Ocean. Explore the western end of the Lewis & Clark trail from China Beach Retreat and its Audubon Cottage near Cape Disappointment State Park and two 100-plus-year-old lighthouses. Selected as one of the 'West's Best Small Inns' by Sunset Magazine. Featured in Martha Stewart Living Magazine in January 2003. "Breakfast to the Shelburne is like art to the Louvre," from the St. Louis Post Dispatch. Three Stars NW Best Places. AAA Three Diamond-rated.

Rates: 13 Rooms $139/$179B&B; 2 Suites $199 B&B. Off-site waterside B&B; two Rooms $199 B&B; 1 Suite $229 B&B. Audubon Cottage: $289 B&B.Group Rates for Business Retreats and lodging/dining packages available Sun – Thurs, Oct – June. Number of Rooms: 19

Cuisine: Gourmet Regional Cuisine features the best seasonal and local ingredients. Restaurant and Pub offer breakfast, lunch and dinner featuring fine NW wines, microbrewed beer and liquor. Innkeepers' Breakfast served daily and offers creative preparations.

Nearest Airport: Astoria, Oregon

"The Mountain State"

Famous for: Appalachian Mountains, Monongahela National Forest, White Sulphur Springs, Harper's Ferry National Historical Park, Smoke Hole Caverns, Apple Butter Festival, Grave Creek Burial Mounds, Country Music, Coal, Oil, Gas.

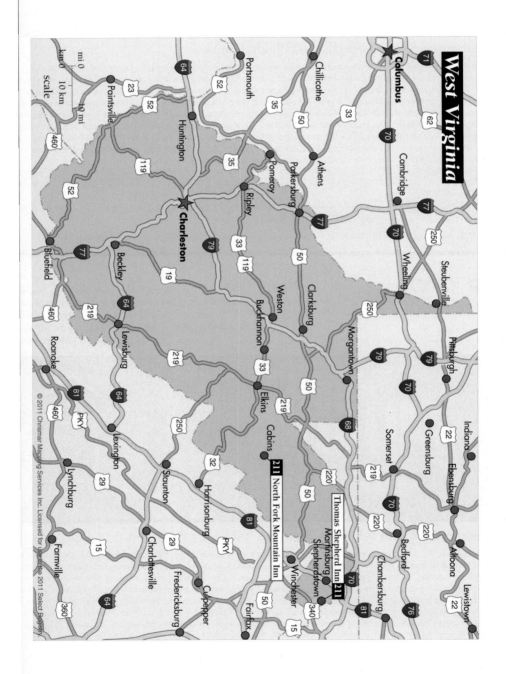

North Fork Mountain Inn

www.northforkmtninn.com
P.O. Box 114, 235 Canyon View Lane,Smoke Hole Road, Cabins, WV 26855
304-257-1108
info@northforkmtninn.com

Member Since 2007

Innkeepers/Owners Ed & Carol Fischer

Come marvel at the breathtaking scenery at an Inn described as "an outpost of luxury in the wilderness." We invite you to come and enjoy the natural beauty of the area in a quiet, relaxing atmosphere. Enjoy a gourmet breakfast as you start your day. Whether you spend the day hiking in the Monongahela forest or enjoying the spectacular view of the mountains and valleys from a rocker on the Inn's wraparound porches, it is like taking a journey back in time to a simpler, slower paced world. Located only three hours from the Washington DC area. The Inn is located 7.6 miles up a paved mountain road with a view of Smoke Hole Canyon and six different mountains. The three story log Inn is of white pine construction with native field stone fireplaces. Each guest room is uniquely decorated with rustic elegance. Guest common areas include comfortable chairs and sofas, book and movie libraries, DirecTV, billiard table, microwave, refrigerator, and board/card games. Excellent fishing nearby. Birdwatching also popular. Finish your day relaxing in the hot tub under a blanket of stars.

Rates: 7 Rooms, $140/$190. Two suites with king bed & loft, $245. 1 Bedroom Cabin with full kitchen, $180. Number of Rooms: 10

Cuisine: Gourmet breakfast included. Fine dining w/wine tasting on Saturday evening, casual dining on other evenings, gourmet picnic baskets available for lunch or dinner. Ed is an award winning chef in Great American Seafood Cookoff in New Orleans.

Nearest Airport: Grant County Airport; Washington Dulles

Thomas Shepherd Inn

www.thomasshepherdinn.com
300 W. German Street, P.O. Box 3634, Shepherdstown, WV 25443
888-889-8952 • 304-876-3715
info@thomasshepherdinn.com

Member Since 2006

Innkeepers/Owners Jeanne Muir & Jim Ford

We invite you to stay in our bed & breakfast inn, with six 'inviting, well kept and beautifully decorated' guest rooms with private baths, central air and wi-fi, all located on the 2nd floor. Built in 1868, the inn offers gracious hospitality to guests for over 25 years. Relax in front of the living room fireplace or on the back porch overlooking the garden; start your day with a generous homemade breakfast. Room amenities include comfy robes and bedside chocolates. Shepherdstown, a hidden gem for weary urbanites, is less than two hours from Washington, DC or Baltimore. The town has a vibrant cultural scene, ranging from premiere plays at the Contemporary American Theater Festival to independent movies at the Opera House to music and crafts festivals featuring local and nationally-known artists. A variety of locally-owned shops and restaurants fill the historic buildings on nearby German Street. Rich U.S. history is only minutes away at Antietam Battlefield or Harpers Ferry. Biking, hiking and rafting abound along the C&O Canal Path, the Potomac and the Shenandoah Rivers.

Rates: $160-$205 Friday/Saturday/Sunday; $125-$175 Monday thru Thursday, not including taxes, double occupancy. Two night minimum stay required on Saturdays and holidays. Not suitable for pets or children under 12. No smoking inside Inn. Number of Rooms: 6

Cuisine: Full hot homemade breakfast daily w/fruit, entree, meat, baked goods; early beverage service w/signature spice biscotti. Hot beverages available all day; afternoon snacks. Walk to several locally-owned fine dining & casual restaurants on German Street.

Nearest Airport: BWI and Dulles airports-70 miles. Parking beside and behind the Inn on Duke Street (corner of German Street).

"The Badger State"

Famous for: Wisconsin Dells, Apostle Islands, National Lakeshore,
Lake Superior, Mirror Lake State Park, House on the Rock (a 1940s retreat
built on a 60-foot rock outcropping overlooking a 450 ft drop), Dairy,
Beer, Cranberry Fest.

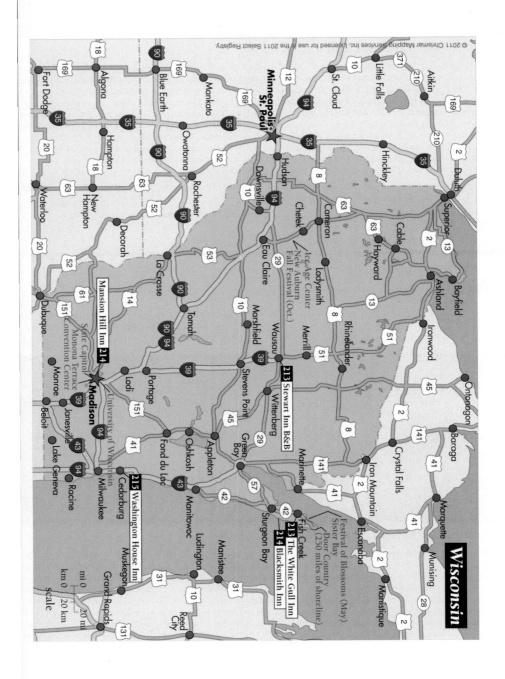

The Stewart Inn Bed and Breakfast

www.stewartinn.com
521 Grant Street, Wausau, WI 54403
715-849-5858
innkeeper@stewartinn.com

Member Since 2005

Innkeepers/Owners Paul & Jane Welter

Located in the historic downtown Wausau River District, the Stewart Inn offers upscale accommodations in an authentic National Register Arts and Crafts masterpiece. Public rooms on the first floor of this Prairie Style mansion retain the incredible architectural detail created 100 years ago by Chicago architect, George W. Maher, a contemporary and associate of Frank Lloyd Wright. The second floor serves as an exclusive five-room boutique hotel where the owners take pride in providing guests with exceptional, unobtrusive service. Each of the newly renovated guest rooms has an extraordinary ensuite bath and tasteful combination of modern amenities and historic charm, sure to please even the most discriminating travelers. The Inn is fully equipped for the business traveler and offers a comfortable, secure alternative to conventional lodging. Restaurants, shops, museums, and entertainment are all within walking distance. If you're traveling with a dog, you'll find the accommodations extremely pet-friendly.

Rates: $150/$195 weekdays, $170/$215 weekends. Business rates available. Number of Rooms: 5
Cuisine: Full gourmet breakfast, afternoon wine and cheese, evening cookies and milk.
Nearest Airport: Central Wisconsin Airport (CWA)

White Gull Inn

www.whitegullinn.com
4225 Main Street, P.O. Box 160, Fish Creek, WI 54212
800-625-8813 • 920-868-3517 • Fax 920-868-2367
innkeeper@whitegullinn.com

Member Since 1979

Innkeepers/Owners Andy & Jan Coulson

Established in 1896, this white clapboard Inn is tucked away in the scenic bayside village of Fish Creek on Wisconsin's Door Peninsula. Antiques, fireplaces and meticulously restored and exquisitely decorated rooms, suites and cottages provide a warm and romantic atmosphere. Several suites feature double whirlpool baths. Renowned for hearty breakfasts, sumptuous lunches and candlelit dinners, the Inn is famous for its traditional Door County fish boils, featuring locally caught Lake Michigan whitefish cooked outside over an open fire. With its back to a bluff and its face to the bay of Green Bay, Fish Creek today is a stroll around village with historic buildings housing numerous art galleries, shops and restaurants. A natural harbor filled with majestic yachts in summer separates the village from Peninsula State Park, Wisconsin's largest and most beautiful park. Within a few minutes of the inn, guests will find spectacular sunsets, theater, music festivals, antique stores and every imaginable recreational activity, from golf and fishing to wind surfing and kayaking.

Rates: 6 Rooms, $160/$235; 7 Suites, $235/$295; 4 Cottages (1, 2 and 4 bedroom), $250/$480. Open all year. Number of Rooms: 17
Cuisine: Full breakfast included. Lunch served daily.Dinner from the menu Monday, Tuesday, Thursday in summer, Saturday through Thursday in winter. Traditional Door County fish boils featuring local Lake Michigan whitefish served other evenings.
Nearest Airport: Austin Straubel Field, Green Bay (75 miles)

Blacksmith Inn On the Shore

theblacksmithinn.com
8152 Highway 57, Baileys Harbor, WI 54202
800-769-8619 • 920-839-9222
relax@theblacksmithinn.com

Member Since 2002

Innkeepers/Owners Joan Holliday and Bryan Nelson

Awaken to waves lapping the shore as the morning light glistens on the water. Linger over breakfast. Kayak the harbor. Hike the nearby Ridges Wildlife Sanctuary. Laze in your hammock. Bike a sleepy backroad to Cana Island Lighthouse. Bask in your whirlpool as you take in the warm glow of the fire. Stroll to village restaurants and shops. Serene water views, private balconies, hammocks, in-room whirlpools, fireplaces, fine linens, down pillows, satellite TV/DVD/CD, DVD library, wireless internet, ipod hook-up, in-room refrigerators and a bottomless cookie jar! Door County offers art galleries, antiquing, music, theater, lighthouses and miles and miles of shoreline. Adults Only.

Rates: Late May-Oct. Rooms $245/$295, Cottage $255/$445; Nov.- Late May, Rooms $145/$235, Cottage $155/$295 Number of Rooms: 16

Cuisine: Guests enjoy a homemade continental breakfast from the balcony overlooking the harbor. "There is nothing simple about the view that beckons each guest every morning," Jill Cordes, Food Network.

Nearest Airport: Green Bay (GRB)- Hwy 172 E. 8 mi. to Hwy 43 N. 5 mi. to Hwy 57 N. 63 mi. (90 min. drive)

Mansion Hill Inn

www.mansionhillinn.com
424 N. Pinckney Street, Madison, WI 53703
800-798-9070 • 608-255-3999 • Fax 608-255-2217

Member Since 1997

General Manager Tania Worgull

Elegance, luxury and charm await you at The Mansion Hill Inn. The Inn's warm hospitality has made it a favorite of business and leisure travelers alike. Lovingly restored and lavishly decorated, Mansion Hill Inn is located in Madison. A masterpiece of Romanesque Revival style built in 1857, it abounds in fine architectural detail and period furnishings. Each of the ten guest suites and rooms are individually and exquisitely decorated to provide the best of antique ambiance and contemporary amenities. Many rooms have marble fireplaces and balconies as well as views of the State Capitol building. The Inn is conveniently located on a quiet corner in the heart of downtown Madison and boasts luxurious accommodations, amenities, and a convenient location. We're close to the campuses of the University of Wisconsin, Madison Area Technical College, Edgewood College and within walking distance of State Street. Valet parking is complimentary.

Rates: Ten Beautiful Guest Rooms including 2 Suites, 4 Grand Standard Rooms and 4 Standard Rooms, ranging from $200 to $375 on special event weekends. Number of Rooms: 10

Cuisine: Many fine restaurants within walking distance. Complimentary wine service every evening. Continental-plus breakfast in our Breakfast Parlour.

Nearest Airport: Dane County Regional Airport

Washington House Inn
www.washingtonhouseinn.com
W62 N573 Washington Avenue, Cedarburg, WI 53012
888-554-0515 • 262-375-3550 • Fax 262-375-9422
info@washingtonhouseinn.com

Member Since 2007

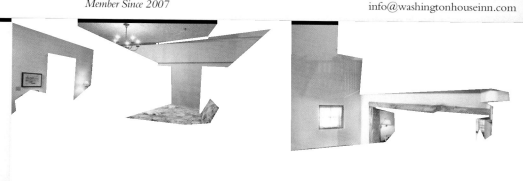

Innkeeper Wendy J. Porterfield

Listed on the National Register of Historic Places, Washington House Inn successfully blends the charm and romance of days past with the amenities and conveniences expected by today's discriminating travelers. 34 rooms with luxury bedding include whirlpools (single and double), steam baths, antiques, fireplaces, flat-screen TVs and free in-room Internet. Guests are invited to enjoy a complimentary evening wine and cheese tasting featuring award-winning wines from local Cedar Creek Winery, and a sampling of Wisconsin cheeses. For a little extra pampering, the inn offers sauna and on-site massages. Located in the heart of Cedarburg's Historic District, the inn offers elegant lodging within walking distance of shopping, dining and entertainment options, including the Ozaukee Interurban Trail (30 miles of paved trail for hiking or biking), making the Washington House Inn the place to stay in Historic Cedarburg. Within a 15 minute drive are five golf courses. The Inn is also perfect for small groups such as wedding parties, family re-unions, small meetings and business retreats.

Rates: Open year round. $125-$315 Friday/Saturday. $100-$252 Sunday-Thursday. Number of Rooms: 34

Cuisine: Enjoy our expanded continental breakfast buffet. Thoughtfully prepared for you each morning by staff bakers and served in our Gathering Room, or if you prefer, delivered to your guest room.

Nearest Airport: General Mitchell International

"The Equality State"

Famous for: Yellowstone National Park, Grand Teton National Park, Devils Tower National Monument, National Elk Refuge.

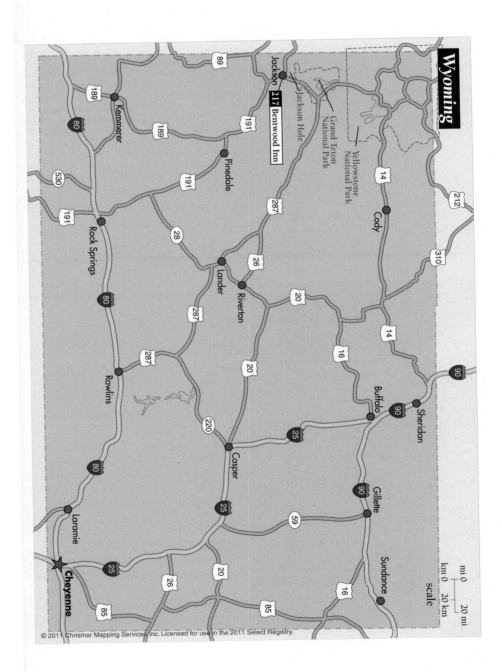

Bentwood Inn
www.bentwoodinn.com
P.O. Box 561, 4250 Raven Haven Road, Jackson, WY 83001
307-739-1411 • Fax 307-739-2453
info@bentwoodinn.com

Member Since 2008

Innkeepers Lee & Deborah Clukey

The Bentwood Inn is a luxury bed and breakfast in Jackson Hole, nestled in majestic old-growth cottonwoods on 3 acres of solitude. The Bentwood is 5 miles from down town Jackson, Jackson Hole Mountain Resort, and the south entrance to Grand Teton National Park. The Snake River is about a quarter mile away. This welcoming, intimate lodge highlighted by the Great Room with its three-story river rock fireplace, was built in 1995 with 200 year old logs salvaged from the Yellowstone Park fire of 1988. The Bentwood boasts 6,000 sq.ft. of Western eclectic decor with five guest rooms each featuring a fireplace, king bed, jetted tub, quality linens, towels and robes, cable TV and private balcony or deck. A gourmet breakfast launches the Bentwood magic for a day of wildlife viewing and activity in the parks on the hills and trails, or being pampered and shopping in Jackson. In late afternoons, guests share the day's experiences and bond while enjoying cheese, appetizers and refreshments on the expansive decks in the summer, or in front of the fire in the Great Room on cooler days.

Rates: Room rates vary by season. Please visit our website to view our "Rates At A Glance" page. Number of Rooms: 5

Cuisine: At the Bentwood Inn we strive to prepare innovative menus. Unique presentations with creative twists on old favorites will satisfy the appetite of the most discerning guests. Enjoy fresh baked goods and fresh fruit every day.

Nearest Airport: Jackson Hole Airport: 18 miles. Idaho Falls Airport: 85 miles, Salt Lake City Airport 200 miles.

SELECT REGISTRY
DISTINGUISHED INNS OF NORTH AMERICA

Gift Certificates

The gift of an overnight stay or a weekend at an exceptional inn or B&B can be one of the most thoughtful and appreciated gifts you can give your parents, children, or dear friends. Employers are discovering that a gift certificate for a "getaway" is an excellent way of rewarding their employees, while at the same time giving them some much needed rest. A few ideas:

- **Weddings • Anniversaries •**
- **Holiday & Birthday gifts •**
- **Employee rewards/incentives • Retirement •**

Our gift certificates are valid at any of our more than 400 member properties. We process orders daily, packaging certificates with our complimentary Association guidebook and your personal message. Certificates may be ordered online or by phone, and expedited shipping is available at an additional cost. The next time you think about gift-giving, think about our Gift Certificate Program—the perfect gift for that special person, **1-800-344-5244** or online at **www.selectregistry.com/giftcertificates.**

From California to Nova Scotia, SELECT REGISTRY represents the finest inns, B&Bs, and unique small hotels North America has to offer. We are proud to include among our members a number of exceptional Canadian properties. To our Canadian guests, we say, "Our innkeepers stand ready to welcome you during your travels, whether it is to the States or within Canada." To our American guests, we say, "Why not see what Canada has to offer?"

In these uncertain times, when crossing oceans is worrisome, nothing beats the exhilarating feeling of visiting an exciting new country in the security and comfort of your own car. Yes, for many millions of Americans, Canada is just a short drive away—and yet it is a whole new world!

No wonder Americans love to travel to Canada: not only do their U.S. dollars go a lot further there (which means a lot more holiday for the same amount of money), but they also get to choose between a multitude of completely different experiences.

De la Californie à la Nouvelle-Ecosse, le SELECT REGISTRY représente plusieurs auberges, cafés-couettes et petits hôtels des plus distingués en Amérique du Nord. Nous sommes fiers de pouvoir compter parmi nos membres plusieurs des plus beaux établissements canadiens. À tous les voyageurs, canadiens-français, nous vous souhaitons de merveilleux séjours dans les auberges de prestige du SELECT REGISTRY.

There are the breathtaking vistas, mountain wildlife, Asian food and totem poles of British Columbia, the "foodie" paradise of the Niagara Peninsula (Canada's Napa Valley) and the Eastern Townships of Quebec, replete with friendly wineries and raw milk cheeses. There are festivals galore, museums, parks and world-class shopping in Toronto and Montreal as well as the fascinating culture of the Province of Quebec where French-Canadians take food and fun very, very seriously. And, never to be forgotten, the bucolic seaside charm and legendary hospitality of Canada's maritime provinces, New Brunswick, Prince Edward Island and Nova Scotia.

Many travelers have experienced all four seasons of the Northland (the winters are sunnier and less cold than you think). Traveling east to west, it would be hard to declare a regional winner. Some Canadians modestly claim to be the most hospitable of innkeepers, and a critic can't easily challenge that assertion.

Superb food, wine and service can be expected at the Canadian inns of the SELECT REGISTRY. Understated luxury, too. But above all, they offer you an exclusive glimpse of the best of Canada: its forests, crystalline lakes, affordable golf and skiing and cosmopolitan, secure and friendly cities. The Northland beckons!

"The Pacific Province"

Famous for: Canadian Rockies, Ferries, Vancouver Island, Spiral Railway Tunnels, Butchart Gardens.

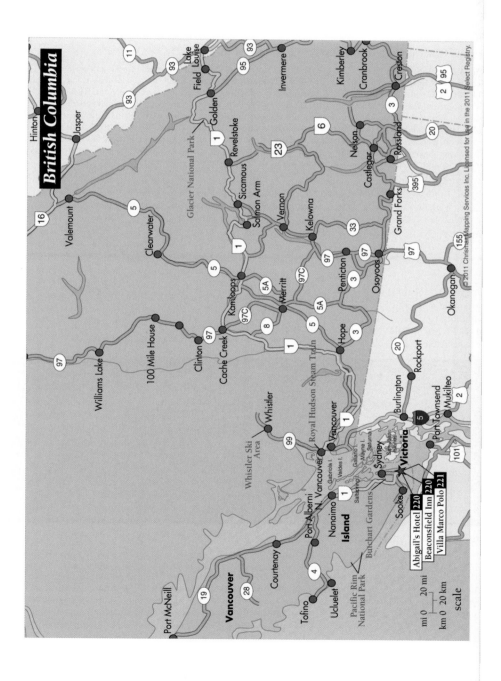

Abigail's Hotel

www.abigailshotel.com
906 McClure Street, Victoria, BC, Canada Canada V8V 3E7
800-561-6565 • 250-388-5363 • Fax 250-388-7787
innkeeper@abigailshotel.com

Member Since 2000

Innkeeper/Owner Ellen Cmolik

This unique and romantic boutique bed and breakfast hotel is conveniently nestled at the end of a tranquil cul-de-sac surrounded by quaint English gardens and friendly residential homes. Intimately housed in a 1930's heritage Tudor mansion, Abigail's blends the romance and charm of the past with all the comforts and conveniences of the present. Each of the 23 beautifully appointed guestrooms has its own characteristic and flair. Many rooms feature marvelous soaker baths, down duvets, rich linens and wood-burning fireplaces. Complimentary appetizers are served each evening in our Library Lounge which guests can pair with local award winning BC wine & champagne. Abigail's is walking distance to Victoria's must-see ocean or city tours, galleries, museums, and restaurants. Each morning the hotel fills with the irresistible aroma of freshly prepared baked goods, and gourmet breakfasts, interactively presented by Abigail's Executive Chef. Wireless internet service, local calling, coffee and tea 24 hours a day and parking are all-inclusive during your stay with us.

Rates: $172/$349 CDN. Seasonal discounts available. Open year-round, reservations available 24 hrs. Number of Rooms: 23

Cuisine: Our famous gourmet breakfast is served each morning in the sunny breakfast room and complimentary evening appetizers served every evening in our fireside library. Licensed premises.

Nearest Airport: Victoria International Airport

Beaconsfield Inn

www.beaconsfieldinn.com
998 Humboldt St., Victoria, BC, Canada Canada V8V 2Z8
888-884-4044 • 250-384-4044 • Fax 250-384-4052
info@beaconsfieldinn.com

Member Since 1994

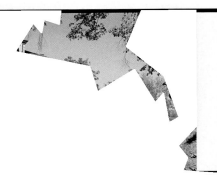

Proprietors Mark and Diana Havin

We invite you to our award-winning Edwardian Inn built in 1905. Located only four blocks from Victoria's Inner Harbor, the Beaconsfield Inn is the ultimate in charm, luxury and romance. Enjoy antique furnishings, stately guest and common rooms, spectacular stained glass windows, feather beds with down comforters and fireplaces in all rooms. Jacuzzis in mosts rooms. The Beaconsfield Inn is situated on a quiet, tree-lined street a short 10 minute stroll to downtown and the inner harbour with all its shopping, restaurants and tourist attractions. Evening sherry hour, late evening coffee and cookies. Awake to our gourmet full breakfasts. The Beaconsfield Inn has been awarded a 5 star rating from Canada Select.

Rates: 5 Deluxe Rooms, $109/$295 CDN; 4 Suites, $199/$299 CDN. Open year-round. Number of Rooms: 9

Cuisine: Full breakfast, Evening sherry. Late night cookies and freshly brewed coffee.

Nearest Airport: Victoria International. Or downtown inner harbour – Float Planes from Vancouver.

Villa Marco Polo

www.villamarcopolo.com
1524 Shasta Place, Victoria, BC, Canada Canada V8S 1X9
877-601-1524 • 250-370-1524 • Fax 250-370-1624
enquire@villamarcopolo.com

Member Since 2007

Proprietors: Eliza Livingston, Clarke Bingham & Liam Morton; Managing Innkeeper: Danusia Quaranta

Escape from the ordinary. . .to the Villa Marco Polo Inn. Built in 1923 as a gift to a young bride, the Villa Marco Polo is an Italian Renaissance mansion that continues to be a romantic setting for special vacations. A reflecting pool visited occasionally by bald eagles, Coopers hawks, and blue herons is the focal point of a classical Italianate garden. Our suites feature double soakers, fireplaces, fine linens, luxurious beds, down pillows, hardwood floors and Persian carpets. In our Spa and Healing Space, guests can schedule facials, manicures, aromatherapy, etc. Generous gourmet breakfasts featuring locally grown produce are served in our lovely sun-splashed dining room. Enjoy afternoon tea or Italian Amarone either in the garden, or in front of the fire in our wood-paneled library. Whether a business meeting requiring WIFI and private telephones, or a celebration requiring the services of an events planner, your experience at the Villa will be memorable!

Rates: Rates range from $195 to $325. Number of Rooms: 4

Cuisine: Gourmet breakfasts feature locally grown organic produce, house-made preserves, organic maple and birch syrups from Quebec and Yukon, organic coffee from Bolivia, and fresh eggs from island farms. With prior notice, we can handle special needs.

Nearest Airport: Victoria International Airport is 28 km from the Villa.

DISTINGUISHED INNS OF NORTH AMERICA

Gift Certificates

The gift of an overnight stay or a weekend at an exceptional inn or B&B can be one of the most thoughtful and appreciated gifts you can give your parents, children, or dear friends. Employers are discovering that a gift certificate for a "getaway" is an excellent way of rewarding their employees, while at the same time giving them some much needed rest. A few ideas:

- Weddings • Anniversaries •
- Holiday & Birthday gifts •
- Employee rewards/incentives • Retirement •

Our gift certificates are valid at any of our more than 400 member properties. We process orders daily, packaging certificates with our complimentary Association guidebook and your personal message. Certificates may be ordered online or by phone, and expedited shipping is available at an additional cost. The next time you think about gift-giving, think about our Gift Certificate Program—the perfect gift for that special person, **1-800-344-5244** or online at **www.selectregistry.com/giftcertificates**.

"The Heartland Province"

Famous for: Wine Country, Niagara Falls, Toronto, the Shaw Festival, Forests, Lakes.

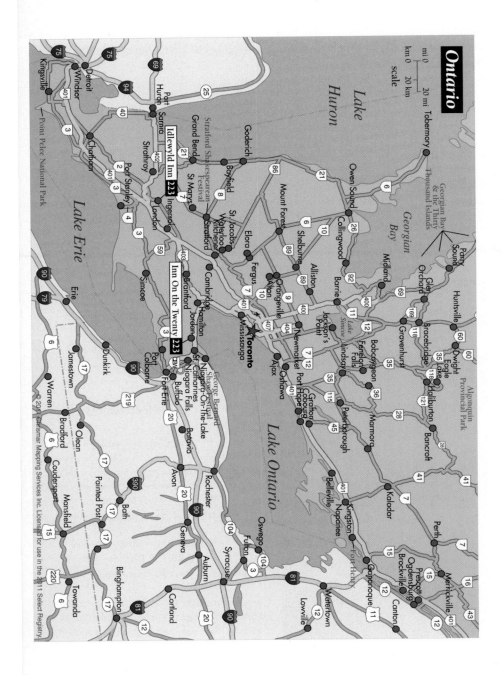

Inn on the Twenty

www.innonthetwenty.com
3845 Main Street, Jordan, ON, Canada Canada L0R 1S0
800-701-8074 • 905-562-5336 • Fax 905-562-0009
info@innonthetwenty.com

Member Since 1998

Innkeeper/Owner Helen Young

This is the heart of Ontario's wine country! Renovated winery buildings boast twenty-seven suites, all with fireplaces and Jacuzzi tubs; antiques and unique art abound. The Inn is located in a charming village with artisans and antique shops and our very own full service spa. Great golf, walking and bicycling opportunities as well as the sophistication of Niagara's famous Shaw Theatre and the not-to-be-missed Falls are nearby. Our restaurant, On the Twenty, is a DiRoNA award winner and a leader in regional cuisine. The Niagara wine route beckons with up to forty diverse wineries within a fifteen minute drive of the Inn. Cave Spring Cellars, one of Ontario's most recognized premium wineries, is our partner and is right across the street from the Inn. Special tasting offers are available to Inn guests. A visit to Canada is a fresh experience and we are thrilled to welcome so many of our US neighbors. We are just 25 minutes from the borders at Niagara Falls and make a great en route stop to Toronto. AAA◆◆◆

Rates: 26 Suites: 7 two-story, 20 one-level, 5 with private garden. $159-$389 Number of Rooms: 27

Cuisine: On the Twenty is a DiRoNA Award restaurant with regional focus. Private Dining Rooms available for up to 135. Ontario wines and beers. Full bar. Cave Spring Cellars Winery on site. Tours and tastings available daily.

Nearest Airport: Buffalo, Toronto, Hamilton

Idlewyld Inn

www.idlewyldinn.com
36 Grand Avenue, London, ON, Canada Canada N6C 1K8
877-435-3466 • 519-433-2891 • Fax 519-433-7178
info@idlewyldinn.com

Member Since 2008

Innkeeper/Owner John & Christine Kropp

Experience Victorian surroundings, exquisite fine dining and service as it was meant to be at London's spectacular boutique hotel. The Idlewyld's signature ambiance of quiet elegance has been captured in the spectacular dining room ~ featuring a menu that is imaginative and inspired ~ and continues into the garden courtyard. Each of our 23 individually-designed rooms offers its own special atmosphere reflective of the Idlewyld Inn experience. Our guests will enjoy complimentary with their stay: wired hi-speed Internet service, on-site parking, nightly turndown service, and morning coffee service, and a full hot breakfast. There is so much to discover in London. You can venture into London's past, which has seen the emergence of a big band legend and the discovery of insulin, or go back further and witness an archaeological dig. To satisfy your artistic interests there is The Grand Theatre, Orchestra London, the London Regional Art and Historic Museum plus an array of special events focused on the visual and performing arts.

Rates: Dinner & Breakfast Package $255/$325 Room with breakfast $149/$225. Number of Rooms: 23

Cuisine: Our chefs use only the finest locally-produced meat, vegetables, fruits and herbs, including AAA Ontario beef, award-winning lamb and pork and the full bounty of garden and orchard. Serving breakfast, lunch, dinner daily and weekend afternoon tea.

Nearest Airport: London International Airport (YXU)

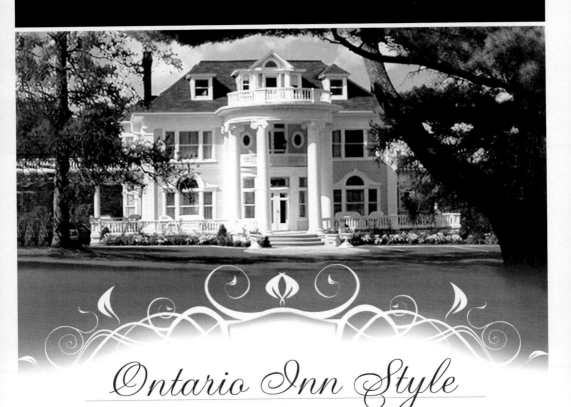

Ontario Inn Style

Discover over 40 of Ontario's Finest Inns and Spas including several Select Registry properties. All of the innkeepers share the Select Registry's philosophy and promise of excellence.

Enjoy true Canadian hospitality along the sparkling Great Lakes, in vibrant, clean cities and throughout quaint villages and quiet rolling countryside.

Attention Spa Goers —Ontario's Finest now offers quality assured spas that feature distinctly Ontario treatments and therapies.

We look forward to welcoming you this season.

ONTARIO'S *finest* INNS · SPAS

Ask for a complimentary map & guidebook at 800-340-4667 or visit

www.ontariosfinestinns.com · www.ontariosfinestspas.com

See you soon in Ontario, Canada!

"La Belle Province"

Famous for: St. Lawrence Seaway, French Culture, Maple Syrup, Winter Sports, Apples, Camping.

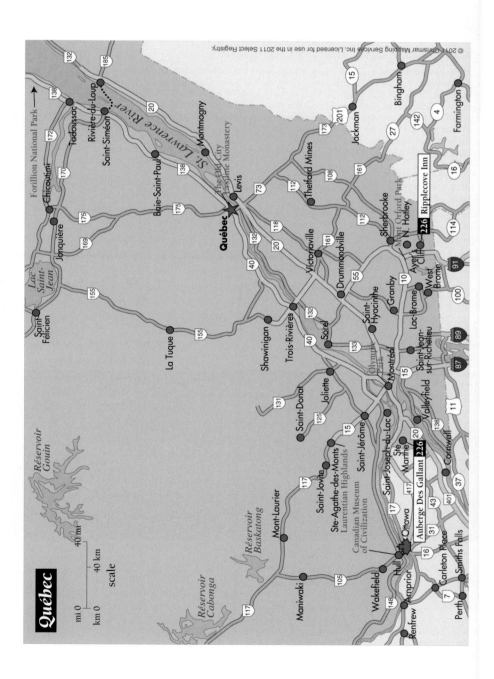

Auberge des Gallant

🍴 🍴 🍴 🍷

www.gallant.qc.ca
1171 St — Henry Rd., Ste-Marthe, Rigaud, QUE, Canada Canada J0P 1W0
800-641-4241 • 450-459-4241 • Fax 450-459-4667
res@gallant.qc.ca

Member Since 1998

Innkeepers/Owners Linda, Gerry & Neil Gallant

Garden and SPA lovers will enjoy romantic Auberge des Gallant (The Gallant Inn) nestled on Rigaud Mountain, between Montreal and Ottawa in the heart of a bird and deer sanctuary. Enjoy award-winning French cuisine and wine list, as well as our spa! We offer comfort zone, Jane Iredale and even maple sugar body wraps and facials. Elegant spacious rooms with real wood-burning fireplaces and balconies overlook our five acres of beautifully appointed gardens, which in summer attract a multitude of birds and butterflies, while the winter promises sleigh rides, cross country skiing and downhill skiing. Our maple sugar house with its 10,000 taps is open from late February to the end of April for traditional maple meals. Maple syrup is available all year round! Next time you are visiting Quebec, Montreal, Hudson and St-Lazare, make sure to stop in and stock up on our maple syrup.

Rates: 24 Rooms w/wood-burning fireplace & balcony, from $150/room for B&B in country room & $175, MAP P.P. for honeymoon suite. Number of Rooms: 24

Cuisine: Breakfast, lunch, gourmet 5 course dinner with wine pairing, Sunday brunch. Extensive wine list and liquor. Maple products available all year.

Nearest Airport: Montreal, Trudeau, 30 miles. Ottawa 70 miles.

Auberge Ripplecove Inn & Spa

🍴 🍴 🍴 🍷

www.ripplecove.com
700 Ripplecove, Lake Massawippi, Ayer's Cliff, Quebec, CANADA
Canada J0B 1C0
800-668-4296 • 819-838-4296 • Fax 819-838-5541
info@ripplecove.com

Member Since 1995

Innkeepers/Owners Debra and Jeffrey Stafford

Since 1945, Ripplecove Inn has been chosen by sophisticated travelers from around the world to get away from it all in an atmosphere of romance and privacy. The Inn resides on a beautifully landscaped 12 acre peninsula alive with English gardens and century-old pines. Guests can choose from 33 designer decorated rooms, suites or lakeside cottages, many with lake view balcony and fireplace. A full service Spa facility offering massage, hydro therapy, facials, 3 private salons and a four season outdoor hot tub guarantee complete relaxation. A private beach with water craft, biking, tennis, heated outdoor pool and lake cruises are also all on site! Rated as one of Quebec's top 10 best places to dine, our Victorian dining room and lakeside terrace offer refined French and international cuisine with vintage wines accompanied by live piano music and sterling silver service. Located only 15 minutes north of the Quebec/Vermont border, Ripplecove Inn is the perfect stop over while on route to either Montreal or Quebec city via Interstate 91 through Vermont.

Rates: 33 Rooms, Suites and Cottages, US $149/$365MAP/person/day including daily dinner, breakfast and gratuities. All rooms offer A/C, TV, TEL and designer decor. Most rooms offer fireplace, private lake view balcony and whirlpool bath. Number of Rooms: 33

Cuisine: Four Diamond Award french and international cuisine is served in a Victorian style lakeside dining room, pub and terrace. A 6000 bottle wine cellar has been awarded by Wine Spectator Magazine as "one of the best restaurant wine cellars in the world".

Nearest Airport: Pierre E Trudeau Airport, Dorval (Montreal), Quebec, Canada, or Burlington, Vermont.

Hôtellerie Champêtre
Auberges et Hôtels du Québec
Québec Resorts & Country Inns

unique
COUNTRYSIDE EXPERIENCE

26 of Québec's finest inns and tons of delightful packages to choose from...

**Book online your next dream vacation at
www.resortsquebec.com!**

**You are just one click away from luxurious escapes
and unrivaled pleasures!**

To know more:
www.resortsquebec.com

SELECT REGISTRY

DISTINGUISHED INNS OF NORTH AMERICA

**Coming in 2011
The New Golden Quill Loyalty Travel Program**

Please go to
www.selectregistry.com/goldenquill
for complete details on the new program
and learn how to register.

Notes

SELECT REGISTRY

DISTINGUISHED INNS OF NORTH AMERICA

Thank you for choosing a Select Registry inn.
Your comments help us to maintain the highest standards in the industry.
We appreciate feedback and the opportunity to respond
(and to facilitate communication, where appropriate, with our member properties
should something during your stay be not to your liking).
Of course, our innkeepers appreciate hearing good things from you, as well!
Please include your name, address and phone number,
so we can respond in a timely manner.
Or, if you would prefer, you can use our convenient online comment card
at www.selectregistry.com/comments.

Name of Inn:_____ State or Province: _____ Date of visit: _____

Your name and address (please print and be aware that we require a name): _____
_____
_____
_____

Your phone number: _____

Email address: _____

Please check ONE box in each category:	Excellent	Good	Disappointing	Poor	Would not return
Bedrooms/comfort/decor	❑	❑	❑	❑	❑
Public rooms/aesthetics/furnishings	❑	❑	❑	❑	❑
Food/restaurant quality	❑	❑	❑	❑	❑
Service quality	❑	❑	❑	❑	❑
Welcome/friendliness	❑	❑	❑	❑	❑
Personality/character of the Inn	❑	❑	❑	❑	❑

Additional comments: _____
_____
_____

As a discriminating traveler who wants to go to the best Country Inns and B&Bs, I recommend the following Inns (please include name, city and state/province, and tell us why): _____
_____
_____

DISTINGUISHED INNS OF NORTH AMERICA

Select Registry Gift Certificate Program

The perfect gift for that special person.
Select Registry gift certificates can be ordered online at:
www.SelectRegistry.com.
Our gift certificates are packaged with a copy
of our most recent guidebook,
and a message from you to the recipient.
VISA, MasterCard, and American Express accepted.
Expedited shipping is available for an additional charge.

Place
Postage
Here

Select Registry, Distinguished Inns of North America
501 E. Michigan Avenue
P.O. Box 150
Marshall, MI 49068